GERRY STUDDS

Gerry Studds

AMERICA'S FIRST
OPENLY GAY
CONGRESSMAN

Mark Robert Schneider

University of Massachusetts Press

Amherst and Boston

ISBN 978-1-62534-285-0 (paper); 284-3 (cloth)

Designed by Jack Harrison
Set in Adobe Garamond Pro with Electra display
Printed and bound by The Maple-Vail Book Manufacturing Group

Cover design by Jack Harrison
Cover art: Gerry Studds in 1985, as photographed by Renée DeKona
for the *Cape Cod Times*.

Library of Congress Cataloging-in-Publication Data
Names: Schneider, Mark R. (Mark Robert), 1948–   author.
Title: Gerry Studds : America's first openly gay congressman / Mark Robert Schneider.
Other titles: America's first openly gay congressman
Description: Amherst : University of Massachusetts Press, [2017] |
Includes bibliographical references and index.
Identifiers: LCCN 2016059945 | ISBN 9781625342850 (pbk. : alk. paper) |
ISBN 9781625342843 (hardcover : alk. paper)
Subjects: LCSH: Studds, Gerry E. | Legislators—United States—Biography. |
United States. Congress. House—Biography. | Gay legislators—United States—Biography. |
Politicians—Massachusetts—Biography. | United States—Politics and government—1945–1989. |
United States—Politics and government—1989–
Classification: LCC E840.8.S778 S38 2017 | DDC 328.73/092 [B]—dc23
LC record available at https://lccn.loc.gov/2016059945

British Library Cataloguing-in-Publication Data
A catalog record for this book is available from the British Library.

For Judith

Contents

Acknowledgments

I had just completed my final book talk for *Joe Moakley's Journey: From South Boston to El Salvador,* when audience member Gregory Williams suggested that I write a biography of Gerry Studds. "Thank you," I said, "but I'm not the man for that job." Studds's biographer probably should be gay, I reflected, or at least know something about fishing and coastal issues. Then I went home and thought about it some more. I didn't really believe that. I had written several books about African American history, and I am not African American. I could learn about the policy matters I didn't know well. Studds was a compelling figure. So—thanks, Gregory, for getting me started.

I googled "Gerry Studds" and then e-mailed Dean Hara, Studds's widower. I didn't expect a reply, but Dean responded immediately, and we arranged to meet at his apartment. Having made some inquiries about me, he'd decided to entrust me with Studds's unpublished "Memoire" and his papers, which he was in the process of assembling for donation to the Massachusetts Historical Society. Dean was my guide and counselor throughout the writing of this book. He arranged interviews with people he knew and suggested others who might be helpful. He volunteered information through several interviews himself. Most important, Dean read the manuscript in process and let me write the book without imposing his own interpretation. I could not have written this book properly without his help.

I probably owe a debt of gratitude to Studds himself, whom I never met. Studds wrote, but never finished, a memoir of his life in the closet. This book is much richer because of that manuscript.

All the informants contributed greatly to the telling of this tale. They generously granted their time, suggested more people with whom to speak, and gave me documentary material that was not in the archive. Many of the informants were Studds's staffers, who toiled in obscurity but made possible his work on complex matters such as the ocean environment, foreign policy, and AIDS funding levels. Special thanks are due to Tom McNaught and Kate Dyer, who each carefully reviewed one chapter. Congressional staffers are the unsung heroes of American political life, and I hope that I have paid them proper attention.

I also thank the people at the Massachusetts Historical Society. I am grateful to Brian Halley and the team at University of Massachusetts Press whose criticisms have improved my book. Special thanks are due to copy editor Amanda Heller, who closely read and corrected the manuscript, and to project manager Mary Bellino. All the errors, of course, are mine.

And finally, thanks again to Judith, my wife, best friend, wisest critic, and fellow writer.

GERRY STUDDS

Introduction

GERRY STUDDS lived the first forty-six year of his life as a closeted gay man, a public figure with a private secret. In July 1983, Studds revealed his secret to the world on the floor of the House of Representatives. While investigating unfounded allegations of recent illicit sexual behavior, a special counsel retained by the House Ethics Committee dredged up information regarding a brief sexual relationship between Studds and a male page conducted ten years previously. Studds agreed that he had made a regrettable personal mistake but contended that he had committed no crime. He further asserted that the affair had been consensual, that the page had been coerced into testifying, and that the affair did not therefore merit investigation. He thus became the first openly gay congressman and, after a dramatic 1984 campaign, the first openly gay candidate to be elected to the U.S. Congress.

Studds later wrote a memoir of his life in the closet, but he never finished it. He could not figure out how to protect the privacy of his partners, and he felt uncomfortable writing about his friends and colleagues. His memoir is personal, moving, and funny, and informs the early part of this narrative. Studds vowed to show the harm that was caused to gay people by the prejudice that forced them to become invisible, and in this he succeeded. He portrayed himself as a young man growing up in a haze of ignorance, confusion, denial, and guilt, finding his professional career blocked by suspicions about his sexual orientation and his basic impulses stifled by the prevailing social climate. Had he been born ten or twenty years later, coming of age after the gay liberation movement emerged in the early 1970s, he might not have suffered the anxiety that he did while maturing during the 1950s. Coming out made him a happier person, and years later he met the man who became his partner, and later his husband. This is the story of a man who spent much of his early life afraid of having his secret discovered, but who lived to be an openly gay public figure, and finally a happy man.

Studds represented the southeastern Massachusetts Twelfth, later Tenth Congressional District from 1973 to 1997. During those twenty-four years, he focused on protecting the ocean and coastal environment and the American fishing industry. He is less well known for his determined opposition to President Ronald Reagan's wars in Central America, but during the 1980s he helped lead the fight against U.S. support for the El Salvadoran dictatorship and the Nicaraguan contras.

Having grown up along the coast, he once told an aide, "Salt water runs in my veins." Young Gerry loved to fish, and learned to sail as a youth. During his boyhood summers, he raked Irish moss off the rocky Cohasset and Scituate ledges, rowing a boat alone far out to sea to find the heavy stuff. He did not have urban street smarts, but he did have instinctive nature smarts, and the environmental movement appealed to his sensibility.

Studds attended Yale during the 1950s, the years of the "Silent Generation." Studds found his voice in the antiwar movement of the 1960s, to which he was immediately attracted. He became faculty adviser to the student protesters while a master at St. Paul's School in Concord, New Hampshire, and he helped persuade Senator Eugene McCarthy to challenge President Lyndon Johnson and run in the New Hampshire Democratic primary in 1968. These two brainy, somewhat aloof anti-politicians had much in common, and McCarthy became a role model for him. Studds was a product of the 1960s radicalization, and his anti–Vietnam War activity led him to speak out against U.S. intervention in Central America during the 1980s.

Yet it is his role as the first congressman who was openly gay that makes his career compelling. Everything about him was conditioned by this central fact of his life. As a young man, he gradually came to realize that society condemned him, in his entire being, as a pervert, a sinner, a criminal, and a potential traitor, simply because of his sexual orientation. This growing awareness radicalized him and made him an outsider. Knowing himself to be a decent man falsely condemned made it easier for him to recognize the rampant hypocrisy throughout society. Growing up homosexual during the 1950s made him a quietly angry young man and gave his personality an edge. Some people found him to be arrogant. He was not the type to go along to get along.

In this sense, Studds's career stood as a symbol for many millions of gays and lesbians of his generation. Most of them held a private secret that they felt must be kept. The radicalization of the 1960s led to the gay liberation movement of the 1970s, during which many gays and lesbians, mostly of the postwar "baby boom" generation, "came out" and demanded an end to the discrimination against them. One of the ironies of Studds's career is that he was born too late to join this movement. Certainly, other men and women of his generation did embrace the gay liberationists. But Studds was already running for the United States House of Representatives in 1970. He had to keep his secret, like millions of others whose co-workers, neighbors, and family members openly declared their anti-gay prejudices. By this point in his life, he had created an identity as a closeted gay man. He considered "coming out" but felt that he could not do it.

Studds often referred to himself as a congressman who was gay, not as the gay congressman. His responsibilities to his district and the nation came first. He collaborated with gay movement leaders, however, and fought in Congress to achieve equality for gay men and lesbians in two major areas: AIDS research, prevention, and care; and ending the ban on gays and lesbians in the military. In addition, at the very end of his congressional career, he spoke out against the Defense of Marriage Act, which would deny federal protection to same-sex couples.

Within the gay movement, Studds excelled as a spokesman. He was a commanding orator, blessed with a keen intellect, a sense of compassion and humor, and a magnificent voice. His most important contribution to the gay rights movement, and thus to American history, was his ability to see ahead. Studds had been a history teacher, and he paid attention to the story of the African American civil rights movement, even though his district was overwhelmingly white. This frame of reference made him patient and helped him to understand that defeats were inevitable, but that victory would ultimately be won. That victory came much faster than even he imagined, and he had a lot to do with bringing it about. He lived long enough to get to the mountaintop, and even to walk partway into the Promised Land.

Most people who have heard of Gerry Studds know about him for the two weeks in July 1983 when publicity swirled around his censure by the House. Yet Studds kept out of the public eye important information that helps to explain his behavior in 1983. Like other gay men of his generation, he was used to keeping secrets. This book tells the full story for the first time.

Let me offer a word on my use of terminology. During the early part of

Studds's life, Americans used the term "homosexual" to describe same-sex-oriented men, and as narrator, I employ that term up to 1970 for the sake of historical accuracy. For most of Studds's career, gay and lesbian activists referred to themselves as gays and lesbians; the term "LGBT" (lesbian, gay, bisexual, transgender) did not appear until later, so I use the terms "gay" and "lesbian" from 1970 on, using just the word "gay" to stand for the wider movement.

1

Wedding Day

"LOVE IS PATIENT, love is kind. It does not envy, it does not boast . . ."
These simple, direct words are spoken by millions of men and women as part
of their wedding ceremony. But they had never, until recently, been spoken
by two men, or two women, in a legal ceremony in the United States. The
arc of the universe was bending toward justice.

"I, Gerry, take you, Dean, to be my spouse, to have and to hold from this
day forward, for better or for worse, for richer, for poorer, in sickness and
in health, to love and to cherish; until death do us part." And Dean Hara
repeated this vow to Gerry Studds.[1]

"By the power vested in me by the Commonwealth of Massachusetts,
I now pronounce you spouse and spouse," minister Tom Green intoned.
Historic words—"spouse and spouse." They were being repeated around the
Commonwealth of Massachusetts in mid-May 2004 for the first time in the
country's history.

Studds never thought that he would see same-sex couples marry in his
lifetime, and certainly never thought that he would be married himself. The
concept of being allowed to marry someone they loved was unfathomable
to gay men of Gerry's and Dean's age. Ever since the landmark November
2003 *Goodridge* decision of the Massachusetts Supreme Judicial Court, the
possibility of getting married was coming close to reality. After months of
political and legal challenges, the first day was to be Tuesday, May 17, 2004.
Studds did not want to get caught up in the inevitable media circus, so early
on the following day, he and Dean filed for their marriage license. The clerks
recognized Gerry, the country's first openly gay congressman, and wished
the couple well.

Gerry and Dean had been together and exchanged rings in 1991, a personal commitment with no legal standing. Now they wanted to perform a legal ceremony as soon as possible, and scheduled it for May 24, the same date when Dean's parents had married.

The wedding was a private affair with only six people present. Tom Green, an ordained United Church of Christ minister and an acclaimed architect, performed the simple ceremony in the Beacon Hill apartment he shared with his partner, David Simpson. Gerry knew Tom and David from Provincetown, dating back to an unhappy period in the summer of 1983. Tom Iglehart, a former student of Gerry's, took the pictures. Another friend then solemnized David and Tom's marriage.

Eight years earlier, Gerry had delivered a stirring address on the floor of the House of Representatives protesting the Defense of Marriage Act, which seemed to shut the door on federal acceptance of same-sex marriage. No one in those heady days of May knew whether or not some federal court would enjoin the Massachusetts marriages.

Gerry and Dean, both over six feet tall, wore dark suits and big smiles. Dean chose a solid blue necktie, and Gerry's sported diagonal multihued red stripes. Seated, they posed for wedding photos with the "flower girl," their black and white English springer spaniel. Standing, David and Tom flanked the happy couple, champagne glasses raised, as light streamed in. The clouds of earlier in the day had parted.

"He was so much in love," Dean remembered, years after Gerry's sudden death just three years after the wedding. "He had been a man desperate for love." For Gerry, this was a happy climax to a private life that had been lived in the shadows and hidden in plain sight until his forty-sixth year. Dean was twenty years younger than Gerry. They had grown up in different times.

"Oh my God," Dean thought that day. "I'm getting married! Growing up gay—you couldn't imagine getting married."

Yet some people *had* imagined it, fought for it, and made it happen. Those people stood on the shoulders of the activists of Gerry's generation, and the commitment of all of them would change the world.

2

A New England Boyhood

THE ALGONQUINS who fished the dangerous waters called it Quonahassit—
"long rocky place" in English. That was the language spoken by the pale-
faced invaders who arrived in a year they denominated 1614. A negotiation
between the white men and natives turned into a fight, and the strangers
were driven off in a hail of arrows, but not before one Algonquin was
wounded and another killed by the white men's guns. Three hundred years
later, the villagers of Cohasset, having Anglicized the Indian name for the
place, erected a commemorative marker on the probable spot of this bloody
skirmish between Captain John Smith of the Virginia settlement and the
native people.

After this first encounter, the Algonquin people began to die of exposure
to European diseases. English settlers arrived at Plymouth in 1620, Wessa-
guscus (modern Weymouth) in 1622, and Shawmut (Boston) in 1630. In
the 1630s, English Puritans established themselves at Bare Cove, which they
renamed for their original home and incorporated as Hingham of Massachusetts Bay Colony. More than a century later, at the southern extremity
of this settlement, some villagers, seeking a church and town meeting nearer
to themselves, organized the separate village of Cohasset, a poor cousin to
Hingham.

The Algonquins had named it well: spectacular granite outcroppings
marked its unique geography, and threatening coastal rocks would sink
many a ship in the following years, necessitating the construction of light-
houses. The townspeople turned to catching lobsters and fishing for herring
and mackerel. In the rich forest they found ample supplies of timber for

homes, boats, and firewood; inland lay arable land for corn, hay, and vegetables, and space for animal husbandry.

By the middle of the nineteenth century, Cohasset was a rural fishing village, connected to the thriving commercial hub of Boston by a railroad. The village green, located between the cove at the Scituate border and the Little Harbor, hosted plain white frame Congregational and Unitarian churches and a town hall. In the 1980s, when a movie company shooting *The Witches of Eastwick* sought a perfect representative of a quiet New England town, they located in Cohasset.[1]

As Boston became crowded with new immigrants beginning in the 1890s, some members of its wealthy Brahmin class began turning their Cohasset summer homes into permanent residences. The attractions of the town's coastline brought visitors for day trips and weekend excursions. Hotels like Kimballs at the cove and the Red Lion Inn in the village still survive today. Circus entertainers including England's acrobatic Hanlon Brothers made Cohasset their headquarters. Summer theater became the South Shore Music Circus on Sohier Street. In 1894 the Brookline real estate tycoon Henry M. Whitney, who was the genius behind the new Boston subway, set up a golf course on his estate; then a yacht club was established. Along the winding Jerusalem Road, wealthy businessmen constructed magnificent homes. Among them was Clarence Barron, the financial writer who founded the eponymous stock market report. These new estates transformed the humble fishing village's identity within the metropolitan area, but by the end of World War II, Cohasset, despite its wealthy newcomers, remained a semi-rural fishing village and modest bedroom community.[2]

This was the town to which Elbridge Gerry Eastman Studds (he abjured the first two names) and his wife, Beatrice, moved with their three children in 1946 from Garden City, New York. Eastman Studds had been born to Colin Auld Studds and Maud Eastman. Colin and Maud had married in 1899 at Nashville's First Baptist Church. "The bride is the representative of old and prominent families of Tennessee," gushed a Nashville society column. Maud "has been admired as one of the handsomest and most attractive members of Nashville society." The groom "is a Virginian and possesses that happy quality of making friends wherever he goes. . . . He occupies the position of District Passenger Agent of the Southeastern Division of the Pennsylvania Railroad."[3]

Probably because of Colin's job, the couple moved to Hempstead, Long Island, a suburb of New York. Soon two sons were born, Colin II and Elbridge Gerry Eastman, named for Maud's grandfather.[4] One of the Eastmans had married a descendant of the illustrious Gerry family of Marblehead, Massachusetts, but there was no direct lineage between other Eastmans and Gerrys. Elbridge Gerry had been a signer of the Declaration of Independence, Massachusetts delegate to the Constitutional Convention, Massachusetts governor, and vice president to James Madison. His name has remained famous in American history for the politically motivated designs he crafted for a North Shore Senate district. A critic branded one such district a "gerrymander," for its salamander-like shape, and the term stuck.

Eastman Studds grew up in Hempstead. In 1915, when he was eleven years old, his father died, and the boys were raised by their mother and her brother. Eastman attended Yale University and established himself as a Park Avenue architect. In 1933 he married Beatrice "Bonnie" Murphy, one of four children of Walter and Clara Murphy of neighboring Garden City. Eastman and Bonnie had been introduced by her brother, a fellow student of Eastman's. Bonnie's father, Walter Murphy, was a wealthy coffee importer whose fortunes sank in the 1929 stock market crash. Although Bonnie had been raised in affluence, her father died penniless. Bonnie was an intelligent young woman who had been accepted at Smith, but her father disapproved of higher education for girls, so she did not go to college. The Murphys were Catholics, and this untraditional Episcopalian-Catholic marriage flew in the face of socially conservative norms, although neither Eastman nor Bonnie was religious. On May 12, 1937, Bonnie gave birth to Gerry Eastman, in nearby Mineola. The boy's first name was pronounced with a hard "G," as in Elbridge Gerry.[5]

Thus the circumstances of Gerry Eastman Studds's birth put him at variance with the person he later seemed to be, through no fault of his own. His name, Cohasset address, elite education, skill at elocution, and dignified bearing suggested that he was an old-line Yankee of proud and comfortable stock. He wasn't. In fact, his bloodline embodied the mid-nineteenth-century Massachusetts Yankee nightmare. In 1854, the American or "Know-Nothing" Party captured the state government by warning against a nonexistent conspiracy between the southern slaveholders and the Roman Catholic Church, both of which, to the old-line Yankees, represented un-American tendencies. Gerry Studds was descended from exactly that lineage.

For young Gerry, Cohasset was an idyllic place in which to grow up. Although his earliest years were spent on Long Island, during World War II Eastman moved the family to Birmingham, Alabama, where he had secured a job. Two more children were born, a sister, Gaynor, in 1940 and a brother, Colin Auld, in 1944. Gerry felt himself to be an outsider among his southern schoolmates and remembered his early boyhood years there as miserable.

After the war the family returned briefly to Long Island. Then in 1946 Eastman took a job in Boston and commuted from Cohasset, picking the town sight unseen. They took up residence in a series of rented homes on Jerusalem Road and later on Elm Street, all right near the village. Their first rental on Jerusalem Road, near the cemetery, overlooked the marshy inner harbor; later, on Elm Street, the family lived closer to the village and the inviting yellow brick Paul Pratt Library. In 1952 Eastman purchased a house at 16 Black Horse Lane, which was to remain the family home throughout Gerry's congressional career.[6] This colonial house on a quiet lane seemed unprepossessing enough from the street, but Eastman built an attractive addition. The side of the building faced a saltwater tidal marsh, and to the rear lay a wood. The Studds family did not move there until Gerry was away at boarding school, but he entered young manhood with the sense of having a permanent home and loving family.

Gerry attended fifth and sixth grades at the town's only school, on Ripley Road. Cohasset was still an intimate village of only 3,700 in 1950, with most of its land dedicated to forest and farm. Some Portuguese American fishermen clustered around the cove, and most of the Yankees worked as farmers and tradesmen. The big estates may have made Cohasset look rich, but it wasn't.[7]

The cove, where the lobster boats lay at anchor, was a short walk past the village. For two summers, young Gerry apprenticed himself to an old lobsterman. Gerry would peg the lobsters as the old man removed them from their traps. Together they harpooned tuna, swordfish, and sometimes even a shark. Then they would retire to the old mariner's quarters, where he would regale Gerry with tales of the sea. The old man had shipped as a cabin boy from Marblehead to Hawaii and later sailed to Cuba once by himself. "There's other kinds o' knowledge that you don't learn at college," the old salt rhymed. Gerry wrote to his Long Island grandmother, informing her that he wanted to be a lobsterman too when he grew up. "Be careful," Gerry's parents warned him. He didn't understand what they meant until many years later, and he felt hurt and confused that his parents seemed to distrust his dear friend.[8]

Gerry remembered his father as a "quiet, gentle, and unassuming man, without the hard, competitive edge necessary to flourish in business."[9] He was a capable architect but apparently delivered such thorough service that he spent too many uncompensated hours with contractors and homeowners. Gerry's mother was loving and sociable, an avid gardener. Having been raised among the elite, Bonnie had grown up with a cook, but as a wife and mother had to learn to run a household herself. Socially correct to a fault, Bonnie and Eastman dressed properly for cocktail hour and dinner.

They wanted the best for their children, especially for their firstborn, for whom they purchased Brooks Brothers clothing, an expense they denied themselves. They joined the yacht club, and Gerry learned to sail. The house was more than Eastman could afford, until his mother moved in and paid off the mortgage with the proceeds from the sale of her Long Island home. Gerry sensed that his parents' fortunes had declined, and that they had invested their own aspirations in him. Throughout his life Gerry worried about money. Like Cohasset itself, Gerry Studds looked richer than he was.

Gerry excelled in school and suffered for it socially. He had been moved ahead one grade, and began committing deliberate errors, the better to fit in with his peers. For seventh grade, his parents obtained a scholarship for Gerry to attend the Derby Academy in Hingham, where academic achievement was prized. Nonetheless, Gerry's lasting memory of the school was of its tedious dancing classes conducted by a prudish octogenarian; already he was a rebellious personality constrained by the strictures of conformity. Gerry played with neighborhood friends, among them Lew Crampton and Barbara DuBois, who joined the Studds family on Christmas Eve to sing Handel's *Messiah* around the piano. Over the years, the Black Horse Lane home became a gathering place for Gerry's companions. Gerry, Gaynor, and Colin lived harmoniously with happily married parents, and the siblings remained friends throughout their lives. As Gerry concluded eighth grade in 1950, his parents obtained for him another scholarship. Their intellectual, nautical son had been accepted at the distinguished Groton School.

Groton

Studds remembered Groton as "close to heaven on earth."[10] He never described the United States Congress, or any other institution with which he was associated, in remotely the same terms. The school was set on four hundred acres in the town of Groton, thirty-five miles northwest of Boston. Its campus was arranged in a circle around a common designed by Frederick Law Olmsted. An American version of an English prep school, this was a place for the academic elite. Its graduates included Franklin Delano Roosevelt and Dean Acheson. Dormitory living was barracks-like so that no boy could flaunt his wealth, a tradition for which Studds was duly appreciative. Its Latin motto emphasizing public service guided headmaster John Crocker and the school's teaching staff. With only two hundred students, academic life was intimate, rigorous, and steeped in the liberal arts tradition. All thirty-eight boys in the graduation picture were white, most bearing Yankee names.

Here young Gerry took flight. Now there was no need to play dumb to fit in. At Groton he mastered French and studied ancient Greek, an early display of a remarkable gift for languages. During senior year, the boys read through the first six abridged volumes of *A Study of History* by Arnold Toynbee. The final four volumes had not yet been abridged, and so for a class project the students completed the job. Gerry's final paper was a fifty-page essay contrasting Toynbee and Marx. The boy was becoming a young man destined for academic work.

Groton educated the whole boy. Although Gerry's religious inclinations declined, he loved the music of the church throughout his life. He particularly enjoyed choir music and the Sunday organ recital. He sang in the choir, moving from soprano to baritone as his voice, which was mellifluous and resonant, matured. After a deliberate negotiation with his parents, they agreed to rent a baritone horn at five dollars a semester so that he could play in the band. "I soon reached the minimal level of competence required to perform without embarrassing everyone else and maintained precisely that level throughout my years at Groton," he remembered, with the dry, self-deprecating wit that characterized his later oratorical style.[11]

Gerry played Deputy Governor Danforth in Groton's production of *The Crucible* by Arthur Miller. Girls from nearby Concord Academy performed the female roles. Now a staple of high school drama, the play was then a controversial attack on the witch hunt of suspected communists by Senator Joseph McCarthy of Wisconsin. As graduation approached, headmaster Crocker invited the boys to his study to hear a comical recording satirizing McCarthy. Gerry's education was liberal in both senses of the word.[12]

Football was another matter. Gerry perceived himself to be gangly and awkward, but every boy had to play a sport, and he guessed that he would be the least inept at football. He did not take to the physical combat demanded by his position, defensive lineman. Yet he determined that despite his lack of ability, he would prove himself in this endeavor too. His coach constantly yelled at him to "stay low," but the injunction seemed counterintuitive to him, and he usually stood fully erect to make the tackle. This formative experience may have taught him to keep his own counsel, a trait that sometimes served him well and sometimes got him into trouble. At six foot one and 155 pounds, he pounded away in practice against classmates who were more solidly built, until, "in tones," he recalled, "that I can remember to this day," the coach, rebuking his young charges, yelled out, "Jesus Christ, if this keeps up, Studds will make the team." That he did indeed revealed another aspect of the boy's character. He could get knocked down, grit his teeth, and get back up for the next play. Gerry won a varsity letter, blocking a punt in a game against Governor Dummer Academy. Among his teammates were Ken Auchincloss, whose family connections would later help Gerry in Washington, and John Demos, later a historian of the Plymouth settlement.[13]

By 1952, Gerry was fifteen years old and politically aware enough to participate in politics as the presidential election approached. The contest pitted General Dwight David ("Ike") Eisenhower against Adlai Stevenson, whose bald dome and intellectual disposition led to the coining of the term "egghead." Gerry's parents were Republicans, and that was good enough for him, so he joined the Young Republicans Club. "We were appalled, however, to find that most of the faculty supported Adlai Stevenson, a phenomenon for which there seemed no rational explanation," the mature Studds, probably chuckling as he wrote, later observed.[14]

Gerry was now old enough to be interested in girls—except that he wasn't. Luckily for him, attendance at a boys' school limited everyone else's interest in girls, and Gerry just assumed that he was more or less like everyone else. Groton held an annual school dance, and the boys typically invited girls from home to attend, or had classmates arrange dates for them. Gerry had played "spin the bottle" at Cohasset, and fancied for a while that his kissing partner, Barbara DuBois, was his "girlfriend." She was his date at the dances, but they never felt desire for each other. This too seemed entirely normal, and in fact conformed more to proper 1950s codes of behavior than an eruption of passion between them would have.

Yet everyone experiences lust in adolescence, and Gerry felt it for a football teammate, Michael Baring-Gould, who, he later surmised, had no idea of his feelings. They were the best of friends at Groton, and often stayed up talking long into the night. Gerry arranged for his sister Gaynor to be Michael's date at the annual dance. Gerry never tried to express the physical desire he felt, although he had "messed around" (as he wrote in his memoir), which probably meant "mutually masturbated" with other boys. He sensed that an attempt on his part at sexual intimacy with Michael would violate their friendship. Gerry was relatively untroubled by his emerging sexual desires, which he still assumed were "normal." Their friendship continued into college until adult life took them in different directions. Many years later the friends, one of them now a professor, married and a father, the other a U.S. congressman, arranged to meet, but Baring-Gould died in a canoeing accident before their reunion could take place.

During one summer, Gerry went into business for himself, becoming a "mosser." He would row his sixteen-foot boat two or three miles off the ledges ringing Cohasset and Scituate, arriving just ahead of low tide. Then he would scrape Irish moss with a long rake while standing in the boat, loading up to a ton of the plant before returning home when the tide rolled back in. On shore he sold the moss to a processor, who transformed the stuff into a gooey mush used in cosmetics, gunpowder, and instant breakfast. The physically demanding work instilled in him a sense of self-confidence, self-reliance, and a love of the sea, and it made him tougher and stronger.

Gerry spent his final high school summer, 1955, at Groton's camp for poor children in Bristol, New Hampshire. His first exposure to urban children from Boston neighborhoods would widen his horizons, and at Yale he would return to this place. As the old lobsterman had foretold, this was "the knowledge they don't teach at college."

Yale

Gerry graduated from Groton with excellent grades and was offered full scholarships to Harvard and Yale; he chose the latter, probably because his father had graduated from Yale in 1925. In New Haven, he applied himself with the same rigor he had shown at Groton and finished his first year at the top of his class. He became disillusioned with the social sciences, which seemed pretentious and pointless to him, a not uncommon experience for people with a liberal arts bent. Apprenticed to a sociology professor who was conducting a "multi-volume study of the drinking habits of American Jews," he concluded that sociology involved too much bean counting to no useful end. He majored in the emerging field of American studies, which brought together his own interests in history, literature, and music. He continued his Groton pursuits by singing in the choir and playing baritone horn in the marching band.[15]

At the start of his sophomore year in 1956, Russian tanks rolled into Hungary to crush the movement against Soviet rule. The death of Stalin three years earlier, the "secret speech" by new Soviet premier Nikita Khrushchev in which he denounced the crimes of the former tyrant, and tough talk by Secretary of State John Foster Dulles had encouraged Hungarians to rise up. American blustering turned out to be empty rhetoric, and soon a stream of refugees was headed to the United States, many of them winding up in North Haven, Connecticut. The local Episcopal minister called on the Yale community to help instruct the refugees in English. Gerry and a fellow student rose to the challenge.

Of course, neither youth had a word of Hungarian, which is one of only a few non-Western languages found in Europe, along with Finnish and Basque. The young teachers began with pointing and charades, an approach guaranteed to yield comic misunderstandings. The students persevered, and as their original group of thirty refugees grew to two thousand, they pressed the university's lone professor of Hungarian into service and recruited more volunteers. They even produced an elementary textbook that became a national model.

Through this effort, the governor of Connecticut created a committee for Hungarian refugee relief, and the group named Gerry its director of education. He traveled around the state organizing local committees to work with the new arrivals. He found administrative tasks less rewarding than teaching. Meanwhile, his grades declined as he barely attended classes for almost five months. At the end of his sophomore year, he wrote his parents a long philosophical letter that showed his personal maturation. By age twenty, he was really absorbing the message of those teachers who encouraged their charges to do useful work in the world. Gerry had heard a speech by the Christian philosopher Paul Tillich, and later attended a talk by Martin Luther King Jr. "Knowledge without wisdom is worthless," Gerry quoted Tillich to his parents. He apologized to them for the lower grades he anticipated, and resolved to apply himself to his studies, but with a deeper understanding of the difference between careerism and seeking a purpose in life.[16]

Also in his sophomore year, Gerry joined Saint Anthony Hall, a nonresidential fraternity which became the center of his social life. He roomed at Saybrook, one of Yale's residential colleges, with fellow Grotonians. Saint Anthony Hall promoted public service, and its members often pursued careers in government, the diplomatic corps, religion, academia, or the arts. The fraternity held a regular Thursday night discussion group downstairs in the basement, known as "the Crypt." These evenings often featured outside speakers but sometimes had an open agenda. The discussions encouraged him to return to Groton's camp for poor children as a counselor. His social conscience was growing.[17]

The following year Gerry won the Robert Staats Millikan Award for Christian leadership. He had initiated a Big Brother chapter to work with emotionally disturbed children in nearby Hamden. This activity no doubt grew out of his camp counselor summers and Saint Anthony Hall conversations about leading a meaningful life. His award was noted in the Yale and Boston newspapers. The young man was distinguishing himself among elite company.[18]

With his fraternity brothers at Saint Anthony Hall, Gerry could also reflect in a general fashion on the emerging major question in his life—his sexual orientation. There he could raise the question of "love" in the shared language of Socratic dialogue as recorded by Plato. These were thoughtful young men who took intellectual life seriously. The students knew about "love" between teacher and student in classical times but could not connect that phrase to their own place and time. He recalled: "Knowing there was something I wanted and needed, but not understanding it, I hinted, I suggested, I wondered, I requested, and very often and in terror of the consequences, I begged. It is a tribute to the genuineness of many of these friendships that they endured even this."[19]

Most likely no one knew what he was really getting at. "I had no idea he was gay," recollected Tim Hogen, a fellow student. "No one even had the concept in those days. He went out with my sister once or twice. I remember him as serious, well spoken, and a deep thinker." Dave Schroeder, a Groton football teammate and Yale contemporary, confirmed this view. "We double-dated a few times over one summer, and I don't think he knew what his sexual orientation was then."[20]

Like so many homosexual young men of his generation, Studds had nowhere to turn. He did not encounter fellow homosexual students, who were also hiding and wondering alone. He did not have a spiritual adviser; his French professor, a devotee of Voltaire, had confirmed his doubts about religion. He was lucky in this, for all major religions condemned homosexuality as a sin, and he would have been counseled to suppress his impulses. Nor was there a homosexual community to which he might have been referred; homosexual activity was a crime as well as a sin. Police departments typically had "vice" squads that routinely entrapped homosexual men. Had he consulted a psychiatrist, he would have been told that he had a medical condition for which the cure was difficult and expensive—lots of talking at best, or electric shocks at worst.[21]

In addition to being branded sinners, criminals, and mental degenerates, homosexual Americans also were regarded as potential traitors and were barred from federal employment shortly after the Eisenhower administration came into power. During the early 1950s, Senator Joseph McCarthy promoted a fear of communists who had supposedly infiltrated Washington and Hollywood. Because homosexuality was illegal, red hunters surmised that communists could blackmail homosexuals in government office. A "lavender scare" caused homosexuals to be hunted out in government departments, and by 1960 the State Department alone had fired one thousand suspects, some of whom committed suicide. During the 1950s, two thousand a year were expelled from the military. A 1951 best seller, *Washington Confidential,* charged that six thousand "pansies" were on various federal government payrolls, posing a threat to security. States conducted their own investigations, and Florida fired one hundred suspects. Even the American Civil Liberties Union agreed that states had the right to pass anti-sodomy laws, which almost all did. In Britain, prominent homosexuals such as the actor John Gielgud and war hero Alan Turing, who had cracked the German "Enigma" code with a precursor to the computer, were arrested. Turing died mysteriously, probably a suicide, in 1954. In America no public figures admitted to being homosexual. While the worst of these atrocities transpired in the early 1950s, by the time Studds, a politically aware young man, was at Yale, the likelihood is that he knew about the status of homosexuality in the political world. The great irony is that McCarthy (likely but not definitely) and Roy Cohn, his chief aide, were homosexuals themselves. They had pursued communists with a vengeance only to see the hysteria they spread rebound against their own secret selves.[22]

Gerry actually cajoled a few heterosexual companions into sexual experimentation, an exercise that wounded those friendships and left him even more lonely and isolated. Late at night he stole into the library, seeking the book that would explain his predicament, only to find the appropriate pages ripped out—a clue that he was not alone. He would probe his roommates, usually awkwardly, for insights into their own personal dilemmas. "Let me know what's wrong with you, so I can help you," he implored his roommate Dave Schroeder, who replied good-naturedly, "Get off my back Studds, I don't need your help." Obviously, this plea wasn't about Schroeder. In his personal life, Gerry felt lost, alone, and confused, like many other homosexual young men of his time.[23]

Gerry never found the counterculture that was emerging among beatnik poets, some of whom, like Allen Ginsberg, were homosexual. As an American studies major, he might have learned something about the sexual orientation of Walt Whitman, composer Aaron Copland, Harlem Renaissance poets like Langston Hughes or Countee Cullen, or their literary descendant James Baldwin, then just gaining notoriety. The year after Studds graduated, literary critic Leslie Fiedler published his startling *Love and Death in the American Novel,* but his ideas were already percolating in the late 1950s as an antidote to the conformist zeitgeist of the 1950s. Drawing on D. H. Lawrence's observations, Fiedler suggested that the true theme of American literature was homoerotic love between men of different races, and he traced these adventures from *The Deerslayer, Moby-Dick,* and *Huckleberry Finn* to the Lone Ranger. In every case—Natty Bumppo and Chingachgook, Ishmael and Queequeg, Huck and Jim, the Lone Ranger and Tonto—American writers were imagining the same story: escape into the wilderness to a world without civilization and its discontents, that is, the restraining influence of women.[24]

Nor did Gerry locate the obscure Mattachine Society, named for medieval masked revelers, which had organized to promote homosexual rights in 1950. He might have ventured into Greenwich Village in New York to find a semi-public homosexual community, but he never mentioned that in his memoir. He did not seem to have discovered *Sexual Behavior in the Human Male,* by Alfred Kinsey, published in 1948, which reported that 37 percent of men had had a homosexual experience. Although this figure was later challenged, Gerry might have found it reassuring, but he doesn't seem to have known about the book.[25]

Homosexuality remained a dark netherworld in the 1950s. As the historian Linda Hirshman reminds us, homosexuals, unlike participants in the civil rights movement, did not have families or communities to turn to for support.[26] Young homosexuals lived alone with their terrible secret. Groton had been near to heaven for Gerry, but for most young homosexuals, almost anywhere in the United States, Yale included, was a hell of isolation and confusion. Gerry Studds would have to face the world on his own upon graduation as the 1950s came to an end.

3

"Bored with Trivia and Impatient with Stupidity"

GERRY STUDDS, Yale '59, surprised his friends and family by pursuing a career in banking. He needed the money—that explained it. In August, he arrived at the Hanover Bank in Manhattan as a trainee for the foreign department. "I enjoyed my first day spent under the tutelage of a tipsy Irish vault keeper," Studds remembered, adding, "He was the last person in the bank that I really liked." After three weeks, Studds ended his career in high finance.[1]

The graduate headed back to New Haven and by October secured a one-year appointment as a permanent substitute teacher for an eighth-grade class in the West Haven school district. Studds had the same class all day for every subject, as in an elementary school. The twenty-five students came from an ethnically mixed blue-collar neighborhood.

The idealistic young teacher soon found himself confronting a hidebound administration, led by a Dickensian principal, Mabel Casner, who was "a living caricature of a conventional public school administrator." Determined to eradicate any hint of creativity shown by either teacher or children, the elderly gray-haired principal stymied Studds's efforts to instill in his students a spirit of self-directed learning. One day the twenty-two-year-old teacher purchased a hundred paperbacks out of his own meager savings for class-room use and found that the students liked to read. The stern Casner was not amused. "Reading," she announced, "is a recreation. I will not have it in my school."

And so the situation comedy proceeded, with the principal cast as Elmer Fudd and the teacher as Bugs Bunny. The confrontation came to one humorous climax when Studds willfully defied the regulations involving air raid drills. The alarm for an air raid required the students to retreat to the basement, while the alarm for a fire necessitated an outdoor evacuation. The alarms sounded alike, so when one went off, Studds took his class outside, guessing that a fire alarm might be real but an air raid was probably only a drill. "Don't get smart with me," Casner snapped when Studds explained his reasoning.

This experience might have driven Studds from the field, but he enjoyed teaching. At year's end the children even took him out for a dinner of meatballs and spaghetti, with allowance money they had saved, to show their appreciation. Studds had found a career.

Unfortunately, he was a mere substitute lacking an education degree and state certification. So Studds applied for and, in March 1960, won a Ford Foundation scholarship for Yale's master's in teaching program, with a concentration in history. One of Studds's history professors (perhaps the renowned Edmund Morgan, the scholar of the American Revolution, or possibly the equally distinguished Robin Winks in European history), disdaining the notion of "teaching" as a discipline in itself, simply circulated a reading list and invited the students to visit him in his office at their leisure. For Studds, who acquired his degree, this was a year well spent.[2]

Meanwhile, Studds was shedding his old skin, at least in one way. By November 1958 he had turned twenty-one and had cast his first vote in the congressional election for Republican Hastings Keith. As the 1960 presidential race got under way, Studds was attracted by the vigor, idealism, and glamour of fellow Bay Stater John F. Kennedy. Like millions of his generation, Studds could see in Kennedy an image of his own aspirations. "I was captivated by his eloquence and his wit," Studds recalled, two qualities that he himself possessed. According to his memoir, he "hung on every word of the Kennedy-Nixon debates," although he did not identify any specific issue that distinguished the two candidates. During the campaign Kennedy promoted himself as a more capable Cold Warrior than his opponent, warned of a nonexistent "missile gap" that he had simply invented, and promised to spark the economy, which was temporarily marked by slow growth. The debates were all about style, not substance; they reflected a Cold War consensus. Studds spent election day driving Democratic voters to the polls.[3]

In other areas of his life, Studds knew what was expected of him and tried to behave accordingly. He dated young women, and in his memoir he did not mention any homosexual experiences during this time. Gerry had a romance with a professor's daughter in which the couple petted and confessed their mutual admiration. Girls were supposed to be virgins, and proper behavior precluded consummation of desire until after the wedding. The couple discussed marriage, and he took his girlfriend home to meet his approving parents, but he declined to take the next step. The young woman likely would have sensed how forced his attentions were. In his personal life, as he watched his college friends begin families, Studds seemed stuck in neutral.

Meanwhile, the changing political situation widened his professional horizons. Millions of young people, inspired by Kennedy's idealism, turned to public service careers. Studds, with his Groton and Yale pedigree, his proficiency in French and experience with the Hungarian refugees, was ready to embark on a career in the Foreign Service. He was temperamentally and intellectually as well suited for this as he was for teaching. In December 1960, he passed the written exam and began studying for the oral interview by reading up on economics, his weakest area, and devouring the *New York Times*.

The fateful day arrived and Studds performed well, until the economics questions. One examiner grilled the young applicant regarding the deficit in the U.S. balance of payments. Studds had a carefully prepared reply for this expected question, but it merely restated the premise by affirming that "large amounts of gold are leaving the United States and going to France."

"Mr. Studds," the interviewer said, "what difference does it make where that gold is?"

"Sir, I don't have the foggiest idea," Studds replied.

He got the job, pending his security clearance. At the interview Studds easily fielded questions about potential subversive contacts (none), personal habits (wholesome), and his politics (registered independent). Studds recounted the one potential trouble spot in his memoir:

"Do you prefer boys or girls?" the interviewer asked.
   "Girls," I responded without hesitation.
   "Let the public service be a proud and lively career," President Kennedy had exhorted. With this, my first official lie, I qualified for such a career.

Camelot

New Foreign Service officers start off with three two-year postings, one in Washington and two abroad. Studds had met a lovely young woman named Ann Giese at a wedding, and he was now courting her, so he requested that his first assignment be in Washington. Ann was a Radcliffe senior whom

Studds remembered as "vivacious, fun-loving and playful," and he believed himself to be in love with her. In addition, he hoped to be assigned to Budapest, and only married men were dispatched behind the Iron Curtain, to preclude "penetration of personnel," as Studds described the policy, with a rhetorical chuckle.[4]

Studds was assigned to the newly established Operations Center in the State Department, a New Frontier crisis management office that monitored cable traffic from key embassies, along with CIA and Defense Department messages. Stephen Smith, the president's brother-in-law, and Theodore Achilles, a career diplomat, served as directors. Studds had known the latter man's son at Saint Anthony Hall. This Yale link would have endeared Studds to Achilles senior.

Studds worked a twenty-four-hour shift, paired with a senior officer, sometimes Smith or the pipe-smoking Achilles, followed by two days off. For a young man turning twenty-five, just two years removed from jousting with principal Mabel Casner, this was pretty heady stuff. The staffers discussed global politics during the long shifts, springing into action only if there was some urgent development, such as the crises in Berlin and the Congo which flared up during his tour. Studds was not making any decisions, but he did get to see how the process worked. Sometimes he attended meetings convened by Secretary of State Dean Rusk.[5]

On his days off, Gerry spent time with Ann. Her expressive eyes were set in an oval face, crowned by an abundant mane of dark hair. Gerry took her home to Cohasset, and again his family encouraged him. "If you don't marry her," his father declared, "I will." Studds had buried his secret deep inside himself, and only his mother suspected his true nature. Ann faced other obstacles with Gerry that might have daunted a less adventuresome spirit. Qualified in French, Studds anticipated that his first assignment would be to Upper Volta, a poverty-stricken Francophone African nation. He called and asked Ann to come with him to Ouagadougou, its capital. She said yes, and the wedding was set for the National Cathedral in Washington. The *Boston Globe* society page carried the announcement of the engagement on Christmas Eve, 1961. Studds dutifully lost his virginity with Ann. The wedding invitations were printed.

Untold numbers of closeted homosexual men before and after Studds had endured this disorienting experience. At last Gerry realized that he could not go through with it. Years later, he wrote frankly about his emotional state: "More disturbing still was the very real attraction I felt for her younger brothers, aged twelve and fifteen. Although there was no question of a physical relationship, there was clearly an intuitive, lyrical, almost chemical component in my response to them that was not present in my feelings for Ann. I became unsettled, confused and frightened." Studds was in Washington, Ann in school at Radcliffe, when he called it off over the phone. "Although we had never discussed what had brought me to this point," Studds later wrote, "it was clear that she had sensed much of what was going on inside me and that she understood, accepted and concurred in my decision. She flew to Washington the next day, and we agreed, amicably and calmly, that we did not have the mutual certainty that marriage deserves. . . . For myself, I had no explanation, none at least that I dared to contemplate."[6]

It is instructive to contrast Studds's life experience to this point with that of two other gay politicians. The first to draw national attention was the openly gay Harvey Milk, elected a city supervisor in 1977 in San Francisco. Born seven years earlier than Studds in New York, Milk knew at an early age that he was a homosexual, and had been arrested in a police sweep of New York's Central Park at age seventeen.[7] He never dated girls, realized that his sexual orientation precluded a public career, and led a resolutely private life far from his parents until the radicalization of the 1960s. In this sense, his life was much simpler than Studds's. Milk had no public persona to defend, and he was unconflicted in his identity.[8]

At the other end of the spectrum, New Jersey governor Jim McGreevey, born to a working-class Irish Catholic family twenty years after Studds, resolutely suppressed his homosexual orientation despite coming of age in the 1970s. Like Studds, he aspired to a political career and went through the public motions of courtship. Unlike Studds, he pursued his genuine erotic feelings in furtive assignations. A believing Catholic, he regarded his own impulses as sinful and did his best to control them, successfully enough to marry and have children. McGreevey's secret exploded when he was blackmailed by a staffer and he decided to resign and confess his sexual orientation. That this drama unfolded as late as 2004 suggests how difficult homophobia made it for gay men, especially those in public life, to come out. Studds certainly did the right thing by calling off his marriage to Ann, and he never made the same mistake again.[9]

Meanwhile, Studds felt his interest in the State Department waning as well. Even in the Kennedy years, the cautious top-down traditions of a sclerotic bureaucracy were all too visible to Studds. "Idealism, energy, willingness to rock the boat didn't seem to last long in this organization," he remembered. Despite the advertised "vigor" of the Kennedy administration, it was exactly this inability to ask searching questions that led it into its two major catastrophes, the Bay of Pigs invasion of 1961 and the decision to send military advisers to Vietnam. Many years later, the major architect of these policies, Secretary of Defense Robert McNamara, identified careerism and a blind "can-do" attitude as contributing factors in the decision to wage war in Vietnam. Studds's top boss, the stolid, unimaginative Dean Rusk at State, never broke from his initial appraisal of Vietnam. Studds, although he was not yet in a position to be making policy decisions, felt constrained and disappointed. On his résumé, he cited "desire for more challenging work" as his reason for leaving the State Department after the eleven months from February 1962 to January 1963. He was applying the lessons learned at Groton and Yale about critical thinking, but he was mired in a bureaucracy that valued conformity.[10]

Luckily, Studds was assigned to serve as special assistant to the secretary general of the International Conference on Human Skills, to be held in Puerto Rico in early October 1962. This multi-departmental working group was directed by Sargent Shriver, another presidential brother-in-law, and head of the Peace Corps. Hoping to counter the popularity of Fidel Castro's revolution, the administration sought to encourage economic growth in underdeveloped nations. Capital investment alone would not do the job. Emerging nations needed more literate and highly skilled workforces to wield the modern machinery of the postwar era. Representatives of forty-three nations from Europe, Latin America, and Africa attended the conference and agreed to set up a manpower training office in Washington. Studds regarded the gathering as a success and changed his return ticket in order to visit the Dominican Republic, Haiti, Jamaica, and Nassau on his way home so as to learn more about some of the participating nations. This was his first meaningful foreign travel.[11]

A few days after the conference ended, the Cuban missile crisis began. These were tense and exciting times for a young man to be working in Washington, and Studds felt frustrated by the plodding nature of his work at State. He shared these feelings with an insider twenty years his senior, W. Don Ellinger. Ellinger was a friend of David Hackett, who knew Attorney General Bobby Kennedy. Hackett told Studds that the president was preparing a new organization, a domestic version of the Peace Corps that would work in poverty-stricken areas of the United States. Ellinger and Hackett pulled some strings and got Studds temporarily reassigned from State to the attorney general's office and later to the Interior Department.[12]

Studds now found himself in meetings with the attorney general, Hackett,

Ellinger, and Richard Goodwin, planning for what they dubbed a National Service Corps. They resolved to mobilize five thousand volunteers and part-time staffers to address the problem of poverty in the United States. Studds was assigned to take the idea on the road in January 1963. Drawing on his own experience working with emotionally disturbed children, minority youth, and Hungarian refugees, he spoke at the University of Illinois and the University of Pittsburgh about the plan. He found much enthusiasm among young people and heard probing questions from professionals about how the new organization would interact with existing social service agencies.[13]

By May, the president had approved the report and appointed Captain William R. Anderson, retired commander of the famed nuclear submarine *Nautilus,* as leader of the effort, and Anderson picked Studds as his executive assistant. They still had to sell the idea to a skeptical Congress, which was dominated by a coalition of segregationist southern Democrats and budget-conscious midwestern Republicans. Studds traveled to Akron, Pittsburgh, and Tampa this time to address men twice his age. Accompanying Anderson, Studds visited Indian reservations in South Dakota and mental hospitals in Maryland and Kansas.[14]

These experiences brought Studds into face-to-face contact with black community leaders. On August 28 he attended the March on Washington, securing a place just yards from the podium. While the march is best remembered for Martin Luther King's passionate "I Have a Dream" speech, the speakers included all the top leaders of the civil rights movement. The most controversial was young John Lewis of the Student Nonviolent Coordinating Committee, who had been beaten and jailed as a Freedom Rider. Studds could not then have imagined that he and Lewis would one day serve together in Congress and become friends. "No event in my life had moved me so deeply," Studds recalled. "I can still feel the intense August heat and the exhilaration of the crowd as they marveled at who they were and what they had done. I can still taste the peanut butter sandwich passed to me by a black family from Iowa whom I had never met." And had Studds known that the unsung hero of that memorable day was a homosexual, forced into the shadows by prejudice, the event would have been even more overwhelming. The march was actually the inspiration of activists senior to King, the labor leader A. Philip Randolph and his aide, the radical pacifist Bayard Rustin. Rustin's 1951 arrest on a "morals" charge convinced the other leaders that he had better keep a low profile.[15]

Three months later, Studds joined his staff colleagues to walk past President Kennedy's casket in the East Room of the White House. He had spent the previous four days, like everyone else in the country, in front of his television set, wondering how it could have happened.

The Kennedy administration had failed to get the National Service Corps bill through Congress, but in 1964 President Lyndon Johnson succeeded, and Volunteers in Service to America (VISTA) was born. Despite Johnson's commitment to the Kennedy agenda, and superior legislative skills that produced the Civil Rights Act of 1964 and the Voting Rights Act of 1965, the atmosphere of idealism was beginning to dissipate. For many young people like Studds, Camelot was over and a confusing, disillusioning new reality was setting in.

Masculinity

Studds was out of a job shortly after VISTA was created. He had been a State Department employee on temporary assignment, but during the National Service Corps campaign, he had quit at State, in a telling fashion. He had been offered a position in January 1963, early in his Interior Department assignment, to return as a junior officer in the European Affairs division. Studds went to an interview at the personnel department, where a staffer told him that his background check for the job revealed a pattern of informants who complained that he was "bored with trivia and impatient with stupidity." Studds, now a headstrong young man, agreed that those characteristics did indeed describe him: "I told [the interviewer] that if I were hiring someone for a position of responsibility, boredom with trivia and impatience with stupidity were characteristics that I would insist on." This determined act showed a self-confidence and lack of diplomacy that would characterize his early career. Studds abruptly resigned from the Foreign Service, burning his bridges behind him. "He was not easily intimidated," former schoolmate Dave Schroeder recalled.[16]

Still wet behind the ears in political terms, Studds rather incredibly began to explore a run for Congress in his home district, a place where he had never lived as an adult. Studds couldn't even identify most of its towns. But Hastings Keith had not voted for the National Service Corps, and Studds was considering taking him on. A dinner with New Bedford Democratic Party leaders, Mr. and Mrs. Sylvester Sylvia, convinced Studds that he would be wasting his time.

Back in Washington, Studds was living with roommates, one of whom was his old Groton classmate Ken Auchincloss, whose grandfather was about to retire as a Republican congressman from New Jersey. This Groton connection gave Studds an insider status that could only increase his confidence. Through Don Ellinger, Studds secured a position as legislative assistant to New Jersey senator Harrison A. Williams Jr.[17] Studds did not realize it, but he had stumbled accidentally into an impossible situation that was nevertheless about to reshape his career.

Williams, a Democrat, had successfully led the fight for the first federal mass transportation act, which allocated funds to states and metropolitan areas. He chaired the Subcommittee on Migratory Labor of the Committee on Labor and Public Welfare; in that capacity he had championed the VISTA bill. Williams was also an alcoholic. His chief subcommittee aide, Frederick Blackwell, controlled access to him, a responsibility that should have rested with newly appointed legislative aide Studds, who was just learning that Williams's office suffered from high turnover because of these problems. As Williams approached the 1964 campaign, tensions in the office boiled over, just as they had before Studds arrived and as they would continue to do, much more disastrously, after Studds left.

Blackwell sent a memo to all the office workers (as committee counsel, he was not on that staff himself), ordering them not to initiate conversations with the senator. During the election campaign, reporters sniffed out that Blackwell, a congressional employee, was improperly participating in the election campaign. Blackwell accused Studds of leaking the information and threatened to fire six staffers, something that he did not have the power to carry out but that he might persuade Williams to do. Studds headed this off, and the story never broke. They had policy differences as well. Blackwell assured Studds in the spring of 1964 that the Vietnam War would be over by the fall. Despite this internal strife, Studds worked twelve-hour days, seven days a week. He submitted his resignation, the fourth legislative assistant to do so in six years, shortly after Williams won reelection.[18]

Williams would be elected two more times. In 1968 he was censured by the New Jersey chapter of the NAACP for making a scene while under the influence of alcohol at its convention. After that, Williams became sober. But in 1981 he was convicted for his role in the FBI "Abscam" sting operation, in which several Congress members were invited to accept bribes from an overzealous FBI agent posing as an Arab sheikh called "Abdul." Williams resigned before the Senate could expel him, and served three years in a federal penitentiary. This sorry story (without Williams's part included) would be reprised in the 2013 movie *American Hustle*.[19]

But that remained many years in the future. After the 1964 election, Studds again found himself on the Washington merry-go-round in search of a job. He secured an enthusiastic letter of recommendation from Williams and anticipated that on the strength of it he should be readily employable. Studds applied again at the State Department. In his preliminary interview, Studds fielded the predictable questions about his loyalty, associates, and possible use of drugs. He reported frankly on his difficulties with Blackwell in Senator Williams's office, but he anticipated that Williams's letter would trump Blackwell's likely opposition to his hiring at State. Over the next few months, Studds's friends called to reassure him, reporting that they had just been interviewed and that they had said all the right things.

As the months passed, however, it gradually dawned on Studds that there was a problem. Finally, he called the State Department and was granted a meeting with the chief of the Division of Special Investigations of the Office of Security. Instead of meeting with Studds, the official led him to an unmarked office and then departed. The receptionist announced that the doctor would see him soon—a psychiatrist, a Dr. Langworthy. Studds felt stunned, tricked, and betrayed. Langworthy began with a series of questions about his feelings regarding his parents, and then turned to Studds's earlier interview, in which the investigating officer had confronted him with the accusation that he was "bored with trivia and impatient with stupidity." Langworthy inquired about Senator Williams and Blackwell. Studds told him that although the two lived together, he did not think they had a homosexual relationship, and that Blackwell, an incompetent, ran the office even though he was assigned to a committee staff, not to the office. At the end of the half hour, Langworthy delivered his opinion: "You seem to have trouble adjusting to authority. . . . The fact remains of your difficulty with interpersonal relations. You know, I've always lived by the philosophy, 'Don't fight battles if you can't win them.'" He said that Studds would soon be informed of the department's conclusion. Studds marched back to the front office and asked why he had been delivered to a psychiatrist. The answer was not reassuring. Studds knew that this stage of his career was over:

> For the first time, I experienced a sensation that was to become increasingly familiar over time—the gnawing and throbbing of a deeply internal wound; a momentary fear of being unable to breathe; a feeling of utter helplessness and vulnerability. They must know something about me, I thought, something potentially humiliating and devastating. But there is nothing I can do about it. There is not even anyone I can talk to about it. . . . [T]he instinct for survival suggested, therefore, that I stuff it deep down inside me, ignore it as best I could, and carry on.[20]

Two days later, on Sunday, Martin Luther King Jr. led thousands of marchers out of Selma, Alabama, on the long walk to Montgomery to demand the
right to vote for the state's disfranchised Negroes. Studds boarded a char-
tered train from Washington filled with spirited activists, black and white
together, arriving for the final days of the protest. "For the first time in my
life," he wrote later, "the only safe place to be was in the black section of the
city; the only safe company to be in was black company; and we spent those
two nights sleeping on the floor of a black church in Montgomery." That
he could join this demonstration so quickly on the heels of suffering such a
bitter personal defeat showed his resilience. He could take a punch and get
back up on his feet. Studds had heard King speak at Yale and had been at the
March on Washington two years earlier. Something inside him—a sense of
being a despised outsider, even if he didn't look like one—was rising within
him. Thousands of marchers thrilled to one of King's greatest speeches.
"How long will it take?" King asked, and answered himself, "Not long!" The
crowd roared its approval. Studds had gone from having a State Department
career to being a protester against the powerful. Later that year, President
Johnson signed the Voting Rights Act into law. Gerry Studds, an astute
observer of history, learned a lesson in the relation between mass action and
effecting social change that would last throughout his life.[21]

A few weeks after returning home, he received his rejection letter from
the State Department. Studds must have suspected that he had been turned
down because he was a homosexual. He didn't even like to admit this to
himself. There is no evidence that Studds was aware that a nascent homosexual rights movement existed in 1965. So in his loneliness and human need
for intimacy, sex, love, and affirmation, during his early Washington years
he reached out to the unlikeliest of people, seeming not to have much of
a sense about the sexual orientation of his own friends. Nobody he knew
talked about homosexuality at the time, except to make demeaning jokes.
"Anyone willing to have dinner and drinks with me was likely to be asked,
after several nightcaps had given me the courage to help in this task," Studds
wrote later. "Everyone, from old friends from school and college passing
through Washington, including Lew Crampton, . . . to new friends, either
in the Foreign Service or acquaintances made in the course of living in
Washington, responded in ways that ranged from awkward to embarrassing
to catastrophic."[22]

Studds probably did not know in 1965, because it was still a secret, that
the State Department was the salient government department guarding
an internal scandal involving homosexuality. This scandal would have

loomed especially large in his superiors' minds because of the uncovering of a British spy ring in the early 1960s, some members of which were Cambridge-educated homosexuals. Also, still abiding in the memory of State Department veterans was the case of Sumner Welles. Named for Massachusetts senator Charles Sumner, and educated at Groton and Harvard, Welles had worked at the State Department for many years, and by 1937 had become an undersecretary of state. In 1940 the married Welles, while traveling by train, propositioned several Pullman porters, who complained to their superior. The story got to the president. Franklin Roosevelt, who regarded homosexuality as a weakness, called for a secret investigation of the rumor, which confirmed its truth. Welles was later forced to resign.[23] This episode formed an integral part of State Department insider lore, but Studds was not an insider.

Homosexuals had been banned from the Civil Service from its inception. After the 1948 publication of the Kinsey Report, and during the McCarthy era anti-homosexual "lavender scare," homosexuals were relentlessly rooted out. According to author and activist Frank Kameny: "In testimony before Congress in 1965, a representative of the department testified that homosexuality was 'an absolute bar' to State Department employment; even a 'latent homosexual' or a person merely with 'homosexual tendencies' was disqualified, even if he had never acted upon his tendencies; anyone who had had even one homosexual experience past his eighteenth birthday was unemployable by the department." Kameny knew this from personal experience; in 1957 he had been fired by the Army Map Service because of his homosexuality. In 1965 Kameny helped engineer a case that reinstated a homosexual man fired from the Labor Department.[24]

Twenty-three years later, Congressman Gerry Studds, having received an offer to write his memoirs, secured the State Department Office of Security's report on him. This document, backed by hundreds of pages of supporting material, began by noting that its subject was "single, and never married, but reportedly once engaged." It observed that one source "expressed doubt regarding STUDDS in area of homosexuality" and another source "recalled hearing jests concerning STUDDS's masculinity." Those two sources, whose names were redacted, were probably Blackwell and an office friend of his. The security officer regretted that he had been unable to contact Senator Williams himself, despite Blackwell's promise to arrange an interview. The rest of the several dozen informants had no doubts about Studds's masculinity, and they probably were all speaking truthfully. The Security Office even interviewed Ann Giese's mother, who entertained no suspicions that Studds might be a homosexual. Reading the report in 1988, Studds probably chuckled quietly as he perused the 1961 interview with principal Mabel Casner, who praised her former employee.[25]

Studds received the March 19, 1965, report of psychiatrist Dr. O. R. Langworthy under separate cover. The two-page, single-spaced document reads like a parody of a psychiatrist viewing normal political conflicts through a distorting pseudo-scientific analytic lens. By the 1980s, Langworthy's report seemed so out of date that it might have been written by an early twentieth-century phrenologist discussing how the shape of a black man's head indicated his mental capabilities: "It is my definite feeling after talking with this man that he has strong paranoid tendencies and great difficulty in getting along with other people. . . . It is also interesting that he tends to accuse the Senator and Blackwell of homosexuality in an indirect way. I certainly do not feel that this is a good candidate for Foreign Service but whether we should turn him down on medical grounds or not would be a matter of consideration."[26] By way of this Kafkaesque bureaucratic logic fused with psychiatric gibberish, Studds was denied a job in the State Department.

Yet in 1965, Studds knew none of this. All he could do was speculate, and the speculation left him with the growing realization that he was a homosexual, a man who was asking his male friends to have sex with him, and who had stopped pretending that he wanted to have sex with women. He had no job and was not sure what he wanted to do next. He was on the outside of society, looking in. It was not impossible that he would grow up to be, as he had written to his grandmother in 1949 at age twelve, just like the lonely Cohasset lobsterman who had taken him out to sea so they could be alone together on his boat.

4

With Gene McCarthy
in New Hampshire

In May of 1965 Gerry Studds reached his twenty-eighth birthday. He was unemployed, had been turned down for a job at the State Department for mysterious reasons, and had little idea how to live life as a man whose impulses were condemned by the wider society. Old friends from school, college, and past jobs drifted away. What would he do next?

A Saint Anthony Hall fraternity brother came to the bewildered young man's aid. Don Welles, now an Episcopal minister, invited him to visit St. Paul's School in Concord, New Hampshire, where he was on the faculty. Like Groton, St. Paul's boasted an expansive campus and an impressive endowment. Its faculty included accomplished graduates of Ivy League schools. He should fit right in, Welles argued. As for the students, "almost every one of these kids will someday be in a position of consequence," he pointed out, "and if you are successful, your impact can be very substantial and very widespread indeed."[1]

Studds took the job. In the 1960s, St. Paul's had 450 students, all boys, and seventy-five faculty members. The "masters" lived on campus and effectively were on duty all day, every day, for nine months of the school year. "I remember the rector telling us to take one weekend off, as if he was being generous," Gerry's colleague Dick Aiken remembered many years later with a rueful grin. Every teacher had responsibilities both for overseeing a dormitory and for coaching a team. The student body was almost all white, and most of the boys came from elite families except for those on scholarship.[2]

Studds taught history and political science. He was a popular, demanding, and brilliant teacher. On the first day of class he passed out a map of the United States and asked the students to fill in the name of each state and its senators, Bill Woodward, one of the scholarship students from New Hampshire, recalled. "I had a huge interest in politics, and I could do more of it than other students." Studds became an inspiring teacher for Woodward, who later worked for him and went on to have a distinguished career as a Washington speechwriter. "He could be tough," Woodward said. "Once he assigned an essay on reapportionment of state legislative districts. I argued that states should be allowed to apportion senatorial districts by county. He just wrote 'balderdash' on it in red ink. I still think I'm right."[3]

Tom Iglehart remembered Studds as witty and engaging in class, using the Socratic method to draw students out and encourage critical thinking. He was also Iglehart's dorm master at Armour House, which attracted artsy, nonconformist students like himself. Studds inhabited a small room there, and students used his place for late-night bull sessions, a safe haven for the offbeat.[4]

The masters were also expected to coach a sport, and "Studds was not very athletic," Aiken, a football coach, recalled. "Also, he got so nervous when he was coaching that he threw up once before a game."[5] The school's fall 1965 pictorial magazine shows a photo of Studds, arms outstretched, as a football appears to bounce off his head and a group of boys giggle in the background. "Sir, you're supposed to use your hands," the caption reads.[6]

Studds coached intramural soccer one year and baseball another. "My baseball team became something of a legend," Studds wrote in his memoir. During one game, an exchange student who had reached third base ran in the wrong direction, back to first base. "Although most [other intramural teams] won more games than we did, very few had as much fun," Studds remembered. His first year went well, and he felt relatively happy. He spent the summer of 1966 taking more history classes, this time at Stanford.[7]

In April 1965, President Lyndon Johnson sent ground troops—not merely "advisers," as President Kennedy had done—to Vietnam. As the death toll in Vietnam began to rise and graduating students faced the prospect of being drafted, protests broke out on many college and high school campuses. College students demanded that their schools end recruitment by the military, ban Reserve Officer Training Corps programs, and cancel research grants from war profiteers. By fall 1967, the antiwar movement picked up steam as the war escalated and nearly half a million troops were fighting in Vietnam.

New Hampshire, a traditionally Republican state, lay far from the turmoil that exploded on American campuses in the mid-1960s. At St. Paul's, the semi-rural location and conservative administration further isolated the school. Yet the generational tension that characterized the 1960s radicalization showed up even there. The antiwar students formed a chapter of Students for a Democratic Society, the nationally organized New Left group that led many campus antiwar actions. The activists included the sons of Secretary of Defense Robert McNamara and Secretary of the Army Stanley Resor. The students sought a charter from the administration and were bluntly turned down. They countered by reorganizing the group as "Student Left," which had no national ties, and this request could not reasonably be rejected. The boys asked Studds, who had emerged as a friend of the rebellious students and an opponent of the war, to serve as their adviser. His acceptance earned him the enmity of the administration and the many conservative senior faculty members.

Student Left organized a contingent to join the dramatic March on the Pentagon in October 1967. Young people faced off against their peers in uniform. An iconic photograph captured a protester placing a flower in a rifle barrel. "Upon my return to school," Studds remembered, "I learned that I had offended the Secretary of the Army," the father of one of his students, "not by joining a march on his office to express opposition to his policy, but by declining an invitation to ride home with him in his limousine for dinner that evening."[8]

The participation of the St. Paul's contingent in the march spurred more intense campus debate. In the school newspaper, Studds called for dialogue and took note of the first St. Paul's alumnus to be killed in Vietnam.[9] The discussion continued in Student Left's publication, *Sinister* (Latin for "Left"), between a conservative master and faculty adviser Studds. The next day, an administrator summoned Studds to his office and told him that the publication would be closed down. "Shortly afterwards," Studds recalled, "I was told by [another] senior administrator that I was 'totally nihilistic and destructive' and 'a disgrace to Groton, Yale, and the Foreign Service.' A free translation, I presumed, was 'a traitor to your class.'" But the upper class was itself dividing over the war, as the administrators soon learned. The father of one of the leftist students served as a trustee, and he protested the censorship of the newspaper. The administrators reversed course, but Studds was becoming the focus of their ire. He began to think about alternative employment. Then in November 1967, the ground under the American political world began to tremble. New Hampshire and Gerry Studds would be at the earthquake's epicenter, and the shake-up would lead Studds to his life's work.[10]

McCarthy for President

The war in Vietnam began as a Democratic project, with its roots in the Harry Truman administration's support of the French colonial war from 1946 to 1954. President Eisenhower continued that policy after the French defeat by imposing the Ngo Dinh Diem regime on Vietnam. President Kennedy sent advisers to the Vietnamese military, and Johnson introduced U.S. ground combat troops. They all believed in the Cold War consensus that communism was evil and had to be fought on every front, that plotters in Moscow were causing all the world's problems, and that one communist victory would lead inexorably to the next—the "domino theory."

The antiwar movement had many different components but might be thought of as divided into two overlapping camps, the liberals and the radicals. Most visible because they were young, confrontational, and militant were the radicals of the New Left. Students for a Democratic Society organized the first anti–Vietnam War march on Washington in April 1965. Shaped by their experiences in Mississippi during the civil rights movement's Freedom Summer in 1964, the New Leftists took as their point of departure the Democratic Party convention in Atlantic City, in which the Mississippi Freedom Democrats—almost all of them black but with a few white allies—were denied fair representation in favor of the regular Democrats, segregationists all. To the New Leftists, the Democratic Party was part of the problem, not part of the solution, as a later aphorism would put it. They saw the war in Vietnam as part of the worldwide anticolonial struggle—similar to that led by Gandhi against the British in India. They argued that the whole system was corrupt, and their strategy was to disrupt the system by any means necessary. The New Left's raucous energy was fueled by the draft, the collusion of academia with the war machine, and the spiraling death toll among Vietnamese and Americans.[11]

The larger, more powerful camp was that led by Democratic Party–aligned antiwar liberals, including such traditional peace organizations as SANE, the anti–nuclear weapons group; Americans for Democratic Action; and the National Student Association.[12] As the war became increasingly unpopular among liberal Democrats, more and more of them turned against it. Some antiwar Democrats saw the war as immoral, but most, such as future House speaker Thomas P. "Tip" O'Neill of Massachusetts, simply thought it was unwinnable, the wrong war in the wrong place. Allard Lowenstein, a former president of the National Student Association, regarded the war as immoral but objected to the hyperbolic rhetoric of the New Leftists. In the spring of

1967 he advanced a plan to "Dump Johnson." To almost everyone, the idea sounded preposterous, but Lowenstein organized student body presidents to agitate within the Democratic Party for an alternative to LBJ. Lowenstein hoped that New York senator Robert F. Kennedy would run. Kennedy was tempted, but he worried that his Senate colleagues would view his decision to run as motivated by personal animus against the president rather than by principled opposition to the war.

After considering other alternatives, Lowenstein turned to Eugene McCarthy, the senior senator from Minnesota and a firm opponent of the war. The two men were quite dissimilar in temperament. Lowenstein was fiery, moralistic, and a workaholic. His frenetic pace and narcissism rubbed some the wrong way, but it took a bold, driven leader like him to crystallize opposition against a sitting president. The senator, by contrast, was cool, cerebral, reserved, and not politically ambitious.[13]

McCarthy, a man of principle, hesitated. He worried that his candidacy would put congressional Democrats on the spot: Were they for McCarthy or Johnson? Either way they invited a primary challenge, potentially splitting the party. McCarthy also worried that Robert Kennedy might still enter the race. And he, McCarthy, had never run a national campaign before.[14]

While Lowenstein searched for a way to "Dump Johnson" in 1968, the same question was percolating among liberal Democrats in the nation's first primary state, New Hampshire, where the election was scheduled for March 12. The state, population 700,000, was traditionally Republican but becoming more Democratic as Massachusetts residents moved in. McCarthy faced formidable obstacles there. The state party hewed to the national party line, and both Democratic governor John W. King and Democratic senator Thomas J. McIntyre strongly supported the president's war policy. The state's Democratic voters, clustered in working-class Manchester, Nashua, and Salem, had shown no overt opposition to the war. New Hampshire had few universities and a relatively small liberal professional class.

While McCarthy pondered these problems, thirty-year-old David Hoeh organized a meeting for Lowenstein in Bedford, a Manchester suburb. Hoeh had attended college in New Hampshire, participated in his first campaign in 1958, and, with his activist wife, Sandra, campaigned for Democratic candidates over the next decade. Hoeh lived in the Hanover area, where he worked at Dartmouth College. Between a dozen and a score of activists listened to Lowenstein speak. McCarthy's New Hampshire supporters had no money, no full-time staff, no clear base, and powerful opponents. They weren't even sure that McCarthy would run.[15]

Studds was just back from the March on the Pentagon. He read the newspaper account of the "Draft McCarthy" meeting and called Hoeh. Studds had worked with David's wife, Sandra, on a 1966 congressional campaign and was increasingly disgusted by the war—and the foul atmosphere at St. Paul's. The two men had lunch at a Concord restaurant. Studds wanted to know if the McCarthy campaign was for real, and Hoeh couldn't answer. "I guess we should give the political system one more try with McCarthy and the New Hampshire presidential primary before we head to the barricades," Studds declared, reflecting the feelings of many.[16]

Studds attended the next meeting of the antiwar Democrats. Lowenstein promised that a McCarthy announcement was imminent, so the group decided to form a McCarthy for President committee, elected a steering committee that included Studds, and agreed to send representatives to the Committee of Concerned Democrats conference in Chicago on December 2. They arranged for McCarthy to give a nonpolitical speech at a university lecture series in mid-December. The next day they held a press conference in Concord, which, absent a declared candidate, generated little excitement.[17]

A few days later, Studds went home to Cohasset over the Thanksgiving break with a stack of recent New Hampshire election returns and tried to figure out what they meant. On twenty yellow legal pad sheets, he compiled in his meticulous hand the vote totals of every hamlet and precinct since 1960. Very few people would have done this in 1968, most especially the slapdash, disorganized crowd around McCarthy, and certainly not the potential candidate himself. The painstaking research allowed Studds to see patterns and make projections. The New Hampshire Democratic presidential primary would elect twenty-four delegates to the national convention from the state's two congressional districts. Studds determined where the Democratic vote was growing, and figured out how McCarthy could generate media coverage reaching 75 percent of Democratic voters in twelve days of campaigning.[18]

Finally, on November 30, McCarthy held a low-key press conference in the Senate Caucus Room and declared that he would enter the primaries in Wisconsin, Oregon, California, and Nebraska. He would reserve judgment on the New Hampshire and Massachusetts primaries. He did not even say that he was running for president. McCarthy's detractors saw the "announcement" as too timid, but his supporters believed he had delivered a principled statement of opposition to the war, in which U.S. combat deaths had now reached fifteen thousand. New Hampshire's Senator McIntyre dismissed

McCarthy's chances, predicting that he could expect between three and five thousand votes if he dared to enter the primary, scarcely 10 percent.[19]

A few days later, Studds and his colleagues flew off to Chicago to join four thousand activists at the Blackstone Hotel to launch the McCarthy campaign. Lowenstein delivered a fiery antiwar introductory speech. Then McCarthy spoke in his imperturbable monotone, quieting passions and appealing to reason. The stylistic difference masked a deeper tension between the two men. Lowenstein, who had wanted Robert Kennedy to be the candidate, mentioned McCarthy's name only once during his introduction. McCarthy thereafter froze Lowenstein out of his inner circle, appointing journalist Blair Clark as his campaign director. Hoeh and Studds vowed that they would not allow anyone to upstage their candidate. Later, they would even sit down with the actor Paul Newman, and the two unknown young men would instruct the movie star on proper campaign decorum.[20]

McCarthy held an important meeting in Chicago with the small New Hampshire delegation, whose members urged him to enter the primary. Studds made a compelling case, reviewing his research and campaign strategy for the senator. McCarthy remained unsure about New Hampshire. But when a reporter approached Hoeh outside the closed caucus room, Hoeh replied, "I bet he enters."[21]

The New Hampshire McCarthy team arranged two university speeches for him, one in Manchester and the other in Durham in mid-December, part of an endowed lecture series. On December 14, Hoeh and Studds drove to Boston's Logan Airport in Studds's Chevelle station wagon. Much to their surprise, a gaggle of reporters had already assembled, awaiting the chance for a scoop regarding McCarthy's possible entry into the New Hampshire primary. McCarthy, true to form, insisted that his visit was nonpolitical, and that his only press conference would be in New Hampshire. Studds, Hoeh, McCarthy, and an aide piled into the station wagon, and the reporters followed along.[22]

Fourteen hundred people, an unheard-of number for that lecture series, gave McCarthy a standing ovation as he entered the auditorium. And then, as Studds, recalled, came a repeat of the Chicago experience. "It was a golden opportunity and it was a disaster," Studds wrote. The speech was part of a series on civil rights and housing, and McCarthy stayed on point. "McCarthy's speech was fine in substance, but it was totally non-political and delivered in the flattest conceivable style." The audience applauded respectfully and filed out. "After the speech," Studds recalled, "I walked with the Senator back to his motel room. . . . And he put his arm around me and said, 'I think we really got them that time. I could feel it.' I said to myself, 'Oh my God. He really thinks he had them in the palm of his hand.'" McCarthy had let the air out of his own balloon.[23]

The senator met with the New Hampshire steering committee that night. Later, Studds and Hoeh drove him to Boston in the station wagon. McCarthy sat in the back with famed journalist David Halberstam. Halberstam pressed McCarthy on whether he would enter the New Hampshire primary. Studds and Hoeh were disappointed to hear him say that he didn't think he would, and dismayed that he hadn't said that to them first, directly.[24]

So Studds retired to Cohasset again over the Christmas break and compiled a succinct memo arguing for McCarthy to campaign in New Hampshire. First, he pointed out that the local people were eager and well organized. Studds predicted that they could recruit an army of college students willing to knock on doors and stuff envelopes. He challenged the national strategy advanced by McCarthy's inner circle regarding New Hampshire, insisting that he would create a three-month media vacuum if he didn't run. Finally, he assured the candidate that Senator McIntyre had lowballed McCarthy's prospective vote total. Then, he recalled, "we closed our argument, prophetically, with the words: 'A victory here, which we think we ought to shoot for and which seems to us far more within the realm of possibility than it did a month ago, would have major national repercussions.'"[25] Studds was pushing on the hinge of history. Would the door swing open?

A few days later, Studds and Hoeh learned in the newspapers that it would not. McCarthy was not coming to New Hampshire. Studds and Hoeh felt "crushed," as well as resentful that they had not been told in advance. A few days later, Hoeh called campaign director Blair Clark to complain and was surprised to hear him say that they were still considering New Hampshire. On New Year's Eve, Clark phoned Hoeh and asked to meet him, Sandy, and Studds to discuss the matter further. On January 2, while they were dining at a Bedford motel, the phone rang for Hoeh. He returned to the table and announced: "That was the Senator. He is coming into New Hampshire." Studds recalled, "Blair's chin nearly fell into his soup, I dropped my fork, and I thought Sandy was going to faint."[26]

Studds had clearly played an important role in this turnabout. In his memoir, McCarthy singles out "the enthusiasm and spirit of the people who were urging me to run" as a significant factor in his decision.[27] Yet the story revealed all the inherent weaknesses of McCarthy's operation. Anyone seriously running for president would easily have decided to run in New Hampshire. His campaign staff should have communicated better with Hoeh and Studds at every step. This maddening lack of coordination with the local people would frustrate Studds and Hoeh over the next ten whirlwind, historic weeks, which would become a formative experience for thousands of young people. In his role as campaign coordinator, the second in command to Hoeh, Studds would set in motion the flood of volunteers who would campaign for McCarthy.

Studds and Hoeh called a press conference the next day, timed to coincide with McCarthy's in Washington. Again, few reporters showed up to hear the expected news that McCarthy would not run in the primary. Studds watched in amusement as Hoeh read McCarthy's telegram, which the two young men had themselves composed the night before. The lucky few reporters had a major scoop.

"So far as I know," Studds remembered, "this was the only time that Senator McCarthy . . . said 'I am running for the Presidency of the United States.' I wrote that sentence. I was determined he would use those words." The next day the story was front-page news all over the country.[28]

The full enormity of what they had done suddenly dawned on Studds and Hoeh. "As we left the press room, Studds and I looked at each other and almost simultaneously said, 'What have we gotten ourselves into now?'" Hoeh remembered. They had $500 in the campaign account, no office, and no phone. Both of them had full-time jobs, and they had little promise of help from McCarthy's barely functioning national office.[29] What if Senator McIntyre was right? If McCarthy badly lost the primary, it would be taken as a sign that the public wanted to fight and win in Vietnam. The liberals would feel demoralized. The battle between Democratic hawks and doves was joined in New Hampshire.

Hoeh and Studds rented the shuttered Ralph Pill electrical store on Pleasant Street in Concord as state headquarters. The place was a huge, filthy wreck, so vast that it would look ridiculous if a reporter showed up to see the lone desk. Over the next ten weeks, Hoeh would drive almost daily fifty miles to Concord, join Studds for dinner, and stay at headquarters until late at night. Studds tried to take a leave from work, presenting a request from Senator McCarthy himself, but was turned down. His relations with the St. Paul's administration deteriorated further.[30]

McCarthy finally arrived on January 26, setting off a day of amateur bungling. In Nashua, Studds had to pull aside two bearded, long-haired young volunteers and ask them to leave before the senator arrived. It was thus Gerry Studds who set the template of "Go clean for Gene" by carrying out this difficult but necessary task. The motorcade proceeded north to

Manchester, where the roof of the local campaign office had caved in. At a scheduled campaign stop at a restaurant, McCarthy declined to interrupt diners at lunch, thinking it rude. Then the candidate arrived at a factory gate a few minutes after closing time, but McCarthy carried on, good-naturedly greeting the few workers still straggling out. In Concord, McCarthy paid a courtesy call on the governor, who was leading the pro-LBJ forces. That night at St. Anselm College, eight hundred supporters packed an auditorium. Despite this success, Studds remembered the day as "a nightmare. . . . I never want to live through anything like that again!" The problems had not been of his making, but they reflected the broader political difficulties that McCarthy faced.[31]

Press accounts ran from neutral reportage to belittling opinion pieces. William J. Cardoso of the *Boston Globe* covered McCarthy's formal meeting with Governor King by recounting the mighty forces and political professionals arrayed on the president's side and the conservatism of the state's voters. "By comparison," Cardoso wrote, "the McCarthy organizers are university theoreticians." He identified Studds as chief of the Concord headquarters, which was "in magnificent disarray."[32]

Events in New Hampshire were immediately overshadowed by dramatic developments in Vietnam. Over Christmas, General William Westmoreland had confidently predicted that military leaders believed they could "see the light at the end of the tunnel" in Vietnam. Then, during Tet, the Vietnamese New Year, National Liberation Front forces struck simultaneously all over the country, even briefly capturing the American embassy. Television viewers watched in horror as a Vietnamese police chief brutally executed a rebel fighter, his hands tied behind his back, with a pistol shot to the head. American military leaders called for an additional 206,000 troops to join a war that the administration had just declared it was winning. Support for the war collapsed.[33]

Volunteers from out of state began to stream into New Hampshire to help McCarthy. New activists took full-time positions in the Concord office and others were dispatched around the state. Hoeh and Studds assumed advising roles, connecting the new arrivals with local activists, putting out the inevitable fires that accompany every campaign. McCarthy made several more trips to New Hampshire, generating positive news coverage as the campaign grew in experience and professionalism.

On election eve a media horde descended on the state. Studds spent election night with the candidate. The final result showed McCarthy with 43 percent of the vote, not a literal victory but a tally that reflected declining support for the war. In conservative New Hampshire, whose Democratic leaders had dismissed McCarthy's chances of winning even 10 percent of the vote, the senator had run almost dead even with the president. Johnson's Vietnam strategy had lost credibility with average voters. Gerry Studds had contributed significantly to this outcome.[34]

Lessons of Chicago

Then came the whirlwind. A few days after McCarthy's "victory," Robert Kennedy announced that he was entering the race. Despite the similarity of their antiwar stances, shared Catholic beliefs, and broadly liberal social views, the two men distrusted each other. Kennedy did not think McCarthy could win. Kennedy had broad appeal among African American and Mexican American voters, while McCarthy attracted educated white suburbanites. Kennedy had on his side the best political professionals in the business. McCarthy had amateurs.[35]

Although Studds had also worked with Robert Kennedy, he had personally bonded with McCarthy, and he felt a special kinship with his fellow academic. "I think we probably got to know him better than people in most of the other states," he wrote. "David and I got to feel quite at home with him. We developed a genuine affection for him."[36] Studds had not burned any bridges with Kennedy supporters, but McCarthy would be the role model and inspiration for Studds's later career.

In mid-March, President Johnson gathered a blue ribbon panel of advisers, known as the Wise Men, to consider the generals' request for more troops. They rejected it and questioned the president's course of continuing escalation. On March 31, Johnson scheduled a dramatic television appearance. He announced a bombing halt and shocked the world by declaring that he would not seek another term. Vice President Hubert Humphrey became the third Democratic candidate instead. A few days later, Martin Luther King Jr. was assassinated in Memphis, and black ghettoes across America erupted in fury. Studds had heard King speak when he was at Yale. He had stood only yards away from him during the "I Have a Dream" speech. He was dismayed by this brutal murder, whose major effect was to intensify racial polarization.[37]

The candidates battled through the primary states during the spring. Studds served as McCarthy coordinator for Maine, New Hampshire, and Vermont but was so busy catching up at school that he could do little. McCarthy won in Wisconsin and Pennsylvania, Kennedy in Indiana and

Nebraska; then McCarthy won in Oregon, but the California primary shifted the momentum to Kennedy. Studds watched the California returns with students at his dormitory apartment until two o'clock in the morning, when they witnessed Kennedy's declaration of victory and then, moments later, his murder. Coming just two months after King's assassination, this new tragedy left millions feeling that the country was verging on a collective nervous breakdown.[38]

In August, Studds set off for the Democratic Party convention in Chicago as a delegate. Ten thousand angry young people gathered in Grant Park to protest the war. The Chicago police infiltrated provocateurs into a crowd that hardly needed provoking; then they charged into the protesters, who chanted "The whole world is watching" as the television cameras rolled. Inside the convention hall, McCarthy's forces were swamped. Controversy surrounded the credentialing of delegations from the South; the Vietnam plank, which backed the president; and the nomination, which Humphrey won on the first ballot. In an ugly coda to the disgraceful behavior of the authorities, a squad of policemen invaded McCarthy's hotel and bloodied his supporters. "Our delegation was advised by McCarthy organizers to be careful on the street, even to hide our delegate badges for fear of the police," Hoeh remembered. Humphrey, beholden to Mayor Richard Daley, failed to condemn this police riot, causing McCarthy to withhold his endorsement until almost the end of the campaign.[39]

"I will never forget wandering in the park across the street from the Hilton each night after the convention adjourned," Studds told an interviewer a few months later. "The kids," he recalled, referring to the demonstrators, "would come up to us, they would see our delegate badges, the New Hampshire identification, and thank us."[40] Studds and Hoeh endured their own bizarre moment on the convention floor that illustrated Mayor Daley's control of the proceedings. Hoeh, suspicious that the credentials confirmation machine at the entrance was fixed to allow anyone to enter, inserted his Dartmouth College I.D. card to see if the machine showed green, which it did. "Look at that," Hoeh exclaimed to Studds. Hoeh went off to find a television reporter to record the problem, but as he did, a policeman grabbed him, handcuffed him, and carted him off to jail. "The malfunction was designed to allow Daley's men onto the floor," Hoeh remembered. "Every aspect of the convention was rigged," Studds told a student reporter in September. This bitter pill caused Studds and his colleagues to have to "bit[e] deep into our tongues" to endorse Humphrey in the fall.[41]

Studds had learned some lessons. He felt discouraged but not defeated. He faced the fact that the McCarthy campaign had been badly organized. The New Leftists snickered behind the backs of McCarthy's people, saying that he hadn't wanted to win, and that it had all been a trick to get the "Movement" off the streets. Studds rejected that conclusion, but he admitted to an interviewer in January 1969 that "there was no excuse for not conducting [the campaign] in a more organized and professional and competent way."[42] His quiet resolve and personal ambition were crystallizing. He, not someone from McCarthy's team, was the one who, through careful analysis, had condensed the evolving realities of New Hampshire into twenty pages of revealing statistics. The impulse to fight for justice through political struggle came from deep inside him. He could do it again.

Antiwar Democrats had no candidate in the fall as Humphrey and his running mate, Senator Edmund Muskie of Maine, faced off against Nixon and Maryland governor Spiro Agnew. The New Leftists raged at Humphrey, chanting "Dump the Hump" outside his campaign appearances. It was his government that was prosecuting the war. Nixon, who had been out of office since 1960, claimed he had a secret plan to end the conflict, and swept to an easy victory in November, polarizing the nation even more intensely.

A Tearful Embrace

Studds had put his personal and professional life on hold during the campaign, and now both unraveled. As he put it: "Meanwhile, at St. Paul's, things went from bad to worse in my relations with senior faculty and administration. The paranoia and resentment intensified, and the daily routine was becoming the daily ordeal." In May 1968 the students rebelled, protesting the dress code, demanding the admission of female students, and arguing for a more liberal scholarship program. These proposed changes reflected changes in society. The faculty conducted an angry debate over whether or not to affirm the existing rules, which they did. The administration blamed the turmoil on Studds. As Studds recalls in his memoir, the rector pressured him to resign, informing him: "You simply would not believe the extent to which great numbers of the faculty hold you personally responsible for the trouble here. To them, you mean SDS, anarchy, disruption, and nihilism. . . . Four men have written to say one more year of the same you and they leave, four very substantial men I cannot do without."[43]

These anonymous accusations from his colleagues stung Studds badly, and he felt compelled to make a personal statement in self-defense before a faculty body. "If any man here seriously thinks that . . . I . . . have used these boys to bring on disorder and/or change, then that man is in trouble," he declared. "He is in trouble because he does not understand what is happening in this school—he does not understand what is happening in this nation—and he does not understand what is happening in this world."[44] Studds had gone from advising a presidential candidate to fighting a minor group of reactionary gossipmongers. He started looking for a way out.

In fact, the reform agitation had its effect. During the summer of 1968, Rector Matthew Warren (Studds never named him in his memoir) called a voluntary convocation to ventilate some of the students' concerns, and many reforms were adopted. Student admissions became more diverse, as did the faculty, and later female students were admitted. Studds was working on the McCarthy campaign and did not attend the convocation, but he had done a lot to bring about the modernization of one of the country's leading preparatory schools.[45]

He was still a closeted gay man with erotic impulses like everyone else. The antiwar movement had also unleashed a sexual revolution. The birth control pill and easier access to condoms were making sex safer. Millions of young people attended coeducational institutions together for the first time and dated free of parental supervision. Eroticism, communalism, and psychedelic drugs flourished. Young people who opposed the Vietnam War associated the pro-war impulse with an uptight society whose puritanical morality fostered aggression; the Beatles and the Rolling Stones provided the background music. On some campuses, teachers and students kissed openly, held hands, and even slept together. Young people flaunted their long hair and sexuality as badges of honor.

Studds felt deeply frustrated in this part of his life too. There were other gay men on the St. Paul's faculty, but Studds did not associate with them. "He didn't give off a gay vibe," student Bill Woodward remembered. "There were other teachers who displayed stereotypical effeminate behavior there, but I didn't associate Studds with them." Studds deliberately kept his distance from them. "There were some people on that faculty who were predators," Tom Iglehart remembers, "but it was only whispered about. There were no guidelines in those days. Years later another graduating class insisted that guidelines be put in place, and they were."[46]

Neither David Hoeh nor faculty friend Richard Aiken suspected that Studds was a closeted homosexual. Aiken could sense Studds's growing unhappiness and isolation. He volunteered the use of his house at the end of a country road in Truro, Massachusetts, the penultimate town on the tip of Cape Cod. "Take off for the weekend," Aiken said, "and bring a friend."

It was, perhaps, a sign of the times that an Episcopal minister could counsel his colleague to loosen up and enjoy a tryst.[47]

"The friend to whom I turned was a student," Studds confessed. The young man was doing poorly in school, was becoming depressed, and had looked to Studds for comfort. In Truro they walked along the beach, and later drove to Provincetown for dinner; it was Studds's first look at the town. They drove home, built a fire, and collapsed in tears in each other's arms. Then they went to bed. "Toward morning," wrote Studds, "when it would become clear that there would be no sexual consummation of this intimacy, I disintegrated. I cried uncontrollably. I cried until my handkerchief and pillow were drenched. . . . This unanticipated, uncontrollable outpouring of emotion was without precedent in my life." Studds was having his own nervous breakdown. On the drive home, he had to stop the car to cry some more. "Clearly, I was out of touch with fundamental parts of myself."[48]

In 1968, millions of homosexuals and lesbians still had no place to go to talk about their sexuality. They had to hide or bottle up their desires. Like every other human being, Studds wanted to have sex and fall in love too, but he couldn't. He felt trapped. Studds also felt guilty. He had broken his own moral code by sharing his bed with a student, even if they hadn't had sex together. In his memoir he apologized, and hinted that he had experienced some sort of intimacy, not necessarily sexual, with other students: "Occasionally, in ways that were human but neither professional nor responsible, my own needs momentarily overwhelmed those of a student, and the man to whom they turned for counsel and strength turned instead to them. They deserved better. I wish it had been mine to give."[49]

Studds had stopped pretending that he might be heterosexual, but he still had no idea how to conduct himself as a homosexual. He told a few students about his sexual orientation and hinted at his availability.[50] His alienation from his homosexual faculty colleagues suggests that he did not feel comfortable with them either. So he turned to the young men around him, establishing a pattern for his future conduct. It should be noted that heterosexual teachers sometimes did the same thing, although less so in high school than at college. In the incident that Studds describes, two people are experiencing genuine, tender emotions together, without the more powerful of the two compelling a consummation. This was not the equivalent of a Catholic priest forcing himself on an altar boy and swearing him to secrecy. No student ever came forward to complain about him. Yet Studds himself acknowledged that his behavior violated his own code regarding sex between teacher and student.

Studds knew that he had to leave. Everything in his life was falling apart. His antiwar activity had alienated the conservative administration and faculty. His candidate had lost, and Nixon was now president, leaving the antiwar Democrats licking their wounds. He had not come to terms with his sexual orientation and was improperly turning to his students in a way that might hurt someone if he continued. He needed to make a change.

His friend Don Welles had brought him to St. Paul's, and Welles found him a way out. He suggested to Studds that the school would be reluctant to fire him but would be glad to see him quit. If Studds wanted to leave, he could even extract a price. Studds took this proposition to the headmaster the next day. The man caught his drift immediately and offered to pay his salary and tuition for a year of graduate school. Studds was soon accepted at Harvard for a second master's in education program. In June, he attended a faculty end-of-the-year dinner party for those moving on. No one even mentioned his name. He had been a thorn in everyone's side and now was treated like a ghost at the banquet. Studds left the room in tears. "'How strange,' I thought, 'that this should hurt so much.'"[51]

A few weeks later, in the early morning hours of June 28, the New York City police raided a Mafia-owned bar in Greenwich Village called the Stonewall Inn. This routine harassment of homosexuals and lesbians had gone on sporadically for years. The raid reminded the patrons that they were second-class citizens whose mere existence was an affront to society. But that night the room was crowded with hundreds of people, and a full-scale riot broke out. Something in the zeitgeist had changed, something born of the antiwar, black liberation, and emerging women's liberation movements. The despised and outcast were rising up and demanding their rights. Soon they would define themselves and build their own revolution. That night, the gay liberation movement was born.[52] Gerry Studds would keep his distance from it for the next fourteen years, but the movement would catch up with him when he least expected it.

5

Studds for Congress

HAVING BEEN RELEASED from his responsibilities at St. Paul's School, Studds departed in the summer of 1969 for eastern Europe, taking along two students, Charles Read and Ned Perkins, as traveling companions. The trio flew to Amsterdam, rented a car, and slapped a "McCarthy for President" sticker on the bumper "so as not to be taken for the wrong kind of Americans," Read recalled. The travelers drove through France and Italy, then north to Trieste and down the Dalmatian coast through what was then Yugoslavia. Camping out and staying in hostels, they proceeded south to Greece, and then back north and farther east to Bulgaria. They arrived in Romania just before President Nixon landed to visit its anti-Moscow communist dictator Nicolae Ceaușescu. Read was astonished to see so many people in a communist country lining the parade route with American flags. In Prague, Czechoslovakia, they could feel the tension in the air as Russian troops, still occupying the country, clashed with protesters. Studds decided that they should depart for East Germany. Then they spent a week in Hungary. Studds was conversant in German and Russian, and even had a little Hungarian from his Yale days. "There was a sense that change was in the air," Read remembered.[1]

This ambitious ten-week journey illustrates Studds's relentless intellectual curiosity. It was a time when many young Americans explored western Europe, but few visited Soviet-dominated eastern Europe. The trip also suggests his emotional resilience. He had just been evicted from his teaching post, having left all his previous jobs under the same dispiriting circumstances. At the lowest point of his professional career, Studds could hardly have imagined while he was exploring Romania that five years later he would be preparing, as a first-term member of Congress, to vote to impeach Nixon.[2]

In the fall Studds came to Harvard, where he was to begin taking courses for a second master's in education, a degree he neither wanted nor needed, for a career he was not sure he wished to pursue. He moved into a second-floor apartment in a Cambridge triple-decker.[3] He had located himself in one of the most exciting cities in the country for young people at a great turning point in national history.

Of all the major metropolitan areas in the country, the Boston area has the densest concentration of students. And among the country's most elite institutions, Harvard occupies a virtually unique position close to its state's political and economic capital. Harvard had also played an outsized role in producing Kennedy administration foreign policy advisers, some of whom had quit the Johnson administration as it escalated the war in Vietnam. In the Boston area, antiwar committees formed on scores of campuses. Boston in 1969 was the unrivaled center of academic life in the country, and a hot-bed of dissent.

In this electric environment, various currents of youthful rebellion swirled. Over the summer, Students for a Democratic Society had imploded. The more moderate Student Mobilization Committee worked with the New Mobilization Committee to advocate massive, peaceful, legal demonstrations. The liberal Democrats, now freed of the Kennedy versus McCarthy tensions, maneuvered for position in the upcoming congressional elections.

The region buzzed with organizing for the October 15 Moratorium to End the War in Vietnam. The Nixon administration had come into office in January with a "secret plan" for ending the war, which was to increase the bombing while withdrawing American troops. As Nixon and his national security adviser Henry Kissinger would soon learn, this plan was doomed to fail because the contending Vietnamese parties would not compromise. Nixon succeeded only in uniting the antiwar Democrats, who were no longer restrained by a Democratic president conducting the war. Studds's former colleagues in the McCarthy campaign conceived the Moratorium to appeal to moderates. The teach-ins and rallies were decentralized and held on a weekday, so as to encourage numerous local protests. Meanwhile, the New Mobilization Committee, led by radical pacifists, some labor leaders, and the Old Left parties, especially the Trotskyist Socialist Workers Party, called for a March on Washington a month after the Moratorium.

The Moratorium challenged the administration's claim that it was backed by a pro-war consensus. Two million people participated in antiwar activities in over twenty major cities and many more in smaller towns. Whole new categories of moderates came over to the antiwar side. Almost a quarter of a million demonstrated in New York's Central Park, and 100,000 people gathered to hear Senator George McGovern of South Dakota call for peace on the Boston Common. The demonstrations were so impressive that Nixon, unbeknownst to the protesters, called off an expanded secret bombing campaign lest the nation explode in anger. On November 3, Nixon gave his famous "Silent Majority" speech in which he condemned the protesters. Antiwar activists responded with the massive March on Washington on November 15.[4]

Gerry Studds heard Nixon's speech and began, incredibly, to consider running for Congress. "I decided it was not a year to be quietly thoughtful," he later told a reporter.[5] He was the most unlikely of candidates, and any political oddsmaker would have laughed off his chances of winning. Studds, just thirty-two, had unhappily resigned from every job he had ever held. He had never run for political office. He was newly returned to Massachusetts, never having lived there as an adult. Scarcely anybody in his home Twelfth District even knew who he was. He had cast his own first vote in 1958 for the six-term Republican incumbent he now hoped to unseat. He had no money and would have to live with his parents. He was an unmarried man keeping his sexual orientation a secret. Of all the quixotic quests in the history of politics, this was among the least likely to end in success. Yet his very obscurity also meant that he had nothing to lose.

Moreover, Studds was encouraged by the atmosphere around him. The political world was rapidly changing. Pro-war Massachusetts congressmen faced gathering opposition in the 1970 primaries. Antiwar liberals had organized Political Action for Peace, whose leaders included businessman Jerome Grossman, scientist Arthur Obermayer, and prominent Harvard faculty members such as John Kenneth Galbraith and Arthur Schlesinger Jr. The peace advocates targeted pro-war Democrat Phil Philbin, whose district included the liberal suburb of Newton. They recruited Boston College Law School dean Father Robert Drinan to enter the primary against him. In 1967 Thomas P. "Tip" O'Neill, of the Cambridge-based Eighth District, had changed his mind on the war, angering President Johnson and Speaker John W. McCormack, his mentor. In May 1970, McCormack, who represented much of Boston, announced his own retirement, and antiwar candidates rushed in to run there too. Finally, in a 1969 special congressional election on the North Shore, antiwar candidate Michael Harrington defeated William

Saltonstall, state senator and son of former governor and senator Leverett Saltonstall.[6]

The Twelfth Congressional District, which stretched along the state's east coast from Weymouth and Hull in the north to New Bedford on the southern coast, contained fifty-two municipalities, divided, like Caesar's Gaul, into three parts: the South Shore, Cape Cod and the Islands, and the New Bedford region. Since the Civil War, it had sent only one Democrat to Congress. The Twelfth was the most Republican and perhaps the most Yankee district in the state. It had little industry, only a few labor unions, and no sizable colleges. Yet the district was changing fast. Outmigration from Boston to the suburbs had given it, by 1970, more registered Democrats (75,378) than Republicans (72,283), but the biggest group was independents (96,931). The right Democrat did have a chance.[7]

The South Shore generally voted Republican but had a few Democratic towns. Some Boston Irish Catholics were moving to Weymouth, the second-largest town in the district. The men often worked in neighboring Quincy at the General Dynamics Fore River Shipyard, a union stronghold. Plymouth, with lower property costs, was attracting the same kind of voter. These workers were often pro-war, anti-abortion, but pro-labor Democrats. The more exclusive, semi-rural old Yankee towns like Hingham, Scituate, Norwell, and Duxbury would probably vote Republican.[8]

The Republican heart of the district was Cape Cod, whose elderly retirees and small business owners catering to the tourist trade were not about to vote for a reformer. A few working-class Irish Catholics had retired to affordable Hyannis; there were some upscale liberals on Martha's Vineyard; and Provincetown's gays and Portuguese American fishermen voted Democratic; but larger Republican towns like Barnstable, Chatham, Orleans, and Yarmouth would swamp them. Senator Ted Kennedy lived in the family compound at Hyannis, and might have been influential with potential Democratic voters, but in August 1969 he had driven off the bridge linking Chappaquiddick Island to the rest of Martha's Vineyard, killing his female passenger. His political influence in 1970 was diminished.[9]

The district's Democratic stronghold lay in its only city, New Bedford, and surrounding towns like Fairhaven and Dartmouth. Historic New Bedford was an old whaling town, now home to the nation's biggest fishing fleet. Many other businesses, such as boat repair, banking and insurance, and food processing, depended on the success of the harvest from the sea. New Bedford also had some surviving textile and clothing factories. In this gritty union town, about 50 percent of its residents claimed Portuguese ancestry. Any successful Democratic candidate for the Twelfth congressional seat would have to roll up a big majority here.[10]

The Massachusetts Twelfth District thus stood culturally very far from Studds's milieu at Harvard. Yet to secure his party's nomination, he would have to win a base of antiwar activists. Studds most likely first floated the idea of running to Ken Auchincloss, his closest friend from Yale. He probably consulted Gus Maffrey, who had taught with him at St. Paul's and was now a student at the Fletcher School of Law and Diplomacy at Tufts University in nearby Medford. He spoke with Congressman Michael Harrington and some wealthy antiwar activists in Cambridge. Then, just as he had done in New Hampshire for McCarthy, Studds ran the numbers, looking carefully at recent returns from each town. By New Year's Day, he had made up his mind.[11]

In February, Studds spoke at an event in Falmouth. There he was approached by Paul Nace, a navy veteran of Vietnam, just back from patrolling the Mekong Delta, and a firm opponent of the war. He offered to help. Nace had grown up in Brooklyn, attended Boston College, and earned an MBA from Columbia University. In the navy he met John Kerry, another antiwar sailor. Within a few weeks, Nace concluded that the war was a mistake and made it his mission to protect his own men rather than to kill the enemy. Soon after meeting Nace, Studds asked him to run the campaign. "We were very different people," Nace recalled decades later, "but Studds figured out that if he was going to campaign in working-class New Bedford, he was going to need somebody with street smarts. And there were a few times later, when he was challenged by pro-war types, he would call attention to me in the back of the room as his manager, a Vietnam veteran, and potential opponents would look at him with new respect." Nace had a hearty laugh and spoke the vernacular; this was a different character from Studds's Groton friends.[12]

Studds had several rivals among the antiwar candidates. These included an aide to Ted Kennedy, a Methodist minister, and a state representative. All were older and better connected than Studds. Studds joined them at a forum in Hingham's Old Ship Church, a venerable institution perched on a rise in the town center, declaring that his major concern was the fate of young people whose lives had been put on hold by the war.[13] A few days later he and David Hoeh appeared on the front page of the *Boston Globe* as he welcomed back to New Hampshire Senator Eugene McCarthy. The story identified Studds as an "unannounced candidate for Congress." This high-profile event signaled to antiwar liberals that Studds was their candidate.[14]

Studds announced his candidacy on March 31, first in New Bedford and then at Boston's famed Parker House Hotel, near the State House. "Americans have seen their country become hopelessly entangled in an immoral and unwinnable war in Asia," Studds declared. Echoing his appeal to the St. Paul's faculty less than a year earlier, he asserted that Congressman Hastings Keith and President Nixon "do not understand either America or the world of 1970." As to his electability, he pointed to the victory of Michael Harrington on the North Shore a year earlier.[15]

Studds had to contend against one remaining antiwar candidate to win the backing of the district's antiwar caucus, assembled in mid-April at Memorial Hall in Plymouth. Studds blasted Nixon on the war and his nomination of former segregationist G. Harrold Carswell to the Supreme Court. He tied Keith to Nixon. Studds captured the caucus's endorsement, and his rival dropped out.[16]

Gus Maffrey brought a fellow Fletcher School student with him to that meeting. Margaret Strayhorn, a twenty-four-year-old Illinois native recently returned from a Peace Corps stint in Malawi, was getting her first taste of radical antiwar politics. Reacting against what she perceived as the caucus chairman's heavy-handed manner, she exclaimed to the woman next to her, "That guy is a jerk!" Strayhorn volunteered to work full-time for the Studds campaign and was dispatched to New Bedford. She arrived at a labor union hall, where she met John Xifaras, the chairman she had found so assertive. "Forty-three years later and we're still married!" Margaret Xifaras later exclaimed.[17]

Studds expanded his platform, which called for better pay for teachers, low- and moderate-income housing, an end to the seniority system, a guaranteed minimum income, and comprehensive national health care. His campaign brochure declared: "He's younger. He's tougher. And he's going to win." A discriminating political professional might suspect that this slogan, highlighting the candidate's sailing, football, and youthful "mossing" prowess, was designed to obscure the detail that he was thirty-three and lived with his parents. His bumper sticker just read "Studds" in black letters on a white field, and it began appearing on cars with the last two letters cut off. Campaign brochures showed him shaking hands at factory gates and senior centers.

The brochure also showed the assembled Studds family at his sister Gaynor's 1962 wedding. The text appealed to independents by noting that his family had been Republicans until Gerry converted them; they looked like the wholesome WASP families that predominated on the Cape and South

Shore. During the campaign, the family home became a campaign headquarters, with Bonnie and Eastman running the place, and Gaynor and
brother Colin campaigning at New Bedford supermarkets. Colin carried a
card in Portuguese reading "Eu sou o seu irmao"—I am his brother.[18]

Three traditional candidates with parochial concerns also secured spots
on the primary ballot. They were Gordon J. O'Brien, a Weymouth World
War II veteran who had worked as an assistant district attorney; Plymouth
County Commissioner John J. Franey of Abington, a teacher backed by his
union; and Robert Hunt of New Bedford. "The Democratic opposition was
not in the same league as Gerry," Paul Nace remembered. "If you were a
traditional politician, he seemed to represent nothing. They never saw him
coming." Incumbent congressmen frighten away more powerful politicians
who will sacrifice their own seat if they challenge in another race and lose.
In the Republican primary, Keith for the first time faced a formidable opponent, State senator William D. Weeks, who would still hold his seat if he lost
the nomination.[19]

On April 30, Nixon announced the expansion of the war into Cambodia.
Campuses erupted in protest, and on May 4, Ohio National Guardsmen
killed four demonstrators at Kent State University. Students on four hundred campuses went on strike, and many colleges canceled graduation. The
Cambodia invasion caused thousands of young people to commit themselves to political action, and volunteers flocked to Studds's banner, just as
they had to McCarthy's after the 1968 Tet Offensive.[20]

Studds set up a temporary headquarters at the Governor Bradford Motel,
across from Plymouth Rock. During the May upheaval, Jim Litton, then a
law student at New York University who had grown up in Brookline and
Plymouth, walked in to volunteer. After the invasion of Cambodia, he had
gone to Washington to see Hastings Keith and joined a delegation to voice
their opposition to the war. "Keith put his feet up on the desk and dismissed
our concerns," Litton remembered. "I asked him if anyone was running
against him, and he said, 'Yes, someone called Jerry Stutz, but he doesn't
have a chance.'" The twenty-two-year-old Litton arrived at the motel just as
Nace and Studds were rushing off; judging by their looks, he guessed that
Nace was the candidate and Studds the manager. Litton returned the next
day and became Nace's assistant. Soon they established a permanent office
at Plymouth's Cordage Park, a commercial complex centrally located within
the district.[21]

In June, a meeting of over a thousand students at the Massachusetts Institute of Technology endorsed Studds and several other antiwar candidates.

Studds's press secretary and former student Bill Hamilton wrote to *New York Times* reporter R. W. Apple Jr., urging him to cover the campaign. They expected to win, Hamilton wrote, knocking out a Republican incumbent on the war issue.[22]

Another volunteer, recent Harvard graduate Mark Segar, captured the atmosphere of the campaign in an article for the *Boston Globe*. Studds "looked like Plastic Man in Sicilian mourning clothes," Segar wrote. He had "a weird name, a weird appearance, no pretty wife, and no money. Things didn't look promising." A campaign adviser told Segar bluntly, "You ain't gonna sell this boy on his sex appeal." Segar campaigned in Weymouth with Studds and Congressman Michael Harrington, whose Irish American bona fides would help there, and with Ted Kennedy on the New Bedford waterfront. At a fund-raising gala on a Woods Hole estate overlooking Cape Cod's Buzzards Bay, Gene McCarthy was the star attraction. Segar had fun. About fifteen hundred others volunteered. This was a time when politics genuinely seemed to be about ideas and when people held those ideas passionately. "We had ten to twelve full-time student volunteers in New Bedford, alone," Margaret Xifaras recalled. "In those days before 'targeted' campaigning, we knocked on every door."[23]

By early September, it began to look as though Studds might actually win the primary. He campaigned relentlessly, visiting every town Democratic committee, winning labor endorsements. "He discovered that he was really good at selling himself politically," Bill Woodward remembered. "He could work a crowd. He was charming, good-humored, and friendly. He could talk to antiwar types, but also to fishermen."[24]

Studds won an astonishing near majority in a four-way race. He took forty-two of the district's fifty-two cities and towns, including all but two on the South Shore. He carried every town on the Cape and came in second in New Bedford. Forty-three thousand people voted in the Democratic primary, more than double the number of voters in 1968. Studds celebrated at his campaign headquarters with a hundred joyous volunteers, declaring victory at one a.m. and driving off to New Bedford, where he planned to meet the morning shift of factory workers. By contrast, Keith narrowly defeated Weeks.[25]

New Politics vs. Old

Yale-educated Studds learned something about working people during the 1970 campaign. New Bedford had a 35 percent high school dropout rate and a housing shortage, so when Nixon vetoed Democratic education and housing bills, Studds made that an issue and tied Keith to Nixon on those policies. He campaigned at the Stetson shoe factory in South Weymouth and a nearby machine shop where wages were under four dollars an hour. "People who know me have seen a change in me since the campaign started," Studds told a reporter. "They say we've changed from a McCarthy-type campaign to a Bobby Kennedy campaign. I guess I saw New Bedford and I got mad. . . . The people there are incredibly poor. It's an emotional, almost populist thing," he said.[26] "He did well with working-class voters," Margaret Xifaras remembered. "He listened well. He was respectful. People were not used to that level of contact with a potential congressman."[27]

Keith was a much more formidable opponent than Studds's primary rivals. His career in Congress provided him with a base of power and friends for whom he had done favors. He was an army veteran, the married father of grown daughters. He held moderate positions, opposing escalation in Vietnam and supporting environmental concerns.[28] Yet Keith ran a routine campaign, underestimating his opponent. "Keith was a 1950s kind of guy who could easily do well at a Rotary Club luncheon," Margaret Xifaras said. "He was an Eisenhower Republican, but not able to distinguish himself from Nixon or his policies." Campaign manager Nace thought Keith "was a nice guy," but "he represented the quintessential congressional vegetable that got us into Vietnam."[29]

Studds won important liberal organizational and financial backing. During the primary, he earned the endorsement of the National Committee for an Effective Congress. In late September, he addressed the state's Americans for Democratic Action convention in Cambridge. There, Studds cautioned the liberal activists that they must patiently appeal to patriotic working-class voters too. There had been pro-war demonstrations by construction workers in New York in May, and that type of voter lived in Studds's district. "Unless . . . an attempt is made to reach the hard hat and the machinist's wife," Studds warned, "the polarization in this country is likely to grow far worse."[30]

Studds emphasized economic problems as the election edged closer. In a *Boston Globe* interview, he said, regarding Vietnam, "I, like most Americans, would like us out tomorrow, or next week, but realistically that's not going to happen." He argued that defense spending caused inflation, and called for an end to the antiballistic missile (ABM) system. He pointed out that unemployment in New Bedford could be mitigated by spending on schools and hospitals. He reluctantly backed import quotas, which would protect

New Bedford's textile and shoe industries, and supported birth control and legal abortion.[31]

Keith still held a commanding lead in the polls in late October. He disputed Studds's claim to have worked in the White House on the Domestic Peace Corps, a matter no one would have cared about, but which raised doubts about Studds, who was just becoming known in the district. Then he tried to tie Studds to supposed radical extremists during his years as a teacher. Despite these personal attacks, the election narrowed over the final week.[32]

Ted Kennedy campaigned in New Bedford for Studds, who would be his congressman if he won. Kennedy was running for his second full term against a token opponent, but Chappaquiddick haunted him, and he wanted to win big. Kennedy instinctively liked Studds and drew him into his circle, doing radio spots and offering advice. They appeared together at Bristol Community College. Just as Studds began his speech, a black student interrupted to protest the killing of a black youth by police. Studds let him finish, then continued as the room fell silent. At the end, two thousand students rose and gave Studds a standing ovation. On another occasion, Studds addressed a crowd at a Portuguese American Democratic rally and vowed that if he won, he would learn to speak Portuguese. Kennedy was impressed.[33]

Studds needed to win New Bedford and Weymouth by two-to-one margins, and he just missed. The final returns gave Keith the win. Campaign manager Paul Nace, a tough Vietnam veteran, broke down in tears when it looked as if it was over. Studds did not concede and called for a recount. The final tally, not completed until the end of the month, showed Keith with 100,432 votes, Studds with 98,910, and 4,426 ballots left blank. It had been the second-closest congressional race in the nation. In Massachusetts, eight Democrats and four Republicans won congressional seats, and the election of Father Drinan in the Third District replaced a pro-war Democrat with an antiwar Democrat.[34]

Round Two

Studds was encouraged by his showing. Only recently he had been an obscure graduate student who had been driven out of a high school teaching job, and he had transformed himself in one year into a strong contender in a House race. He noticed, too, that a Vietnam referendum on many Massachusetts ballots showed strong antiwar sentiment. "Win the war" gained

268,025 votes, planned withdrawal scored 822,955, immediate withdrawal won 517, 350 votes, and 434,757 voters abstained. An antiwar candidate stood a good chance in the next Massachusetts congressional election.[35]

Studds was ready to try again. With the help of Senator Kennedy, he secured a job at the University of Massachusetts as associate staff director to a committee preparing a report on the future of the university. Late in May he held a big fund-raiser at Hull's Surf Ballroom on Nantasket Beach to retire his 1970 campaign debt. A thousand people attended a party significantly billed as a "staying alive" bash, joining Senator Kennedy and antiwar veteran John Kerry. According to *Boston Globe* columnist David Nyhan, "Studds came out of nowhere in that race and built an organization that is convinced its time will come in 1972."[36]

In February, Nixon expanded the war. With U.S. backing, South Vietnamese troops invaded neutral Laos in an effort to interdict North Vietnamese aid to the South. Although U.S. casualties were declining, 335,000 troops were still on the ground. Antiwar veterans held an inquiry into war crimes that drew a great deal of publicity, and in March, Lieutenant William Calley was tried for the My Lai massacre, in which U.S. troops killed three hundred unarmed civilians. In April, half a million protesters marched on Washington and another 150,000 paraded through San Francisco's streets to Golden Gate Park. Ironically, because there was no violence, the media scarcely covered the demonstrations.[37] All the energy was on the antiwar side now; there would be no more pro-war marches by construction workers.

Studds finished his job in September and embarked upon an intensive six-week Berlitz course in Portuguese. "Anybody who tells me that what I am going through at Berlitz is a political gimmick gets a punch in the mouth," he joked to a reporter. In November he left for six weeks in Portugal, the Azores, and Cape Verde.[38]

While Studds was away, the Massachusetts legislature gerrymandered the state's congressional districts. With naked partisanship, the Democrats removed from the Twelfth District eight Republican towns that Keith had won and placed them in Republican Margaret Heckler's neighboring Tenth District.[39] Keith announced that he would not run again.[40] The Old Guard was on its way out.

Shortly afterward, Gerry's father, Eastman, died at the early age of sixty-seven. He had been dressing for a party and suffered a brain aneurism, calling out to his wife and falling to the floor. Gerry's brother and sister were married now and both living in Buffalo. Gerry phoned to tell them what had happened, and the family gathered for a private service at St. Stephen's Episcopal, a lovely old stone church set on a rocky ledge just off the town green.[41]

Studds threw his hat in the ring six weeks later and ran unopposed in the primary. He announced that he would not just preach to the choir but was going to appeal to working-class voters who needed convincing to stay in the Democratic column. Speaking at a Cambridge fund-raiser a week after announcing, he said, "We must refrain from the ultimate arrogance in assuming that people who vote for George Wallace [the segregationist Alabama governor, who was running for president] are some different kind of people."[42]

William Weeks, the Republican nominee, came from a distinguished lineage. His grandfather John W. Weeks had been a congressman, U.S. senator, and secretary of war in the Warren Harding administration. Sinclair Weeks, William's father, had also been a senator, and then been appointed secretary of commerce in the Eisenhower administration. William Weeks had attended Harvard and the University of Virginia Law School, had served in the military during World War II, and was a partner in a prominent Boston law firm. At forty-six, he had served for six years in the state Senate, and was married with children. Despite his diminutive physical stature, Weeks looked the part of a handsome congressman, with his square jaw and confident manner. He knew lots of wealthy people, and by campaign's end he would spend almost a quarter of a million dollars. While Weeks supported Nixon, he was a moderate on most issues. His résumé suggested that he should easily beat an unemployed bachelor living with his mother who had never won an election.[43]

Nor was the war in Vietnam necessarily a losing issue for Weeks. By 1972, Nixon was winding it down. The country was exhausted by the war as a political issue. To be sure, this was the central question for millions of young people who enthusiastically backed George McGovern, the antiwar Democratic nominee for president. McGovern had served as a bomber pilot in World War II, yet Nixon succeeded in painting him as a weak figure, a pacifist who would surrender Vietnam to the communists. Nixon had scored a remarkable coup by his 1972 visits to China and the USSR. Meanwhile, the number of American soldiers being killed was decreasing as the U.S. combat role switched mostly to bombing, which produced fewer U.S. casualties. Finally, the image of black people in the white imagination had shifted from

one of devout Christians led by Martin Luther King Jr. to that of violent
rioters. McGovern looked like too nice a guy for the dangerous times the
country faced. This too represented an advantage for Weeks.

Studds located his campaign office in Hingham because he and his campaign manager, Jim Litton, figured that the South Shore would determine
the outcome. Litton scheduled house parties on the South Shore, mostly
organized by women. "The house parties won the election," Litton said years
later. "They built a base, and the participants got out their neighbors' vote
on Election Day."[44]

Weeks and Studds both fought hard. Studds "would have to be labeled
an extremist, based on his positions in the past," Weeks declared early on.
Weeks's big issue was opposition to "federal control over our affairs," and
he presented himself as the candidate who understood local concerns. "He
was attuned to the issues from his state Senate district," Margaret Xifaras
remembered, "but he was not attuned to wider national issues." In fact,
Weeks circulated different campaign literature town by town, as if he were
running for selectman in each separate locale.[45]

Studds attacked Weeks on this when they finally met in their lone televised debate. Studds called Nixon's peace rhetoric "a patent fraud" and
demanded immediate withdrawal from Vietnam. Weeks charged that
Studds was "to the left of McGovern." Studds argued that Nixon's stance of
making peace contingent on the prior release of U.S. prisoners while continuing the bombing would only "create more prisoners," and he noted that
two pilots had just been captured. When Weeks deferred to the president's
wisdom, Studds challenged him by asking, "If winning is so important, why
are we getting out?" Studds pounded away on domestic national issues, too,
decrying Nixon's vetoes of jobs and education bills, and backing Ted Kennedy's call for national health insurance.[46]

As the election neared, Weeks was running ahead in the polls. In Weymouth, Democratic state representative Robert Ambler formed a "Democrats for Weeks" committee, a dangerous sign because it indicated that
Studds was too antiwar for many working-class voters. State senator Alan R.
McKinnon backed Studds, but the same fissure showed up in the New Bedford area, too, whose Democratic state representatives largely stayed neutral.
The cultural divide that would drive many white working-class voters into
the Republican Party was beginning to emerge.[47]

Studds prevailed upon state leaders to bring the renegades back into line.
He asked House speaker David Bartley to rebuke the Democratic House
whip, William "Biff" McLean, from the New Bedford area, who was also

pro-Weeks. McLean refused to back off. "One more thing like that and Studds will see my picture in the paper with my arm around Weeks," he told a reporter. Studds deliberately kept his distance from George McGovern, whose campaign stalled right after the Democratic convention. In the polls, Studds held a lead with younger voters, Weeks with those over forty-five.[48]

And then, according to Litton, Studds's campaign manager, "Weeks screwed it up." Weeks circulated a new campaign brochure, titled "Be Selfish," urging voters to think only of their narrow local interests. "If my opponent believes that the people of Massachusetts will respond to his call to 'Be Selfish'" Studds declared, "then he has forgotten the lessons of our heritage." This appeal to idealism would help turn out Studds's base, and Weeks's appeal to parochialism alienated some who might otherwise have voted for him. This was still Massachusetts, a "Commonwealth" whose founders had hoped to build "a city upon a hill." That is what Studds meant by "our heritage," and that deft turn of phrase may have put him over the top.[49]

Studds campaigned hard in New Bedford, hoping for a two-to-one margin of victory there. He joined the lone state representative who actively supported him, Ron Pina, at a North New Bedford restaurant, where partisans munched on codfish balls and malasada pastries. "Gerry even knows how to swear at me in Portuguese," Pina said to laughter. Studds took calls on a radio show in Portuguese. This forgotten constituency deeply appreciated his show of respect for their language and culture.[50]

In the final week, Ted Kennedy joined Studds at a New Bedford factory gate. Looking like the happy warrior of old, Kennedy called out in a booming voice for the workers to come over and meet their candidate. He said to a national reporter of Studds, "He's really good, isn't he?"[51]

The campaign volunteers gathered expectantly on election night at the appropriately named Dreamworld nightclub in Scituate. The race was very, very close, but Studds had a slight edge. Hingham, a Republican town, suffered a counting snafu, and the race was not decided until the following day. Studds won by 1,207 votes, 117,754 to 116,547. Studds had made gains throughout the district, narrowing the gap on the Cape and in Republican South Shore towns. He had lost Falmouth on Cape Cod by 952 votes in 1970 but by only 72 in 1972. "Winning politics is about getting good splits everywhere," Margaret Xifaras said many years later. Studds had done exactly that.[52]

Weeks demanded, and got, a recount. "Entire issue Newsweek delayed for outcome your race," old friend and now editor Ken Auchincloss telegraphed a week later. "Editor furious. Undersigned nervous wreck. For

Studds surrounded by family and friends at 1972 election night victory party. *Photograph by Ken Wilson, courtesy Dean Hara.*

God's sake hurry up and win." A month later, with the race still undecided, Studds wrote back, humorously teasing his friend because *Newsweek* still hadn't covered him: "Incidentally, I think we won. Our opponent, who was brought up to believe that if you fail to inherit something, you should certainly buy it, has difficulty grasping this fact and a recount is still under way." Studds and Auchincloss shared the same sense of humor, a kind of P. G. Wodehouse sensibility regarding the social class that Weeks and Auchincloss had been born into, and that Studds inhabited when it suited him. In the interim, congratulatory letters arrived from such luminaries as Republican governor Frank Sargent and Harvard professor John Kenneth Galbraith, who wrote, prophetically, "I hope you have a good time in Washington, stay for a long while, and become chairman of a major committee without benefit of the seniority system." Finally, on December 14, Weeks conceded, leaving Studds the victor by 1,100 votes, the second-closest congressional race of 1972.[53]

The new force of the antiwar movement and generational revolt was gradually but noticeably changing the direction of Massachusetts politics. With Studds's victory, only three Republicans remained in the twelve-member Massachusetts congressional delegation, and Republican senator Ed Brooke was as liberal as the Democrats. In the Ninth District, which covered Boston, Joe Moakley, running as an independent, ousted the anti-busing champion Democrat Louise Day Hicks. Nixon won a smashing victory over George McGovern despite a horrific bombing attack in North Vietnam over the summer. In late October, Secretary of State Henry Kissinger had announced that "peace is at hand," thereby undercutting McGovern's main issue. McGovern carried only one state, which would later give birth to the famous bumper sticker "Don't Blame Me, I'm from Massachusetts." Nixon did carry one Massachusetts congressional district—the one that would now be represented in Congress by Gerry Studds, whose closeted gay sexual orientation no one ever hinted at during the election.

6

The Sacred Cod

GERRY STUDDS was sworn in as a member of the Ninety-third Congress in January 1973 by the diminutive speaker, Carl Albert of Oklahoma, as Tip O'Neill, dean of the Massachusetts delegation and majority leader, looked on. Albert appeared even smaller than he was, sandwiched between the six-foot-one Studds and the bulky O'Neill. Gerry's mother, Bonnie, and brother Colin came to Washington for the ceremony.[1]

Studds joined a new class of thirty freshman representatives that was about to shake up the status quo in a sclerotic institution. Powerful committee chairmen, all of whom had achieved their position by seniority, ruled their committees by fiat and were routinely reelected by bringing home the bacon to their districts. Many freshmen wanted to democratize that system. They represented the radical impulses of the 1960s. The times, as the Bob Dylan song had it, "were a-changing" faster than anyone realized.

Driving the new mood in Congress was the generational revolt inspired by the war in Vietnam. Studds's victory in a district that had also voted for Nixon exemplified the confused sensibility of the war-weary public. In the short time between Nixon's election and his second inauguration, the president had unleashed the most horrific bombing campaign of the entire war against North Vietnam, leaving its factories and hospitals in rubble and its land pockmarked by bomb craters and poisoned by Agent Orange. In mid-January the parties signed a final agreement that provided for the withdrawal of U.S. forces, an exchange of prisoners, the establishment of a demilitarized zone, and the installation of a shaky coalition government in South Vietnam—the same outcome that might have been negotiated in

1965. To the antiwar activists, over 1 million Vietnamese and 55,000 Americans had died to satisfy the deluded imperial dreams of the older generation, who had mistaken the nationalist desires of the Vietnamese for a communist conspiracy. Every president from Truman to Ford had deployed the "domino theory" to justify the war. They argued that if "the communists" won in Vietnam, a global conspiracy to dominate the world would threaten all of Southeast Asia. The theory was so bogus that no one could ever say whether Moscow or Beijing was calling the shots in Vietnam; actually it was neither.[2]

Ironically, as Studds took office, the period of "the 1960s" that had begun with the civil rights sit-ins was coming to an end. The national mood had changed. The antiwar activists and Vietnam veterans were now putting the war behind them and starting their careers and families. Two years later, when the Saigon regime folded as National Liberation Front and North Vietnamese troops advanced, the American population watched in mute, exhausted silence. World communism would collapse sixteen years later. The whole bloodbath had been for nothing.

The Imperial Presidency

Studds's freshman congressional class included the first significant contingent of congresswomen: Yvonne Burke, Marjorie Holt, Elizabeth Holtzman, Barbara Jordan, and Patricia Schroeder. The election of Jordan and Burke ended Shirley Chisholm's status as the sole African American congresswoman. Just after they were sworn in, the Supreme Court blocked the states from banning abortion in the *Roe v. Wade* case, and the sense of urgency that had animated the women's liberation movement dissipated. The new congresswomen pushed the Equal Rights Amendment to the Constitution out of the Judiciary Committee and onto the floor, where it passed. The states failed to ratify it, but its passage was a clear sign that the character of Congress as an old boys' club was changing. Between 1968 and 1974, more African Americans were elected to the House, including Julian Bond, Ron Dellums, Charles Rangel, Louis Stokes, and Andrew Young. These feminist activists and veterans of the civil rights struggle changed the composition of the Democratic caucus and Congress itself.[3]

Sitting for his first *Boston Globe* interview in March, Studds told the reporter that he was "appalled" by both the state of Congress and its relationship with the executive branch. The Democrats held a big majority in the Ninety-third Congress, 244–191, but were still unable to pass reform measures. Studds objected in particular to the Democratic caucus's rejection of two such measures, one requiring committee chairmen to step down at age seventy-five and a second making caucus votes public. Some significant changes had taken place in the two short months of Studds's tenure which loosened the seniority system, but Studds was not mollified. The following year, when the same reporter found Studds in a similar frame of mind, an unidentified New England colleague snapped, "Maybe when he's been down here for a while he'll smarten up." Indeed, Studds displayed a measure of arrogance and defensiveness that alienated some of his colleagues, no doubt fueled by the fact that he was guarding a personal secret.[4]

Another procedural problem Studds identified was that "Congress has lost its power to declare war . . . and this very definitely represents a major constitutional crisis." Although the Americans had withdrawn from Vietnam, Nixon continued bombing Cambodia to suppress the resupply of rebel units in South Vietnam. In May, Studds added his name to a lawsuit filed by the Center for Constitutional Rights to challenge the constitutionality of the bombing campaign. Later that year, Congress passed the War Powers Act, which required the president to secure congressional authorization before initiating hostilities, and placed a sixty-day limit on the use of force without authorization. Studds thus helped enact the first significant restriction on presidential power since the growth of the postwar imperial presidency.[5]

Another bright spot was that Studds got the committee appointments he had requested. The party leadership, probably recognizing that he had squeaked into office and might be vulnerable in his coastal district in 1974, assigned him to Merchant Marine and Fisheries, and Public Works. He sat on three subcommittees on the first committee—Oceanography, Merchant Marine, and Fisheries and Wildlife Conservation—and four on the second. He hired six staffers for his Washington office, including Bob Francis, a trusted boyhood friend from Cohasset, as his administrative assistant.[6]

Back in his district, Studds established three offices, one in each region: in Hanover on the South Shore, in Hyannis on Cape Cod, and in New Bedford; his predecessor had maintained only one. Studds immediately embarked on a hectic work regimen of sixteen-hour days, scheduling visits to the district on alternate weekends, during which he held several town meetings a day, patiently taking questions from constituents. Over the course of his career, he would visit every town twice a year, a remarkable outreach that earned him respect even from Republican voters. His district staff quickly gained a reputation for delivering superior constituent service. The Washington office put out a "Weekly Report to the People" that explained his votes, pending legislation, and district issues. Using House recording facilities, Studds made weekly audiotapes in his magnificent baritone voice. Local radio stations were happy to play them. By contrast, Hastings Keith had been barely visible in the district.[7]

Studds delivered his first floor speech on a favorite theme, the imperial presidency. Yet he approached the issue of impeaching the president warily during the unfolding Watergate scandal of 1973–74. As the nation watched in stunned disbelief, the Watergate burglars implicated the White House staff, Nixon's two top aides resigned, and Vice President Spiro Agnew was forced to quit in an unrelated bribery scandal. Because Studds's district was the only one in the state to have voted for Nixon, he maintained a cautious silence until the "Saturday night massacre" in October 1973, when Nixon attempted to fire Watergate special prosecutor Archibald Cox, leading his attorney general, Elliot Richardson of Massachusetts, to resign. Richardson was the kind of upright Yankee that Cape Cod Republicans respected. When only a quarter of the respondents to a Studds questionnaire on the scandal checked "no need for an inquiry," *Boston Globe* political reporter Bob Healy noted the implications for Nixon. Studds finally issued a statement calling for the president's resignation. When Nixon resigned in August, Studds declared that "President [Gerald] Ford comes to office with an unprecedented reservoir of good will."[8]

The Two-Hundred-Mile Limit

"I remember as a kid seeing the Russian fleet coming into George's Bank; they looked like the New York City skyline with their huge superstructures," Jeff Pike, a member of Studds's staff, recalled about cod fishing in the early 1970s. Pike sailed out of Harwich with his uncle in those days. He was a wiry, tough, smart young man, and fishing attracted him early on. The Russian factory trawlers would drag huge nets off their sterns, pulling codfish up into their enormous holds.[9]

The Russians were among the last to come to the banks off the Atlantic coast of North America, a thousand years late to the game. The first were the Basques, who arrived sometime after the turn of the first millennium. Later came the Vikings, and after them, sailors from western Europe. One explorer, Bartholomew Gosnold, would call the bent-arm-shaped peninsula off the coast of what is now Massachusetts "Cape Cod" for its abundant fish stocks, and he would name its largest offshore island for his daughter Martha. For almost the next four hundred years, fishing vessels would reap the ocean's seemingly limitless bounty.[10]

The initial settlers soon turned to the sea themselves, establishing fishing stations at Plymouth, Naumkeag (Salem), Gloucester on Cape Ann, and Boston. Succeeding generations of Pilgrims and Puritans became wealthy Yankee fishermen and captains of merchant vessels. By the eighteenth century, they were getting rich by participating in the triangular trade involving sugar, rum, and slaves, as well as cod and iron goods. When the American Revolution concluded, the thorniest issue at the Paris peace talks involved cod fishing rights for the New England fishermen. Thus the cod became "sacred" in Massachusetts, its image suspended above the state legislative chamber in Boston and the city celebrated in verse as "the land of the bean and the cod."[11]

By the 1970s, the haul of groundfish (cod, haddock, and flounder) off the Grand Banks, closest to Canada, and Georges Bank, about seventy-five miles east of Massachusetts, began to run low. Dramatic changes to a thousand years of relatively static fishing technology, and a process soon to be dubbed "globalization," had transformed a core relationship between man and beast on the planet. The nineteenth- and twentieth-century innovation of steel-hulled petroleum-powered vessels, organized into fleets, that could catch, refrigerate, and globally transport the cod began to suck the sea dry. The codfish, a three- to five-foot long omnivorous predator, was being eaten out of existence by the most relentless predator of all.

Gerry Studds very rapidly processed this transformed situation. "It's hard to over-emphasize how smart he was," Bob Francis, his first administrative assistant, recalled. Francis and Studds had sailed together as teenagers, and had won prizes in local competitions. Studds applied his powerful intellect to this problem with a sense of urgency.[12] "Gerry said that salt water ran in his veins," Jeff Pike, the Harwich sailor, remembered. Pike had gone to see Studds regarding fishing issues in the mid-1970s, and after a few years the young fisherman, now armed with a master's in public policy, became Studds's fisheries policy adviser. "He had sailed as a kid. He had a one-master, the *Bacalhau*. That's 'cod' in Portuguese, but he would go out and set lobster traps. Once he came out with my crew for two nights' fishing off the Nantucket shoals. I remember him, a U.S. congressman, cutting bait at two a.m. as we long-lined for cod."[13]

By 1973, the New Bedford fishermen understood that the cod wasn't going to last forever. New Bedford was Studds's base, and the fishermen, many of them Portuguese Americans, were the heart and soul of New Bedford. Their family-owned commercial vessels, over two hundred of them, dragged nets for groundfish, or pulled rakes along the bottom for scallops, the two

Studds greeting fishermen on a New Bedford dock. *Photographer unknown, courtesy Dean Hara.*

major sources of income for fishermen. The fishing industry accounted for a significant part of New Bedford's total revenue, and its fleet was the largest on the East Coast. But New Bedford was also the poorest major city in the state. If its fishing industry were destroyed by foreign fishing, New Bedford would sink with it.

The obvious solution was to assert American territorial rights up to two hundred miles from U.S. shores, thus barring foreign vessels from Georges Bank and the American section of the Grand Banks. In 1973, most nations claimed only a three-mile limit, but a "cod war" between Iceland and Britain, important NATO allies of the United States in the early 1970s, led to Iceland's declaration of a fifty-mile zone for itself; Britain retaliated, and the idea of a two-hundred-mile limit began to circulate.[14]

Studds was uniquely positioned by his district and committee assignment to press for this measure. Not everyone wanted it. The American Pacific fleet based at San Diego fished for tuna off the shores of Chile and Peru. If the United States adopted the expanded limit, the Latin American nations could do the same thing, so the National Fisheries Institute opposed the measure. The U.S. Navy objected as well, fearing that another nation might retaliate by closing its waters to American naval vessels. The Nixon and Ford administrations therefore opposed the idea. In general, American big business was also leery of protectionist measures, which could produce unanticipated consequences.

In the House, Studds collaborated closely with fellow committeeman Don Young, an Alaska Republican. Young, a hardy outdoorsman from Fort Yukon, seven miles above the Arctic Circle, had fished and trapped professionally and worked as a tugboat captain before being elected mayor and then congressman. A jovial bearded man with a big smile, he hung a huge polar bear hide on his office wall. The Alaska fishing fleet, based at Kodiak, faced the same problems as the New Bedford fishermen. "We had Russians, Poles, Chinese, and Japanese twelve miles off our shore," Young remembered. Echoing Pike's description of the East Coast waters, he said, "It looked like a city out there."[15]

At the same time, Senate Commerce Committee chairman Warren Magnuson of Washington and Ted Kennedy, another sailor, introduced a similar bill as an interim measure, pending a resolution of global fishing issues by an international Law of the Sea conference. In his House floor speech, Studds pointed out that haddock were "virtually extinct" and flounder stocks "seriously depleted." The Canadians, who had the world's largest fishing banks within their zone, were also discussing the two-hundred-mile limit; the two North American allies had their own bilateral agreement, but no one else was bound to respect it.[16]

Although Studds and Young secured sixty-nine co-sponsors and Magnuson got seventeen in the Senate, the bill did not move out of the House subcommittee during the first session of the Ninety-third Congress. Momentum built, however, in the following year as Studds made his case before the public and his legislative colleagues. The administration still wanted to wait until the Law of the Sea conference resolved the issue, but Studds objected. "Any agreement would take until at least 1980 or later for ratification," he warned. "By that time all the haddock will be wiped out." In May he testified before the Senate Commerce Committee, arguing that foreign fishing fleets were destroying the stocks. The world catch was down 8 percent as a result of past overfishing.[17]

In June 1974 the fishermen themselves took matters into their own hands. They organized a "Sail on Washington," starting in Maine and picking up more boats as they moved down the coast, much like Coxey's Army of unemployed workers in 1894 and the Bonus Marchers of 1932. These seamen made a dramatic presentation before Studds's subcommittee. They displayed the fine mesh nets used by foreign vessels that snared juvenile fish before they could mature and reproduce. Shipyard owners, seafood dealers, and others testified that they needed protection now.[18]

After Nixon resigned, Studds reintroduced the bill, this time with 168 co-sponsors. President Ford still backed the State and Defense departments, which lobbied senators against the expanded limit. Studds once again condemned "the spinelessness of this institution as we have seen again legislative policy dictated . . . by the executive branch." This overstated the case. In October, President Ford received Studds and five colleagues at the White House for a discussion. "We stressed that we are not representing just our parochial constituencies, but global concern regarding over-fishing," Studds reported.[19]

Later that month Studds flew to San Pedro, California, where the subcommittee held hearings in the capital of the tuna fishery. Studds assured industry leaders that tuna, a migratory species, would be exempt from the bill. Studds and Young were making progress. As the Ninety-third Congress ended, the Senate Armed Services Committee reversed itself and passed the measure, 8–6. Studds was admitted to the Senate floor, joining Kennedy and Magnuson, to watch the bill pass, 68–27. New England fishing industry leaders cheered. Studds had high hopes for future success.[20]

Having handily won reelection in 1974, Studds filed again right away in the Ninety-fourth Congress. Meanwhile, he kept his two committee seats, but moved from Merchant Marine to the Coast Guard and Navigation Subcommittee, a more appropriate seat for a fishing district. In March, the subcommittee held new hearings. Studds was particularly impressed by the testimony of a Lithuanian immigrant fisherman, an eyewitness to the over-fishing by foreign trawlers. By July, the subcommittee finally approved the two-hundred-mile limit almost unanimously, and the full committee voted, 36–3, to send the bill to the floor.[21]

Studds spoke before the International Relations Committee in September and on the floor in October, when the measure was finally debated. He reassured skeptics that the bill, because it was an interim measure pending ratification of an international treaty, would not jeopardize access for military vessels to strategic straits. Meanwhile, "the rape of the fisheries off our coasts is still continuing," he insisted. The total catch off the East Coast was now 1 million tons, far above a sustainable level, yet the U.S. share of the total had dropped from 92.9 percent in 1960 to 50 percent in 1974. And on Georges Bank, just seventy-five miles off the coast of Massachusetts, the U.S. share of the catch had declined from 88 percent in 1960 to 10 percent. After five hours of debate, the House approved the measure, 208–101.[22]

In the Senate, the bill passed by a vote of 77–19, and President Ford announced that he would sign it, pending negotiations regarding the start date. "This is unquestionably a very great victory," a delighted Studds told a reporter. "This should signal a rebirth for one of our oldest and most important industries." The result marked a personal victory for Studds as well. It is unlikely that his predecessor, a Republican loyalist, would have bucked the opposition of a Republican president. "Almost total credit is due to Representative Gerry Studds whose bill was passed last October after nearly three years of working doggedly to get it through," the *Boston Globe* observed on its editorial page. "New England fishermen owe Representative Studds an A-plus for effort and effectiveness," the *Globe* opined, and for the rest of Studds's career, that is what they would do. A few months later the president announced that he would sign the bill with a March 1, 1977, start date. Hailing Ford's decision, Studds stressed the need for Americans to regulate the catch and take responsibility for preservation. "The President's action today assures that we can begin to conserve and protect these valuable marine resources off our shores with a sound, uniform management program," he declared.[23]

"Studds knew more about fishing than any other East Coast congressman," Young recalled. "Nevertheless, because the Senate always predominates, the law became known as the Magnuson Act, but Studds and I wrote it. He would come up to Alaska and say, 'It should have been called the Young-Studds Act,' and that always got a laugh. As for the fears about the bill's possible negative consequences, there turned out to be nothing to worry about." The two men became friends and fishing buddies, an example of the House at its bipartisan best. Their staffers organized a softball team and called themselves "the Young Studds."[24]

The Oil Lobby Smells Fishy

Concurrent with the political crisis that gripped Washington during the Nixon-Ford years was the emergence of an energy crisis. Gasoline had been cheap since the appearance of the affordable automobile in the 1920s. After the creation of the Organization of Petroleum Exporting Countries, known as OPEC, the price of gasoline shot up to over a dollar from its usual price of thirty-five cents, and long lines formed at gas stations because of supply shortages. American oil companies promised that, given the opportunity to drill off the nation's coasts, they could produce enough oil to restore normal pricing. Pressure began to mount in Massachusetts to allow drilling for oil off Georges Bank.

In April 1974 the Council on Environmental Quality identified Georges Bank as a promising area for new offshore drilling. President Nixon instructed the Interior Department to prepare a report justifying the lease of 10 million acres. "There is no question [President Nixon] wants to drill out there," Studds warned. "I've got dozens of questions. They are clearly trying to accelerate the process." Studds became even more suspicious when he saw that the report ignored the possible impact to the marine environment, and its nineteen thousand projected jobs seemed like a number plucked out of thin air.[25]

Since there was no congressional committee with obvious oversight responsibility for offshore oil drilling, Speaker Albert created a new fifteen-member ad hoc committee in April 1975, to which he appointed Studds. The committee heard testimony from the governor of Louisiana, who questioned whether the benefits to his state, where there had been drilling for two decades, matched the infrastructure costs covered by the taxpayer. Studds came away convinced that the federal government had to compensate the states by creating coastal zone management programs. Moreover, he concluded that the exploratory and production aspects of drilling had to be managed separately so that the public could be heard on licensing issues if oil was struck. Otherwise, every oil site would be drilled regardless of the environmental consequences.[26]

Studds sent his aide Richard Norling on a fact-finding mission to the British and Norwegian drilling sites in the North Sea, a location whose rocky bottom and rough seas resembled conditions at Georges Bank more than the placid Gulf of Mexico. Norling discovered that the British political environment was as different as the nautical environments were similar. The U.K. fishing industry had its own representative on the national planning commission. (This was, after all, a country whose national dish was fish and chips.) The British government took 75 percent of net profits; the U.S. government was currently getting 16. Yet Massachusetts saw some upside in the possibilities; its Energy Office estimated that the 2 to 6 billion barrels off its shore could produce 5,400 jobs over a twenty-year period. When Studds opened hearings in Boston a few months later, the panel heard from Governor Michael Dukakis and Governor Meldrim Thompson of New Hampshire, as well as representatives from the petroleum and fishing industries and environmentalists. Studds reiterated that he was not opposed to drilling. "The question is, under what circumstances, and who will receive the benefits?" he asked.[27]

Exploratory drilling began on Georges Bank in April 1976. The Interior Department had leased a likely site to a consortium of the major oil companies. Studds doubted that the necessary regulatory regime could be crafted in time if the drillers struck oil. Citing the pressure on legislators and bureaucrats to move the process along, he fretted, "Perhaps we should hang *three* lanterns in the steeple of the Old North Church—because this industry is coming by land *and* by sea." He proposed that regulators adopt guidelines for further leasing that would include the establishment of regional advisory boards. The boards, which would represent the fishing industry, should require detailed drilling plans and create an oil spill liability fund. There were fifty full-time oil industry lobbyists on Capitol Hill, Studds warned; they all gave assurances that nothing could go wrong. It all smelled fishy to Congressman Studds.[28]

By late July, Studds scored another victory in his campaign to protect the American coast. After ten hours of debate, the House passed comprehensive offshore drilling legislation. The bill ensured that the bidding process would not exclude small companies, that state governments would be involved in leasing and drilling plans, that developers would be liable for spills, and that the exploration and development phases would be separated. The Senate had passed a similar measure, and the differences would have to be worked out in conference. They were. Then the slightly revised version was voted on again in October. "Big Oil Defeats Safe Drilling Bill," the *Globe* headline read. In the interim, the lobbyists had gone to work, and the measure was defeated in the House, 198–194. Studds vowed to re-file the bill the following year.[29]

Two months later, on December 15, 1976, the *Argo Merchant,* a Liberian-flagged oil tanker with a Greek crew, ran aground twenty-seven miles off Nantucket. Over 7 million gallons in its hold spilled into the sea and oozed toward the island. In 1969 another vessel had leaked 22,000 gallons of refined oil off Woods Hole, at Cape Cod's western end, and the damage was not yet undone. Now volunteers flocked to Nantucket to head off the giant crude oil slick, hoping that the shifting currents would spare its beaches. Massachusetts state legislators introduced emergency legislation to assess the cleanup costs. No, said the oil companies, we don't want to deal with fifty different state laws. Let there be one federal cleanup law. Studds introduced one and the lobbyists opposed it. Since the *Argo Merchant* spill had occurred in international waters (the two-hundred-mile limit applied to fishing only), the damaged parties would have to sue in a Liberian court. Studds told a reporter that the U.S. taxpayer would probably get stuck with the bill. "God knows what the seals are supposed to do," he lamented.[30]

As luck had it this time, the slick floated toward the open sea, away from Nantucket, but it still had to be cleaned up there. It was the worst oil spill in U.S. history. "We can't even find out the real owners [of the ship]," Studds fumed.[31] He now had his next project, one that would last until a more dramatic tanker spill thirteen years later.

The prospects in this fight were looking better. In the 1976 election, Democrat Jimmy Carter had defeated incumbent president Gerald Ford. In the House, Tip O'Neill, who had stood beside Studds as he took the oath of office for the first time, replaced Carl Albert as speaker. The times, they were a-changing.

7

The Congressman
in the Closet

During the election campaigns of 1970 and 1972, Gerry Studds stifled his personal life. He campaigned long days, and was driven around by aides to events covered by reporters. Had Studds visited a gay bar, or been seen in some other compromising situation, he would have lost the 1972 election. Not even his closest advisers, including Bob Francis, his childhood friend, knew that Studds was gay. It crossed the minds of many people, but each privately rejected as too unlikely the idea that a homosexual would run for public office.[1] English literature offered a few stereotypes of the eccentric bachelor, a category to which Studds seemed to belong: Sherlock Holmes and Henry Higgins might come to mind. In 1972 there were no openly gay elected or appointed officials.

"It is between difficult and utterly incomprehensible for the average person to understand the behavior of a closeted gay person and the apparent irrationality of things that he does and risks that he undertakes," Studds began a brief disquisition on "Risk Taking" in his memoir. In it, he recalled flirting with an airline steward, to whom he gave his card, realizing too late that it identified him as a congressman. Or on another occasion, he panicked when he learned that the man he was chatting up was a journalist.[2] Not every gay person faced such dilemmas in the 1970s, but a congressman in the closet certainly did.

In Washington, Studds felt free of the constraints that he encountered at home. Reporters hardly notice freshmen congressmen. Newly anonymous, Studds tried to develop intimate personal relations. He did not seem to have a sense of who was gay and who was not, a discriminating ability for which gay people later invented the term "gaydar." When he went out to Washington watering holes, sometimes with staffers after work, he would offer promising young men a ride home and then suggest that they come up for a drink. Probably most said no. Years later, two seventeen-year-old congressional pages would describe Studds employing exactly this gambit. Both separately accompanied Studds to his apartment, at which point he poured some drinks and then made an advance, which both young men declined.[3]

Another seventeen-year-old accepted. They went up to Gerry's Georgetown apartment and talked and drank into the early morning hours, whereupon Studds declared that he was too inebriated to drive him home. Studds drank heavily in these situations, vodka being his drink of choice, probably not so much for the purposes of seducing a vulnerable partner as for steeling himself to do something he knew he shouldn't. On this occasion the page, later identified in a congressional report as "X," stumbled into bed with Studds. X liked Studds enormously for his intellect, charm, and wit. Ten years later he would tell an investigating committee that he enjoyed Gerry's company and had acted of his own free will, and that their relationship would have been regarded as normal in another society. Most likely X was referring to ancient Greece, a notion that he probably got from Studds. X and Studds repeated this experience two or three more times in the summer of 1973.

The legal age of consent in Washington was sixteen, and the page did not work for Studds. Yet as Studds would later recognize, the power relation between the two of them was seriously misaligned; that he, not the page, had instigated their relationship; and that therefore what he was doing was wrong. In many cases, such behavior is predatory and reprehensible. Yet untold numbers of teenagers have had sex with older adults, willingly, and none the worse for the experience. This was one of those cases. Each partner treated the other with respect, and neither had the illusion that they were in love. Emotionally, X said, he was never hurt. Their relationship in this regard was quite different from that between Bill Clinton and Monica Lewinsky in that Lewinsky became infatuated with Clinton.

Studds then pushed the envelope of this relationship way too far. He invited X to be his driver on a vacation to Portugal, and X accepted. Just as he had done at St. Paul's, Studds allowed his own needs to override his adult responsibilities. When his aides realized what was happening, they urged their boss not to go, but he insisted. This was a vacation, not a fact-finding mission, and each of them paid his own way. For Studds, the vacation also served a political purpose, in that he would be able to describe his journey through Lisbon, Viseu, Coimbra, Braga, Bragança, and the Serra de Estrela mountains for his constituents, which he did in his newsletter. Every few nights, congressman and driver had sex together. When they returned to the United States, X told Studds that he wanted to break off their relationship, and they went their separate ways as friends. Studds probably concluded that his staff had been overly protective and that he could ignore their future warnings, just as he had once disregarded the advice of his Groton football coach to "stay low."[4]

Studds did not see that sexual mores were changing to protect young people and subordinates against predatory behavior by their elders and superiors. President Kennedy had conducted numerous affairs while the Washington press corps looked the other way, but after Watergate, journalistic norms changed. This development was encouraged by feminists who insisted that "the personal is political," and that enhanced scrutiny of a public figure's private behavior belonged in the public square. The lines regarding private and public behavior began to blur. If a public figure, for example, committed adultery, should it be reported? These questions were about to explode in American public life in periodic "scandals."

One day in 1974, Studds granted reporter Vera Vida of the Republican-leaning *Quincy Patriot Ledger* an interview for a human interest feature. A woman reporter writing for women readers in those days had to ask about the personal life of an eligible bachelor. What kind of woman was Studds looking for? Was he dating? Studds replied with some evasive answers, and lamely allowed that he "saw people" when he could, but that, as the article's headline put it, "Congressman Studds Has No Time for Cupid," and when he did return to the district, he stayed with his mother. Anyone who cared to read between the lines might conclude that they were reading about either a closeted gay man or a social recluse.[5]

In the following year, Studds bought a condominium at Waterfront West on Commercial Street in Provincetown's West End. The evidence began to mount that Studds was not simply a "bachelor." It was becoming untenable for him to stay at his mother's home in Cohasset when he returned to the district as he began to develop a private life as a gay man in Washington. "He was torn about wanting to be open, but terrified," his chief of staff, then a reporter for the *Cape Cod Times*, Peter Fleischer, recalled. "What about my mother?" he wondered aloud. Bonnie Studds, Fleisher noted, was "fairly regal in her demeanor," and "she loomed large in his life." Bonnie suspected that her son was gay, and had once approached her husband with her suspicions. Eastman had run out of the room in denial. After Eastman died, Gerry called his mother daily to check on her.[6]

Meanwhile, in Washington, Studds met "T," as he calls him in his memoir, a handsome young waiter with an artistic bent, when Studds was out with his staff in the fall of 1975. Their eyes locked in mutual interest, T passed Studds his phone number, and Studds called, nervously, a few days later. As they strolled over a Potomac bridge, "I found myself surprised, then fascinated, and in short order, overwhelmed by waves of emotion I had never known," Studds remembered. "It seemed I could dispense with the bridge and leap the river, I was at once focused and giddy. 'Thirty-eight going on sixteen' I mused to myself, only slightly sobered by the realization of how little I looked the part of the smitten teenager."[7]

T was in his early twenties, an aspiring writer and artist, holding a night job until he found his footing in the arts. T set the congressman in the closet loose emotionally, if not entirely free. "For the next three months, I was a person transformed," Studds wrote. "Clearly I was in love, and it appeared that he was too. . . . More than once that fall, we could be observed saying good night and embracing, standing beside his car on Pennsylvania Avenue at two thirty in the morning. And more than once I wondered who might be watching." T accepted Gerry's offer to use the Provincetown condo for a writer's retreat, and the two drove off together in caravan, their cars loaded with T's furnishings. Studds's narrative then trails off unresolved, but their relationship soon ended.

A detached observer can read all the unspoken obstacles into the story. Studds lived a very busy, highly scheduled public life, and would have had to give it up to develop a committed relationship with a young waiter who lived under no such constraints. They could not be seen in public together for fear that Gerry's sexual orientation would be exposed. Studds wrote on the first page of his memoir that he wanted heterosexual readers to understand how isolating and painful anti-gay prejudice made life, especially for gay men who chose public careers, and this relationship probably failed for those reasons.

Another factor may have contributed to the end of this love affair. Studds hinted at it when he admitted "how little I looked the part of the smitten teenager." Certainly the age and power difference between a thirty-eight-year-old congressman and a waiter in his early twenties would be limiting, but Studds was also running himself into the ground. Jeff Pike, who met Studds a few years later, remembered: "He smoked. His refrigerator was full of bad food. He didn't do any exercise."[8] Studds would give those habits up only when he turned forty, but he never gave up drinking, and only later would he discard the old-fashioned 1950s-style horn-rims that, along with his thinning hair, accentuated the appearance of a middle-aged man out of step with the disco-dancing 1970s. That makeover transformed him in his forties into a much younger-looking, vigorous man than he appeared to be in his thirties. And T probably awoke in Studds a buried desire to just "lighten up." Studds recalled T saying about himself that he wanted "to fly." Many years later, after he was out of the closet, Studds would find the person who taught him to take wing, but that was still years away.

Meanwhile, other gay people were making their own choices in those years. "Coming out" took many different directions, which may be over-simplified into two categories. Most visible were the flamboyant gay libera-tionists. The politically minded among this group hoped to change society fundamentally, to bring the whole anti-gay matrix down by demonstrating in the streets and living their lives openly. Gay men by the thousands flocked to San Francisco's Castro District and transformed it into the capital of gay America. San Francisco in the 1970s became what Harlem, Detroit, or Chi-cago of the 1920s had been for African Americans. Gay San Franciscans felt the same sense of liberation. Some gay writers, like some Harlem Renais-sance novelists before them, announced that sexual repression was the bane of Western civilization and that their culture could free its prisoners of their discontents.

The more politically oriented radical gay men and lesbians of the early 1970s were influenced by the antiwar, civil rights, and women's rights move-ments to challenge the constraints of patriarchal Western civilization, in which traditional gender roles prevailed. They mocked those conventions openly, stressing their differences from what seemed to them to be oppres-sive heterosexual norms that imprisoned everybody. "Gay liberation" took its name from the National Liberation Front of Vietnam, by way of the women's liberation and black liberation movements.

A different, sometimes overlapping current of committed activists focused on changing the law. In 1972, every aspect of same-sex activity was illegal almost everywhere in America. Gays could be fired without cause and were barred from the military and civil service. Immigrants at the border who were suspected of homosexuality were examined by medical doctors and turned away. To paraphrase the words of the Dred Scott decision of 1854, gay people had no rights (except the vote) that heterosexuals were bound to respect.[9]

In May 1974, New York congressional representatives Bella Abzug and Ed

Koch introduced a bill that would ban discrimination in most places on the basis of sex (the word we would now use is "gender"), and also on the basis of marital status or sexual orientation. The measure thus joined feminist and gay concerns. Abzug circulated a "Dear Colleague" letter looking for co-sponsors.[10]

Studds faced a very different electorate than did Abzug or Koch, both of whose liberal districts contained gay communities. Studds threw the letter out right away. He felt terrible, but he did it. He was worried about his first reelection campaign. That November he defeated his Republican opponent, 138,779 to 46,787, an almost unbelievable margin in what had been a Republican district. Studds benefited from the post-Watergate landslide, in which his party gained forty House seats. Among the newcomers were "New Politics" types who, like Studds, were issues-oriented, rather than old-style politicians bent on dispensing patronage to their coterie. Yet some of the "Watergate babies" were not New Deal economic liberals like their predecessors. Concerned with budget balancing and honest government, they presented themselves as sober pragmatists rather than as fighters for the poor.[11]

Encouraged by the 1974 election results, Studds changed his mind and agreed to co-sponsor the gay rights bill in 1976. When his stand became known, Edmund Dinis, the Portuguese American son of a popular New Bedford politician, entered the primary with nothing but the gay rights issue on his agenda. Dinis had served in the state legislature and as Bristol County district attorney. His roots ran deep in the heart of Studds's base, Democratic New Bedford. Studds was still a new face.

Dinis's first press release declared that "Mr. Studds wants to make homosexuality an acceptable way of life." He mailed it to the members of all the local unions and school committees. He warned that homosexuals should not be allowed to teach children, implying that they were inclined to pedophilia. "Furthermore, this [bill] gives them the right to marry," Dinis insisted. In 1976 this was an unimaginable possibility that no one advocated. The rest of this low-minded campaign suggested by innuendo that Studds was himself homosexual. "I felt certain that no one in politics could survive such allegations in 1976," Studds remembered. His worst nightmare had come to life.[12]

Meanwhile, the just emerging gay civil rights movement had made some gains, and this set off alarm bells among social conservatives everywhere. At the 1972 Democratic Party convention, Jim Foster of San Francisco gave the first speech by an openly gay activist to a national convention. In 1974,

Elaine Noble was elected to the Massachusetts legislature; she was the first openly lesbian or gay person elected to public office. Her district included the Fenway and South End, home to a significant gay community in Boston. The following year, a Minnesota state senator, Alan Spear, came out. In the military, a brave air force sergeant, Leonard Matlovich, announced that he was gay and challenged the military's exclusion policy in court. California repealed its sodomy law.[13] These encouraging signs might have persuaded Studds to come out himself, but he didn't. His district was very different from Elaine Noble's, and he judged that the wisest course was to keep his private life out of the public discussion. This is the closeted gay progressive's dilemma: if you don't feel that your sexual orientation is relevant to your performance as an elected official, why allow other people to make it an issue? So Studds simply ignored Dinis.

Studds received mail from haters and allies both. "I lived in constant fear that Dinis or one of his supporters would come up with a picture of me or some other tangible evidence that I was gay, and leak it to the press, thus ruining not only my career but, as far as I was concerned, my entire life," Studds wrote in his memoir. Dinis, however, stagnated in the polls. "This is dirty politics," the *Boston Globe* quoted one school committee member who had received Dinis's letter. Dinis ran a full-page ad on the day of New Bedford's Portuguese American festival that blared: "Homosexual teachers: Studds says OK, Dinis says No! Studds cosponsored a bill, H.R. 5452, that would give homosexuals the right to teach our children! And run our jails! And our police departments! And our Armed Forces!" The ad included a quote from a *New Bedford Standard-Times* editorial rebuking Studds for co-sponsoring the bill, and a statement by advice columnist Ann Landers decrying homosexuality as "a severe personality disorder," echoing the judgment of the American Psychiatric Association. Dinis was correct that Studds, by backing the gay civil rights bill, was proposing a major change in American life.[14]

Studds and Ted Kennedy both marched that day in the Portuguese American parade. Studds thought he got an especially warm reception. He speculated that some people in the crowd might have felt embarrassed that Dinis, one of "their own," was acting like a schoolyard bully, and they didn't like his tone.

Just before the primary election, a New Bedford reporter called John Sasso, a Studds staffer, with a question: "On the record Dinis has called Gerry a fairy. Do you have any comment on that?" Sasso snorted and gave a "beneath our contempt" answer, but under the bravado, Studds and his people were worried. To his relief, Studds won an even bigger victory than he had in 1974, carrying New Bedford and the district by 85 percent. Studds himself was stunned. There was no Republican challenger in November. "It was the clearest indication yet, to me, of the fundamental decency of that constituency," he wrote. "Even so, I took a long time to recover from being so scared."

8

The Mashpee Wampanoag and the New Bedford Portuguese

WHEN JIMMY CARTER assumed the presidency in January 1977, the Democrats held a House majority of 292–143 and had sixty-one senators. Yet Carter had run as an outsider to Washington, not as a champion of New Deal or New Politics values. In the primaries, Studds had supported Arizona congressman Morris Udall, a strong environmentalist, but he told his constituents that he was "very pleased" with the inaugural ceremony, to which Carter walked, a gesture that reflected Studds's own sensibility. Tip O'Neill became speaker of the House, and Ted Kennedy was among the Senate's most respected members, so Massachusetts held outsized power on Capitol Hill. But in his first term with the new speaker, Studds was about to discover the truth of O'Neill's dictum that "all politics is local."

The Mashpee Wampanoag

While Studds was contending against Edmund Dinis, a bitter controversy that had not surfaced in the campaign reached a climax. In August 1976, the Mashpee Wampanoag native people filed suit in federal court against the New Seabury Corporation and other developers in the town of Mashpee on Cape Cod to reclaim eleven thousand acres of land worth $30 million.

The Wampanoag were the main tribal group on the Cape when the Pilgrims landed. They had worked out a modus vivendi with the white settlers under their first chief, Massasoit, but after his death a fierce conflict, known as King Philip's War, broke out, ending in massacres of the Wampanoag and their defeat. The survivors were settled in an area of western Cape Cod that later became the town of Mashpee. In 1790, during the presidency of George Washington, the first Indian Non-Intercourse Act was passed, requiring that all land purchases from native peoples be approved by Congress. The government of the new United States did not want the states to provoke any wars with the natives through bogus land purchases. Prior to the town's incorporation in 1842, however, the Mashpee common land was divided into parcels among tribal members, who then sold it to non-natives, without the consent of Congress. In the 1970s, when land developers began building homes and golf courses at an accelerated rate, the Mashpee Wampanoag, aided by the Native American Rights Fund, brought land reclamation suits on behalf of their tribe and native peoples in Maine. While the Massachusetts lands were valued at perhaps a manageable sum, the Maine lands equaled two thirds of the state and were valued at $25 billion. The legal principle was the same: in neither case, in clear violation of the 1790 law, had Congress approved the land transfer.[1]

The developers and property owners exploded in anger. With a suit in court that placed every land title in question, homes could neither be bought nor sold, nor mortgages secured. The situation was complicated by the ethnic complexity of the town. More than half the townspeople had some Indian ancestry. The tribe itself was divided about the wisdom of the suit. Many people weren't sure if they themselves were tribal members. It was not even clear whether the Mashpee Wampanoag constituted a tribe. One thing was certain: white business owners, developers, and homeowners were howling mad, and they wanted their government to fix the mess.

That was the situation when Congressman Gerry Studds came to Mashpee Town Hall in December to address four hundred angry residents. The developers and homeowners were led by Samuel Sirkis, a wealthy adviser to sports celebrities, and the Mashpee Action Committee, to which the New Seabury Corporation had contributed $15,000 as a start. Sirkis personally hated Studds, and to raucous applause he lambasted the congressman as a do-nothing who fiddled while Mashpee burned at an Indian stake.[2]

Sirkis wanted Studds to file a bill to indemnify the town for the $30 million. The local state representative, a Republican, had done that in the Massachusetts House, but the bill wasn't going to pass there. Studds explained that passing federal legislation would be even more hopeless, because a Massachusetts bill would trigger a move to indemnify Maine. In reality, few bills become law, and this idea stood no chance in Congress. Studds could have pulled a fast one and gotten ahead of the parade. He could have shared his constituents' anger, vowed to file a bill, made some speeches denouncing the lawsuit, and shut Sirkis up while the "bill" languished in a subcommittee. He didn't. He told voters the truth, even though they weren't going to like it. "I will not be a demagogue to you," he declared. "I will not file legislation just so that I can come here to Mashpee and tell you that I filed it."[3] The real solution was for the town and the tribe to sit down and negotiate a compromise.

Over the next year, Studds, working with Senators Ted Kennedy and Ed Brooke, tried to accomplish that. In February, they urged that the president appoint a federal mediator, and in March, President Carter did so. In April, Studds proposed that the Small Business Administration help out Mashpee businesses that were having trouble securing loans. By September, the mediator, having met with all sides, threw in the towel. Studds didn't want to give up, but the Mashpee selectmen would not meet with the tribal leaders. In October, Studds and the Massachusetts senators filed emergency legislation to protect homeowners with less than an acre of land from losing their title should the Indians prevail in court, but the court ruling was handed down before the bill got anywhere.[4]

The outcome that Studds regarded as the worst possible was finally at hand. In January 1978, a federal jury found that although the Mashpee Wampanoag had been a tribe when their land was sold in 1834 and 1843, they had not in fact been a tribe for one hundred years and therefore had no standing to make a claim. The Wampanoag's attorneys appealed the verdict, which did not decide on the substance of the case, but the appellate court upheld it the following year. The suit had cost the Wampanoag $350,000 in legal fees.[5] The verdict ended another tragic chapter in the sad history of Indian relations with the whites who had invaded tribal lands.

"Once the case was resolved, it was devastating for the tribe," recalled Mark Forest, who worked on Cape Cod for Studds. "They went into a cocoon; they became invisible." Years later, Studds worked out a compromise for the Gay Head Aquinnah on Martha's Vineyard. Because the Aquinnah did not file a lawsuit, Studds was able to pass federal legislation that reserved some land and cash for a tribe that, like the Mashpee Wampanoag, had been despoiled of its rights over a century earlier.[6]

The Ocean Environment

During the Carter years, Studds emerged as a champion of ocean environmental issues and became chairman of a subcommittee, Oceanography, serving under the new chairman of the Merchant Marine and Fisheries Committee, John Murphy of New York. While Studds generally admired Carter, who earnestly called the country's attention to the need for conservation, he became disappointed by the president's energy program, which he saw as relying too heavily on the free market. Studds fought, with varying degrees of success, for measures that might have prevented three of the worst disasters in environmental history. First, he attempted to balance preservationists' concerns against the economic imperatives of commercial fishing. Second, he worked to ensure that offshore drilling did not pollute the oceans, and to promote alternative energy sources to reduce the need for drilling. Third, he got an oil tanker safety bill through Congress, warned about ocean dumping, and fought for a robust Coast Guard. Studds came up against the power of the oil lobby, which influenced southern Democrats from coastal states. Had Studds's warnings been heeded, New England fishermen might not have depleted groundfish stocks, the *Deepwater Horizon* disaster of 2010 might have been prevented, and the 1989 *Exxon Valdez* tanker spill might never have happened.

Counting the Fish

The Magnuson Act took effect on March 1, 1977. The new law designated the Coast Guard and National Marine Fisheries Service as enforcement agencies. In the frigid March winds, Coast Guard sailors began boarding Soviet trawlers. Some licensed fishing in specified amounts was still permitted to foreign vessels, and the Russians tested those limits. The Coast Guard cutters would signal the slow-moving trawlers, and the sailors, wearing rubberized suits to protect against the cold, clambered up rope ladders to poke their noses into the holds and inspect the nets, as good-natured Russian fishermen looked on. The Coast Guard impounded the *Taras Shevchenko* and the *Geroy Eltigen* until the proper penalties could be assigned in U.S. District Court. To Studds's consternation, the Carter administration short-circuited the policing. Secretary of State Cyrus Vance was negotiating an arms control agreement in Moscow, and the administration didn't want to antagonize the Soviets. Studds approved of the arms control talks but didn't see any linkage between the two processes. To make matters worse, the State Department classified its memos to the White House. By the end of April, one of the ships was sailing back home after posting a $1 million bond, and the Russians finally got the message, but Studds was grumpy about having to buck the State Department in a matter whose resolution seemed obvious to him.[7]

Studds issued a cautionary warning a year after the two-hundred-mile limit went into effect. The results were better "than I dared dream just one year ago," he wrote. The foreign ships were gone, and the fish had begun to regenerate faster than anticipated. The New Bedford fleet, whose 250 boats at its peak had declined by half in the 1970s, had just ordered twenty new vessels that would provide eight hundred to one thousand new jobs. The New England catch had increased by over 20 million pounds, pumping $25 million into the regional economy and spurring further investment. Times were good.

Success, however, might contain the seeds of catastrophe. Studds had conceived of the two-hundred-mile limit as a conservationist, not a protectionist, measure. The original act established eight regional fisheries management councils, whose job was to monitor the fish stocks, and these had "imposed strict quotas on American fishermen as well," Studds reminded council members. He warned that the targets had been designed not to restore peak levels but only "to prevent further reductions in the population of each stock."[8] Tensions between scientists and policy makers on the one hand, and fishermen on the other, were to persist over the next forty years, leading to temporary total bans, further declines in fish stocks, and reduction of the New Bedford fleet to pre-two-hundred-mile-limit proportions.

Drilling in the Sea

The energy crisis spurred by the OPEC cartel encouraged many Americans to desire independence from foreign imports. Oil companies took advantage of this sentiment by pressing for barely regulated offshore drilling. Studds became a leading spokesman for careful controls. His policy represented the interests of New Bedford fishermen and Cape Cod environmentalists.

In 1977, the Interior Department readied a million acres of the Atlantic Ocean off New England for lease to oil companies. As a regulatory measure passed by the Senate made its way through the House as H.R. 1614, Studds described the clear principles that should apply to leasing. He insisted that state and municipal governments must have a seat at the table when leases were approved. Safety concerns regarding blowouts must be addressed in advance. Furthermore, he wanted the lease lots to be small enough so that smaller developers might compete. Developers would have to compensate localities that provided onshore access to drilling platforms. Finally, he wanted maximum coverage for damage to fishing vessels to exceed the

$5,000 allowed by early federal guidelines. These principles won the support of local New England interests regardless of political party. Former Republican governor Frank Sargent even contributed a newspaper op-ed headlined "Studds Rightly Sounds Oil Drilling Alarm." Sargent was skeptical about claims that a lot of oil would be found at Georges Bank, citing a study that estimated its total capacity at merely six months' worth of U.S. demand.[9]

Studds had fully expected H.R. 1614 to pass. It had the support of President Carter and Interior Secretary Cecil Andrus. To his disgust, the bill was strangled in the Rules Committee. He blasted "the most blatant example of special interest power politics I have ever seen in five years of Congress." Five Democrats had defected to join the five Republicans to keep the bill off the floor. "I simply witnessed an incredible abuse of power by the major oil companies. They'll have to learn to play our way or not at all," Studds fumed, but so far it was Exxon, Conoco, and Shell that were making the rules. There would be no reforms to the leasing or regulatory regimes in 1977.[10]

In the next session, Studds's Outer Continental Shelf bill got fast-tracked to victory. The overwhelming support for the bill, 291–91, suggests that the oil lobbyists realized that they had overreached during the last session. The new measure provided a liability fund for damage claims, regulated the bidding system, and gave an increased role to state and local governments. Drilling plans had to be more detailed, leases might be suspended once issued, and a flexible financing system for bidders encouraged smaller companies to participate. "We're very happy," Studds said, expressing his satisfaction. The oil companies decided to live with these provisions as the bill went to a conference committee and finally passed, 338–18, in August.[11]

The Outer Continental Shelf Act of 1978 did not close the issue. Studds monitored offshore drilling throughout his career. In 1979 he traveled to Corpus Christi, Texas, where he saw the damage that could be caused by a blowout. Studds did not live long enough to witness the nation's worst drilling disaster, the British Petroleum *Deepwater Horizon* spill in the Gulf of Mexico thirty years later. Had the tough regulations that Studds insisted on been in place, that catastrophe might have been avoided. As for Georges Bank, the explorations went forward, but "they found a little gas and not much oil," staffer Jeff Pike recalled decades later. The initial projections had been overblown.[12]

As a critic of the oil lobby, and a representative of Northeast energy consumers, Studds felt a responsibility to put forth his own energy program, which stressed conservation and alternative energy sources. The wider context for this discussion was Carter's energy program. The president took a big risk by telling the public the painful truth that they too had a role to play in conservation, in the much-mocked but honest "malaise" speech of 1979. Yet Carter also felt responsible to his party's southern wing, whose Louisiana, Texas, and Oklahoma House members received money from oil lobbyists, and whose constituents worked as roughnecks, pipefitters, and engineers. Carter proposed a free market policy which, he expected, would promote exploration, creating a temporary price hike but then a fall as supplies rose over time. The blizzard of 1978 raised the stakes for New England congressmen, who demanded price controls and aid to seniors unable to pay for home heating oil. This problem increased tensions between Speaker O'Neill and President Carter, but they did their best to negotiate a compromise.[13]

Studds finally told his constituents that the "Carter energy proposal is a disaster," as consumer prices spiked too high. Matters got more worrisome after the Three Mile Island nuclear accident in Pennsylvania in 1979. He joined a losing fight to deny licenses to new facilities that did not have adequate evacuation plans. Concern grew on Cape Cod that if the Pilgrim reactor in Plymouth experienced a problem, there were only two bridges leading off the Cape. Over the rest of his career, Studds would promote wind, solar, conservation, and ocean thermal alternatives to both fossil fuel and nuclear energy. By the 1990s he began to warn, ahead of most of his colleagues, about the dangers of global warming.[14]

Spill Bill Thrills Hill

Studds had a much easier time getting tanker safety standards approved. The shipping industry was a less formidable opponent than the oil lobby, and its case was not helped by the standard practice of registering what were actually American ships under Liberian flags to avoid U.S. taxes and regulations. In fact, 94 percent of imports came to U.S. ports under foreign colors. Studds re-filed his tanker safety bill immediately after the 1976 *Argo Merchant* spill. It cost the U.S. taxpayer $1.5 million for the Coast Guard to clean up that mess. The *Argo Merchant* had been an ancient rust bucket with an incompetent captain and a terrible safety record—a perfect poster child for all that was wrong with oil tanker shipping.[15]

The Tanker Safety Act of 1977 set minimum safety requirements for ships entering U.S. waters and gave the Coast Guard enforcement responsibilities.

It assigned liability for cleanup costs by adding a three-cent-a-barrel import tax to create a compensation fund. The bill included new provisions that mandated modern navigation and collision avoidance systems and required that ballast and liquid cargoes be stored in separate compartments. The president's staff agreed. In the following session, in September 1978, it passed, 366–6, and later became law.[16]

Oil tanker safety was one piece of a larger puzzle regarding how the industrialized world was fouling the sea. A related problem of the global commons had to do with mining in international waters. Studds was in the congressional vanguard on these and other environmental issues that threaten the very existence of life on the planet. As chairman of the Oceanography Subcommittee, which was charged with protection of the marine environment, he worked in a variety of ways to study and protect the seas. He read voraciously, and was briefed by scientists at the Woods Hole Oceanographic Institute on Cape Cod.

Studds also promoted regulation of ocean dumping. Scientists estimated that between 35 and 50 million tons of garbage were being tossed annually into unregulated international waters. People started to notice the problem when medical wastes washed up on the New Jersey and Long Island coastlines. Studds got an ocean dumping bill through the House in 1980 that set rules for U.S. ships. Unfortunately, this problem only metastasized over the following decades as international trade expanded and a garbage swirl the size of Texas poisoned the Pacific Ocean. The best Studds could do was to pass several coastal zone management bills limiting development and aiming to improve water quality. In February 1980, his committee held hearings that called attention to water quality in Boston Harbor.[17] Studds would monitor this issue throughout his career, but without consistent presidential and international leadership, the oceans have been severely compromised.

Studds also maintained a seat on the Coast Guard and Navigation Subcommittee, and there he became an effective advocate for this important police force and safety patrol. The Coast Guard served as a rescue agency for vessels in distress and saved many lives. In 1979, one accident killed several New Bedford fishermen. Studds wanted to minimize such catastrophes. He helped the Coast Guard improve its recordkeeping and passed a hoax call bill that set stiff penalties for pranksters calling in false alarms. Studds fought throughout his career for adequate Coast Guard funding. He joked that landlubber congressmen wanted to keep it "*semi-paratus,*" a Latin pun on the Coast Guard motto *"Semper Paratus,"* "Always Prepared." Studds was especially proud of the Coast Guard's rescue swimmer program, one that has saved thousands of lives over the years.[18]

From New Bedford to Central America

By a strange series of developments, Studds's work representing the city of New Bedford led him to the second great achievement of his life. In the 1980s, Studds would become a leading opponent of President Ronald Reagan's wars in Central America. He came to that position in a roundabout and unanticipated fashion, one that derived from the unique history of New Bedford.

New Bedford, lying along the west bank of the Acushnet River, began as a Quaker farming village and later became a whaling center. In January 1841, the young Herman Melville shipped out from there and turned his experience into the novel *Moby-Dick,* later to be recognized as one of the classics of American literature. Among Melville's fellow sailors were men from the Azores Islands, and these Portuguese speakers became part of New Bedford's ethnic fabric. When the discovery of oil in Pennsylvania sent the whaling industry into decline, New Bedford's whalers took up fishing. In 1913 the city fathers unveiled in front of the main library a statue of a harpooner in action, bearing the inscription "A Dead Whale or a Stove Boat."

New Bedford's Quaker heritage made it a leading center of antislavery sentiment prior to the Civil War. The escaped slave Frederick Bailey from Maryland arrived there around the same time Melville did. To protect his identity, he changed his surname to Douglass, and it is fair to say that the great abolitionist orator created his new identity there. During the Civil War, Frederick Douglass recruited many black residents of New Bedford for the Massachusetts Fifty-fourth Infantry. In 1986 the city added a companion statue to that of the harpooner, depicting Lewis Temple, African American inventor of the toggle harpoon, inspecting his creation.

During the late nineteenth century, Portuguese mainlanders joined their Azorean cousins and took jobs in the textile mills, clustering in the city's north and south ends. In 1958, an earthquake devastated the Azorean island of Fayal. Massachusetts senator John F. Kennedy won legislation expanding Portuguese immigration, becoming a hero to that community. Many new immigrants, fishermen at home, joined the New Bedford fishing fleet, making the city the capital of Portuguese America. The 1970 census identified about one third of all the nation's Portuguese immigrants and second-generation descendants as living in Massachusetts, and most of them inhabited New Bedford and nearby Fall River. Because they were new immigrants, and dark-skinned relative to other "whites" such as the Irish, the Portuguese retained their language and sense of community to a greater degree than other European ethnic groups did.

By the 1970s, foreign fishing vessels had swamped the family-owned New Bedford fleet, and the city's African American community suffered every possible urban ill. Many textile factories had closed down and shifted operations to the South. Hastings Keith had ignored the city, and many residents felt forgotten. New Bedford languished.

Then "they see a man with Gerry's name, and his looks, and he gets up to speak, and they hear Portuguese," Maria Tomasia remembered. "He was paying attention to them. He showed them respect, and they made him one of their own." Studds hired Tomasia, the twenty-three-year-old daughter of a factory worker, as his local immigration staffer. Tomasia was born on São Miguel in the Azores and came to New Bedford as a child. She typified the community. People began turning to the congressional office for help with visa problems, and Tomasia's part-time job became full-time. Word got out among Portuguese American fishermen, housewives, and factory workers. Studds met with the leaders of the various Portuguese American organizations. He maintained a good relationship with this underrepresented community and had special knowledge about an overlooked foreign country.[19]

Then in 1974, left-wing military officers overthrew the hated dictatorship established by António de Oliveira Salazar, and Portugal's importance soared. The Portuguese Empire, the last vestige of European colonialism on the face of the earth, began to crumble in Cape Verde, Angola, and Mozambique. By 1976, when Mário Soares, a socialist, put together a governing coalition, the State Department feared that the Russians and Cubans would influence the outcome in Portugal's former African colonies.

Only one Portuguese American held a seat in Congress, Tony Coelho of California, but Coelho didn't speak Portuguese. So the chairman of the House Foreign Relations Committee asked Studds to join his committee, which he did, yielding his seat on Public Works and Transportation. Studds was also one of the few congressmen who had previously worked in the State Department, and with his wide-ranging intellect, this assignment was a perfect fit for him. In June, Studds met again with the leaders of Portuguese American organizations, and in July made an eight-day trip to Portugal and the Azores. There he met with Prime Minister Soares, Ambassador Frank Carlucci, and civil society leaders. Continuing on to the Azores, he was joined by Tomasia, who showed him around her home territory. Studds became convinced that Portugal could not hold on to its empire and voted against any appropriation that would pit the United States against independence fighters in Africa, regardless of their leftist political colorations.[20]

Studds took two subcommittee assignments: International Security and Scientific Affairs, which, before the creation of a separate Intelligence Committee, oversaw the CIA; and International Development, which monitored foreign aid and the Peace Corps. Studds was especially concerned with the imbalance between funding for military and humanitarian aid. In May 1977 he delivered to the president a letter calling for a redress of this imbalance in favor of economic aid. Studds noted in his newsletter that he agreed with the president's emphasis on human rights as a component of U.S. foreign policy, but added that administration spokesmen who appeared before the newly renamed International Relations Committee did not always share that perspective.[21]

A case in point was the Carter administration's support for right wing, pro-U.S. dictatorships that dominated Latin America from Guatemala to Argentina. Studds tried to amend the 1978 military aid bill on the House floor in May 1977, singling out Argentina, which faced a leftist insurgency, as "one of the most repressive regimes in Latin America," in which torture by the secret police was routine; the United States had trained the director. Studds proposed an amendment to eliminate military aid to Argentina, but it failed by thirteen votes. A month later he weakened the measure and it passed. Studds also told his constituents that he was "deeply disappointed" by the administration's support for military aid to the dictatorship of the Somoza family in Nicaragua, and he quoted President Carter's humanitarian rhetoric against him.[22]

Studds agreed with the president regarding his new treaty with Panama. Carter understood that it would be easier to maintain calm in the Canal Zone if Panamanians had greater authority over the canal and received more revenue from it. President Ford had supported the same policy. But in the 1976 Republican primary, Ronald Reagan attacked Ford for doing so, whipping up a patriotic fervor among conservatives that played into their fears about American decline after the communist victory in Vietnam. Studds reported on the debate and the canal's history in his newsletter. Among his constituents was the historian David McCullough, a resident of Martha's Vineyard, who came to Washington to visit senators and his own congressman; McCullough's recent book *The Path between the Seas: The Creation of the Panama Canal, 1870–1914*, would later win a Pulitzer Prize. McCullough told Studds that he had sent Carter a letter claiming that even the arch-imperialist Theodore Roosevelt knew that change was inevitable and would have approved the Panama treaty. The treaty barely passed in the Senate and became a major issue in the 1980 campaign.[23]

Over the next two years of the Carter administration, Studds agreed with the president on some matters and disagreed on others. He devoted increasing space in his newsletter to international relations, treating his constituents as intelligent people who could think for themselves about complex foreign policy matters. Studds expressed skepticism about Carter's support for the shah of Iran, and about the sale of arms to repressive regimes such as that of Saudi Arabia. When that kingdom's neighbors North and South Yemen went to war with each other, Studds presciently urged that "we should stay out of inter-Arab conflicts." He praised Carter for bringing Israel and Egypt together at Camp David, but pushed to reduce military aid to Israel by the amount that it spent policing the occupied West Bank.[24]

Studds's passion was most engaged by the emerging revolutions in Central America. He was among the few congressmen who understood that the United States had intervened repeatedly in the region to install brutal dictatorships that protected American economic interests, and that the poor of those countries often saw the United States as their enemy. During the 1920s and 1930s, the United States had helped impose the regime of Anastasio Somoza García in Nicaragua. By the 1970s, a broad-based movement, divided between leftists and liberals, was on the brink of overthrowing Somoza's son, Anastasio Somoza Debayle. The dictator had a bloc of anti-communist Democratic allies in the U.S. Congress, and Carter hesitated before cutting off aid to the Somoza regime in February 1979. Studds hailed this as a "courageous decision . . . to defend the principles in which the United States believes." When the leftist Sandinista movement triumphed in July, Studds opposed a move in the House to cut off economic aid to them. "I can think of no quicker way," he wrote, "to drive these people into the arms of the Soviet Union and Cuba than to refuse them assistance during a period of grave economic crisis." He deplored military aid to the equally repressive governments of Guatemala and El Salvador, which were to erupt in revolution as well. This debate among Democrats foreshadowed the splintering of their party over the next decade, with Central America policy the most divisive of issues, and Gerry Studds one of Congress's most penetrating minds and outspoken defenders of human rights.[25]

9

Knocks on the Closet Door

THE GAY RIGHTS MOVEMENT took some noticeable steps forward during the Jimmy Carter administration. In the 1976 primaries, candidates Morris Udall, Birch Bayh, and Carter all declared that they opposed discrimination against gays. Bayh even attended a gay rights fund-raiser, a historic first. Activists fought openly, if unsuccessfully, for a gay rights plank at the 1976 Democratic convention. Carter's aide Midge Costanza arranged meetings for some gay leaders at the White House. These developments represented the possibility that gays and lesbians might yet be included in the body politic.[1]

The most dramatic events transpired in California. By the late 1970s, San Francisco's gay and lesbian population had grown to about a quarter of the city's total. Gay Democrats organized their own club, which worked with liberals to promote their inclusion into municipal departments. These liberal activists, who in any other city would have been seen as extremists, soon faced a challenge from radicals led by Harvey Milk, who argued that gay people had to win elections themselves. Milk was seven years older than Studds and in many ways his opposite. Milk had never doubted his homosexuality or dated women to protect his identity. He was out, proud, and militant; stylistically Milk was as emotional, Jewish, and New York as Studds was cerebral, WASPy, and New England. Milk led chants at demonstrations urging gay people to "come out." He ran in and lost three elections for the San Francisco Board of Supervisors before finally winning in 1977.[2]

By that year, forty municipalities had passed gay rights protection ordinances. Among them was Dade County, Florida. Actress Anita Bryant championed a referendum campaign for repeal, and it passed by a vote of

202,319 to 89,562; soon after that, St. Paul, Minnesota, voted to repeal its gay rights ordinance. Gays lost these first important fights but noted that merely being on the agenda represented progress. Republicans, on the ropes since Watergate, now had a winning issue. They could count on a powerful new ally, the religious right. Newly prominent preachers like Pat Robertson and Jerry Falwell backed Republican politicians. They hastened the departure of white southerners out of the Democratic Party by espousing traditional "family values." The gay rights issue drove a wedge into the Democratic Party. Would its candidates risk losing election by supporting this unpopular cause?

Smelling blood, California Republican state senator John Briggs led a campaign to bar gays from teaching. Oklahoma had already passed such a measure. The literature promoting the new law argued that gay teachers would molest their students. The proposed law was so overtly discriminatory that former president Ford, President Carter, and former California governor Ronald Reagan all opposed it. The Briggs Amendment lost by a big margin. A few weeks later, erstwhile San Francisco supervisor Dan White shot and killed Harvey Milk and Mayor George Moscone in their City Hall offices. The gay movement had its first martyr. The following year, when White was convicted only of manslaughter after pleading that his junk food diet had caused him to lose control, gay people rioted at City Hall. This horrific chain of events raised the national consciousness about gay rights and infused the movement's activists with new determination.[3]

They expressed this militancy at the first national gay and lesbian civil rights march in Washington, D.C., on Sunday, October 14, 1979. For many gay people, this mass action provided a thrilling, transformative experience. Participation in the march communicated to them that they were not alone, should take courage, could come out if they were hiding, and should know that they were on the right side of history. Speakers included fringe figures from the arts, such as beatnik poet Allen Ginsberg, as well as political leaders Ellie Smeal of the National Organization for Women and New York congressman Ted Weiss. There had been only one prominent gay figure in American life, and it took his murder to bring the marchers together.[4]

Gerry Studds had been to demonstrations before, but he could not bring himself to attend this one, and it did not persuade him to "come out." Instead, he modified his jogging route to bring him to the demonstration, so that he could observe it while claiming not to be a participant.

During the weekend of the march, Studds's friend Bill Damon invited him to dinner with gay activist Brian McNaught. "Is he gay?" McNaught asked. "No one asks him that," Damon replied. But McNaught did ask, and Studds told. Studds became friendly with McNaught and his companion and attended their Christmas party that year.[5]

Studds also met Lewis Gannett, a Cambridge writer who had grown up in Washington. He came to the demonstration with friends, one of whom, Larry McCreedy, a therapist, knew Studds from Provincetown. They went over to Studds's office to say hello. Gannett had never heard of Studds and was astonished to find that a congressman from a neighboring district was gay. Gannett noticed, too, that Studds was reading *The Homosexual Matrix* by C. A. Tripp, the first major book to reject Freudian conceptions that homosexual behavior was aberrant, an illness to be treated, and to argue that homosexuality was normal. "Studds invited me out to dinner right away," Gannett remembered. "I could see that he was torn between being a public figure and being gay. It was killing him." The National March on Washington was unleashing bottled-up energy in thousands of people. Studds later hired Gannett as his driver in the district.[6]

Yet the problem of being a gay public figure in a conservative district seemed insurmountable to Studds. In late 1977, Studds's staffer Chris Sands received a letter warning that Studds was about to be "outed." A former page named Steven Richards Valentine was "preparing a gossipy tell-all about slightly disguised gay congressmen," and was threatening to give it to the *Washington Post*. The informant, now Valentine's boss, fired him because he was writing it during work time on the company's typewriter, and he was giving Studds, through his aide, a warning. "I saved Gerry's ass on this once, in the original situation. . . . I stopped some trouble," the informant told Sands.[7] This was a clear reference to Studds's visit to Portugal with a congressional page. Studds had a secret, and he knew that he had better watch out.

Cautiously, when Studds returned to the district on alternate weekends, after his meetings he sometimes went with Gannett to stay at his Cambridge apartment on Saturday nights. They were friends, not lovers; Gannett was seeing someone else. Gannett introduced him to the gay world that Studds had been missing out on during the 1970s. He had never been among openly gay people before, not even in Provincetown. They went to Buddy's in Boston, a disco joint, and Studds just watched, completely agog. Hardly anyone recognized him, and the few who did were also in the closet; everybody's secret was safe here. One night Gannett threw a party for gay friends, another first for Studds. His world was expanding.[8]

Studds began to take a few more risks in his personal life. Sometime after the gay rights march, in late 1979 or early 1980, he went to a Dupont Circle gay bar, the Frat House, which had a western theme and was decorated with a somewhat incongruous moose head. There, through a mutual friend, he met a tall, handsome young man who was looking for a job on Capitol Hill. Dean Hara, a recent college graduate from Minnesota, was then working at the Pan American Development Foundation, which did private sector development work in Latin America. Studds agreed to help Hara, and the two met a week later at a French bistro on Wisconsin Avenue in Georgetown to discuss Hara's job prospects.[9]

Hara didn't have a car, so Studds picked him up in his loud orange Saab. Hara only knew that Studds worked on Capitol Hill. Since Hara was the job hunter, Studds asked most of the questions.

After a while, Hara asked Studds a few questions of his own and learned that he had gone to Groton and Yale, and had run for Congress in 1970.

"What happened?" Hara asked.

"I lost," Studds said.

"Then what happened?"

"I ran again."

"And?"

"That time I won."

Hara realized that the circumspect gentleman sitting across the table was gay and a congressman. Studds had trusted Hara with a secret. He didn't have to say, "Don't tell anyone." That was understood.

The two began seeing each other, discreetly, dining at Gerry's Watergate apartment about once a month, a casual relationship in which, perhaps because of their twenty-year age difference and Gerry's impossible schedule, neither expected to blossom into a full-fledged romance. The two drifted apart, and by 1981 Hara was dating a man his own age.

Back in his district in the early 1980s, Studds started entertaining guests at his Provincetown condo. Lewis Gannett and his lover or Larry McCreedy and other friends would come over, and they would all take the *Bacalhau* out on the bay. In a photo taken by Gannett, Studds looks relaxed, happy, even youthfully goofy, leaning back bare-chested in the wind and sun. "He was the funniest guy I ever knew," Gannett remembered. "Years later he told me that his mother told him that I was his only driver who wasn't gay. We both got a good laugh out of that."[10]

Meanwhile, the election of 1980 was about to change Washington's political complexion in a manner that would limit job possibilities for young Democrats like Hara for the next twelve years. On November 7, 1979, Ted Kennedy announced at Faneuil Hall in Boston that he was running for president. Kennedy believed that Carter's refusal to fight for a national health care plan, when he had Democratic majorities in both houses, represented a failure of leadership. Also, Carter had needlessly antagonized Speaker Tip O'Neill, who might have mobilized the House to achieve this significant change in American life, but it hadn't happened. Events off-stage, however, doomed Kennedy's campaign. Three days earlier, radical Iranian students had seized American hostages in Tehran, and the country rallied around its president. Then Kennedy's early television interviews revealed a surprisingly inarticulate man who could not explain his program. The shadow of Chappaquiddick reappeared because of his failing marriage, an open secret. The antagonism between Carter and Kennedy infected the mood in Congress and at the State House as well.[11]

Studds wholeheartedly backed Kennedy. He shared Kennedy's enthusiasm for a single-payer health care system. Both men were sailors, both Ivy Leaguers. Studds was Kennedy's congressman. During the Massachusetts primary, a race that Kennedy had to win big to stay credible, the state's politicians were divided. The congressional delegation backed Kennedy (O'Neill, as speaker, had to remain neutral), but Governor Ed King and a few score of state representatives backed Carter.

As primary day neared, Kennedy scheduled a big event at a Hyannis hotel but uncharacteristically developed laryngitis. He could only croak in a hoarse voice, so he called Studds in Washington, requesting that he speak for him. Gannett picked Studds up at the airport and at his boss's instruction raced toward Hyannis.

"What if we get stopped for speeding?" Gannett worried.

"We're going to an event for Ted Kennedy in Massachusetts," Studds reassured him. "They'll give us a fucking escort if they have to."[12]

Studds and Gannett arrived on time and were hustled up to the hotel ballroom through a freight elevator by Secret Service agents toting big guns. Kennedy boiled over with energy in the enclosed space, frustrated by the temporary loss of his voice. Studds stayed cool as a cucumber and delivered an eloquent address. Kennedy won the primary.

Observing this election so closely inspired Studds to file four bills affecting the political process. They had no chance of passing, but he hoped that they might stimulate debate. First, he proposed a constitutional amendment that would limit presidents to one six-year term, an idea that had been considered during the original Constitutional Convention. The purpose was to reduce the executive's personal ambition. Next he proposed to eliminate the Electoral College. This anachronistic institution, developed in an eighteenth-century nation with impassable roads and only local news-papers, made some sense in 1789, but two hundred years later only inertia kept it alive. His third measure would soon be seized upon by conservative populists—term limits for congressmen, which Studds set at twelve to eigh-teen years. Finally, he suggested that presidential primaries be conducted by region, four of them in rotating sequence so that the political process would not be subject to the arbitrary schedule that privileged New Hampshire.[13] His proposed reforms were similar to Progressive Era measures to curtail the power of ethnic-based, boss-run political machines. In the midst of a presi-dential campaign and the Iran hostage crisis, no one noticed these ideas.

In May, Kennedy initiated the first campaign fund-raiser for a presiden-tial race in the gay community. He sent his operatives to other gay events and promised to end antigay discrimination in the federal government. For gay activists, Kennedy's move marked one small step into the mainstream of American politics. At the Democratic convention in Madison Square Gar-den, Kennedy gave his dramatic "The dream shall never die" speech. On the platform, Kennedy shook the victorious Carter's hand but never raised his arm, "a tableau of Democratic division," Kennedy's biographer concluded.[14]

Studds met Gannett's friend Sean Strub during the convention. Strub took them out to some nightspots, including the city's well-known Anvil bar. Later, in Washington, Strub asked Studds if he'd thought about coming out. "I've thought about it a lot," Studds said.[15]

When he was in Washington, Studds would on occasion visit gay bars in Baltimore, where he figured he would not be recognized. "He would drive there in his orange Saab," staffer Jeff Pike remembered. "We told him he might try going there in something less noticeable."[16]

Studds still had his reasons for staying in the closet. He did not believe that an openly gay man could be elected to Congress, and he did not think that his sexual orientation bore any relation to his job performance. The taboos against homosexuality seemed so overwhelming, and his closeted behavior was so well established, that he could not conceive of himself publicly declaring that he was gay. Harvey Milk, and the San Francisco gay community that produced him, were a unique case. His own circumstances were entirely different. He represented a socially conservative district. His signature political appearance was at a Catholic religious procession, the Portuguese *festa* in New Bedford, not at a Gay Pride parade.

Studds was in an election campaign, too, and nervous about the outcome. This time the challenger was a Republican who echoed the conservative themes of his party's presidential nominee, former California governor and movie star Ronald Reagan. Paul V. Doane, a Cape Cod investment broker, was calling for increased defense spending, few restrictions on offshore oil drilling, and bringing online a second nuclear plant at the Pilgrim site in Plymouth. He backed the MX missile, opposed abortion and the Equal Rights Amendment, and supported the "supply side" tax cuts that Reagan's running mate, George H. W. Bush, had once dismissed as "voodoo" economics. Doane's program held scant appeal for Massachusetts voters, and he stagnated in the polls. Doane went negative, running a radio advertisement that highlighted his life as a family man. Studds could simply have ignored the radio clip. Instead, at a debate in Hingham, Studds, according to the *Boston Globe,* "lashed out at his opponent, chastised him, lectured him, and all of it with an anger that would seem to indicate the contest is a close one."[17] Clearly, Doane had struck a nerve.

The election wasn't close. Studds won by a landslide, 195,791 to 71,620. The one change in the delegation was that Barney Frank, an acid-tongued liberal, replaced Father Robert Drinan, who had been ordered by the Catholic Church to give up his position in Congress as incompatible with membership in the priesthood. The Massachusetts congressional delegation of 1981 would have a more socially liberal and anti–Cold War complexion than that of 1971. Joe Moakley, Gerry Studds, Ed Markey, and Barney Frank typified this transformation from the likes of Louise Day Hicks, Hastings Keith, and Phil Philbin. In the Senate, Democrat Paul Tsongas had in 1976 replaced liberal Republican Edward Brooke, the first African American elected to the Senate since Reconstruction.

Ronald Reagan defeated the sitting president, Jimmy Carter, barely carrying liberal Massachusetts with 41.9 percent of the vote to Carter's 41.7 percent. Third party candidate John Anderson, a liberal Republican senator from Illinois, won 15.2 percent. Reagan did very well in the Twelfth District, winning two to one in Barnstable County on Cape Cod, earning a majority in the South Shore's Plymouth County, and coming close even in Democratic Bristol County (New Bedford).[18] Many Studds voters had also voted for Reagan, who promised to rebuild the military, solve the energy crisis, spark the stagnant economy, and punish Iran. These same voters knew and trusted Studds. They voted both for the president who would make war in Central America and ignore the AIDS epidemic, and the man who would be among the new president's fiercest critics on both issues.

10

"The President Has Certified That . . . Black Is White"

ON THE MORNING of January 4, 1981, John McAward, the national director of the Unitarian Universalist Service Association in Boston, was packing for a trip to Central America when his phone rang. A friend in El Salvador told him that two American land reform advisers and their Salvadoran colleague had been murdered the night before at a hotel restaurant. The gunmen had walked into the restaurant, coolly opened fire, and departed like assassins with nothing to fear. A few days later, McAward led a congressional delegation to the region that included Bob Edgar of Pennsylvania, Barbara Mikulski of Maryland, and Gerry Studds.[1]

Studds was accompanied on this trip by staffer Bill Woodward, his former student. Woodward, a Goldwater Republican when he started school, became radicalized during the 1960s. In college at Columbia, Woodward opposed the war in Vietnam and grew his hair so long that it flowed beneath his shoulders. He graduated just after Studds was elected, and Studds hired him on the condition that he cut his hair.

For ten days the representatives toured Honduras, Costa Rica, and Nicaragua, avoiding El Salvador as too dangerous, but they met with Salvadorans while in Nicaragua. Studds was the only member of the Foreign Affairs Committee to make the trip, so it was Woodward who drafted the delegation's report. His nuanced analysis would serve as a template for the left-liberal critique of the Reagan administration's Central American war policy. Neither Studds nor Woodward had ever been to Latin America

before. "That trip hooked him," Woodward remembered.[2] The report raised
Studds's profile in the American peace activist community.

The account, "Central America, 1981: Report to the Committee on
Foreign Affairs, U.S. House of Representatives," began with Nicaragua,
whose Sandinista revolution had set off shock waves throughout the isth-
mus.[3] In July 1979, the Sandinista National Liberation Front overthrew the
brutal dictatorship of Anastasio Somoza Debayle. President Jimmy Carter
had turned against Somoza, especially after one of the dictator's national
guardsmen murdered an American television reporter as his cameraman
filmed the event. Studds and his colleagues met with almost every important
government, business, media, and religious leader and members of the U.S.
embassy staff. They toured a poor barrio and saw that Nicaragua remained
devastated by a 1977 earthquake and the effects of its civil war; near the capital, Managua's, lakefront, destitute people still inhabited the ruined remains
of a former office tower. The Somoza family and its clique had looted the
treasury for years and absconded with foreign aid money. Woodward's report
praised the restoration of peace in the country, the government's commitment to establishing a mixed economy, and its efforts at social reform on
behalf of the poor. Yet it also noted the country's military buildup and the
Sandinista party's conflation of its own role as a political movement with
the government itself. Studds visited a prison and observed the terrible conditions there. He called attention to limitations on freedom of the press—
worrisome, but so far tolerable. He noted that Nicaragua sought positive
relations with the United States and did not want to replicate Cuban-style
communism and dependence on the Soviet Union. Studds advised that the
United States offer economic aid with no strings attached, and maintain
an attitude of patiently encouraging political pluralism. Nicaragua had "no
single charismatic leader," like Cuba, and it would be a mistake to provoke
authoritarian tendencies there by pursuing a hostile course toward its leftist
but noncommunist revolution.

Of all the countries of Central America, Guatemala endured the worst
suffering in the 1980s. The inaccessibility of its mountainous regions, and
the cultural remoteness of its Mayan population, made it difficult for reporters to cover the story of its 200,000 casualties during the civil war that lasted
from 1966 to 1996. Studds met with four refugee Guatemalan labor leaders
in Costa Rica, who told him that two hundred of their key activists had
been killed. Studds concluded that "the United States should not renew any
form of military sales or assistance to Guatemala," and urged that it expose
the human rights violations committed by the country's American-trained

military. The report also discussed conditions in Costa Rica, the lone democracy in Central America, and Honduras, a poverty-stricken banana republic bordering Nicaragua, Guatemala, and El Salvador.

The most pressing emergency in the region was occurring in El Salvador—the one Central American nation without a Caribbean coast, a coffee rather than banana exporter, and the country with the most autonomous and ruthless oligarchy. El Salvador is roughly the same shape and size as Massachusetts. In January 1980, rightist military officers staged a coup. Confronted by popular organizations and much of the Catholic Church, the military killed priests whom they denounced as communists. In March a death squad murdered Archbishop Óscar Romero as he celebrated mass. Soldiers fired on his funeral procession, killing and wounding scores of mourners. Moderate dissidents fled the country or joined one of the guerrilla groups that united to form a five-member front known by its Spanish acronym, FMLN. The man behind Archbishop Romero's execution, the former army major Roberto D'Aubuisson, gave impassioned television speeches denouncing union leaders, priests, and politicians, whose mutilated corpses would be found the next day on the streets. When Ronald Reagan was elected president, elite Salvadorans, whose "fourteen families" owned virtually everything in the country, were delighted. Soon afterward, the military killed five top opposition politicians. In December, four American churchwomen disappeared near the airport, and their violated corpses were later found in a shallow grave. By January 1981, when the American labor advisers were murdered and Studds arrived in Central America, nine thousand Salvadorans had been killed, almost all by right-wing death squads. The leftists had established their own territory in the northern mountains.[4]

In Costa Rica, Studds met with exiled Salvadoran Christian Democratic and leftist political leaders. In Honduras, Mikulski and Edgar traveled to a refugee camp on the Salvadoran border. There, witnesses related graphic details of barbaric atrocities committed by the army. Studds's report recommended a cutoff of military aid, a suspension of the land reform program because it was being used for the opposite of the purpose for which it was intended, and an inquiry into the killing of the Americans. It further urged the United States to cooperate with international organizations and the region's neighbors to encourage a peace process. In an insightful conclusion, Studds pointed out: "If there is any lesson to be learned from Vietnam . . . it is that good intentions are not sufficient to make good policy. . . . Outside agitation there may be, but the causes of violence remain uniquely Salvadoran in origin." He refused to interpret the situation through a Cold War prism in which Soviets and Cubans fostered world revolution, but rather saw it as a struggle against local oligarchies which had begun long before 1917 or 1959.

The Hard-Liner in the House

President Reagan had a Republican majority in the Senate. Hard-liner Jesse Helms now chaired the Foreign Relations Committee. Chris Dodd, a freshman from Connecticut and a former Peace Corps volunteer, led the opposition in the upper chamber and was often joined by Massachusetts senator Paul Tsongas. In the House of Representatives, many, including Majority Leader Jim Wright of Texas, agreed with the president on Central America. House liberals sensed that Reagan intended to start a war, but Tip O'Neill, with a diminished majority, was reluctant to split his already divided party over foreign policy. The Democrats picked a new subcommittee chair for Inter-American Affairs, Michael Barnes of Maryland, who was then starting only his second term. "Tom Downey and Toby Moffett asked me to do it," Barnes recalled, naming two of his young liberal Democratic colleagues. "We've got the votes, you're in," they reassured Barnes. He and Studds took their assignment seriously and liked each other from the start. Committee members Stephen Solarz and Jonathan Bingham of New York, George Miller of California, and David Bonior and George Crockett of Michigan saw things much as Studds did. Studds became the strongest voice on his committee for a "no support" policy toward El Salvador's military. Barnes, like most Democrats, was persuaded by Salvadoran president José Napoleón Duarte that his nation should get some support, albeit conditional, from the United States.[5]

Studds, Mikulski, and Edgar sent a "Dear Colleague" letter on January 27 seeking "Legislation to Terminate Military Aid to El Salvador" (H.R. 1509). Reprising the salient observations from their trip, they stressed the evidence of atrocities committed by the regime and the fact that moderates were abandoning Duarte and no effort was being made to find the killers of the four churchwomen. They warned that giving guns to El Salvador's military could lead to another Vietnam.[6]

The oppositionists, however, could muster only about fifty votes for a cutoff of aid to El Salvador. Most Democrats worried that if aid was terminated, and the military was overthrown by "communist" rebels, they would be blamed for "losing" El Salvador. Reagan's simplistic worldview, willfully indifferent to countervailing evidence, presented the events in Central

America through a Cold War, evil-Soviets-versus-good-Americans prism.[7] In addition, Reagan was determined to reverse the "Vietnam syndrome," which supposedly caused most Americans to oppose foreign wars. Finally, the Mariel boat lift from Cuba in 1980, during which tens of thousands of Cubans fled the island, caused some congressmen to fear that Salvadorans might run to the United States if the FMLN won. In fact, over a million would do exactly that as a result of Reagan's policy.[8]

At the end of February, Studds, Mikulski, and Edgar took their case before the Foreign Operations Subcommittee of the Appropriations Committee. They quoted a military commander who had told them, "What we have done in the north [the mountainous region where the war was being conducted] is to dry up the ocean so we can catch the fish easily." This murderous policy had already created 200,000 refugees. Studds insisted, "There is absolutely no reason to believe that supplying these forces with more weapons will lead to anything other than an escalation of the violence." Most Democrats agreed that President Duarte represented a moderate center, but Studds reminded them that Duarte's Christian Democratic Party had crumbled, and that "important decisions are determined by the military and the military alone." Studds and his colleagues offered seven policy recommendations: the junta should negotiate with the rebels; and the United States should stop military aid, demand that the junta stop throwing peasants off their land, inquire separately into the killing of American citizens, back the UN refugee aid program, stop the deportation of Salvadorans in the United States by granting "Extended Voluntary Departure" status to them, and work with Mexico to develop a joint policy.[9]

By March, Studds had secured only seventy-one co-signers for H.R. 1509. In a subsequent letter, Studds argued that Reagan's policy echoed Soviet behavior toward Poland, where the independent labor movement was challenging the communist dictatorship; both were cases of Great Powers ruling weaker neighbors through puppet governments. A false analogy, scoffed Edward J. Derwinski, Studds's Republican colleague on Foreign Relations, who cited the Catholic Church's support for Duarte as evidence of his centrism. Studds, Derwinski postulated, was suffering from "an aberrational stream of thought brought on by an overdose of the Bay State's cranberry juice. In view of his deserved reputation as one of Congress' most scholarly members, no other explanation makes sense." In fact, the Salvadoran church was strongly critical of the government that had murdered its archbishop.[10]

Anti-interventionists crafted the best compromise they could get. They responded to Reagan's request for $107 million in military and economic aid to El Salvador by insisting that the president biannually "certify" that progress was being made in five specific human rights and political areas; in effect, it attached strings to the aid to El Salvador. Bill Woodward recalled that he and one of Barnes's staffers worked out stronger language which was adopted by the House Foreign Affairs Committee in a 26–7 vote at the end of April. The wording insisted that in exchange for the aid, the Salvadoran government had to put an end to human rights violations, show that it had "substantial" control over the military, make progress on land reform, schedule genuinely free elections, and negotiate with the rebels. "I moved to end military aid for 1982," Studds declared in his newsletter. "The time has come in El Salvador to stop the killing and start the talking." But because Republicans held a majority in the Senate, the final language stated only that the administration had to show "progress," not identifiable changes in policy or targeted achievements. The Reagan administration could easily live with the Senate language, which was later passed.[11]

In his weekly "Report to the People" Studds attacked a State Department "white paper" called *Communist Interference in El Salvador.* Based on captured guerrilla documents, it had garnered a great deal of media coverage. The paper argued that Moscow was sending hundreds of tons of arms to the El Salvador guerrillas through Cuba. The media paid very little attention in June, however, when a diligent reporter fact-checked the white paper against the captured documents and found that none of it was true.[12]

Studds and Woodward worked with a Salvadoran exile named Leonel Gomez to expose the death squad operations. Gomez, a land reform activist, had luckily arrived late to the meeting at which his boss and the two American labor advisers had been killed. Gomez won political asylum in the United States and became a key source of information about El Salvador; he had contacts among a wide variety of people. Gomez encouraged the disillusioned Roberto Santivañez, who had been D'Aubuisson's superior in military intelligence, to tell what he knew. CBS News's Walter Cronkite interviewed him. In shadow and with his voice disguised, Santivañez exposed the ties between the death squads and the regime, and then told the same story to the House and Senate intelligence committees.[13] Woodward worked in concert with human rights activists to illuminate what the Reagan administration was deliberately obscuring.

Studds did the same with regard to Guatemala, where the situation was even worse. Guatemala had the biggest population in the region and historic links to the United States through the operations of the United Fruit Company. The corporation had engineered the overthrow of Guatemala's democratically elected government in 1954 when it embarked on a course of land reform. The Carter administration had cut off military aid to Guatemala, but Reagan proposed to deliver "nonlethal" aid such as trucks and jeeps. Studds would not allow this camel's nose under the tent. "Nearly every local or national leader of any opposition group of any size has been murdered," he pointed out. He recruited roughly the same fifty liberal congressmen in a protest letter to Secretary of State Alexander Haig, insisting that the vehicle delivery constituted a "clear violation of congressional intent to ban the shipment of U.S.-made weapons or defense-related supplies." In July 1981, Stanley Rother, a courageous American priest working in Guatemala, was murdered after receiving death threats from the military. A State Department official testified before Inter-American Affairs shortly after this and defended the vehicle sale. "I believe it's illegal," Studds insisted.[14]

Late in September, Salvadoran president Duarte came up to Capitol Hill. Duarte offered mixed messages regarding certification of his country's compliance with the conditions of the aid agreement. Studds called attention to the twenty thousand Salvadorans who had been killed in this one-sided bloodbath. Duarte was "devoted to democratic principles," Studds acknowledged, but was "operating at present more on simple hope."[15]

Thomas O. Enders, the new assistant secretary of state for Western Hemisphere Affairs, arrived next. The six-foot-eight Enders, scion of a wealthy Connecticut banking family, and a Yale graduate like Studds, wanted the Salvadoran military to clean up its act. Reagan's hard-liners—Secretary of State Haig, CIA director William Casey, and U.N. ambassador Jeane Kirkpatrick—simply wanted to wipe out the leftists militarily. They opposed negotiations with people they perceived as communist enemies, and did not encourage land reform or the human rights blather that they associated with Jimmy Carter. Several key Reagan advisers, including James Baker, Ed Meese, and Michael Deaver, shared Enders's "moderate" perspective. Enders communicated his views to Studds's subcommittee in conciliatory language in September. Studds grilled Enders carefully. He pressed him on whether or not the administration backed negotiations, and Enders evaded the question, wrongly asserting that the rebels were refusing to negotiate. When Studds asked if Enders would condemn a rumored military coup in Honduras, he declined to do so.[16]

In November, El Salvador's defense minister José Guillermo García appeared before the House Foreign Affairs Committee. "There is not much point in being gentle with García," a Studds staffer recommended before the hearings. "He is a killer." García did not disappoint, insisting that his government was winning the war. Next came Secretary of State Haig. Studds asked him the same questions he had asked Enders. No, Haig said, we don't want negotiations with the rebels, and we don't care if there is a military coup in Honduras.[17]

Studds deployed the understated wit that was becoming his trademark. "Mr. Secretary," he told Haig, "as you know, we don't often agree, but I want you to know that I defended you the other day. Col. García . . . , when he suggested that those who would use the term 'stalemate' with reference to the situation in El Salvador were subversives, I said that was an unfair characterization of my Secretary of State and that I would not tolerate that."

"Colonel García and I couldn't have agreed more on every area we touched on," said Haig.

"I am sorry to hear that," Studds replied. "I knew the agreement wouldn't last long."

The substantive climax of this confrontation occurred when Studds pressed for an unequivocal declaration that the administration was not trying to overthrow the Nicaraguan government and would not do so.

"No, I would not give you that assurance," Haig said. "It seems to me, Mr. Studds, that you should be concerned about the mounting evidence in Nicaragua of the totalitarian character of the Sandinista regime."

"In my judgment, if it is material, many of the actions of the current government of Nicaragua are indefensible," Studds allowed. But he did not see that as a reason to overthrow the government. Reporting on this exchange to his constituents, Studds concluded, "Every time I hear Alexander Haig speak, my unease grows."

This testimony complete, the House voted in early December to approve a foreign aid bill that included the certification protocol for military aid to El Salvador. "I voted for the foreign aid authorization bill primarily because it will for the first time place conditions on US aid to El Salvador," Studds told his constituents. Yet he worried that the president would not act in good faith in making his reports. President Reagan signed the bill into law, knowing that he only had to certify that "progress" was being made—an easy bar to hurdle by pointing to words rather than deeds. Over the course of Reagan's term, he would do exactly that.[18]

The Massacre at El Mozote

Just as Reagan was signing the foreign aid bill into law, on December 11, 1981, soldiers of El Salvador's elite U.S.-trained Atlacatl Battalion committed one of the worst massacres of unarmed civilians in the modern history of the Americas. As the army swept through the guerrilla-held northern mountain town of El Mozote in Morazan Province, the guerrillas slipped away. The Atlacatl Battalion assembled the terrified men, women, and children of the village and killed 767 of them. The military intended that there were to be no survivors. One woman, Rufina Amaya, did escape and crawled away in the night, listening to the screams as her family was massacred. Later the guerrillas contacted human rights organizations in San Salvador, which alerted courageous American reporters. Ray Bonner and photographer Susan Meiselas of the *New York Times,* and, separately, Alma Guillermoprieto of the *Washington Post,* trekked into the village and surveyed the still unburied corpses a month later. Their shocking eyewitness accounts appeared on January 27, 1982.

The next day, President Reagan certified that El Salvador was making progress in all the areas specified by the foreign aid bill restrictions. Three days later, the army committed another massacre in San Salvador, killing twenty-seven civilians, whose bodies were discovered with their hands bound. The women among them had been raped. The military claimed victory in a battle with the guerrillas.

Shortly afterward, Assistant Secretary Enders appeared before the Western Hemisphere Subcommittee. He strongly defended the Salvadoran military and what he described as a bipartisan foreign policy. Enders showed that the body count from 1981 had gone down from 1980, a clear sign of progress. As for the "alleged massacre" at El Mozote, Enders asserted that that there had been a battle, not a massacre, and that the newspaper accounts could not be believed because the reporters had been escorted to the scene by guerrillas and therefore were biased. The State Department could not verify them.

Then chairman Mike Barnes turned the microphone over to Studds, who dismantled Enders's obfuscation of the plain facts. "If there is anything left of the English language in this city after your long assault by your immediate superior, it is gone now because the president has certified that up is down and in is out and black is white. I anticipate his telling us that war is peace." He didn't ask any questions as he struggled to control his fury. The State Department's statistics, Studds told Enders, who was already aware of it, had been culled from El Salvador's controlled press, which did not investigate atrocities committed outside the capital. "Bodies have turned up every single day of the year, as you know, in El Salvador," Studds lectured Enders. "What I would like to know is . . . how long you can downplay, as you did in your earlier remarks, killings such as those which occurred at El Mozote and the Rio Lempa before that, the murders of the churchwomen, the killing of the Archbishop, and an assassination in cold blood in November 1980 of the entire leadership of the opposition." Studds demanded to know if Enders was satisfied, to which he replied, "No, sir."[19]

"You take empty rhetoric and call it reform. . . . You look at a fourteen-month gap between a murder and the application of a lie detector test and call it an investigation," Studds lectured. Everything that had been building up inside him since his trip to Central America came bursting through in controlled rage: "You . . . have resurrected the State Department approach to Vietnam: if it doesn't work, do more of it." By certifying "progress," in El Salvador, Studds insisted, the administration had sent a clear message to the El Salvador military that "they can do virtually anything they choose to do and the United States will continue to support them." When Studds concluded his speech, a round of applause erupted from the gallery, and Barnes had to pound his gavel to restore order.

Studds did not focus on El Mozote. The story seemed too unbelievable. The *Times* later fired Bonner for unbalanced reporting. But after the war ended in 1992, an Argentine forensics team unearthed all the bodies. The story was recounted in a stunning book by Mark Danner, *The Massacre at El Mozote,* which laid bare the full horror of the event and the cold-blooded fashion in which Haig and Enders covered up the crime.

That same day Studds introduced a new, clearly doomed resolution to declare Reagan's certification "null and void." It suspended aid to El Salvador until the House and Senate agreed that the conditions of the law had been fulfilled. Studds declared that none of the five conditions had been met, and that according to the Catholic Church's El Salvador office, 11,723 people had been murdered in 1981, not the low figure the administration claimed. He cited an angry letter to President Reagan from William Ford, brother of one of the slain churchwomen, asserting that right after the murders, the investigating office in El Salvador took a two-week vacation. The land reform program had distributed no land. No steps toward negotiating with the rebels had been made, but the Salvadoran army had just published a list of 138 "traitors" whom they vowed to "relentlessly pursue." Ambassador Deane Hinton's claim that the U.S. embassy could not confirm that a massacre had occurred at El Mozote showed only that the embassy didn't want to know what happened.[20]

Studds's cross-examination of Enders earned him a spot that evening on the Public Broadcasting System's *MacNeill/Lehrer Report,* one of television's most respected news shows. Host Jim Lehrer introduced Studds by noting recent gains by the rebels in Usulután Province, where they had regrouped when the army devastated nearby Morazan. "Why shouldn't Reagan have certified human rights progress?" Lehrer asked.[21]

"Well, for the very simple reason that it's not true," Studds said, and described the discrepancies between the reports of the human rights groups and the administration's claims. "I think that 1984 arrived two years early." He argued that Haig and Enders saw the whole situation as part of a "Cold War chess game. It's not." Studds saw "a revolution within an individual country" and reminded the audience of the Vietnam precedent. "We are getting deeper and deeper into a quagmire," he warned.

Given the bleak human rights climate, Studds felt skeptical about what might happen in the elections scheduled in El Salvador for March 28. They "will reveal very little about the true political views of the Salvadoran people," he told his constituents. Studds sent them a questionnaire. Nine thousand people returned them, showing 78 percent opposed to military aid to El Salvador. El Salvador generated more mail from his district than any other issue, and it was running twenty to one against sending military aid. Studds tried to move his "null and void" resolution out of his own subcommittee, which decided to wait until after the El Salvador elections.[22]

Six weeks before the election, the Salvadoran hard-liners formed a new political party, known by its Spanish acronym as ARENA. Its main candidate, death squad leader Roberto D'Aubuisson, denounced Duarte as a communist. Leftist leaders feared for their lives and would not return from exile, and even Ambassador Hinton suggested that they should campaign only by videotape. The guerrillas in the FMLN therefore vowed to disrupt the elections, a counterproductive policy. Hoping to achieve peace, and with only two major candidates, the people turned out in larger numbers than expected and gave Duarte a plurality of 40 percent. Five rightist parties split the other 60 percent and were about to make D'Aubuisson the president when a high-level congressional delegation, led by Majority Leader Jim Wright, warned the rightists that if D'Aubuisson were chosen, military aid might stop. A colorless alternate candidate became president, while D'Aubuisson became head of the Constituent Assembly.[23]

Studds viewed the results with clear eyes. He was not a friend of the guerrillas. He saw, correctly, that the large turnout showed a widespread desire for democracy among the populace, and that the guerrillas had been rebuked. Duarte's Christian Democrats had been weakened and the far right strengthened. This new situation, he reported to his constituents, was even more unpalatable than what had preceded it.[24]

The Empire Strikes Back

Before the Salvadoran elections, Studds and chairman Barnes co-sponsored a resolution to bar covert operations against Nicaragua. They knew that the CIA was organizing five hundred paramilitary counterrevolutionaries—"contras"—at a base camp in Honduras to invade Nicaragua. Studds was no more enamored of the Sandinistas than he was of the FMLN, but he understood that American military threats would only encourage authoritarian tendencies among them. "How can we threaten to invade them and then criticize them for their military build-up?" Studds implored in his newsletter. He pointed out that the Sandinistas would see American intentions through the prism of U.S. intervention against the elected governments of Guatemala in 1954, Cuba in 1961, and Chile in 1973.[25]

The contras were in fact being trained in Honduras by the Argentine military with CIA coordination. Studds had long called for cutting off aid to this military dictatorship, which had "disappeared" nine thousand leftists in a dirty war that began in 1976. U.N. ambassador Jeane Kirkpatrick openly admired the Argentine generals and approved of using them as trainers of the contra forces in Honduras. Emboldened by their support from the Reagan administration, the Argentine generals invaded the offshore Falkland Islands (to Argentines, the Malvinas), occupied by Great Britain since 1833. Confronted by a war between two allies, the Reagan administration sided with Britain. "The Empire Strikes Back," ran the cover banner of a weekly newsmagazine, echoing the title of a popular movie.

Even still, Studds could not get the House Foreign Affairs Committee to cut off aid to Argentina and its ally Chile. The "Committee continues to beat plowshares into swords," Studds glumly wrote to his constituents. The foreign aid bill increased U.S. arms aid by $1.2 billion globally. The Reagan administration watched passively as Britain smashed the Argentines. In a grand irony, Nicaragua backed Argentina's claim to the islands, and in gratitude, the Argentines pulled their advisers out of Central America. The CIA would have to pick up the slack.[26]

Meanwhile, Reagan's El Salvador policy had been strengthened by the March elections. Studds bolstered the certification protocol to require a separate report and vote on the investigations into the murders of the Americans. In February, a colleague of the slain land reform advisers from the American Institute for Free Labor Development appeared before the Western Hemisphere Subcommittee with new evidence regarding the killings, implicating high-level military officials. Studds's measure passed in the subcommittee, but administration officials leaned on House Republicans to stymie his effort. A weaker nonbinding measure was approved in July as the second certification deadline loomed. This time Enders made a more nuanced case, but he still insisted that the March elections showed that El Salvador deserved more military aid.[27]

Studds tried fruitlessly to get this finding declared "null and void" again in July, rounding up eighty-four congressmen willing to cut off military aid. The same stubborn problem would not go away—fear of "losing" El Salvador to the communists and enabling the bloodbath that Reagan promised was sure to follow. That there was already an ongoing bloodbath committed by U.S. allies, and that no such event had happened in Nicaragua, didn't matter. Studds pointed to the realities on the ground. Prisoners were frequently tortured in the headquarters of the national police. The fake land reform had led to almost ten thousand evictions. The murders of the Americans had gone unsolved. "At some point we have to be willing to cut off aid," he insisted at the hearings. Without that certainty, "nothing we do by way of conditions will have any credibility down there."[28]

Over the next ten years, the war in El Salvador would grind on and the country's woes would fade from the news, until the regime committed another barbaric massacre in 1989. The urban murder rate declined, simply because all the opposition leaders had fled or been killed. Studds had lost every important vote, but his intransigence had helped set the outer limit of Reagan's options. The number and role of the American advisers were limited, the aid was less than Reagan wanted, and the question of a U.S. combat role never even surfaced. Moreover, Studds publicly encouraged the U.S. peace movement, while Woodward cooperated with its leaders behind the scenes.

As Studds challenged the second certification in July 1982, only a handful of people knew that his private world had been shaken to its core that month. In a bizarre twist of fate that barely missed exploding into the headlines, an event from Studds's forgotten past threatened to come to the surface. Gerry Studds's secret was about to be revealed.

11

The Fisherman's Friend
Caught in a Net

CONGRESSMAN GERRY STUDDS woke up with his boyfriend at his Provincetown apartment on July 1, 1982. Studds was beginning to feel deep stirrings of attachment to Michael, a Capitol Hill staffer whom he had met through a friend a few months earlier. "I don't think I've ever been happier with you," Michael had confided the night before on Gerry's moonlit deck. Gerry replied that he felt the same way. Tomorrow they would spend the day on Gerry's boat, the *Bacalhau.*

On the winter night when they met, they had gone out to dinner, felt a mutual connection, and in early spring escaped together on a weekend getaway to New Hope, Pennsylvania, a lovely town on the Delaware River. Then over Easter weekend they drove through a fierce squall from Boston to Provincetown that blanketed Cape Cod with snow. Gerry and Michael reveled in the seascape, huddling indoors by the fire burning in the woodstove. In May, the couple saw *Torch Song Trilogy* at an off-Broadway theater in Greenwich Village. The publicly reserved Studds trembled with emotion as the players acted out scenes from his hidden life. Studds laughed aloud and cried openly as he recognized characters just like himself represented onstage. Better still, he was sharing this breakthrough moment with the man he loved.

Every love affair contains its unique ballet of attraction and withdrawal. Michael, Gerry worried, was even more closeted than he was himself, a public figure risking career-ending exposure every time they went out together. Michael was obsessed by fear that being revealed as gay would lead to the loss of his job. He insisted that they arrive and depart separately at Washington's National Airport and sit apart from each other on the airplane. Love might conquer all, Gerry reflected once, or it might not.

At 9:30 that July morning the phone rang, and Gerry Studds's life changed forever.

The caller was his press secretary, Steve Schwadron, a loyal and protective aide. Reporters had come to the office, Schwadron said. They wanted to interview Studds about the allegations made by a congressional page on the *CBS Evening News* the night before that congressmen were having homosexual relations with pages. While Studds had not been named on the air, the reporters had other sources related to Justice Department and FBI investigations that listed Studds as one of the persons of interest.

"What the hell are you talking about?" Studds demanded. He hadn't been watching television. He felt a sickening sense of nausea, disgust, and pain in the pit of his stomach.

"Gerry, every reporter in this town is working on some kind of rumor about you. The bottom line seems to be that you're one of the congressmen named by the pages."

Stunned, Studds instructed Schwadron to keep him posted. With his head spinning, he took a shower and emerged just as Michael was waking up.

Schwadron called again.

"Do you know any black pages?"

"Why the hell do you ask that?"

"Because one of the two on CBS is black, and according to the NBC reporter, he says he had sex with you in the Watergate."

"Jesus Christ! I've never even met a black page."

"What should I say to the reporters?"

A look of terror spread across Michael's face as he overheard this conversation. "Don't say a goddamn thing!" Studds barked into the phone and slammed the receiver down. Michael was shaking with fear. His lifelong secret was going to come out too.

The phone rang again. This time it was a television reporter. Trying to disguise his easily identifiable voice, Studds told him that the congressman was not there. He knew that once he denied anything, the questions would keep coming. The reporters would remember the innuendo from the Dinis campaign in 1976. And of course, here he was in Provincetown with a man. They both had to escape, so they quickly dressed and began packing.

Studds recruited his downstairs neighbor, Russell Lukes, as lookout. Russell called a moment later to warn of a journalist approaching, notepad in hand. A moment later there was a knock at the door. Both men froze, hunted prisoners in Gerry's own home. After the reporter left, they looked out and saw a television truck parked outside, and then the Boston TV4 news helicopter buzzed overhead. More television trucks showed up. Russell mobilized a few friends to give the reporters false information regarding Studds's whereabouts, and after a while they dispersed. He then pulled up in Gerry's car so Studds could drive off, leaving Michael to be driven to the airport by another confederate.

Alone in his car, Congressman Gerry Studds realized he had nowhere to go. Reporters would probably show up at his mother's house in Cohasset, his official address. So as he drove toward the Sagamore Bridge, Studds stopped at a pay phone and made a call.

"Mother," he said, "I don't have much time—but there is something very important that I have to tell you."

Except for chance meetings on Capitol Hill, Gerry never saw Michael again.[1]

A Call to Califano

Studds drove to Cambridge, where he hid out for a few days at the apartment of Lewis Gannett, his friend and trusted driver. Studds was distraught and needed a sympathetic ear. One of his staffers showed up soon after and took some of the pressure off Gannett. Yet Gannett observed that at some level "[Studds] was excited. It was as though he had been waiting for this his whole life. He had a sense of history in the making. And he was amazingly competent through this crisis, very quickly reaching out for legal counsel."[2]

Studds soon learned that CBS had interviewed two pages (later identified as Jeffrey Opp of Colorado and Leroy Williams, the African American, from Arkansas) on camera but in shadow. Opp alleged that he had had sex with a congressman, that this was not uncommon, and that there was drug dealing on Capitol Hill involving pages and members. Williams charged that he had had sex three times with an unnamed congressman at the Watergate. That was where Studds lived. He had never heard of either young man.[3]

Over the following days, the newspapers reported that Opp had earlier told a staffer for Representative Patricia Schroeder, a Colorado Democrat, that he had been "homosexually harassed," and that Schroeder had referred him to the Justice Department, which had begun an investigation. Meanwhile, another Democrat, Representative Louis Stokes of Ohio, chairman of the House Committee on Standards of Official Conduct, known as the

Ethics Committee, announced that he would seek a resolution enabling an investigation. The FBI, as well as District of Columbia and Capitol Hill police, initiated their own probes of the drug charges. This information came from Representative Bob Dornan, a California Republican who kept a detective on his staff. Dornan told reporters that six congressmen had been named, and that he knew who they were. The following day, July 8, columnist Jack Anderson wrote that nine present and former congressmen had been implicated as cocaine users, and that one was from Massachusetts. Anderson cited "a 'confidential memo' prepared by law-enforcement officials," though it was probably from Dornan's gumshoe. Finally, a dodgy former page named Steve Valentine told the *Indianapolis Star* that he knew of one congressman who had tried to coerce at least three male pages into having sex with him. Valentine was the man who had been compiling the tabloid article in 1977 that Studds was warned about. His last charge would have sounded ominously familiar to Studds because it applied to him, except for the word "coerce."[4]

A few days later the House approved by a 407–1 vote a resolution, H.R. 518, directing the Ethics Committee to investigate the charges having to do with drug use, improper sexual conduct, and the offering of special privileges to pages, employees, and members in relation to drugs and sex. The resolution gave the committee the authority to retain a special counsel with subpoena power, and to coordinate its investigation with the Justice Department. The committee and special counsel were endowed with a certain amount of discretion by the use of the term "may" rather than the occasionally used "shall" in the description of their duties. Most important, the resolution directed that on the basis of "recent investigations by the Department of Justice," the focus of the inquiry was "to determine whether members, officers, or employees of the House of Representatives have violated the Code of Official Conduct or any law, rule, regulation, or other applicable standard of conduct."[5] The committee engaged Joseph Califano, former secretary of health, education and welfare in the Johnson administration and now a high-profile Washington attorney, as special counsel.

The language of the enabling resolution gave Califano some latitude. It did not limit whom he could investigate, although it did posit that he should inquire about events no earlier than 1980: H.R. 518 referred to "recent" investigations by the Department of Justice. Troubled by this overly broad instruction, Califano privately sought the counsel of a Jesuit ethicist, who suggested the following legitimate subjects for his probe: illegal sex, immoral acts committed publicly, the abuse of office to procure such acts, blackmail, illegal drug use, and preferential treatment. Califano resolved to pursue only allegations involving pages, not members of Congress and adult staffers. These were thoughtful guidelines.[6]

Why did Congress investigate these nebulous charges at all? Congressional leaders had a range of choices in this matter that were conditioned by recent history. The years since Watergate had produced a series of embarrassments that discredited the legislative branch just as Watergate had diminished the presidency. In October 1974, two months after Nixon's resignation, the Washington police stopped a car containing a drunken chairman of the House Ways and Means Committee, Wilbur Mills of Arkansas, and a stripper, Fanne Fox, known as the "Argentine Firecracker," who attempted to escape arrest by plunging into the nearby Tidal Basin. Mills quit in disgrace. In May 1976 the *Washington Post* revealed that Wayne Hays of Ohio had retained an unqualified secretary whose real job was to serve his sexual needs; Hays, too, submitted his resignation. These comic escapades gave way to more serious transgressions. In October 1976 the *Post* reported that several congressmen had received payments of over half a million dollars for helping to advance South Korean business investments. Sensing an opportunity, an ambitious FBI agent launched a sting operation later that year in which six congressmen were duped into accepting cash from FBI agents masquerading as Arabs seeking favors similar to those received by the South Koreans. None of the six had initiated the contacts, and all were entrapped, yet they met different fates in the courts. One was expelled; others failed to gain reelection. Among the ensnared was John M. Murphy of New York, chairman of the Merchant Marine and Fisheries Committee, who lost his next election. The biggest fish caught in this net was New Jersey senator Harrison Williams, in whose office Studds had unhappily labored in 1965.[7]

This context of public mistrust encouraged congressional leaders to investigate the televised charges of sexual misconduct and drug abuse. Did they do the right thing? Surely their primary and quite reasonable motivation was to protect young pages from predatory behavior by their elders. While every parent of a page signed a release form that presumably immunized congressmen from civil lawsuits, no parent could countenance the sexual harassment of his or her offspring. Yet in this case, congressional leaders actually had very little to go on. They might have waited for the criminal investigations, which turned up nothing, to unfold before proceeding with an internal inquiry. After all, they had only the words of two teenagers whose charges lacked specificity. It was the mere fact that their words had been broadcast on television that lent the accusations any weight.

The second contextual factor was that the pages charged not just sexual misbehavior but homosexual misbehavior. Homosexual acts themselves were still illegal in a majority of states. Gays and lesbians who achieved distinction almost universally disguised their sexual orientation. The country had no publicly identified gay figure in the arts, sciences, sports, journalism, or any other field. The small number of openly gay elected officials held only local offices. Worse yet was the emergence of a strange new disease that was killing gay men. The as yet unnamed affliction had sparked a wave of hysteria and condemnation against all gay men.

The Secret of Election 1982

After the 1980 census Massachusetts lost one seat in Congress. As a result, the Twelfth District was expanded and became the Tenth. Demographically, however, it remained an overwhelmingly white middle-class district. Republican candidate Jack Conway, a real estate broker, had the requisite credentials to pose a serious challenge to Studds. Conway was a handsome, gregarious fellow with a sunny personality, in some ways everything the cerebral, reserved Studds was not. His company sign hung on scores of houses up for sale in every town in the district, so his name recognition was high for a non-politician. Nor was Conway an extremist. He didn't bash the unemployed, and he called on President Reagan to fire Interior Secretary James Watt, a man who never saw a public resource he wouldn't sell to an oil company.

So why was he running? That was Conway's biggest problem. His complaints were that Studds talked about Central America too much and had lost touch with the district, was a big spender, and was too liberal. It just wasn't enough to attract any interest. Moreover, Conway made all the usual rookie errors. He accused Studds of being "un-American" for his position on Central America, a charge that probably struck some potentially persuadable voters as overreach. And then there were tactical blunders, like the day he joined a town parade in rural Plympton that marched through an uninhabited forest. "He wasn't a bad candidate," Studds staffer MaryLou Butler remembered years later, "but he wasn't good. It's harder than it looks."[8]

Studds pounded away at his themes—that Reaganomics, with its tax cutting and extravagant spending on useless military programs like the "Star Wars" missile defense system, had proved to be a fake that had driven the economy into recession and piled up a huge deficit. He spoke of his environmental and fishing industry credentials. His pro-choice stance helped against Conway's opposition to a woman's right to choose. Studds debated Conway several times and exposed Conway's lack of knowledge in each contest.

Throughout, Studds worried about what might leak out of Califano's committee. Conway, a decent man, refused to play the homophobia card. At one live radio debate, a caller demanded to know if Studds was a homosexual. Studds sat stunned at the microphone, paralyzed. Conway could have let the silence go on forever, but instead he declared that candidates' private lives were their own business. "What are you going to do," Conway told a reporter a few years later, "let the guy fry?"[9]

As the election neared, district staffer Maureen Garde and driver John Meunier lightened up Studds's mood, which was probably more anxious than they knew, by knocking on his Cohasset door on Halloween dressed as Barney Frank and Margaret Heckler, two incumbents who, as a result of the redistricting, were facing off in a close race in the neighboring Fourth District. Studds looked at Garde's blond wig and cracked up.[10]

Despite being outspent two to one, Studds won by a large margin. He carried the South Shore and the Cape comfortably, and won New Bedford with 80 percent of the vote. "This district voted for Ronald Reagan two years ago," Studds told an enthusiastic crowd at a Marshfield restaurant as the vote count was finalized just before midnight. "These figures tell me that the voters did not mean what Mr. Reagan told them they meant two years ago."[11]

For Studds, this was a night of triumph. But the biggest crisis of his life lay dead ahead, and there was no way the veteran sailor could steer around it.

The Net Tightens

Califano, to his credit, minced no words in his December 14 report to the Ethics Committee. In effect, he blamed CBS for cooking up a hoax. The pages backtracked as soon as his investigators grilled them. For unknown reasons, they had simply retailed gossip that they had heard and then reinterpreted friendly words from members as sexual advances. When Opp went to Schroeder's office with his story, her staffers doubted his veracity. It was only when the CBS reporter told the staffers he believed there was substance to the tales that they referred Opp to the Justice Department.[12]

Investigations can take on a dynamic of their own. That had been the case in the FBI inquiry into the allegation that Martin Luther King Jr. was consorting with communists, a charge that led Attorney General Robert F. Kennedy to authorize a wiretap on King's phone. The FBI discovered instead that King was having an affair, and the bureau fiendishly began sending him anonymous messages suggesting that he commit suicide or face exposure.[13]

Califano might have heeded this lesson. He was charged only with investigating "recent allegations." To be thorough, he interviewed many pages, some of whom came forward with information unrelated to the original charges. Califano might have disregarded them and still have done his duty. Yet an expensive investigation that comes up empty always raises the question "Why then did we bother to spend so much time and money on it?"

When the new Congress convened, a continuing resolution, H.R. 12, was passed to wrap up the unfinished ethics business. Califano uncovered an affair between a page and Congressman Daniel Crane of Illinois. Crane was married, and a Republican champion of family values. In her testimony, the young woman unambiguously declared that she was a willing participant in the affair, and at seventeen, she was legally of age in the District of Columbia, where the age of consent was sixteen. Crane had, however, committed adultery, a crime in the District, for which he was never prosecuted.

What was Califano to do? Under the guidelines of the enabling resolution, and the further reflections of the Jesuit ethicist, Califano might have done nothing. This was a private matter between legally consenting adults. No special favors were given, no coercion was involved, no illegal drugs were purchased. The young woman herself had not come forward to complain. Nor are pages employees of individual congressmen, unlike staffers; pages are in effect fellow employees who work in another department. The Jesuit ethicist's private recommendations to Califano might have persuaded him to desist; nothing in this story matched those guidelines. Califano, however, charged Crane with "improper sexual conduct bringing discredit on the Congress" and recommended a public reprimand.

Califano also learned that Gerry Studds had traveled overseas with an unidentified male page in 1973. Not knowing who that page was, Califano identified the traveler as "Page X." He could not even say for certain if Studds and X had had sex together. Califano could have dismissed the story as hearsay, stale, and beyond his original mandate, but persevering, he plugged diligently away to ferret out the "crime." In addition, Califano turned up the two other pages whom Studds had unsuccessfully propositioned in 1973.

Califano's staff interviewed Page X twice. Yes, X confirmed, he did go to Portugal with Studds, but no, they did not have sex. That too might have ended Califano's inquiries. But he chose to depose X under oath, no doubt warning him of the consequences should he be caught in a lie. Under oath, Page X admitted that, yes, they had in fact had sex. They had met by

chance in a restaurant; Studds offered him a ride home; they went instead to
Studds's place and talked politics, and after they had both consumed several
glasses of vodka and cranberry juice (a "Cape Codder"), the congressman
announced that he was too drunk to drive him home. X spent the night, and
they had sex in an unspecified manner. This happened two or three more
times. In August they went to Portugal together and had sex every two or
three days.

Califano tried hard to get X to play the victim, which he refused to do.
For example, he was asked:

Q: Did you feel intimidated?
A: No I did not. I would like to state at this time [that Studds] was an intelligent, witty, gentle man with I think a high level of insecurity. He did
   nothing to me that I would consider destructive or painful. In another
   time, in another society, the action would be considered acceptable, perhaps even laudable. Unfortunately this is not the case. I have no axe to
   grind with him. I have nothing negative to say about the man. In fact, I
   think that he provided me with one of the more wonderful experiences
   of my life, if we exclude the instances of sexual experience which I was
   somewhat uncomfortable with. But I did not think it was that big a deal.
Q: You said you felt uncomfortable with it, did you continue with it because
   he was a congressman, because he was someone you were impressed
   with?
A: No. Well, I kept company with him because he was an intelligent man,
   someone who was fun to be with. If I could have had my druthers, I
   would have had the friendship with the man without the sex. And I
   mentioned that to him.[14]

The next set of questions elicited clear responses that Studds had offered
no special favors or threatened any form of coercion. X had paid for the trip
to Portugal himself, as had Studds. The statement "if I could have had my
druthers" did suggest, however, that X had had to be talked into the sexual
part of the relationship, and Studds's enemies would later reprise that line
and omit the rest of the testimony.

With this information in hand, the committee next interrogated every
Studds staffer on the Hill. In February, the members requisitioned from
administrative assistant Peter Fleischer all of Studds's travel records from
1973 to 1979 and deposed him.[15] In subsequent months, they interviewed
staffers one by one. "They hauled me in before the committee," fisheries
adviser Jeff Pike recalled with obvious distaste. "There was one member from
Ethics there, but Califano's lawyers asked all the questions. I didn't even have
any representation. 'Did he touch me inappropriately?' 'Did we have sex?'

The whole thing made me so disgusted I quit. I couldn't stand even being in Washington."[16] Staffer Bill Woodward felt much the same way: "I wasn't part of the legal strategy but, yes, they called me in. [The details of the investigation were] supposed to be a secret, and I kept it."[17]

The interviews with the staffers clearly went beyond the mandate of the enabling resolution and Califano's own guidelines. He was to investigate only matters relevant to congressional pages, and said explicitly in his own memoir that he didn't have time to investigate every office romance. More important, Califano had an additional problem in Studds's case. Unlike with Crane, this affair was ten years old, and X was now a mature adult who unambiguously asserted that he was not making a complaint himself. Califano again might have refrained on these grounds, but he chose to push ahead.

As this inquiry proceeded behind closed doors, more wild allegations by journalist Jack Anderson again hit the newspapers in late April and early May. "Columnist Names Kennedy, 8 More in Hill Cocaine Case," blared a *Washington Times* headline. Anderson's sleuths cited an unspecified "investigative document" regarding drug abuse on Capitol Hill. Though the specifics were vague, the report named four sitting congressmen, all Democrats—Parren Mitchell of Maryland, Charles Wilson of Texas, Ronald Dellums of California, and Gerry Studds of Massachusetts—and four retired representatives. How these names surfaced, or what the "investigative document" was, remained unclear, and Anderson soon backed off. These were smear tactics maliciously designed to destroy reputations and, in the case of Mitchell and Dellums, appeal to racist stereotypes. "It's ludicrous," Studds's chief of staff Peter Fleischer declared. "I've known Gerry personally for seven years, and he's never done drugs. Anyone who knows him knows he wouldn't even know what cocaine was if it were lying out in front of him."[18]

In May, a media storm broke out about the mysterious disease that was killing gay men, known as "acquired immunodeficiency syndrome." Early that month gay activists staged candlelight marches to commemorate the lives lost to the epidemic. A congressional committee led by Henry Waxman of Los Angeles demanded to know why the Reagan administration was low-balling its budget requests for research on the disease. Alarm bells sounded on the other side of the issue as well. The American Medical Association warned that the disease could be spread by routine household contact, and some demanded that the victims be quarantined. Conservative columnist Patrick Buchanan, a favorite of the Reagan administration, sneered, declaring, "The poor homosexuals—they have declared war on nature, and nature has extracted an awful retribution."[19]

Gerry Studds's appointment with the Ethics Committee unfolded in an atmosphere of hysteria about gay men spreading a deadly disease. Studds had retained counsel quickly. He chose the firm of Mahoney, Hawkes & Goldings, perhaps because Charles Francis Mahoney, like Studds, was a closeted gay man.

Mahoney and Goldings made an unusual pair. "Mahoney might have become governor had he not been gay," Studds's friend Brian McNaught believed. "Mahoney was a prim, fastidious Bostonian, and Goldings was fat and sloppy," press aide Steve Schwadron recalled. Mahoney had been secretary of human services when Ed King was governor of Massachusetts. Goldings was a Harvard-educated First Amendment specialist whose major clientele were Boston "Combat Zone" strip club owners. Yet they formed a formidable duo, whatever their resemblance to the Broadway *Odd Couple* characters.[20]

Mahoney and Goldings held a strategy meeting in late February 1983 at Mahoney's Gloucester home along with McNaught and another friend of Studds's, therapist Larry McCreedy. Studds was going to have to deal with more than a legal and political problem. He might have to tell the world his deepest secret and "come out" as a gay man.

Four months later, a communication from Califano appeared to offer a way to avoid public exposure. On June 13 he sent the attorneys a four-page summary of his findings, assured them of Studds's rights before the House, and laid out his recommendations for a private procedure before the Ethics Committee. The attorneys and Studds would appear on June 22. Studds worked on a draft of his statement with speechwriter Bill Woodward. He did not dispute the committee's prerogative to investigate. Nor did he challenge the facts of the matter. He asked for no special consideration as a gay man. He did, however, urge the committee to consider that his relationship with X was "mutual and voluntary, without coercion, without any preferential treatment, express or implied, without harassment of any kind; and that it was private." He asked not that he be absolved but that any reprimand be issued privately. He described the descent of reporters on his apartment and urged the committee to reread the testimony of X, which Studds felt exonerated him. He had committed no crime, he said, and had hurt no one.[21]

In summary, Goldings put forward a careful appeal, offering what amounted to a plea bargain: "While they may be found to be improper under Rule 1 of the Code of Official Conduct, the facts constitute neither improper sexual conduct as set forth in the Resolution nor such conduct as defined by the Committee and hence do not justify a public finding against the Member of Congress." Goldings emphasized the staleness of the complaint and urged consideration of X's privacy. He further argued that there was no relation between the original mission of the investigation and the charge against Studds; that pages were not employees of congressmen; that no one had come forward to complain about Studds; and that the committee had been endowed by the House with considerable discretion.[22]

Mahoney, for his part, summarized his recent conversations with X, who had not contacted Studds or his attorneys during the inquiry and urged that his privacy be respected. Mahoney concluded with an appeal to precedent in a 1973 federal case in which the Supreme Court had acted to protect the privacy of a young man.

Over the next few weeks, a flurry of legal correspondence passed among Studds, his attorneys, members of the Ethics Committee, and Califano. Studds restated his case to the members of the committee, insisting that their choices included rejecting Califano's recommendation for reprimand or, more likely, finding against Studds *in camera,* with a letter placed in his file. Should he be publicly disciplined, Studds argued, his political career might be irreparably damaged despite his twelve years of service, which should weigh in his favor. His lawyers emphasized that Studds must be given the right to contest the charges at a closed preliminary hearing. They further insisted that, contrary to Califano's claim, Congress did not legally act *in loco parentis* in relation to pages because the parents had signed a waiver.[23]

Neither Califano nor the Ethics Committee was moved. From their perspective, they had before them a man who had gotten a boy drunk and then had sex with him; no matter how tolerant they might be, that seemed reprehensible. While there was no explicit rule stating that congressmen should not have sex with pages, members of the Ethics Committee had to presume that this principle was implied in Clause 1 of the Standards of Conduct for House Members, which insists upon conduct that will not discredit the House. The implied rule had to be enforced; it would have no meaning if Studds's transgression were swept under the rug. And what if Studds did it again? Would they not look like the judge who failed to issue a restraining order against a child molester who then repeated his crime?

Bastille Day

Studds now faced the greatest challenge of his life. On July 14 he would appear before his assembled colleagues. He was caught between the Scylla of wishing to clear his name—which would have to be done in public, given the committee's interpretation of the rules—and the Charybdis of accepting a public reprimand. The first alternative meant dragging the names of the pages into a public proceeding. The second alternative was equally troubling to Studds. Throughout the process, he had been gradually abandoning his public identity as an "unmarried man" and assuming the identity of an "out and proud" gay man. How could he stand up in public, newly a representative of the gay community, and beg forgiveness for what would seem to be the crime of being gay?

On Tuesday, July 12, key staffers and his attorneys conducted an evening meeting. The lawyers held firm. They advised Studds to fight and win. The staffers knew that such a victory would be a Pyrrhic one. The hearings would focus on sexual behavior that would appear depraved to many voters. No parent could imagine sending his or her child into a potential den of seducers should Studds assert his right to proposition seventeen-year-olds by arguing that they were adults. Legally he might be innocent, but politically, he should admit he had done wrong and apologize. Studds listened as his advisers laid out the likely outcomes of each scenario.

The normally cool Studds broke down in tears. When he recovered, he declared that he would fight and would not apologize, but couldn't say just how. Studds went home, drank a lot of vodka tonics, ate half a box of Triscuits, and fell into a troubled sleep.[24]

The next morning, the day before the scheduled reprimand, the situation looked clearer. The staff was right. He couldn't drag the pages into the public eye, and even if he won legally, he would lose politically and personally. Studds had to end it. The former history professor noted to his staffers that the next day was Bastille Day. In one sense, Studds might have been imagining his reputation, if not his actual head, held aloft on a pike by news reporters, the modern *sans culottes*, decapitating a man they perceived as a debauched aristocrat. On a deeper level, however, Studds was imagining himself as a prisoner who had been given the key to his freedom. He was OUT.[25]

Studds had been huddling separately with speechwriter Bill Woodward throughout the week to prepare for the awful moment. "We worked and reworked that statement," Studds recalled in his memoir. "Bill was always an exceptionally eloquent writer, and he was as eloquent as ever on this occasion. Yet again and again he would include some type of apology in his text, and again and again I would cross it out."[26]

Woodward remembers reading the statement to Studds and the staff and Studds, his friend, former teacher, and boss, exclaiming, "You bastard," when he heard an apology included in his draft. Steve Schwadron wondered how a man who was so brilliant could have found himself in this situation.[27] Studds was in too much pain to see that Woodward, Fleischer, and Schwadron were right. He was in the process of asserting a new identity, a man who was different from people who did not share his identity, like a black man among white liberals. He was gay, he was proud, and he would say so. No apologies.

On the fateful day, Studds entered the chamber and took his seat. To his consternation, he learned that Califano and Stokes had conducted a news conference outside, announcing that they would recommend that Crane and Studds, now named for the first time, be reprimanded. The committee vote had been 11–1. The story dominated the news for the next several days. Stokes entered the House chamber as William Dannemeyer, the most homophobic member of the House, happened to be making a speech on agriculture. Stokes asked him to yield and made his report. Studds then rose and asked Speaker O'Neill for a point of personal privilege. Dannemeyer technically still had the floor and, in a coincidence of supreme irony, yielded to Studds.

"All Members of Congress must cope with the challenge of initiating and maintaining a career in public office without destroying entirely the ability to lead a meaningful and emotionally fulfilling private life," Studds began. "These challenges are made substantially more complex when one is, as am I, both an elected public official and gay."

Congress now had its first openly gay sitting member.

After calling attention to the ten-years-old staleness of the charge, Studds admitted that his behavior constituted "a very serious error of judgment on my part." In six succinct paragraphs, he explained why he would not contest the charges, while personally believing that they did not meet the threshold of "improper sexual behavior" as defined by the House resolution. Finally, he dropped his own bombshell in the last sentence, the one that would draw the most attention in the media storm that followed: "In doing so, however, I repeat that in my judgment, the mutually voluntary, private relationship between adults, which occurred ten years ago, should not—by any conceivable standard of fairness, rationality, rule or law—warrant the attention or action of the House of Representatives of the United States."

Should Studds decide to run for office again, that declaration would give any opponent fresh ammunition. "In that statement, I affirmed my own existence as a gay man," Studds recalled in his memoir. "In words that struck some as arrogant, I essentially told my colleagues that the mutual, voluntary relationship of a decade ago was none of their business. Within a matter of moments, all hell broke loose."

"All hell" was the media scrum. Studds had not game-planned it. Luckily, his colleague and friend Tony Beilenson of California, who coincidentally looked like Studds, ran interference while Studds scooted off the floor, dodging the cameras as Schwadron's car sped him away.

The House still had to vote on the committee report the following week. Studds had to escape the media again. Friends reported that cameras were waiting for him at his mother's house in Cohasset, in Provincetown, even at the airport. Studds took the train to New York, where he hid out at the home of Larry McCreedy. At Penn Station he saw a tabloid headline referring to him and Crane: "Sex Twins Flee City." Like a fugitive, he had kept his head buried in a newspaper during the train ride.

Later Studds stayed with Brian McNaught in Brookline, a Boston suburb. That night a fire, perhaps set by an arsonist, broke out in the adjacent building, the Brookline Women's Health Center, which did abortion referrals. Smoke billowed into the apartment, and as they fled to the street, to Studds's dismay, reporters showed up with the fire trucks. Nobody noticed him. The next day McNaught made a New Hampshire cabin available, and Studds retreated to that locale.[28]

During that week prior to the vote, an unheralded backbencher, then the only Republican from Georgia, made headlines by objecting to the recommendation for reprimand. While calling for the expulsion of both men, he aimed all his fire at Studds. "The relationship he had was not with adults but three schoolchildren," said the representative, Newt Gingrich. "It is, to say the least, disgusting." A teacher in such circumstances would certainly be fired, Gingrich insisted, and should the two congressmen fail to resign, they should be expelled. Gingrich had been content to accept the reprimand recommendation until Studds's speech, which he found "arrogant" and lacking in "remorse," inspired him to seek the most extreme penalty. Moreover, Gingrich noted that Studds was from Speaker Tip O'Neill's state of Massachusetts, and the reprimand recommendation smacked of a pattern of "abuse by Democrats."[29]

Gingrich started working his caucus. Here was a chance to politicize the issue. Crane held a safe Republican seat, but Studds had always seemed a Democratic anomaly in a conservative district. Mysteriously, the vote was put off on Tuesday. Studds sensed the gathering of ominous clouds. On Wednesday he obtained a meeting with Speaker O'Neill and urged him to bring the matter to the floor quickly so as to put it behind them.

The vote came the next day, July 20. Louis Stokes read the charge and received a standing ovation. House members appreciated how difficult his task had been; few congressmen relished serving on that committee. Stokes and Floyd Spence, the ranking Republican, argued for reprimand. Gingrich took the floor and spoke against reprimand as insufficient. Minority Leader Robert Michel moved to amend the committee recommendation to censure, a more serious penalty that required the member to stand in the well of the House as the charge was read. In addition, Democratic caucus rules compelled a censured member to surrender any chairmanships. Only twenty members had been censured previously, mostly for intemperate remarks about colleagues; this would be the first censure for sexual behavior in the House's history. The votes to amend were taken separately. Each member would have to consider not just the rightness of his or her vote but how an opponent in the 1984 election would parse it. In Crane's case the vote to amend to censure was 289–136. Studds had few friends on the other side of the aisle. Only eight Republicans joined the minority of Democrats holding out for reprimand in Studds's case; the vote was 338–87. As Studds explained to his staffers, by calling for expulsion, Gingrich had positioned censure as the middle ground, and it was bound to carry.

The lengthy debate on Crane's case came first. The vote to censure was then taken and passed, 421–3, with Crane himself voting in favor. Crane entered the well and faced his colleagues with his back to Speaker O'Neill. Crane made a tearful apology. Unlike Studds, he had committed adultery and had to apologize to his family as well as his constituents and his colleagues. He had not spoken a week earlier on Bastille Day.[30]

Studds listened in agony as the committee made its case against him. During the intervening week he had received a lot of mail from gay men and women praising him for his courageous affirmation of his sexual orientation. One letter, signed by hundreds of people in San Francisco, quoted a lyric from the musical *Carousel*, "When you walk through a storm, hold your head up high, and don't be afraid of the dark." Studds hummed it to himself as the report was read. He sat surrounded by his Massachusetts colleagues. The vote was 420–3, with Studds voting "present." The no votes came from three African Americans—William Clay, Parren Mitchell, and Mervin Dymally.

Studds was among the most knowledgeable members regarding parliamentary procedure. He had thought ahead to the problem of which way to face when the speaker read the finding. The House parliamentarian had advised him that the proper course was to face the person speaking to him. So

Studds stood in the well, his hands clasped behind his back, facing Speaker O'Neill. Later, hostile commentators would contrast Studds's behavior with Crane's, criticizing the direction in which he faced and his failure to make an apologetic speech.[31] Califano, in his memoir, also condemned Studds for this, but he confused the directions faced by the two men, a sign that Studds was damned by his opponents whatever he did.

After completing his report, Califano had met privately with Tip O'Neill in his office, who, Califano recalled, "tremble[d] with rage." Recovering himself, O'Neill said: "I always knew you got the luck of the Irish from your mother. Only someone with a shamrock could end a House sex investigation by nailing a conservative Republican with a girl and a liberal Democrat with boys."[32]

This story raises the question of the extent to which the entire process was driven by political considerations. O'Neill's remark to Califano suggests that Studds's transgression might have been ignored if not for the discovery of Crane's. What happened in the Ethics Committee is unknown, because Califano and Stokes, with the admirable intention of protecting the identities of the people they investigated and cleared, deliberately "lost" the committee's records, because "destroying" them would have violated House rules.[33] In retrospect, it seems probable that had the original allegations never been aired on television, Congress would not have investigated them. They were unspecific, and proved groundless. Moreover, had Studds followed Woodward's advice and apologized for sexual behavior that most adults would surely condemn, both he and Crane would probably have suffered the lesser penalty of reprimand rather than censure. It was only Studds's defiant speech that caused Gingrich to press for expulsion.

Finally, it is worth considering the evolving legal gray area into which Studds and Crane had stepped. Their sexual partners were legally adults in some senses but not in others: they were above the age of consent but were too young to vote, drink, or be drafted. The youth of the willing partners weighed heavily against Studds and Crane. Yet few would dispute that among the members voting for censure, at least some may have been sleeping with their employees—people they hired and fired. Years later it would emerge that Newt Gingrich was in exactly that situation, technically a case of sexual harassment, during the Clinton impeachment, an infraction for which he was never disciplined. Political considerations always influence such prosecutorial discretion.

This time, Studds went out onto the Capitol steps and faced a bank of microphones and cameras. He read a statement thanking his supporters, apologizing to the media for sequestering himself during the week, and promising to be more forthcoming in the future. "All members of Congress are in need of humbling experiences from time to time," Studds said. "I hope . . . to emerge from the present situation a wiser, more tolerant and a more complete human being."[34]

Newt Gingrich surely learned a lesson from the whole story as well. Push for the maximum; get a favorable compromise. Draw attention to oneself as a champion of family values. Years later he would apply this lesson to dealing with the president of the United States.

And now Gerry Studds faced the next big decision in his life. He declared that he would not resign. But should he run again? He could decline to run and enjoy a quiet private life. Or, as a proud gay man, he could stand for office and make his case on the issues his constituents cared about, despite the calumny that was sure to be hurled at him in the weeks and months ahead.

12

A Gay Man Runs for Congress

AND SO IT WAS OVER. Gerry Studds's secret was out. It had unfolded like a nightmare—the common bad dream in which the sleeper is exposed as an impostor. This nightmare had really happened, and it was reported in newspapers and on television all over the country. Many people expected that Studds would resign.

That was one of the options after Bastille Day. Studds considered it only briefly. He would have been an unlikely congressman even if he had been straight and married. He had only a few good friends among his colleagues. Studds was an inner-directed, somewhat introverted intellectual in a world of exuberant extroverts who were comfortable in their own skins. He could walk away, return to private life, and live openly among gay people.

His family had stayed loyal to him throughout the censure. When Gerry called his mother, Bonnie, on July 1, 1982, she already knew that he was gay. In the late 1970s Studds had told his sister Gaynor, who lived in Buffalo with her husband, about his sexual orientation. His brother Colin's wife, Mary Lou, had suspected that Gerry was gay shortly after meeting him in the late 1960s. Right after Bastille Day in 1983, Mary Lou took her two children to Cohasset's Sandy Beach and noticed that a few women deliberately turned their backs on her, as in a scene from an Edith Wharton novel. Then a pornographic magazine published Bonnie's number, and she started getting obscene calls. Despite the harassment, the family all rallied around Gerry.[1]

Studds told reporters that he wouldn't quit. He didn't know whether he would run again, but he wouldn't quit. He felt no shame. Yet with a little distance, he could now admit to his critics that his behavior had been improper, even if he fell short of apologizing. But he felt proud of his record in the ten years since. "A decision not to run would be generally interpreted as a concession of defeat and withdrawal in some shameful fashion. That I could not do," Studds wrote in his memoir.[2]

So for Studds, Bastille Day had inaugurated the best of times and the worst of times, and the worst was now over. He felt liberated and looked animated in newspaper photos. There would be no more days like July 1, 1982, when he had hidden in his Provincetown condo while reporters pounded on his door. He told journalists that he felt great. "Rep. Gerry E. Studds (D-Mass.) was relaxed, relieved, and almost buoyant yesterday as he talked about being finally able to 'look people in the eye,' and free to 'no longer hide' a part of his life," began the *Boston Globe* story. "My lifelong ambition has not been to be censured by Congress," he joked, but added that "personally this is the best time of my life." Studds granted that it was wrong to have had the relationship because pages were wards of Congress, and he added to his admission of poor judgment the concession that "it was utterly improper," a more conciliatory phrase that implied an apology. "I wish I could take the moment back."[3]

Studds now felt free to explain himself. "To grow up and enter adulthood as a gay person in this country is to be in a situation where all the messages one receives with respect to the deepest feelings inside one tell one that those feelings are not legitimate at best and that they're sinful and evil at worst," he declared, like a man unburdening himself. Studds said that his isolation had been so profound that on entering Congress "in 1973 I was 36 years old and at that point to the best of my knowledge I had not yet met another gay human being."

Like millions of other gay men, Studds had been caught in a web of genuine impulses contradicted by societal norms; having disentangled himself, he was eager to help others similarly situated to move out of the shadows. His office received three thousand letters in the weeks after the censure, running ten to one in his favor. "We got letters from all over the country," staffer MaryLou Butler remembered. "Some people came out as a result of it, and some of them were disowned" by their families. "We got letters that would bring tears to your eyes."[4]

Studds had been so deeply closeted that he was relatively clueless about who else might be gay. Two related stories illustrate that point. Studds's office was right next to Joe Moakley's. Studds once asked one of Moakley's staffers, a married man, to come up for a drink, an invitation that seemed to carry an agenda. Meanwhile, he had had lunch several times with a closeted gay staffer who recalled, "Oh, I had no idea that Studds was gay and I don't think he knew that I was."[5]

Studds's reaction to being caught in a "scandal" bears some similarities and some differences in comparison to the cases of other gay congressmen of his era who had been "exposed." The most prominent of these was Robert Bauman of Maryland. Bauman, a well-known conservative, was married when he was arrested for soliciting a male prostitute just before the 1980 election. He had struggled to control his homosexual tendencies and denied that he was gay, despite the arrest. He lost the election, and his marriage fell apart, but by the summer of 1983 he publicly acknowledged that he was gay and had made peace with himself.[6] Two other closeted gay congressmen, Jon Hinson, a Mississippi Republican, and Fred Richmond, a New York Democrat, had resigned during the early 1980s as their secrets unraveled.[7] So for gay people, Studds's coming out was the first public affirmation that a congressman could be gay and proud.

Three major local newspapers urged Studds to resign—the South Shore's *Quincy Patriot Ledger,* the *Boston Herald,* and the *Cape Cod Times.* Some writers at the *Boston Globe* echoed their concerns. One sign of progress was that none inveighed against homosexuality. They all concluded, however, that Studds had deserved the censure, and that by refusing to apologize, he had failed to acknowledge that he had crossed a line. The *Cape Cod Times* argued that "Studds is no longer perceived as the same man who was over-whelmingly elected for a sixth term last year." The *Globe* held that Studds deserved the censure but fell short of calling for his resignation. Studds was front-page news for the last two weeks in July; many of the region's papers ran "man in the street" interviews whose respondents mirrored the same gamut of opinions.[8]

The gay press was overwhelmingly supportive. Studds's friend Brian McNaught, writing in the *Globe,* was even more defiant than Studds himself, who had at least acknowledged an error in judgment. McNaught bluntly challenged his readers to consider whether an adult's relationship with a seventeen-year-old, or an employer's relationship with an employee, was always wrong. Studds's defenders generally would answer yes. They urged only that his indiscretion be balanced against the staleness of the charge and the fact that X had testified only under duress. McNaught answered no. It sometimes happened, he wrote, that these were positive, affirming experiences for the young people involved, and they did not always regret it. McNaught postulated that Studds had acted with "a pure heart" and asserted, "That is why he objected to the intrusion by Congress into his private life." In the year to come, X himself, unbeknownst to the public, would lend McNaught's view more weight. This was in fact one of those cases.[9]

Fair Skies but a Gathering Storm

The initial test would come in New Bedford. Every August since first winning election, Studds had joined the parade celebrating the Feast of the Blessed Sacrament. At the Madeiras Club prior to the parade that summer, Studds was warmly received by hundreds of participants, who sat separated by gender, the men clad in white and the women in turquoise. One state representative did walk out in protest.

Anticipating a possible hurled tomato, Studds had put on his cheapest suit, a blue seersucker, along with a fish-patterned tie secured by a scrimshaw pin. As he walked past the crowd, the spectators erupted in cheers and Studds smiled brilliantly, waving and flashing a "V" for victory sign. For two miles Studds marched down Acushnet Avenue, flanked by the Portuguese consul, New Bedford staffer Maria Tomasia, and community leader Mary Theresa Silvia Vermette. Studds endured scattered boos, and reporters noted two dissenters carrying a "Homo Resign" banner, but this was a tremendous day for Studds. "The warmth of the reception was very moving indeed," he told a reporter. "Needless to say that affection and respect is mutual." When the parade ended, Studds addressed the crowd, first in English and then in Portuguese. People applauded for a full minute and a half. The front-page headline in the *New Bedford Standard-Times* read, " 'We're with You,' Crowds Tell Studds: Outpouring Thrills Gay Lawmaker," splayed above a picture of the beaming congressman. Who could have envisioned such a development just three weeks previously?[10]

A few days later Studds held his first community meeting, at which he could field questions from constituents in another supportive town, Tisbury, on Martha's Vineyard. Three hundred residents packed a school gym, sitting on folding chairs in a scene painted by Norman Rockwell. Studds got a strong ovation as he entered the hall. The first questioner asked him to reassess the censure. Studds was candid and less defensive than he had been on Bastille Day, stressing that X may have been legally an adult but agreeing that the affair was "stupid" and "indefensible." Yet he insisted that he would be more effective in Congress now that he was out, happy, and more relaxed than he had ever been in his life. At the evening's end, the crowd delivered a standing ovation.[11]

Studds enjoyed further signs of encouragement a few days later when he attended the Cape Cod Democratic Council annual picnic. Senator Paul Tsongas and Governor Michael Dukakis, the nation's two leading Greek American politicians, welcomed him to a Greek Orthodox church. Studds hinted that he would run again.[12]

These early demonstrations of support alarmed the conservative opposition. Studds had effectively stolen a march on them; but at a meeting of six hundred people at the mid–Cape Cod town of Dennis, they went on the attack. Outside the Nathaniel Wixon Middle School, a crowd of angry picketers appeared with signs saying, "Get the Gay Out," "Censure Is Not Enough," and "Resign Now." These were religiously motivated people who objected to homosexuality itself. One newspaper photo showed the chairman of the Dennis Board of Selectmen, George Fallon, shouting through a bullhorn to a line of stern-faced picketers. Inside the hall, Fallon led off the question period by reading a petition calling for Studds's resignation on the grounds that he was a "practicing homosexual." Studds deflected the critics with low-key humor but a firm commitment that he would not resign. Finally, an elderly man walked directly up to Studds and pointed a bony finger at him. "I think you should hang your head in shame," he declared, and quoted the biblical verse prescribing death for sodomites. Without missing a beat, Studds responded, "You better go easy quoting that chapter on Cape Cod because it also says that it is equally sinful to eat shellfish." Others rose to Studds's defense: a former page, a Vietnam veteran, a Catholic priest concerned about Central America, and the town health inspector. Boos and cheers punctuated the tense atmosphere.[13]

"Oust the Youth Sodomizer" and "Studds Resign" signs greeted him at the next stop a few days later at Marshfield's Furnace Brook School. Another line of picketers, more news cameras, and a crowd of over six hundred were waiting, this time nastier in spirit. The *Quincy Patriot Ledger* ran a front-page picture of a downcast Studds staring moodily away from a "Youth Abuser" picket sign as he prepared to enter the auditorium. "Studds reviews damage," the page-one headline blared, and the reporter concluded that "Studds . . . got an unmistakable taste of the kind of objections he doubtless will face if he seeks re-election." The questioners were so vituperative, and Studds's partisans so angered, that the congressman remonstrated, "We need to call a truce here or we'll never get anything accomplished." Studds rebuked one opponent's reference to Sodom and Gomorrah by citing the biblical injunction to love one another. "That type of love produces the disease AIDS," someone in the audience called out. Jack Conway, Gerry's 1982 opponent, joined the chorus and pledged to bankroll the 1984 Republican candidate. "I resent the man," Conway said of Studds. "He's got to be beaten." This was no longer a political matter for some but an urgent question of morality.[14]

Studds knew that an election campaign would put him in face-to-face confrontations with angry opponents. Could he endure a series of meetings like the ones in Dennis and Marshfield during a campaign against an opponent who would probably be backed by national Republican money? Years later, Studds aide Steve Schwadron, recalling the Marshfield meeting, said: "You couldn't find a lot of human beings who could take what was thrown at him. His goal was to respond cerebrally rather than emotionally, and that's what he did. Gerry was coming to a real strong place about his sexual orientation and self-respect."[15] After six weeks of facing his constituents as the autumn of 1983 approached, Studds decided that he would run again, and announce in January.[16]

Studds vs. the "Mudslinger"

This historic decision made Studds the first openly gay man to run for Congress. He did so as the public was becoming aware of the AIDS crisis. Moreover, he was not just any gay person, but a legislator who had been censured during the run-up to an election year in which a popular president of the opposing party would be running for reelection. Studds might easily lose. It took a certain amount of courage to do it.

Throughout the late summer and fall, before Studds announced, rumors swirled about who might challenge him in the primary. The Massachusetts Democratic Party was divided in the early 1980s between its social conservatives and social liberals. This split, over issues like abortion, gun control, and affirmative action, had been sharpened by the Boston school busing battles of the 1970s, which accelerated the departure of urban Irish Catholics to the South Shore suburbs. The divide was exemplified by the 1978 and 1982 contests for governor, pitting Ed King from the conservative wing against Mike Dukakis for the liberals, King winning in 1978 and Dukakis in 1982.

Plymouth County sheriff Peter Flynn had organized King's campaign. On Bastille Day, Flynn watched the news coverage of Studds's speech while having a beer with friends at the Golden Dome Pub near the State House. He felt disgusted. "I'm running," he told his friends.[17]

Sheriff Flynn was a former Bridgewater State College football player, a big, burly, "tough on crime" guy who had won the county election in a landslide. He could be expected to use his wife and two teenage children to strike a contrast between his personal family values and Studds's presumed immorality. Flynn had served in the Massachusetts legislature for eight years and was well connected statewide. Like many local officials, he didn't have any interest in national affairs. He just hated Studds's guts, a feeling that had to be shared by some percentage of the electorate.[18]

In his memoir, Studds described Flynn as "a cartoonist's version of the worst possible scenario I could envision." He scoffed at Flynn's contention that he was not opposed to gay rights, and in the memoir charged him with hypocrisy, noting that he had opposed gay rights measures in the legislature. Yet Studds did observe that Flynn's circumspection regarding homosexuality in general was "also a back-handed indication of just how far we had come."[19] It was. Studds himself as a congressman in 1974 had refused to back the first anti-discrimination legislation. Flynn, whatever his private feelings might be, never argued that Studds should be defeated because he was gay.

When Flynn finally announced, he had to explain why he was running. Flynn thought there was too much traffic on Route 3, the Coast Guard should be better funded, the elderly should be better cared for, and the environment could be improved—sentiments as controversial as the wish that the Red Sox would win the World Series. Flynn saved the red meat for a rally that night in Plymouth. Studds "broke the trust of the people that gave him the right to represent them in Congress," Flynn thundered. "He went to Washington and he betrayed us." One headline blared, "Flynn: I'll Talk about Studds Affair."[20]

Flynn's problem was that Studds wouldn't talk about it. Campaign chairman Peter Fleischer just gave a "no comment" anytime he was asked about Flynn. Studds's position was made easier by a young third candidate, Christopher Trundy. Trundy generally agreed with Studds on policy, declared that Flynn was a "mudslinger," and presented himself as Studds without the baggage. Trundy also discussed another issue to which no one was then paying any attention: he thought that computers were collecting too much information on people and ought to be regulated.[21]

Flynn tried to take a higher road after his announcement. He charged that Studds was overly concerned about Central America at the expense of local issues. He called for tougher penalties for drug dealers and talked vaguely about transportation problems. Polls showed Flynn trailing significantly.[22]

So Flynn went back to homophobia, his only real issue. "When a man continually lies about his deserved censure for seducing a young boy and calls it homosexual rights . . . it is time to call him what he is: a liar. . . . Anytime when you take a youngster . . . and ply that youngster with alcohol, get him drunk and use that individual for your sexual pleasures, it certainly is to my way of thinking child molestation and child abuse," Flynn told an interviewer late in June.[23]

Page X to the Rescue

Unbeknownst to Flynn, or even to most of Studds's campaign staffers, that youngster, now twenty-seven, had felt so angry about being forced to testify against Studds on pain of being charged with perjury that he had on his own initiative volunteered to be Studds's driver. He had always liked and respected Studds. Because the driver assignment didn't involve making policy or going to meetings, Studds just assigned X to the job himself.[24]

This posed a dilemma for campaign staffers, who had to consider the implications of Studds's decision. "We had some hesitancy about [X]'s participation," Peter Fleischer recalled. "The plus side was, if his identity came out, it would show that Studds had not harmed anyone. The minus side was that it might call attention to the issue. On the campaign staff, there was a certain black humor about it."[25] X was never publicly identified; drivers never are.

Studds had hired a polling firm whose confidential report exuded confidence. Studds got very high job approval ratings from his constituents. The most important finding regarded the censure. Fully 83 percent agreed with the statement "There has been enough publicity about Congressman Studds' homosexuality and I'm tired of hearing about the matter." A district-wide *Patriot Ledger* poll conducted at the same time also showed Studds way ahead, but with two thirds of the voters still undecided.[26]

The New Bedford working class felt the same way. "Workers Still Loyal to Studds," the *New Bedford Standard-Times* found in forty interviews at factory gates. New Bedford, with nearly half its workers holding industrial or fishing jobs, was the most blue-collar city in the state by 15 percent. Every major union endorsed him. Most interviewees disapproved of Studds's behavior but said it wouldn't affect their vote. One reporter, searching the pier for a negative view of the congressman, was told to beat it before he found himself in the water.[27]

The climax of the primary campaign occurred at the first debate on August 28, 1984, three weeks before the election, at the United Fishermen's

Club hall in New Bedford. The congressional debate was preceded by the Democratic senatorial debate. In that race, four candidates were contending for the seat being vacated by Paul Tsongas, who was retiring after being diagnosed with cancer. When Studds arrived, driven by X, the hall was surrounded by crowds of campaign activists waving placards. He could see the familiar buses from fundamentalist churches; they had come only because of him. A vast throng of cameramen and reporters milled about. Police had to lead the candidate and X through the crowd.

To get to the stage, Studds and X had to pass through a long, narrow backstage corridor. Studds revealed what happened next in his memoir: "Without warning, and no one in front of me, I found Sheriff Peter Flynn coming straight at me. I was about to hold out my hand for a conventional greeting when I realized that this was not to be a normal encounter. He walked right up to me, arced his hand in a karate-like motion, and gave me a blow in the chest that came close to knocking me back off my feet, but was carefully modulated to simply stun me. He said through gritted teeth, 'I'm going to get you tonight.'" Studds kept his cool. X had been just a step beyond him, and acting as a bodyguard, blocked Flynn like a football offensive lineman and drove him against the wall. Studds observed that Flynn was "clearly taken aback" and gave way. X was a big guy himself, and Flynn didn't scare him. The irony was enormous. Flynn had just been beaten in physical battle by the "child" whose life, he had been suggesting to the public, had been ruined by Gerry Studds.[28]

The hall was packed by a thousand spectators and bathed in television lights. Flynn overplayed his hand the first time he opened his mouth. Asked by one of the reporters about the spiraling federal deficit created by Reagan's "supply side" economics, Flynn replied: "I think there's a question that's on everybody's mind, and I think that's the censure. I think we should get it on the table right now." The room exploded in a hail of boos and catcalls. Flynn had literally spoken out of turn, rudely ignoring the reporter's question. The audience response suggested that the voters would vote on the day's issues, not on Studds's behavior eleven years earlier.[29]

For the next hour, Trundy, Flynn, and Studds fielded a battery of questions on the fishing industry, the New Bedford economy, the environment, cuts in welfare spending, the increased military budget, and Central America. The final segment allowed candidates to interrogate one another. As the packed assembly held its breath, Flynn, jabbing his accusatory finger, pressed Studds to justify his behavior with the page.

"That's the easiest question I've ever been asked," Studds said. "It wasn't anything that I'm proud of. It was a damned stupid and inappropriate thing to do, and I never said it wasn't."

"The hall erupted," Studds remembered. "My supporters were cheering. And Flynn, who had time remaining to ask additional questions to me, was so flustered not to have elicited a defensive response that he ended up yielding the balance of his time. He turned away, shook his head, and said nothing else. That brief exchange made the television newscasts. In the view of many it was the effective end of Flynn's candidacy."[30]

The newspapers agreed. "Voters 'Censure' Flynn" and "Flynn Misses Mark in Debate," read the *Cape Cod Times* headlines; "Studds Dodges Shot from Flynn: Homosexual Censure Issue Fizzles in Forum" in the *Brockton Enterprise* was typical. "Flynn Shifts Focus of Attack," read the Brockton paper's headline after the next debate, in Scituate. Flynn's *raison d'être* had collapsed. As the election approached, among the Boston newspapers, Flynn was endorsed by the *Herald* and Studds won the *Globe*.[31]

Studds spent election eve with his family and X at his Pembroke campaign headquarters. By 9:30 the results were in: 59 percent for Studds, 37 percent for Flynn, and 4 percent for Trundy. X drove them to the North River House restaurant in Hanover, where hundreds of campaign supporters and television crews waited. The crowd cheered wildly as Studds made his way to the podium. "Many people were in or close to tears," Studds remembered. "I wondered briefly whether my composure would crack and the emotions of a lifetime, to say nothing of the campaign, came pouring forth." Studds collected himself, thanked all his supporters for their work, and rallied the troops for the general election in November. Studds had carried forty-two of the district's forty-five towns. From Hanover, Studds and X drove off to New Bedford, where they got a few hours of sleep at a motel, rose before dawn, and went off to a garment factory to shake hands as the morning shift came on. The New Bedford paper carried a front-page photo of the victory party. Studds was grinning from ear to ear.[32]

In the Senate race, Lieutenant Governor John Kerry won the Democratic nomination. The Republican race was sharply contested and supremely significant, as businessman Ray Shamie defeated Elliot Richardson, the attorney general who had stood up to Nixon and resigned in the infamous "Saturday night massacre" of 1973. Shamie overwhelmed Richardson by championing President Reagan's policies and burying his rival in a blizzard of TV ads. The Massachusetts Republicans, once the conscience of the nation

A jubilant Studds celebrating his 1984 primary victory—the first congressional campaign conducted by an openly gay man. *Photograph by John Goldie, courtesy Dean Hara.*

during the antebellum slavery crisis, had morphed into their opposite in the age of stretch limousines and ostentatious wealth—Gilded Age II.[33]

An Old Boyhood Chum

There had also been some drama in the Tenth District Republican congressional primary. A most unlikely candidate among three contestants had emerged. Lewis Crampton of Cohasset, boyhood friend of Gerry Studds, bested two more conservative candidates. Crampton was an Ivy Leaguer, a China specialist, an environmentalist, and an urban planner. He had worked as a community organizer for the Boston Model Cities program and was Massachusetts commissioner of community affairs under liberal Republican governor Francis Sargent. This was not the sheriff of Plymouth County.

There was more, however, that did not get listed on the résumé. Crampton had freaked out during the late 1960s. He had grown his hair long and moved to Roxbury to hang out with a commune that published an irreverent alternative newspaper, leading to his arrest for distributing obscene material. In all, this was, for the 1960s, a not uncommon detour on the road to life as a well-adjusted middle-class adult.[34]

"He was practically a member of our family when we were kids," Studds told a reporter. "The basic difference is that we were both Republicans and I grew out of it." Speaking to the same correspondent, Crampton downplayed his relationship with the Studds family. The person who was the most shocked was Gerry's mother, who had often cooked dinner for young Lew. "She was so hurt that Lew would run against Gerry," Studds staffer Mary-Lou Butler recalled.[35]

During the Republican primary, Crampton's opponents threw his radical past in his face. In a devastating article that equally lampooned Studds and Crampton, conservative columnist Howie Carr quoted one of Crampton's rivals, who dismissed him as "a hippie in a three-piece suit." Some potential Republican voters were probably going to stay home.[36]

Crampton's problem was not lost on Studds. When the *Patriot Ledger* asked Studds about Crampton's views, the quote that made the headline was "in far closer agreement with me than Reagan." Crampton was liberal on environmental issues, and he supported the nuclear freeze and the Equal Rights Amendment. Crampton called Studds a big spender, but Studds replied that it was Reagan who was busting the federal budget with a huge arms buildup and tax breaks for the rich. Studds also reminded readers worried about his effectiveness that he would regain his committee chairmanship in a Democratic House, whereas Crampton would be the delegation's most junior member, always a powerful argument for incumbents.[37]

The national Republican Party ignored Crampton. It produced neither money nor elected officials to campaign for him, and Crampton languished in the polls. By the end of September, Studds had raised $357,176 to his rival's $188,407. Studds was now getting big donations from the national gay community and even had one staffer focused on just that project. Republicans wanted to see a smear campaign against Studds before writing any checks. Crampton would not sink to Flynn's level during their debates, which were issue-oriented and produced no fireworks. Media attention focused instead on the Kerry-versus-Shamie Senate race.[38]

The final numbers told a strange story. Studds won with 143,466 votes, 56 percent of the total. In the Senate race, Kerry beat Shamie by a similar margin. But so did Reagan, who trounced Walter Mondale in the Tenth District with 59 percent of the vote nationally, on his way to sweeping forty-nine states.[39] The most obvious explanation for this outcome is that the economy had rebounded and voters were ratifying the status quo; the incumbents

(Kerry holding Tsongas's place for the Democrats) had won. The one sign of change was that Studds lost the South Shore. This was still a Republican district, if one went by the presidential vote. *Boston Globe* columnist Ian Menzies observed that "Studds is facing a new South Shore voter who has moved out from Boston, is of Irish Catholic extraction and is in more and more cases voting Republican."[40]

An unrecognized aspect of Studds's principled politics was his discussion of Central American peace issues. That question virtually never surfaced during the election unless Studds brought it up himself. He emphasized the issue in his responses to a League of Women Voters questionnaire. His consistent advocacy won him the support of Hollywood's peace activists, and the star of the popular television show *M*A*S*H,* Mike Farrell, came to the district to raise money for Studds. If not for the minority of congressmen like Studds, this important moral question would have stayed beneath the public's radar.[41]

Cognizant of the lack of public interest, Massachusetts peace activists placed a question calling for an end to military aid to the contras and the El Salvador government on the ballot in a nonbinding referendum designed to strengthen the hand of congressmen like Studds. In the Tenth, the question appeared in seventeen of the Cape and Islands' twenty-three towns. Of 100,515 voters, only 46,529 voted on the question, but they passed it overwhelmingly, by 28,916 to 17, 613.[42]

Most important, Studds's victory marked a historic milestone for gay rights. This went almost unnoticed in the swirl of national media coverage that focused on Reagan's landslide. That Studds could win the primary and a general election, not just as a candidate who was gay but as one who had been censured by his colleagues, suggested that in Massachusetts, even in its most Republican district, most people were tolerant of homosexuality. A final ironic note to Studds's victory was that Dan Crane, the Illinois congressman caught in Califano's investigation, lost his seat. Yet even in the national gay community, this milestone was passed with little notice. Gerry Studds had now joined Joseph Rainey and Jefferson Long, the first black congressmen, Jeannette Rankin, the first congresswoman, and Shirley Chisholm, the first African American congresswoman, in history.

13

Plague of Silence

FOR THE SEVENTH TIME, Gerry Studds took the oath of office. His mother, Bonnie, stood at his side. This time was special: he was being sworn in as the nation's first openly gay congressman, and one who had survived a scandal at that. "There was a little extra warmth in the greetings of [my] colleagues" he told a reporter. "Obviously, the last two years are very wonderful to have behind me." He was "out," had been reelected, and felt relieved.[1]

Ronald Reagan had won in a landslide. Republicans had lost two seats in the Senate but still held a 54–46 majority there. In the House, Republicans had gained fourteen seats, making the party division 253–182, but many of the southern Democrats were conservatives as well. The Republicans felt ebullient. Reagan had campaigned on the growing economy and the end of inflation. His slogan, "It's Morning Again in America," reflected his sunny disposition and buoyant optimism that "a rising tide lifts all boats." Reagan appealed to traditional values of hard work and inveighed against the moral hazard posed by granting welfare to the needy or succor to those who had caused their own problems by bad behavior. For most Americans, Reagan's message jibed with their lived experience.[2]

For those outside that majority, however, the times felt perilous. African Americans and Hispanics knew that Reagan's anti-welfare rhetoric and criminal justice policies were directed against them. Nor were their boats rising as blue-collar wages stagnated. But of all the outcasts in American life, none were more alarmed than gay men. For them, 1985 marked midnight in America, a stormy darkness of terrifying nightmares from which there would be no awakening.

Beginning in 1981, a strange new disease had appeared in the United States. The Centers for Disease Control in Atlanta reported 159 cases of it that year, leading to twenty-six deaths, mostly among gay men. By the following year, researchers had named it "acquired immunodeficiency syndrome" and noted that it also appeared among hemophiliacs and intravenous drug users. By the end of the year there had been 771 cases and 618 deaths. At the start of 1985, scientists identified the human immunodeficiency virus (HIV) as the cause of the disease and recorded 7,239 cases and 5,596 deaths.[3] Yet the president had not said a word about AIDS. Although some health professionals in the government bureaucracy identified it as the nation's number-one health problem, Reagan himself shrouded it in a cloak of silence.

History thus placed Gerry Studds in a remarkable position. He became the nation's first openly gay elected congressman at a time of crisis for the gay community. He had won election, however, while defending himself against charges of sexual immorality. His district did not include a major center of gay activism, and with the exception of tiny Provincetown, its demographic was overwhelmingly white, older, and socially conservative. His committee assignments—Merchant Marine and Fisheries, and Foreign Affairs—were unrelated to AIDS. The two subcommittees that addressed the emerging AIDS crisis in the House were Health and the Environment, chaired by Henry Waxman of Los Angeles, and Intergovernmental Relations, chaired by Ted Weiss of Manhattan. Studds had no position of power within the committee system from which to address the crisis. He was a congressman who was gay, not the gay congressman.

Studds began by deliberately adding a Washington staffer who was a member of Boston's gay community. Mary Breslauer, a lesbian, and Robert Nickerson, a gay man, worked in district offices, but their jobs focused on constituent services. For the Washington staff, Studds hired Tom McNaught, who had worked for five years in Boston mayor Kevin White's administration. His brother Brian had known Studds since 1979 and was a prominent leader of the Boston gay community. Tom McNaught, then thirty-five, had a ruddy, handsome face, upbeat manner, wide smile, hearty laugh, and Irish Catholic background. He had been a student at Marquette, a Catholic university in Milwaukee, at the time of the early gay liberation movement in the late 1960s and was more comfortable with his sexual orientation than Studds had been. McNaught was hired as a press aide but was also tasked with working on the AIDS crisis and other issues affecting the gay community.[4]

While many gay staffers worked on Capitol Hill, the first to "come out" was Tim Westmoreland. Westmoreland, a cherubic, mustachioed preacher's son from Boone, North Carolina, was a Duke graduate attending Yale Law School when he took a job in 1979 as counsel to the Health and the Environment Subcommittee chaired by Henry Waxman. His passion was helping poor people. Waxman's district included the influential West Hollywood gay community. He never asked Westmoreland about his sexual orientation, but when the AIDS epidemic emerged, Westmoreland, whose job included monitoring the Centers for Disease Control (CDC), told him. A stroke of luck had placed these two passionate advocates at the epicenter of the congressional response to the AIDS crisis.[5]

Tom McNaught met with Westmoreland and asked him to brief Studds, which he did. Westmoreland remembered, when the scandal broke, being "astonished that any member would mess around with any page," but felt mollified when he learned that the affair had been consensual. Westmoreland and Studds became friends and played bridge together. McNaught met with leaders of gay advocacy organizations in Washington that were lobbying for an appropriate response to the AIDS crisis. He met with Vic Basile of the Human Rights Campaign, Jeff Levi of the National Gay and Lesbian Task Force, and Steve Endean of the Gay Rights National Lobby to offer Studds's assistance. "Aha," Levi observed, "the mountain comes to Mohammed." Levi was accustomed to pleading for meetings with busy staffers, not to eager staffers seeking him out at his office. The gay leaders did not urge Studds to change his course dramatically. They understood that Studds was breaking down stereotypes simply by doing his job, and they agreed that it would be helpful for him to speak at fund-raisers when his schedule permitted. AIDS activists around the country were setting up counseling centers, testing facilities, and support services for people with AIDS, and they all needed money.[6]

Meanwhile, Studds and McNaught carefully followed the contentious debate in Washington over AIDS funding. The Reagan administration offered no leadership on combating the disease. Reagan's physician later told a writer that the president thought AIDS was like "measles and it would go away." Reagan appointed conservative hard-liners like William Bennett, Gary Bauer, and Patrick Buchanan to responsible positions. "These were not just homophobes," McNaught said. "That word implies merely 'fear of homosexuals.' They were haters." To these people, gay men were stereotypical limp-wristed, effeminate fairies whose weak character led them to choose a life of debauchery. The work of devising a budget for AIDS research and care fell to Office of Management and Budget (OMB) officials and Health and Human Services (HHS) Secretary Margaret Heckler, who had been appointed to the cabinet after losing her congressional race to Barney Frank. Reagan's inner circle distrusted her as being too liberal.[7]

Early in February 1985, OMB stunned AIDS activists by cutting funding for research and care from $96 million to $85.5 million. A mere $250,000 was earmarked for education and prevention, and was to be administered locally, not by a coordinated national education campaign. Later that month, Waxman and Weiss held joint hearings of their subcommittees. They were now armed with a new 158-page report by the Office of Technology Assessment (OTA) that highlighted the lack of presidential leadership despite HHS's agreement that AIDS was the nation's top health priority. Many thousands of people would die if the administration did not change course, the report implied. "The Reagan administration has pretended that AIDS is only a blip on the charts, a statistic they hope will go away," Waxman grimly announced at the start of the hearings. The committee entertained a parade of administration officials who lamely pointed to the modest scientific progress that had so far been made. Some, like CDC director James Mason privately acknowledged that, in the words of AIDS chronicler Randy Shilts, the funding was "woefully inadequate." Despite the dramatic implications of the OTA report, the hearings were barely covered in the media, appearing on page fourteen in the *New York Times* and not at all in the *Washington Post*.[8]

Studds did what he could. He used his "Weekly Report to the People" to warn of the dangers of inaction. In May, he summarized the findings of the First International Conference on AIDS, recently hosted by the CDC in Atlanta. There had been two thousand more cases in 1983, eleven thousand to date, and the figure was expected to reach forty thousand by the end of 1987. Massachusetts had confirmed only 242 cases so far, but that number too would rise. "Absent a vaccine, a cure or an effective treatment, our only weapon against AIDS is education," Studds wrote, pointing out that the disease could not be transmitted by casual contact. Yet Reagan and Heckler had shown "an appalling lack of leadership," he charged, forcing state and city governments to foot the bill. Studds had co-sponsored legislation to establish a $60 million revolving fund for emergency treatment, but that "paltry" sum was the best that could be hoped for in Congress, despite predictions that fifty thousand people might die by 1990. No one knew it at that early stage, but by 1990, 120,453 Americans would be dead of AIDS.[9]

Studds, McNaught, and South Shore staffer Bob Nickerson came up to Boston in the summer to meet AIDS activists and people with AIDS (PWAs) at the AIDS Action Committee in the Fenway district. The center, founded by Larry Kessler and Peter Lombardi, included a residence for PWAs, and Studds and his staff met with a number of residents. "Gerry, Bob, and I all had a glass of water there," McNaught remembered. "We knew the science said the disease was transmitted by the exchange of bodily fluids, and although we knew it was safe to drink, even we were terrified. I remember being concerned as we accepted our glass of water." But it mattered that the country's lone gay congressman would venture out of his district to encourage people on the front line.[10]

McNaught booked Studds to speak at a number of fund-raisers that summer. In Key West, he told a reporter that since coming out he was "more pleasant to be around—I was miserable before." In Detroit, where three hundred people attended, he said that if there were a secret ballot, a gay rights bill would pass two to one. Studds was becoming a new figure in a national movement.[11] He was increasingly in demand in Boston. Studds received a standing ovation at a September 1985 fund-raiser for the AIDS Action Committee at City Hall. Four hundred and fifty guests paid $50 each to attend. "You people are so nice that I'm not going to read a message from the president," Studds joked. Another sign of his emerging visibility in the gay community was his own fund-raising, which had netted $586,000 in 1984, much of it from wealthy gay people outside the district.[12]

Studds criticized the president in a fall 1985 newsletter article titled "AIDS: We Deserve Better." Twenty new cases of the fatal disease were being reported daily, for a total of thirteen thousand since 1979. Asked about the crisis at a recent news conference, the president claimed that the government had allocated nearly half a billion dollars for research. "I regret to tell you that this is not the case," Studds wrote, and showed that the $389 million that had been spent had been appropriated by Congress against the administration's wishes, and fell far short of what scientists were demanding.[13]

Not everyone liked what Studds had to say. *Boston Globe* columnist David Farrell had been a consistent critic of Studds. Farrell's views matched those of the growing number of people in the Tenth District who had supported Peter Flynn—socially conservative Catholics who believed that homosexuality was a sin—and it was through that prism that they viewed the AIDS crisis. Studds had still not properly apologized to his constituents for the page incident, Farrell insisted, and was in no position to criticize the president. There was no reason why PWAs should get special attention. "Abstinence is the best preventive," Farrell advised. To some, Studds would always wear a scarlet letter.[14]

A few weeks later, a *Globe* reporter assessed Studds's stature in Congress. During the 1984 election, Flynn had charged that no member would co-sponsor Studds's legislation for fear of being associated with a child molester. "No congressman has ever survived disgrace so immaculately, although a number of House members, mostly southerners, are said to be unwilling now to cosponsor legislation authored by Studds," the reporter concluded. Two of his Massachusetts colleagues, Ed Boland and Chester Atkins, told the reporter that Studds was highly regarded for his work on maritime issues, and another, Joe Moakley, said that he seemed more "easy-going" since coming out. An unidentified friend, however, detected a "new bitterness in his attitude toward Congress." All these observations were probably accurate.[15]

"If there are any members who have difficulty dealing with me it is not directly, subtly or otherwise, apparent to me," Studds told another reporter. "On the contrary, I would say there is more ease." In support of this conclusion, the article quoted Studds's colleagues Stewart B. McKinney, a Connecticut Republican, and Nick Mavroules, a Gloucester Democrat, attesting to his continued effectiveness. Although McKinney never admitted that he was gay, like several others in Congress, he died of AIDS after retiring. Here was the great irony and tragedy. As more and more gay men died of this disease, the hostility of their colleagues and friends toward homosexuality waned. The AIDS-related death that October of actor Rock Hudson, a friend of the president and first lady, caused millions to realize that many people, including perhaps some they knew, were in the closet. AIDS activists felt mixed emotions as Hudson's death drew widespread media coverage when the deaths of other Americans had received no attention.[16]

Studds enjoyed two more personally validating moments during the following year. In March, he gave the keynote speech at the Northeast Gay Student Union, convened at Brown University. Five hundred students gave him a standing ovation. "Every one of us has been broken in one way or another," Studds said. "Now, let's be strong."[17] On Memorial Day, 1986, Studds joined Massachusetts governor Michael Dukakis, Boston mayor Ray Flynn, and four thousand others at the AIDS Action Committee's first annual six-mile walkathon. Thus far the disease had afflicted 515 Massachusetts residents, half of whom had died, executive director Larry Kessler told the crowd. The march raised $350,000. The presence of Dukakis and Flynn indicated that public opinion was shifting as more and more people became ill and died.[18]

Nevertheless, the Reagan administration stoked people's irrational fears. In June, the Justice Department ruled that civil rights legislation did not protect people with AIDS from being fired by their employers. Studds spoke out on the House floor and told his constituents that the ruling was unjust because AIDS was not spread by casual contact. "The Attorney General has given his blessing to a policy not based on facts, but on fear. And fear—far more than AIDS—is a contagious disease." Later that year he told a reporter that he was reading Albert Camus's *The Plague* in the original French. Studds was an unusual congressman.[19]

"This Is an Epidemic": Studds Mails the Koop Report

Rock Hudson's death caused a change in the administration's behavior. In February 1986, Reagan assigned Surgeon General C. Everett Koop to write a report on AIDS. To the surprise of many, Koop released a blunt, plainspoken document in which he predicted that at the current rate of spread, 179,000 would die of AIDS by the end of 1991. He urged abstinence, monogamy, education, and the use of condoms as the remedy. The latter two approaches ruffled the feathers of administration conservatives. Reagan's homophobic trio of advisers, Bennett, Bauer, and Buchanan, like millions of other Americans, insisted that homosexuality was a sinful lifestyle choice that undermined "family values." They argued that the government should not advocate the use of condoms: sex was for procreation only, not pleasure. Nor should the government get into the business of sex education; that was for churches and families. The idea that the government should promote a report that explicitly discussed sex was repugnant to them.[20]

Studds was enraged by this attitude, and he knew that it ran deep in Reagan's outlook. He didn't care if Ron and Nancy had gay friends in Hollywood. "Reagan should have been tried for negligent homicide," Studds's aide Tom McNaught declared years later. "He let 25,000 people die before he uttered a word about [AIDS]. He surrounded himself with haters. The more Gerry realized this, the angrier he got."[21]

After the 1986 release of Koop's report on the AIDS epidemic, the Reagan administration did nothing to publicize it. Meanwhile, people continued to become infected. By the end of the year, 28,712 cases had been reported, and 24,559 people had died. In San Francisco, AIDS activists began stitching together a massive quilt, each of whose squares commemorated the life of a deceased person.[22]

Reagan finally adopted guidelines for AIDS education and prevention on February 11, 1987. These differed from Koop's guidelines, which included sex education for children and the use of condoms. William Bennett, the secretary of education, insisted that sex education be locally, not nationally, mandated, and that "any health information developed by the Federal Government . . . should encourage responsible sexual behavior . . . placing sexuality within the context of marriage." Bennett, who was neither a medical doctor nor a public health advocate, thus trumped Koop, who was.[23] "Family values" proponents in Congress such as Senator Jesse Helms, a former segregationist, and Representative William Dannemeyer routinely attached anti-gay riders to appropriations bills, mandating that nothing be said to "promote" homosexuality. AIDS activists dubbed this tactic "No promo homo."[24]

Studds took matters into his own hands. In May his staff laboriously mailed the Koop report to all 268,000 homes in the district. Studds told Koop, "I can say things that you can't and I would like to embarrass the administration into carrying out their public health policy." He urged every congressman to follow suit and reported that three European governments had already taken similar steps. Such a mass mailing was highly unusual, "but this is an epidemic," Studds insisted. Unlike most of his colleagues, Studds personally felt the urgent need to take action.[25]

Meanwhile, the Reagan administration continued to do nothing. "One reporter asked me about the possibility that the report will be picked up and read by some children," Studds told another journalist. "I said that's the whole point."[26] When Public Health Service director Otis Bowen declared that "the American response to AIDS has been inspiring," Studds told the media that "if anyone other than Dr. Bowen has been inspired by the performance of this Administration on AIDS, he has yet to come forward," and asked that the General Accounting Office investigate why there was still no mailing. He contrasted the federal government's stalling with the progress being made in Massachusetts, where sex education workshops had been held across the state. Washington's inaction "now verges on criminal negligence," Studds fumed.[27]

After a few months, some of his colleagues followed suit. "By sending out the mailing, Studds created a snowball that became an avalanche," Tim Westmoreland remembered. Lowell Weicker, a Connecticut Republican, and Tom Harkin, an Iowa Democrat, later pushed through a measure allocating $20 million toward a national mailing.[28]

"With reference to your recent mailing and your pious pronouncement concerning the spread of AIDS, you would be much more effective were you to publicly renounce your homosexual life style," one constituent informed Studds. But writers in the *Boston Globe, Quincy Patriot-Ledger, New Bedford Standard-Times,* and *Cape Cod Times* praised the mailing, as did most of

Studds's respondents. One woman from Plymouth told Studds her story about a friend dying of AIDS, whom she had nursed. "The haunting part is that on his last Thanksgiving on Earth, his aunts, uncle and brother gathered together but excluded him from their table. That's their legacy because of fear and ignorance."[29] The AIDS epidemic touched millions of people, reinforcing prejudice for some, but causing many others to reconsider the notion that homosexuality was a "lifestyle."

The Second Openly Gay Congressman

Just after Studds mailed the Koop report, Congressman Barney Frank came out. His Fourth District bordered the Tenth at their southern extremities in Bristol County. Each man had known of the other's sexual orientation at least from the time when Frank first arrived in Washington in 1981 after winning the seat formerly held by Father Robert Drinan. He had worked in Mayor Kevin White's administration after graduating from Harvard, and served for eight years in the state legislature during the 1970s. Not seeing a way forward in politics as a gay man, Frank took a degree at Harvard Law, expecting to go into private practice. He changed his mind when Drinan resigned. "It was no big deal," Frank recalled about meeting Studds as a fellow congressman. "We had heard reports about each other."[30]

Besides sharing generally the same liberal politics, they both deployed devastating humor, although Frank was more quotable. Other than that, they formed a study in contrasts. Frank came from gritty Bayonne, New Jersey, and, despite his Harvard pedigree, he never lost his urban Jewish style, developed in plebeian public schools. Frank smoked cigars and once declared about himself, in a celebrated understatement, "Neatness isn't everything." If Studds challenged people's stereotypes about how a gay man behaved, Frank exploded them. There was nothing of the aesthete about him. Studds dressed in handsomely tailored suits, his necktie fastened with a scrimshaw pin. He spoke in a beautiful baritone voice with perfect diction that suggested his Cohasset roots and Groton education. Frank spoke in a rushing, slurred style that, many years later, he compared to that of Boston's mayor Tom Menino, whose detractors called him "Mumbles."

"Gerry was very self-contained," Frank later accurately observed. Frank was irrepressible, combative in style, and he made good copy. He considered Studds "an odd political figure. Gerry ran for office out of a sense of duty, because of the war in Vietnam, and he forced himself to do something that was unnatural for him, that he didn't enjoy very much." The

Massachusetts House delegation had a street-smart Irish Catholic flavor to it that might have made two gay men, neither Irish nor Catholic, seem out of place among colleagues named Moakley, O'Neill, Shannon, and Donnelly. Studds sometimes did seem like a fish out of water. McNaught, trying to be helpful, once told Studds, "People think you are arrogant and aloof." Studds comically drew himself up to his full height and, looking down at the shorter McNaught, replied in a deadpan patrician manner, "I am not *aloof*." The implication was that he granted "arrogant."[31]

Frank fit in better. Bayonne was culturally a lot closer to Joe Moakley's South Boston than it was to Cohasset. Moreover, Frank loved politics, from the crafting of policy to the horse-trading that translated the policy into action—and colleagues like Tip O'Neill and Joe Moakley appreciated this about him. Studds felt at home in the more formal New England town meetings at which he greeted his constituents from behind a podium. "I'd rather walk barefoot over hot coals," Frank joked years later.[32]

Frank had expected to come out earlier, but Studds's 1983 scandal delayed his plans. In 1986 former Maryland Republican congressman Bob Bauman published a regretful tell-all about his life as a closeted gay man. Bauman mentioned that Frank attended Gay Pride parades wearing a tank top, which in effect "outed" him.[33] Frank wasn't hiding, but he never saw a reason to call public attention to a private fact. Two other events conditioned Frank's decision. The media had recently broken a story about presidential candidate Gary Hart's marital infidelity, and it drove the front-runner out of the race. And former Connecticut Republican congressman Stewart McKinney had died of AIDS. The private was becoming public as journalistic norms shifted. Frank discussed the matter with Studds, and then he told O'Neill what he was planning to do. "Tip was emotionally supportive," Frank recalled, "but sad for me. All my straight liberal friends tried to dissuade me, because I'd be less useful in our common cause, but gay people were happy."[34]

O'Neill, out of touch with contemporary culture, later told a colleague that "Barney is going to come out of the room," and the episode presented further comic aspects. By chance, there was a Massachusetts delegation meeting around that time, and before Frank and Studds arrived, Worcester representative Joe Early was grousing about the fact that Massachusetts now had the nation's only two gay congressmen. Joe Moakley from South Boston planted a kiss on Early's cheek and said, "Sure it's only two?"[35]

Studds was sympathetic to Frank and reminded reporters why gay people in public life, especially elected officials, stayed in the closet—"sheer terror" at the thought of reprisal at the polls, Studds said—and to lighten the mood

regarding his censure paraphrased Abraham Lincoln: "As a general proposition for the person being tarred, feathered and run out of town, if not
for the honor, I'd rather have walked." But as Boston AIDS activist Larry
Kessler pointed out to Frank, if you don't come out, you look like you are
ashamed.

AIDS and the 1987 March on Washington

Just after Frank came out, the two congressmen spoke at the AIDS Action
Committee's second annual walkathon. "It was ninety degrees at nine
o'clock in the morning," event organizer Larry Kessler remembered. Frank
got a two-minute standing ovation from the thousands gathered on Boston
Common. Studds again criticized the president, whose silence on AIDS was
deafening. "Just say something!" Studds implored Reagan. Later, the crowd
set off for a ten-kilometer walk through the Back Bay neighborhood, raising
hundreds of thousands of dollars by their efforts.[36]

In mid-October 1987, Studds joined the March on Washington for Gay
and Lesbian Rights. Gay activists were furious at the *Bowers v. Hardwick*
Supreme Court decision of the previous year. The case first came to court
when the police, arriving on an unrelated matter, arrested a man in Georgia
for sodomy in the privacy of his own home. Michael Hardwick appealed
his conviction, and the Supreme Court upheld the state law. Careful legal
scholars noted that this was a 5–4 decision, and observed some ambiguity in
the ruling. Activists used it as an incentive to build the march.[37]

Unlike at the 1979 demonstration, which the closeted congressman had
jogged past incognito, this time Studds accompanied a contingent of constituents from his district. March organizers claimed that 600,000 participated in the largest gathering to date of gay people and their supporters.
The march had a twofold aim: to get a civil rights bill passed, and to respond
energetically to the AIDS crisis. Same-sex partnerships were still illegal, gays
were banned from the military, and they enjoyed no protective legislation
against arbitrary discrimination. Studds told his constituents, "I can personally attest to the powerful impact of such gatherings—particularly on
those who participate in them."[38] One of the great distinguishing differences
between gay rights demonstrations and those of all other movements was
that gay people had previously been invisible, even to one another. Now
they could see their numbers and potential power.

Studds and Frank did not address the rally, but they were introduced, and
Studds, in an uncharacteristic gesture, held his arm up in a clenched-fist

salute. Presidential candidate Jesse Jackson spoke, as did Dan Bradley, the former director of the Legal Services Corporation, now a man living with AIDS; National Organization for Women president Eleanor Smeal; and Virginia Apuzzo, former executive director of the National Gay and Lesbian Task Force. Lesbian folksingers performed, and movie stars waved to the crowds.[39]

Judy Van Handle, a columnist for *Bay Windows,* the Boston gay and lesbian community newspaper, observed Studds at the demonstration. "Some scenes I'll never forget," she wrote, included "watching a beaming Gerry Studds wave to the participants. You couldn't help think back to 1979, when Brian McNaught met Studds and wrote later of Studds' absolute terror of coming out."[40] A new, more self-confident and determined gay body politic was gathering.

Finally, in April of the following year, the administration mailed out a pamphlet called "Understanding AIDS." Studds, Koop, and the dean of the Harvard School of Public Health previewed and approved the document. "It's far better than I expected," Studds told a reporter. The pamphlet went out to 107 million households at a cost of $17.4 million. Studds's pioneering effort had at last borne fruit on a national level.[41]

Studds also collaborated on a private education venture, a book called *You Can Do Something about AIDS,* a compendium of advice from celebrities, doctors, patients, and others. The project was initiated by Sasha Alyson, a publisher whom Studds was then dating. Studds solicited literary and financial contributions for the book, and a million copies were printed over several editions. Studds called the Book of the Month Club, where a leading executive had died of AIDS, and the club sent the book to all its members.[42]

In May, Dr. Anthony Fauci, the country's most prominent AIDS researcher, testified before a congressional committee that AIDS treatment drugs had been delayed by over a year because of short-staffing. He had sought 127 positions to facilitate the release of new drugs and gotten eleven. A black market therefore had developed for pentamidine, the aerosol treatment for the pneumocystis pneumonia that killed most patients. Meanwhile, the death toll was spiking. "What we have now learned is an outrage beyond my power to articulate," Studds reported. "This administration has not only failed to launch an all-out effort against AIDS, it has gone out of its way to conceal this fact from the Congress and the American people." The struggle to get the Food and Drug Administration to expedite the release of new drug treatments inspired a direct-action group called ACT UP to demonstrate on Wall Street, at the FDA headquarters, and at the White House. The first antiretroviral drug, AZT (azidothymidine), had finally been made available in 1987, but its cost at the time made it the most expensive drug in history.[43]

President Reagan ignored the issue to the end. What little he did, he did reluctantly and under pressure. When the president's own commission on AIDS, whose original appointees did not include a gay man until Nancy Reagan insisted on it, recommended an anti-discrimination law to protect AIDS patients from arbitrary dismissal, the president referred the idea to the Justice Department, which had just fired one such employee. Disgusted, Studds wrote: "The President has now lost his last opportunity to offer any semblance of leadership. . . . His silence grows ever more deafening."[44]

During Reagan's last months in office, the House passed a comprehensive AIDS legislation measure. The bill directed the administration to move forward on treatment and vaccine protocols and funded 780 new jobs at the National Institutes of Health. It encouraged voluntary AIDS testing, but did not sanction the mandatory testing that conservatives hoped would lead to quarantine of the afflicted. Studds was disappointed that conservatives deleted an anti-discrimination measure from the bill; the floor debate, he protested, was characterized by "demagogic rhetoric" from its opponents.[45] Nevertheless, Reagan signed it into law. "Reagan's principal legacy in dealing with AIDS," concluded a respected chronicler of his administration, "was one of missed opportunity."[46]

14

Studds versus the Contras

IN ONE OF THE GRAND IRONIES of Studds's career, the House was coming around to his position on Nicaragua just as it was moving toward disciplining him. Ed Boland of Springfield, Massachusetts, chairman of the House Intelligence Committee, had secured a law known as the Boland Amendment that precluded efforts by any U.S. agency to help the contras overthrow the leftist Nicaraguan government—the Sandinistas. To get around this nuisance, Reagan argued that the CIA was only trying to interdict arms shipments from Nicaragua to El Salvador, not to overthrow the Sandinistas. In early 1983, that transparent falsehood began to unravel. The CIA pumped enough money into the operation so that the contra army based in neighboring Honduras swelled to ten thousand men, while Director William Casey refused to say how large it might become. In addition, the CIA funneled money to rebels based in Costa Rica and on the Atlantic Coast, far from El Salvador. Intelligence Committee members became convinced that the Boland Amendment was being flouted.[1]

In April 1983, as he was girding for the release of the Califano report, Studds fought against Reagan's request for an additional $86.5 million for El Salvador's military, arguing that the money would do more harm than good, and he won a partial victory in his subcommittee. He inveighed against U.S. aid to the military regime in Guatemala, then in the midst of a genocidal campaign against its indigenous Maya population in the northwestern provinces. "I spoke at greatest length against U.S. support for covert military action against the government of Nicaragua," Studds reported to his constituents. He insisted that the contra operation was illegal under the charter of the Organization of American States, that it would "demolish"

U.S. credibility in the court of world opinion, and that it was unnecessary and doomed to fail. Later, Studds drafted a letter to Boland, signed by sixty-five colleagues, urging him to further tighten the language of the Boland Amendment, which he did.[2]

Opinion polls showed opposition to Reagan's policy running at 60 to 80 percent. To persuade Congress, Reagan addressed a rare joint session and mixed his familiar Cold War framing of the issue with appeals to patriotism, inflation of the "threat" to the mainland United States, and misrepresentations of the contras—a pastiche of half-truths and lies. "It reminds me of one of the final scenes of the movie *The Wizard of Oz*," Studds wrote his constituents, "in which Dorothy has discovered at long last that the Wizard is not the source of all power and wisdom, but is in fact quite ordinary, barely equal in knowledge and experience to herself."[3]

Reagan's pitch didn't work. The full Foreign Affairs Committee agreed to continue funding the El Salvador regime in May, but by June had voted to terminate money for covert aid to the contras while allowing overt aid only for arms interdiction. When Foreign Affairs met in June, Studds reprised the whole miserable history of U.S. attempts to overthrow governments in Latin America and pointed to the brutal regimes in Guatemala and Chile as the result.[4]

Ten days before appearing secretly in front of the Ethics Committee, Studds, as a prominent leader of the congressional opposition, published a *New York Times* op-ed, titled "Bipartisan Consensus: A Mirage." Responding to pundits who had hailed congressional compromises on El Salvador and flight-testing of the MX missile, Studds pointed out that the public's support for Reagan personally did not extend to his Central America policies, and he urged Democrats to drop the bipartisan façade they had adopted out of fear of Reagan's popularity. "United States democracy stands to profit far more from a blunt, forthright debate between its two major political parties over the issue of Central America and arms control than it does from timid formulations or false consensus," he concluded.[5]

On the day before the vote to censure Studds, the House convened a rare closed session to discuss a CIA report on Nicaragua. The report confirmed that the arms interdiction effort was useless and that the contras were just attacking civilian targets. Yet the Pentagon had announced new U.S. military maneuvers scheduled for Honduras, Operation Big Pine II, in a thinly disguised effort to keep the Sandinistas pouring money into defense rather than development.[6]

Afterward the House voted, 228–195, to tighten the Boland language.

Studds reminded his constituents that Reagan was waging a proxy war against a government with which the United States was at peace. Studds found the vote "extremely encouraging. I was once in a small minority," he concluded, "but not anymore."[7] An odd observation for a man who had just been censured by his colleagues, but it was true.

A week later, Reagan's new assistant secretary of state for Western Hemisphere Affairs, Langhorne Motley, testified before the Western Hemisphere Subcommittee. Undaunted by his recent censure, Studds lit into Motley, telling him that Reagan should stop the Big Pine maneuvers, end the covert war against Nicaragua, and talk with Central American leftists. He mocked Reagan's recent warnings that a vast migration of Central Americans would descend upon U.S. borders should the contras not get arms. This was already taking place, Studds asserted, with half a million Salvadorans but very few Nicaraguans now in the country as a direct result of Reagan's policies.[8]

Reagan tried again on a contra aid package and failed by a 243–171 margin. "I prepared perhaps the strongest statement I have yet made with respect to the course of the Reagan Administration policy toward Central America," Studds reported. He pointed out that Reagan's policies mirrored those of the USSR in Poland and Afghanistan, which the Soviets justified in the same language Reagan used. "The covert military operation against Nicaragua," he declared, "constitutes one of the most cynical, brutal and reckless enterprises ever conducted in the name of the American people."[9]

Then a horrifying series of events, having nothing to do with Central America, breathed new life into the contra program. On October 23, a suicide bomber blew up the U.S. Marine barracks in Lebanon, killing 243 marines. Two days later Reagan invaded the Caribbean island of Grenada, whose leftist government had been overthrown by a rival faction. Reagan made a dramatic speech claiming that American students at Grenada's medical school were at risk, and the invasion was a rescue mission. Studds watched the televised speech on the House floor with his Maryland colleague Mike Barnes. "What?" Studds gasped in mock horror. "We're invading Spain?" Reagan had mispronounced the English-speaking nation's name, pronouncing it with a short "a," as the Spanish city's name is pronounced. "I'm going to introduce a resolution saying we shouldn't be allowed to invade a country whose name the president can't pronounce." Barnes and Studds shared a similar sense of humor.[10]

The Grenada invasion deflected attention from the tragedy in Lebanon. Studds condemned it vigorously, calling the invasion "bizarre and deeply disturbing." Noting the lack of consultation with Congress and the press blackout, Studds pointed out the obvious. The invasion violated the Organization of American States treaty and had been denounced by most Latin American governments, none of which, especially Cuba, was a friend to the new Grenadian regime. Grenada did not pose a security risk to the United States, nor had there been any threat to the U.S. students. "The foreign policy of the Reagan administration has become a shambles," Studds concluded.[11] Predictably, the invasion of Grenada was wildly popular with the public, which bought the rescue narrative. The boost in Reagan's popularity spooked enough congressmen to keep the contra aid package on life support. The contras would live to fight another day.

The Nicaragua Problem

Nicaragua still posed a difficult problem for the administration. The Sandinista government was recognized by all countries. Even authoritarian Latin American regimes disapproved of the Yankee "big stick." Nicaragua's government included no communists but several Catholics. The government was less than democratic, but it did not deploy death squads or practice torture. Compared to the other Central American regimes except Costa Rica's, the Sandinistas were more democratic, transparent, and progressive. So Secretary of State Alexander Haig and his successor, George Shultz, routinely misrepresented the Sandinistas, calling them "Marxist-Leninists" while ignoring the social progress they had made in land reform, education, and public health.

The minority Senate Democrats, led by Robert Byrd, reached a compromise with Reagan's goals, making a conference with the House necessary. Three House subcommittees—Appropriations, Intelligence, and Foreign Affairs—all disapproved of funding the contras. That did not prevent CIA director Casey, emboldened by the Grenada success, from secretly organizing the mining of Nicaragua's harbors, an act of war. When several foreign ships were damaged, including a Soviet naval vessel, an international hue and cry caused House liberals to check the president's course. In October 1984, the Intelligence Committee again reported, and the House passed, a measure closing all existing loopholes. The only course open to the president now was to win majority votes in both houses to appropriate money transparently.[12]

Reagan's 1984 landslide reelection opened that possibility. Administration spokesmen came to Capitol Hill seeking $14 million in nonlethal aid. This paltry sum could not shift the balance of power, but if the request was adopted, it would put the camel's nose inside the tent. In January, Studds confronted Motley again when he came before the Western Hemisphere Subcommittee seeking the money. "Whether you like it or not, CIA support for the rebels is dead," Studds told him.[13]

Secretary of State Shultz, who had replaced the more confrontational Haig, came calling in February 1985, just after the president had described the contras as "freedom fighters" in a radio address. In contrast to his mercurial predecessor, Shultz bore himself with an appearance of probity. It irritated Studds that an educated man like Shultz could shill for the simpleminded "good guys vs. bad guys" nostrums that the president spouted. Regarding Reagan's speech, Studds complained to Shultz: "I thought for a moment that Lewis Carroll had been brought back to life and hired as a speechwriter at the White House. Can't we do better than this?" In fact, the speechwriter was Patrick Buchanan, a far-right conservative. Buchanan typified the second-term personnel shifts that had removed the moderate trio of James Baker, Michael Deaver, and Ed Meese from Reagan's inner council. Shultz argued that the United States had a "moral duty" to oppose the imposition of a "Communist totalitarian regime" in Nicaragua. Studds derided the contras as "a mixed group of mercenaries and thugs and democrats seeking to destroy a wretched regime in a poor country. . . . It isn't a fight for freedom."[14] Studds held a nuanced view of both sides in Nicaragua and steadfastly denied the prerogative of the United States to impose its preferred outcome.

The Senate approved Reagan's request for $14 million, and the issue came before the House in April. In committee hearings prior to the vote, Studds argued that "the question for Congress is whether it ought to be the policy of our government to seek the violent overthrow of Nicaragua's government, or whether wiser alternatives exist." He and his colleagues put specific questions to former CIA director Admiral Stansfield Turner about the mining of Nicaragua's harbors and a widely publicized "murder manual" written by a CIA training operative for the contras. Turner was disgusted by both.[15]

The floor debate was polarized and nasty. It lasted two days. Reagan, riding his recent electoral triumph, lobbied individual House members. The Democrats rallied behind the proposal of Mike Barnes and Lee Hamilton (Boland's successor as Intelligence chairman), a moderate substitute that accepted $10 million in humanitarian aid, but distributed it through the International Red Cross so that the money would be secure, and $4 million to further the "Contadora" peace process, named for the resort at which its Latin American crafters first met. The Republican plan, sponsored by House

Minority Leader Bob Michel, called for distributing the $14 million through the Agency for International Development. This narrow difference masked the deeper implications of the vote, and the passions around it were demonstrated by the hawkish Newt Gingrich, who vilified his opponents and brandished an unloaded automatic weapon on the House floor as a prop. Ultimately, neither bill passed, as liberal Democrats joined Republicans to defeat their own bill on a final vote because they did not want anything going to a conference committee with the Republican-controlled Senate.[16]

Studds spoke against the Republican bill on the floor. He urged his colleagues not to take sides in Nicaraguan politics, and to reject the idea that the United States should intervene militarily in another country's civil war. Studds ridiculed the notion that the Sandinistas posed a military threat to the United States, or that the contras were fighting to interdict arms being sent to El Salvador. And while he refrained from praising the Sandinistas' domestic policies, he did point out that "Nicaragua has shown, through its participation in Contadora, that it does care about its reputation within Latin America."[17]

In his newsletter Studds spelled out the problems with the Sandinista government as he saw them: there had been a suspension of habeas corpus; the press was censored; the electoral laws favored the party in power; and the military, by its denomination as "Sandinista," was becoming the armed wing of one party, not the nation's defense against foreign attack. Studds argued that these repressive measures were encouraged by American threats against Nicaragua, but he did not agree that the Sandinista response was justified.[18]

After the vote, Studds joked to a reporter, "We broke the law of averages—we won one." The vote against the Michel bill had been a squeaker, however, 215–213, with many moderate Democrats crossing party lines. President Reagan vowed to keep the pressure on and come back with more requests again and again.[19]

To exert economic pressure on Nicaragua, Reagan persuaded Mexico to sell oil to Nicaragua at market price, not at discount rates. This forced the country's leader, Daniel Ortega, to seek help from the Soviet Union. Republicans howled that this proved Ortega had secretly been a communist the whole time. Yielding to this pressure, a group of over two dozen moderate Democrats, led by Dave McCurdy of Oklahoma, introduced their own alternative, a $27 million nonlethal aid measure, in exchange for a promise from Reagan not to seek the overthrow of the Sandinistas.[20]

Studds spoke with controlled fury during the June 12 floor debate. Putting aside his prepared remarks, he addressed the contra supporters directly.

"Some members are offended that Ortega went to Moscow," he said. "But tomorrow the Prime Minister of India is here, and he just went to Moscow and got a whole lot more money, and nobody cares." He pointed out that the contras had support neither inside Nicaragua nor among the other Latin American governments. "In 1927, [the humorist] Will Rogers questioned what we were doing in Nicaragua, and he'd be asking the same question today." Studds was probably one of the few members who understood Nicaragua's history. He denounced the McCurdy proposal as "a horrendously stupid policy which will not work." Reagan's contra war proposals, which remained unpopular with the public, were nonetheless driving a wedge between southern Democrats and the rest of the party. Four votes were taken on competing measures, and in the end, McCurdy won, 248–184. Related measures allowed the CIA to share intelligence with the contras. The camel's nose was now inside the tent.[21]

Reagan's problems were far from over. Later in 1985 and early in 1986, the Sandinistas decided that the Americans were not going to invade after all, so they pulled their best troops off the Pacific coast and moved them to the Honduran border, where they began dealing the contras defeats. Much of the "humanitarian" aid money to the contras unaccountably disappeared, while undeniable reports surfaced showing that the contras, not the Sandinistas, as Reagan had claimed, were running cocaine from Colombia into the United States. Late in February 1986, the administration came back to Congress, seeking an additional $100 million for the contras. On the House floor Studds reminded his colleagues that the four Contadora nations opposed contra aid. "The administration," Studds scoffed, "says we should disregard what Latin American leaders publicly say, and heed instead what we are told they privately believe." He ended on an eloquent note: "In the name of law, history, justice, effectiveness, humanity and common sense, let us vote down this proposal today, and begin tomorrow the task we should have started years ago—of helping Nicaragua become not necessarily what we want it to be . . . but instead what the people of Nicaragua themselves determine what it should be." This time the Democrats, with Tip O'Neill leading the way, rallied and turned down the request.[22]

On April 10, Studds introduced a deliberately provocative declaration of war against Nicaragua. He presented it during Special Orders, a period when representatives bloviate before television cameras to an empty chamber. Studds read his speech with the quiet dignity appropriate for a former history teacher. He began by summarizing Reagan's position: that without sufficient aid to the contras, all Central America would go communist, and soon after the barbarian hordes would move north to invade the United States. Yet, faced with this imminent catastrophe, the president was conducting a secret war without naming it. If the stakes were as high as the president suggested, said Studds, Congress should vote on a declaration of war. He concluded by referring to the 1964 Gulf of Tonkin Resolution legitimizing the undeclared war in Vietnam, which had been opposed by only two senators.[23]

Studds was followed by a fellow history professor, Newt Gingrich, who had been his most vocal accuser in 1983. Gingrich conceded Studds's seriousness as a principled "McGovernite" but argued that liberals did not grasp the full import of the communist threat emanating from the Kremlin. In short, the apocalypse was at hand, and justice demanded that the Americans do battle for their "freedom fighter" descendants, the contras. The grand irony of this April 1986 speech is that it came six months after Reagan's first summit meeting with the new Soviet premier, Mikhail Gorbachev, in Geneva. "I had to admit . . . that there was something likable about Gorbachev," Reagan later said. "There was warmth in his face and style." In fact, the Soviets were not interested in Latin America, and Gorbachev would go on to preside over the removal of Soviet troops from Afghanistan, a series of arms control agreements, and the collapse of the Soviet empire. Studds proved to be the better student of history.[24]

Reagan had lost the last vote for the $100 million by 222–210, so he needed to change just seven votes this time. Unfortunately for the president, the General Accounting Office had monitored the $27 million McCurdy appropriation and found that most of it had already disappeared into accounts in the Cayman Islands. George Shultz dismissed the GAO report as misleading, and Republican congressmen accused the Democrats of aiding the enemy by spreading false information. "Our Founding Fathers did not maintain bank accounts in the Cayman islands," Studds shot back.[25] Nonetheless, momentum shifted as the Republican caucus solidified behind the president. The Democratic leaders therefore backed a weak compromise crafted by McCurdy that offered nonlethal aid immediately, and lethal aid later, to be voted just before the 1986 election. The appropriation passed, 221–209, and later passed the Senate.[26]

"I fear that this body has just made a mistake of truly monumental and historic proportions," said Studds, according to the *Congressional Record*. "It may well be the historic equivalent of the Gulf of Tonkin resolution and I fear there may be blood on the hands of this body. . . . You cannot blunt the appeal of Marx by giving millions more to the contras: the Marx brothers of counter-revolution."[27] A memorable line, but the metaphor was more poetic than apposite. There were no Marxists among the Sandinistas, who neither nationalized the means of production nor installed a dictatorship of the barely existent proletariat. And the real Marx Brothers act was being played out in the White House basement.

Iran-Contra

The Iran-contra affair, rumors of which had circulated among reporters for months, exploded across the front pages in October 1986 when a contra supply plane was shot down over Nicaragua and an American CIA contractor survived the crash. The sole survivor, whose plane was aptly named *The Fat Lady*, began to sing to Nicaraguan authorities, and in the following year a Senate committee would uncover the incredible story of what would become known as the Iran-contra scandal. National Security Council director John Poindexter and his aide Oliver North had arranged to supply the contras with money gained by selling American military equipment to Iran, in violation of sanctions. The supply flights originated at an El Salvador military base, confirming the exact opposite of what Reagan had been claiming for six years. Rather than the Soviets supplying the El Salvador rebels, the Americans were supplying the Nicaragua rebels.[28]

A few weeks later, just before the U.S. elections, Assistant Secretary of State for Inter-American Affairs Elliott Abrams appeared before the House to defend the administration. This was to be Mike Barnes's last meeting as chairman; he was running for the U.S. Senate. "Tell [Barnes] Central America wouldn't be the bastion of peace and tranquility that it is if not for his efforts," Studds's aide Bill Woodward joked. But Abrams's testimony was more laughable; he simply denied that the administration knew anything about the affair. "A wry smile crossed Congressman Gerry Studds' face last week as he confronted Assistant Secretary of State Elliott Abrams," *Time* magazine reported. "If the U.S. is not paying for this, who is—the A-Team?" Studds demanded, referring to a popular television show.[29]

Privately, President Reagan was obsessively determined to win the release of Americans held hostage by Shiite terrorists in Lebanon, who hoped to exchange them for colleagues imprisoned in Sunni nations. Reagan administration officials violated various laws by selling arms to the terrorists' Iranian sponsors and then using the proceeds to fund the contras. This complex plot, which the National Security Agency orchestrated from the White

House, led the news from November 1986 through August 1987, when televised congressional hearings on the matter concluded. There has been no more dire governmental scandal in American history. Unlike Watergate, this secret campaign led to thousands of deaths in Nicaragua, and probably many among Iraqi soldiers as well. Two directors of the National Security Agency, Robert McFarlane and John Poindexter, were convicted for their roles in the affair, as was their underling, marine colonel Oliver North. Several civilian arms dealers were also convicted of crimes. Nevertheless, because the American people retained their faith in the president's good intentions, and because no government official acted out of financial greed, personal vindictiveness, or sexual impropriety, this cautionary tale has slipped into obscurity.[30]

Making the story even more extraordinary was the contemporaneous slow-motion implosion of the Soviet Union, which unfolded from 1985, with the ascension of Mikhail Gorbachev to the premiership, until 1991, when the USSR dissolved into its constituent republics and the Communist Party withered away. Reagan and his foreign policy team found themselves confronted by an antagonist determined to disarm, and to outdo them in the struggle for peace. Yet with regard to Central America, Reagan behaved as though nothing had changed since the Cold War, and Moscow were planning to invade Texas by way of Managua.[31] The administration continued to seek money from Congress for the contras.

Studds was almost dumbstruck by Reagan's duplicity. In November 1986, the president made a speech that to most reporters seemed disingenuous at best, followed by a disastrous press conference. Journalist Lou Cannon, a man whom Reagan trusted, later wrote of the news conference, "Almost every answer that dealt with a question about the Iran initiative was at variance with the facts." Studds was astonished when the 1987 State of the Union address ignored the subject entirely. "Hypocrisy and political cowardice" marked the speech, Studds reported, adding that the Reagan administration looked to be in disarray. At the time, no one comprehended what an understatement that was. Secretary of State George Shultz and Secretary of Defense Caspar Weinberger, who usually disagreed about everything, had told Reagan in a crucial December 7, 1986, meeting that the Iran policy being conducted behind their backs by Casey, McFarlane, Poindexter, and North was doomed to fail and must now be publicly abandoned. This Reagan was unwilling to do. By March 1987, his self-delusion and incompetence led him to admit: "A few months ago I told the American people I did not trade arms for hostages. My heart and my best intentions still tell me that's true, but the facts and the evidence tell me it is not."[32] Few presidents have ever made such a staggering admission of prevarication.

Despite the Iran-contra scandal, Reagan, Shultz, and Weinberger continued to seek arms for the contras. They appeared before Studds's committee on behalf of Reagan's foreign aid budget, whose touchstone was a $900 million total increase in military assistance and a $250 million decrease in economic and humanitarian aid. "I suggested to [Shultz] during questioning, that he might be advised to direct his pleas to the president," whose backing of the budget-cutting policy of Senators Phil Gramm and Warren Rudman made the administration's request unfeasible. We have had "six years of beating ploughshares into swords," Studds concluded, and he wasn't going to countenance any more of it.[33]

In March, Congress voted on the dispersal of the remaining $40 million in contra aid from the $100 million appropriated in 1986. David Bonior of Michigan, a member of the Democratic leadership team, and now the most powerful anti-contra spokesperson in the House, crafted the vote as a six-month moratorium on all contra aid. This formulation was approved on a 230–196 vote, but it still left open the possibility for Reagan to access the money later. Studds spoke on the floor, demanding to know why, since there had been no accounting for the money gained by the illegal weapons sales to Iran, the contras needed still more. The nefarious "Enterprise," as Oliver North's money-laundering operation was known, constituted a "diseased policy" that was "illegal under international law and which has been carried out in violation of domestic law." Reagan had to put the contra resupply operation on hold, especially with the Iran-contra hearings about to begin in May. The contras continued to avoid battles with the Nicaraguan army, but in an April attack on a border town, contra fighters murdered a young American solidarity volunteer. Elliott Abrams returned to Studds's committee and blamed the young man's death on the Nicaraguan government for having allowed Americans to travel there.[34]

By August 1987, the Iran-contra joint committee had concluded its investigation, and in November it issued separate majority and minority reports, signed by eighteen bipartisan and eight Republican members, respectively. The reports differed dramatically in tone and substance, heralding a new era of partisanship in American life that would only intensify over the following quarter century.[35]

Meanwhile, Latin American leaders crafted a new peace plan at the initiative of Costa Rican president Óscar Arias. Their document insisted on internal changes that would democratize the Sandinista government. The Reagan administration apparently changed course and seemed to accept it. Newly elected House speaker Jim Wright promoted the plan, which became known as the "Wright-Reagan plan."[36] Studds smelled a rat. If it was genuine, he wrote, it represented "a complete reversal" of previous policy. It looked to Studds like fake propaganda for the benefit of Congress. The following month, Reagan's special envoy to the region, Morris Busby, testified before the Western Hemisphere Committee and announced that Reagan would persist in seeking to arm the contras. When he claimed that administration policy prevented his speaking directly with the Nicaraguan government, Studds reminded him that the United States regularly negotiated with the Soviet Union. Studds and a few dozen of his colleagues signed a letter calling on the administration to negotiate, but Reagan rejected that course.[37]

On October 13, 1987, the very day that President Arias was awarded the Nobel Peace Prize, George Shultz came before the Foreign Affairs Committee seeking an additional $270 million for the contras. The hearing room was packed, and reporters clustered expectantly in front, recording devices at the ready. Shultz, with his craggy face, bushy eyebrows, and unflappable demeanor, had the unenviable task of reconciling the Arias peace plan, which he praised, with his own mission to fund the "freedom fighters," although the Arias plan forbade such outside interference. Shultz focused on undemocratic measures taken by the Sandinistas, even though the Democrats granted his point.

Studds, impatiently tapping a pencil, asked Shultz rhetorically: "You say the only way for Nicaragua to avoid US intervention is to have complete political freedom. One wonders . . . when might we expect an invasion of Brunei, South Korea and Saudi Arabia?" He continued: "But my real question is [this]. You describe [the Arias plan] as a 'bold step in the right direction.' President Reagan calls it 'fatally flawed.' Which one of you is speaking for the United States?" Studds asked if he saw a contradiction, and Shultz lamely replied, "No."[38] Later the full Foreign Affairs Committee held a breakfast meeting with El Salvador's president, José Napoleón Duarte, who reaffirmed his commitment to the Arias peace plan. The plan's acceptance by all the other Central American nations suggested that the initiative lay with the region's governments, not with the United States.[39]

Undaunted, the Reagan administration pressed ahead. Because the votes on military aid were always close, Speaker Wright and David Bonior in February 1988 devised a new strategy to forestall further military aid. They allowed for a small amount, $16 million of nonlethal aid to the contras, adopting a complicated procedure in the Rules Committee that maximized the possibility of its passage: if the bill passed, no moderate Democrat or liberal Republican would later have to vote *against* military aid. Some liberals, like Studds, therefore faced a quandary. He had never voted for any contra aid, lethal or nonlethal. Now, his own leadership, including the anti-contra Bonior, was asking him to do so, and for the first time Studds cast a reluctant vote in favor. Nonetheless, Republicans were so outraged by the procedural maneuvering that they all, along with some anti-contra liberals, voted the bill down, 216–208.

"The contras were stunned," historian William M. Leogrande, then a congressional staffer, observed. The vote had unintended consequences for the Reagan administration's plans. The contras and Sandinistas immediately began peace talks, something the Sandinistas had previously refused to do, and declared a truce. The Sandinistas needed to end the contra threat because the war was destroying the Nicaraguan economy. Shortly thereafter, the House approved a $45.4 million nonlethal aid appropriation to facilitate the peace process, on a 345–70 vote. Studds voted against, convinced that the money was fungible and would be used to support the contra cause. The vote "sends an utterly inappropriate message to the parties in Central America," he informed his constituents.[40]

The vote nonetheless marked the beginning of the end of the contra war. The administration, badly damaged by the Iran-contra scandal, could do little to help its murderous clients. The Sandinistas, battered by the war, agreed to end the state of emergency and schedule elections, which they lost, and then handed over power to the non-contra opposition. This outcome had been declared theoretically impossible by the Reagan team for the past eight years because, they had averred, the Sandinistas were totalitarians. Many years later, Sandinista leader Daniel Ortega returned to power, and no one in the United States even noticed. Gerry Studds had played an important role in the struggle for peace. Yet his interests were changing. Throughout the final two years of the Reagan administration, Studds was gravitating more toward working on the gay rights and environmental issues that affected his local and national constituencies more directly.

15

Provincetown

GERRY STUDDS was happier now in his personal life, which, even though he was out, he still kept private. Since he acquired his condo in 1975, Provincetown had become his real home, though he listed Cohasset as his official address. On visits to the district, he would spend the night there. The Portuguese fishing village had morphed into an artsy gay tourist mecca, full of nightclubs, restaurants, and inns. In summer it exploded with vacationers and day-trippers, but off-season the town retained its quiet charm. Gerry's best friends in Provincetown were gallery owner David Simpson and architect Tom Green, a stable couple. Simpson had deliberately sought Studds out to offer support when the 1983 scandal broke. Tom and Gerry would go out on Studds's fishing boat, setting and pulling lobster traps.

Studds deepened his connection to Provincetown by building a house on the parking lot abutting Waterfront West, the 91 Commercial Street condo building. He bought out Russell Lukes's share of the space and sold his Watergate condominium in Washington. After rejecting an initial design that seemed too "busy," Studds asked Tom Green to simplify it. The house backed on the bay, and Gerry could hear and see the water from his deck. He hung out there with Tom, David, Curt Decker, and Lukes, the neighbor who had engineered Gerry's escape from the reporters on July 1, 1983.

During the summer of 1984 and 1985, Page X stayed in Provincetown with this group of friends. He loved the outdoors too, and joined Studds on the *Bacalhau*. X was artsy, and fashioned sculptures that soon adorned all their homes. Green and Simpson knew who he was, and so did Gerry's brother Colin and Colin's wife, Mary Lou. They knew him from the 1984 campaign as Gerry's driver. Now he was also Gerry's boyfriend. Studds guarded X's identity from political associates. He never introduced him to staffers or colleagues as the man who had testified "against" him in 1983. This was another secret that Studds kept. He never used X's friendship with him as evidence for his exoneration.[1]

Gerry's relationship with X blossomed in summer 1984, during the campaign, and the following summer. After a while, though, they drifted apart. X decided that he wanted to be a sculptor and live in a rural setting; that was not going to happen with Gerry. They parted on good terms, and X later married a woman.[2]

Among Studds's Provincetown visitors was Congressman Peter Kostmayer, a close colleague and friend. Kostmayer represented a Philadelphia suburb and, like Studds, had won his first election by a very narrow margin. Their interests overlapped; both served on the Western Hemisphere Subcommittee, and Kostmayer had made his own visits to Central America. Kostmayer was a landlubber and never ventured out on the *Bacalhau;* they kidded each other about that. Kostmayer had been defeated in 1980, and then reelected; the experience persuaded him to stay in the closet. The two congressmen had dinner together weekly in Washington. On Bastille Day, Kostmayer helped Studds escape the media onslaught, but when he saw the cameras focused on his friend, he decided he had better not put himself in the picture. This act of discretion troubled Kostmayer for years afterward, and he worried that Studds might not have forgiven him for it, but they did remain the closest of colleagues. "Gerry really wanted a relationship," Kostmayer recalled. "That was so important to him."[3]

During the mid-1980s, Studds volunteered to have lunch with the winner of a raffle to raise money for AIDS. The winner was Sasha Alyson, the former publisher of *Bay Windows,* Boston's gay and lesbian community newspaper, and they soon began dating. Alyson owned the small press that published *You Can Do Something about AIDS.* They spent their limited time together out of the public eye, in Provincetown on weekends, relaxing in Gerry's condo as the house was being built. Gerry caught bluefish, and they grilled it fresh. He took Sasha to the 1987 White House Christmas party.[4] That marked a new era in American social history, even if few noticed— social change unfolding step by quiet step. Studds called this the "Triumph of the Routine," the idea that little by little, more straight people would get to know more gay people, causing their prejudices to erode.[5]

Alyson and staffer Peter Fleischer connected Studds to an editor, Ash Green, at Knopf, which gave him an advance to write a memoir. Studds worked on it desultorily, in fugitive moments. He never completed it. Whenever staffers inquired about his progress, he would snap, "I'm working on it!" The memoir was personal, confessional, and focused on his early life as a gay man in the closet. He wrote about himself with insight, honesty, and humor, but could not bring himself to write about others, likely out of his deep New England reticence and sense of modesty, for fear of giving offense. He kidded people that he was calling it "I Should Have Been the Driver," but the unfinished draft is titled simply "Memoire."[6]

When Alyson ended their relationship, Studds felt hurt and abandoned. Despite his professional success, Studds still carried within himself an element of wounded vulnerability. Simpson thought Alyson to be a bit childlike and wondered why Studds was so attached to him. Studds pouted in the aftermath. "Gerry was incredibly sensitive," Simpson recalled. "To some in the public, he had a veneer of arrogance, but underneath that he was easily hurt." Studds drank too much to ease the pain. Black Russians gave way to vodka martinis, imbibed "impeccably dry," at local watering holes such as Larry's Bar, Front Street, Lorraine's, or Franco's.

In his loneliness, Studds felt sustained by his wider circle of Provincetown friends. "Our Provincetown crowd was Gerry's family," Simpson recalled. This was also a community in sorrow as the AIDS epidemic claimed its victims. "I lost almost everyone I knew and loved in the eighties," Simpson remembered with a sigh. Studds knew many of these people too. He was able to direct congressional funding to the Provincetown AIDS committee, which established a hospice.[7]

One tragicomic aspect of Gerry's Provincetown life was that he had a stalker, a deranged woman who was obsessed with him. She would appear on the beach behind the house and shriek, "I want to have your baby!" apparently oblivious to the fact that Studds was gay. Studds would joke about this, but despite the annoyance, he never threatened her with arrest.[8]

Coast Guard and Navigation

Provincetown had a Coast Guard station in the West End, and other district towns had such stations as well. During Reagan's second term, Studds chaired the Coast Guard and Navigation Subcommittee, giving him the opportunity to advance coastal and local issues. When the administration lowballed the Coast Guard's budget, Studds rose to its defense. "Anyone who thinks this budget addresses the problem of budget deficits is probably partaking of an illegal substance," he wrote in February 1985. "But the

Coast Guard [budget] is being cut, so they don't have to worry about being caught." A few months later, the joke was on the chairman when a Coast Guard vessel hailed the *Bacalhau* off Provincetown Harbor as Studds, sailing solo, was hauling in his lobster traps. The crew, looking for drug smugglers, was startled to discover whom they had just pulled over.[9]

The comedy continued as Massachusetts representative Silvio Conte pushed for an $18 annual boat owner fee to pay for Coast Guard services. Conte came from inland Berkshire County, and few of his constituents owned boats. Many recreational boat owners lived in Studds's district, however, so the idea was a non-starter for him. As a joke, Conte arrived at a Coast Guard and Navigation hearing dressed as a rich yachtsman in a ridiculous gold-braided captain's hat, purple pants, and an ascot; Studds was ready for him, sporting a working fisherman's yellow rain slicker. He puffed a seaman's pipe and tooted a boatman's horn to open the session as spectators cracked up. "[Conte] is in danger of losing his visa to Cuttyhunk [Island] in my district where he likes to come and fish," Studds teased. The user fees went nowhere. A few months later, the House voted to maintain Coast Guard funding at the level Studds desired.[10]

The subcommittee also regulated ocean dumping. This issue remained beneath the radar for the public, but it grew worse over time despite Studds's efforts to rein it in—a classic problem of protecting the global commons. "Aqua-litter bugs deposit more than one hundred million pounds of plastic trash into the oceans each year," Studds said as he opened committee hearings. "It is the mortal enemy of seabirds, marine mammals and fish." An array of witnesses from the Coast Guard, National Oceanic and Atmospheric Administration (NOAA), and environmental groups detailed how the practice was killing fur seals in Alaska, pelicans in Florida, and much else in between. "We've got a lot of work to do," Studds noted, and promised to draft legislation and promote pending international treaties in the next Congress.[11]

Studds also defended fishing vessel owners against what he saw as a predatory legal guild on the issue of liability. Studds advocated a bill that would cap awards at $500,000, except in cases of negligence. Working fishermen backed it because trial lawyers routinely charged injured fishermen a third to a half of their awards. Fishing was still among the most dangerous jobs in America; its fatality rate was seven times higher than that of other workers. The bill, which included a new code of safety standards, lost on a floor vote. "The trial lawyers ran a highly visible and subtle campaign," Studds said, and a staffer added that the trial lawyers contributed to virtually every congressman who voted with them. "[The lawyers] have no interest in safer fishing vessels, because injuries are good for their business," Studds told a reporter.[12]

Perhaps the thorniest issue Studds faced on fishing industry regulation had to do with U.S.-Canadian relations and each side's access to fishing grounds and markets. Canada subsidized its fishermen, and U.S. fishermen wanted international bodies to level the playing field. In May 1985, Studds traveled to Ottawa, Montreal, and Nova Scotia to meet with Canadian officials, and learned that Canada gave unemployment insurance to fishermen who worked as little as ten weeks a year. "The Canadians don't know what the hell you are talking about," Studds explained to his fishing constituents, who were accustomed to the demands of American-style individualism. Studds and aide Jeff Pike did promote a higher tariff on imported Canadian fish the following year. Later, he commended a split decision by the International Trade Commission that restricted imports of whole Canadian fish but not fillets. "The Whole Fish, and Nothing but the Whole Fish, so Help Our Cod," Studds reported in his newsletter. It mattered to Massachusetts fishermen that they had a congressman who understood their problems.[13]

Throughout his first term as an openly gay congressman, Studds worked primarily on his district's issues. "I remember two phones literally ringing at once in our office," media staffer Tom McNaught said. "One was the *New York Times,* and the other was the *Cape Cod Times.* [Studds] told the *New York Times* to call back and took the call from Cape Cod." Studds developed legislation to protect striped bass for recreational fishermen, establish an oil spill cleanup mechanism, resolve Superfund hazardous waste disposal problems, create coastal zone management councils, and oppose construction projects near wetland areas. He led the passage of federal compensation for the Gay Head Wampanoag on Martha's Vineyard, funded the Cape Cod National Seashore Advisory Commission, monitored regulation of the Pilgrim nuclear plant in Plymouth, and helped to clean up groundwater in Falmouth that had been contaminated by toxic degreasing compounds used at Otis Air Force Base. Studds won an easy reelection victory in 1986.[14]

Campaign 1988 and a New Romance

In 1985, Governor Mike Dukakis's Department of Human Services established a foster care policy that privileged heterosexual couples. It did not ban gays from adopting but ruled that sexual preference should be one factor in determining the suitability of prospective parents.[15] Even as homophobia declined, same-sex orientation seemed, to most heterosexuals, to challenge traditional family values. Most religious denominations agreed, but many gay people did not feel that way. The tenor of their movement was changing. Although the 1980s were mostly characterized by confrontational demonstrations organized by ACT UP on the AIDS issue, for many the movement was shifting from the idea that "we are different from heterosexuals—we are libertine and free" to the idea that "we are responsible, monogamous, stable, and mature." Bay State gay activists demanded that the state change its policy and "foster equality."[16]

In April 1987, Dukakis announced that he was running for president. This exposed him to attack from all sides, and one of those sides was the left. On the night of the governor's "State of the State" speech, hundreds of demonstrators gathered on the State House steps to protest Dukakis's foster care policy. Dukakis had already lost one election in liberal Massachusetts to socially conservative Ed King, and it would be extremely difficult for him to get out in front of public opinion while running for president. Studds had no particular tie to Dukakis, although his former district director John Sasso was running the governor's campaign, and Bill Woodward became Dukakis's speechwriter. Studds favored reversing the foster care policy, and felt unenthusiastic about Dukakis's self-presentation as a non-ideological technocrat, but he was likely out of sympathy with such provocative demonstrations by gay rights activists. "I really like Kitty [Dukakis's wife]," he'd say, when asked about Dukakis.[17]

After his breakup with Alyson, Studds ran into an acquaintance, Bill Dugan, at J.R.'s, a Washington gay bar, in September 1988. "What's he doing here?" Dugan wondered. He had first met him in 1980, when he was a political science major at Georgetown, and invited Studds, his congressman, to debate a State Department spokesperson on Central America. Dugan's father had been chairman of the Weymouth School Committee, and his parents had campaigned for Studds in 1970 and 1972. Dugan was one of eight children, a freckled Irish Catholic guy with politics running through his veins. Just before Bill was born, his father, then a Weymouth schoolteacher, worked nights at a South Boston market to make ends meet, and one night in 1961, two armed robbers held the place up. They got caught, and Assistant District Attorney Ted Kennedy put Bill's father on the stand and won the case; the Dugan clan loved Ted Kennedy forever after. Although Dugan had heard rumors about Studds being gay while in high school, he recalled, "I didn't even know that *I* was gay." Now Dugan was working as Washington editor for several business self-help magazines; he had been married, had a child, divorced, and embraced his sexual orientation. Studds and Dugan began dating.

In Provincetown, Dugan and Studds would go out to sail and catch lobsters on Gerry's new vessel, *Mr. Boat,* which had replaced the *Bacalhau.* The new one was a motorboat, a Boston Whaler. Once they went with Lester Hyman, Gerry's lawyer and the former Democratic Party state chairman, sailing far out of sight of land, toward Stellwagen Bank. In a transcendent moment, a humpback whale swam up to the boat and spouted through its blowhole in playful greeting. Dugan was falling in love with whales and the man who showed them to him.[18]

To the surprise of many, Mike Dukakis won the Democratic nomination. Gary Hart, the frontrunner, dropped out when reporters challenged him about his marital fidelity, another milestone in the process of the private sphere becoming public. Bill Woodward wrote Dukakis's stirring convention speech, which included a section spoken in Spanish. This marked the highlight of the entire campaign, and the governor emerged from the convention with a sixteen-point lead over Vice President George H. W. Bush. Bush went on the attack, choosing to run negative ads against Dukakis. Appealing to the fears of white voters, the ads showing the menacing countenance of Willie Horton, a black man who had raped a white woman while on furlough from a Massachusetts prison. In fact, some small percentage of furloughed prisoners committed serious crimes in every state. Dukakis, too proud to respond to such demeaning attacks, was soundly defeated.[19]

As the historian Sean Wilentz has noted, in the 1988 campaign both Bush and Dukakis ignored the new reality that the Soviet Union was collapsing and that this historic transformation presented an opportunity for world peace. Just as Bush was baiting Dukakis as "soft on communism" during the campaign, President Reagan entertained Premier Mikhail Gorbachev, who announced vast reductions in the Soviet military.[20]

There were implications in these episodes for Studds. They suggested that a negative attack might be used against him, too, and in his next two races that was exactly what happened. But not yet. Studds cruised to victory in 1988. His Republican opponent, Jon Bryan, an airplane pilot and management professor at Bridgewater State College, had never held public office. The *New Bedford Standard-Times* endorsed Bush, stayed neutral in Ted Kennedy's reelection bid, yet backed Studds. He won all forty-five towns and carried the election by two to one and New Bedford by four to one. Dugan flew up to Hyannis and surprised Studds by joining him and the senator at dinner. "Gerry was shocked that I came up," Dugan remembered.

"That cemented our relationship." Later the Studds team celebrated at the Twin Piers Restaurant in New Bedford and announced victory early in the evening. Bonnie, Colin, Mary Lou, and Bill were all there.[21]

Then Gerry and Bill went back to Provincetown. A few days later they found a note scribbled on a check stub stuck in the door: "We were in town, stopped by to say hello—TK." For a few weeks they wondered who "TK" was until Studds ran into Ted Kennedy in Washington. "Hey, did you get my note?"[22] he asked. Studds always felt a special responsibility, especially to Cape Cod, as Kennedy's congressman, and Kennedy often returned the sentiment.

On Inauguration Day, 1989, Studds and Dugan moved in together with Dugan's housemate and the housemate's sister at 1615 21st Street in Washington. It was the first time Studds had lived with a man. Dugan's brother advised him that he had better tell their parents he was gay, now that he was living with their congressman. He was delighted to find that they were completely accepting, and received Gerry graciously. Dugan's young son adored Gerry too.

Studds went out of his way to make Bill happy. Early in the relationship, Dugan mentioned that he loved wristwatches, and for Christmas, Gerry bought him an expensive Cartier. They danced together at the 1988 White House Christmas party—the first gay couple to dance there, Studds thought. Although Studds had no interest in baseball, he took Bill to a Capitol Hill reception for baseball commissioner Bart Giamatti, at which the couple posed with former Red Sox star Dom DiMaggio and Giamatti. They were happy together, and perhaps more than anything else, it was Provincetown and the sea that made it work.[23]

16

Spilling Oil, Spilling Blood

IN JANUARY 1989, Studds accompanied national leaders of the United Auto Workers, the Amalgamated Clothing and Textile Workers Union, the International Association of Machinists, and the Association of Federal, State, County, and Municipal Employees to El Salvador and Costa Rica. These powerful officials, representing millions of workers, decided to visit El Salvador because they believed that labor rights were being violated there. Despite briefings by Salvadoran officials, including military chief of staff Colonel René Emilio Ponce and air force general Juan Rafael Bustillo, they came away convinced that their counterparts were being killed and imprisoned and the unions broken up. Meanwhile, as the Central America news during Reagan's second term focused on the Iran-contra affair, the war in El Salvador dragged on in a tense stalemate. Over a million refugees fled the country, and they were beginning to show up in the U.S. workforce.

José Napoleón Duarte was again the president of El Salvador, but his Christian Democrats were expected to lose the March 1989 elections to Alfredo Cristiani's rightist ARENA party. Behind the scenes, the military made all the important decisions. Cristiani was backed by Roberto D'Aubuisson, the death squad leader, but he tried to distance himself from the man who had ordered the murder of Archbishop Óscar Romero in 1980. The civilian leftists, led by Guillermo Ungo and Rubén Zamora, also planned to run in the elections. After meeting with Duarte, Cristiani, and Zamora, Studds concluded that, despite the billions of U.S. dollars spent on guns and attack helicopters, the money had bought no influence with El Salvador's brutal military leaders.

El Salvador labor trip, January 1989. Left to right: Studds, Amalgamated Clothing and Textile Workers Union president Jack Sheinkman, Colonel René Emilio Ponce, International Association of Machinists president William Winpisinger. *Photographer unknown, courtesy Dean Hara.*

Studds and the union officials also met with Salvadoran labor leaders. Still accused of being communists, these people feared for their lives. Ten unarmed *campesinos* had been killed by the Salvadoran army the previous September and nothing had been done about it. Unemployment stood at 50 percent, income from the coffee harvest was down 40 percent, and wages ranged from $2 to $3.60 a day. Meanwhile, the guerrillas had contributed to the collapse of the economy by attacking the power grid, sowing land mines, and assassinating pro-government mayors in the countryside. Many people blamed the Christian Democrats and the guerrillas for the stalemate, so Cristiani, a new face representing the business class, whose interests were diverging from those of the militarists, was expected to win the election.

Studds saw a glimmer of hope in that the civilian leftists planned to run and that the FMLN guerrillas pledged to honor the results if the election was fairly contested. "I will encourage the Bush administration to make judicial reform and respect for human rights an absolute precondition to continued U.S. military support for El Salvador," Studds promised. "For eight years the military has called our bluff. The time has come for us to call theirs."[1]

Another reason for optimism was that the administration of the newly elected president, George H. W. Bush, was more pragmatic and less ideological than the Reagan administration had been. In the places formerly occupied by Cold Warriors such as Al Haig, John Poindexter, and Elliott Abrams now sat Secretary of State James Baker, National Security Agency chief Brent Scowcroft, and Assistant Secretary of State for Latin American Affairs Bernard Aaronson, a Democrat. When Baker came up to Capitol Hill in February, Studds was impressed. He found him to be "cool and rational." The new foreign policy team, mindful of the historic changes unfolding in the Soviet Union, was focused on European affairs and the withdrawal of Soviet troops from Afghanistan.[2]

Cristiani won the March election and visited Washington in April. He met with Studds, who was still taking a hard line on aid to El Salvador. The Western Hemisphere Subcommittee voted tough new certification requirements, conditioning further aid on progress toward a negotiated end to the war and improvements in human rights. By summer, the measure passed the House, but the Senate approved $90 million in military aid. Senator Chris Dodd, usually in Studds's camp, had been convinced by Cristiani that the aid gave the United States leverage with his government.[3]

Regarding Nicaragua, Bush tried to keep the contras intact but not on a war footing. On March 24, Secretary Baker signed the Treaty of Washington, agreeing to forgo military but not nonlethal aid for a year, until the February 1990 elections. Studds dissented. When the House approved $66 million in nonlethal aid for the contras, he voted no. He still saw the money as fungible, and pointed out that there was no accounting for how it would be spent. Meanwhile, the contras continued to stage hit-and-run attacks on civilian targets. The funding decision represented "one of the most wrongheaded and immoral foreign policy mistakes of my lifetime," he concluded.[4]

March 24, 1989: Prince William Sound

Around midnight on the same day as the Nicaragua vote, the oil tanker *Exxon Valdez,* with a cargo of 55 million gallons of crude oil extracted from Prudhoe Bay, ran aground on Bligh Reef in Prince William Sound, Alaska. Eleven of its sixteen containers burst and oozed an estimated million gallons each into the sea. Eventually the spill would cover 1,300 miles of coastline and 11,000 square miles of ocean, and kill at least 100,000 seabirds, 2,800 otters, three hundred harbor seals, and a pod of orcas. The herring fishery had to be closed down and salmon fishing redirected out of the danger zone. It was the worst oil spill in world history, a record that stood until the *Deepwater Horizon* blowout in the Gulf of Mexico in 2009.[5]

Studds's friend and fishing buddy Alaska congressman Don Young got the call while he was in an airplane. "Burn it!" he told the Coast Guard. The EPA didn't agree, and the ten-hour window within which that response might have worked passed. No protocols were in place to establish who was in charge.[6]

Coast Guard and Navigation held its first hearing on the disaster two weeks later. The members had before them House Resolution 1465, a comprehensive oil spill liability bill, which the House had passed in an earlier session but which the Senate had killed. This lengthy, complex piece of legislation contained many provisions that Studds dearly wished to see passed into law. Now he was in a position to do something about it. Thirteen years earlier, wind and current had spared the Nantucket coast in the *Argo Merchant* wreck, but Studds had warned then that the country might not be so lucky next time. Now that time had come.

Chairman Billy Tauzin of Louisiana opened the hearings by raising several questions. None was more compelling than "How did this happen?" It had not taken the press long to discover that captain Joseph Hazelwood had been sleeping off a drunken binge as the third mate steered the ship onto the reef. Hazelwood's New York driver's license had been suspended three times. He had simply lied on his pilot's license application, and the licensing board didn't have the manpower to check it.

Coast Guard commandant Paul Yost sat before the committee, a calm man with an aquiline nose and a receding hairline, dressed in a modest blue uniform. His aide stood before a flip chart with maps, pointer in hand, in those last days before PowerPoint presentations. Yost had gone to Alaska immediately with his boss, Secretary of Transportation Samuel Skinner. The Coast Guard had boarded the tanker within three hours, but in the dark of night, the vessel could not be secured. Yost fielded a series of questions regarding the radar system, the ship's routing, and the status of the cleanup. Then Studds's turn came.

He went right after the questions that had been bugging him ever since his staff had tried in 1976 to ascertain even the simplest facts about the *Argo Merchant*, beginning with who owned it. "Who is responsible for the damages?" Studds wanted to know. Of course it was Exxon, Yost replied. "Could they somehow stick Uncle Sam with the bill?" Yost wouldn't rule it out. Studds said that this possibility showed why the country needed a new oil spill liability law. Yost nodded in agreement.

Studds prodded gently on the next matter. "The captain wasn't on deck, right?" When he asked whether the Coast Guard had been changing the regulations to permit that procedure, Yost, with an uneasy grin, replied, "Not at this moment!" and the whole room exploded in laughter. They were locking the barn door after the horse had run off, and they knew it. Yost had to leave for the Senate hearings. "We wish you well on your trip to the Senate," Studds reassured him. "Go as heavily armed as you can."[7]

In August, Studds went to Alaska for further hearings. He concentrated on learning about the effects of the spill on the fishing industry, a natural area of concern for him. Massachusetts and Alaska were the two leading fishing states in the nation, and New Bedford and Kodiak were the two biggest fishing ports. After the spill, herring and salmon boats had been pressed into service for the cleanup efforts. The mayor of Cordova told the panelists, "Whatever you do, go back and never let what happened here occur in the place that you are from." Studds and Young worked together to include in the legislation provisions that would tighten personnel licensing practices, require double hulls in new ship construction, bar tankers from environmentally sensitive regions, and establish standing emergency strike teams to clean up future spills. Studds especially wanted to ensure that there would be no limit on liability for oil transport. President Bush signed the Oil Pollution Control Act, which included most of Studds's recommendations, into law the following year.[8]

"That was a good law," Don Young recalled with satisfaction. "Before it, no ports had emergency response teams. Now, every major port does. Republicans and Democrats worked together to make it happen."[9]

Studds had begun 1989 by working on a different environmental issue, a matter that seemed obscure at the time—something called global warming. He had signed a letter to the president, joining only two colleagues and six senators, warning that global warming represented "perhaps the most serious and far-reaching environmental problem we face in the world today." A few weeks later he offered an amendment that would require federal agencies to monitor carbon pollution. After the *Exxon Valdez* spill, the administration did pass a significant Clean Air Act, but global warming would remain off the national agenda until many years later.[10]

The Jesuit Murders

Studds heard about the murders of six Jesuit priests in El Salvador from his aide Bill Woodward, who had heard from Lisa Murray, another Studds staffer. Murray was then dating Jim McGovern, who worked for Joe Moakley. McGovern had gotten an early morning call from El Salvador shortly after the bodies were discovered. The guerrillas had launched an offensive a week earlier, hoping to force the Cristiani government to negotiate an end to the war. The guerrillas' success stunned everyone, especially the military leaders. On the morning of November 16, a gardener at the University of Central America in San Salvador discovered the bodies of his wife and daughter, eyewitnesses to the murder of the priests, whose corpses lay in the courtyard. A scrawled message on the wall of the destroyed Jesuit office claimed that the FMLN guerrillas had committed the crime. The murder weapon was a Kalashnikov, the weapon used by the guerrillas. But why would the FMLN do this?

The victims were internationally recognized leaders in the Jesuit order—five Spaniards and a Salvadoran. They had published widely, attended conferences, and were well connected. Father Ignacio Ellacuria, the most prominent among them, had been negotiating separately with Cristiani and the guerrillas to end the war. A divide was growing between the business class and the military. The war had wrecked the Salvadoran economy. Internationally, a few weeks earlier the Berlin Wall had fallen, and in the United States, the more pragmatic Bush had replaced the ideological Reagan. Under these new circumstances, the Salvadoran coffee growers and bankers felt that they should broker a peace. If peace came, however, and there was an accounting for the crimes of the past, the generals could lose more than their jobs. Everybody knew this. Few people believed that it was the guerrillas who had wanted the Jesuits dead.

Woodward and McGovern discussed what their bosses should do. Joe Moakley, born and raised in South Boston, had become an unlikely champion of Salvadoran immigrants. He had been working since 1983 to pass legislation that would allow them to stay in the United States while the war ground on. Moakley was a World War II veteran, not a 1960s antiwar type. He did not advocate a complete cutoff of military aid to El Salvador, as Studds did. Moakley had just risen to the chairmanship of the powerful House Rules Committee, and his unassuming manner had earned him the respect of his colleagues on both sides of the aisle. Woodward and McGovern proposed a Speaker's Task Force to monitor the Salvadoran investigation into the Jesuits' murders. If some element of the military, or a paramilitary death squad, had committed the crime, and the investigators were covering that up, the U.S. taxpayers who were buying their guns had a right to know the truth.

Speaker Jim Wright had resigned from Congress after an ethics investigation six months earlier. Studds went to the new speaker, Tom Foley, and suggested that Moakley chair the task force. Foley called Moakley, who told him that he lacked the foreign policy experience for such a sensitive job, but he soon changed his mind. Moakley had met two of the victims in the course of his work on behalf of the immigrants. He was an observant Catholic, and he instinctively hated bullies. As it turned out, Studds had set Moakley, now sixty-two years old, on the great adventure of his life, one that would continue until Moakley's death in 2001.

The Speaker's Task Force was a Democrats-only body. The reason for this was that its work would have to be discreet and free of partisan wrangling. Task force members and staffers were going to have to ask dangerous people some delicate questions, and could not afford to have Salvadoran officials playing individual Americans off against one another. By December 6, Foley had named nineteen members, Studds among them, who began holding closed-door hearings. Witnesses included a female janitor who, from across the street, had seen Salvadoran army soldiers surround the Jesuit compound. She had escaped from El Salvador with the help of the Jesuit order.[11]

At the same time Studds was attending these hearings, the United States invaded Panama. The nation's ruler, Manuel Noriega, had reneged on an earlier promise to allow the Americans to retain military bases that were supposed to revert to Panama. The previous spring, as votes in the national election were being counted and it seemed that Noriega might lose, he nullified the results. Noriega had been a CIA asset during the contra war against the Sandinistas, and the Americans had pretended not to notice that he was also a drug smuggler. Now he was an ugly puppet in revolt against his handlers. The United States staged a provocation, and President Bush used the pretext to send in the marines. His popularity soared as the troops landed. Most Americans would have been hard-pressed to explain why the United States had invaded, but Noriega played the part of the swaggering thug so well that no one was sad to see him go, even if the legality of the operation seemed questionable.

Studds joined a congressional delegation on a two-day visit to Panama in January. He felt conflicted. The invasion, he told his constituents, "was like punching someone who richly deserved it in the mouth. It's not necessarily smart; it's not necessarily mature; it's not necessarily legal; and it may have unintended consequences—but it feels very good at the time." He found that Panama had lost six hundred dead in the fighting and suffered a great deal of physical infrastructure damage; twenty-three Americans had been killed. "The Panamanian people seem to have mixed feelings about the invasion," Studds reported. "They are pleased with the results, embarrassed that it was necessary, and eager for the U.S. forces to go home." Panama was a unique case, Studds believed, and he worried that the action might become a template for future U.S. invasions against other dictators that might not end so well. Bush had invaded Panama, Studds concluded, "not so much because he *had* to, but because he wanted to."[12] Some observers would use almost the same words in 2003 to describe the motivations of the president's son George W. Bush when he invaded Iraq.

While Studds was in Panama, there was a break in the Jesuit case. A Salvadoran officer bragged to an American adviser that he knew who was responsible: the head of the military academy. After the adviser informed his superior, the Salvadoran military itself, not the Salvadoran prosecutor's office, named nine soldiers as the perpetrators, among them four officers. The highest ranking among them, however, the superintendent of the military academy, Colonel Guillermo Benavides, was a follower rather than a leader. Moakley, Studds, and other task force members suspected that the colonel had received his orders from higher up, and that he was dutifully taking the rap in exchange for a light sentence.

This was not the administration's position. On January 24, Undersecretary of State for Latin American Affairs Bernard Aaronson came before the Western Hemisphere Subcommittee, sitting jointly with the Human Rights and International Organizations Subcommittee. Studds acted as chair for his subcommittee. In his opening remarks, Studds asked Aaronson if he still believed, as he had said in a 1983 speech, that aid to El Salvador should be conditioned on its progress in human rights and land reform. Aaronson made a stark contrast to his predecessor, the neoconservative Elliott Abrams. He spoke in a thoughtful tone and acknowledged divergent points of view respectfully. Yet he hewed to the administration line that the guerrilla offensive was the cause of all the trouble. He pointed to FMLN murders of mayors in the countryside as justification for continued military aid to Cristiani's government. The military, he asserted, was working diligently to bring the perpetrators of the Jesuits' murders to justice and had charged nine people with the crime. Finally, addressing Studds's question, he declared that he did agree with his earlier statement, that El Salvador had in fact accomplished some land reform and, by conducting several democratic elections, had demonstrated the utility of American aid to the government. As Aaronson spoke, he was dramatically interrupted by several members of the audience, who, one by one, rose and stood, silently pointing an accusatory finger; some shouted denunciations as they were escorted out.

Studds listened carefully, a forefinger extended beneath his nose in an expression of pensive discontent. Here at last was a worthy opponent who appealed to reason and evidence, but Studds remained unconvinced. None of those goals had been achieved, he told Aaronson, and he didn't approve of pointing to FMLN crimes, which Studds did not dispute, to gloss over the Salvadoran government's depredations. "This administration shows an unwillingness to recognize that El Salvador is sick, not just at the political margins, but sick at its center," he insisted. The murder of the Jesuits showed that. "Given what we know about . . . the apolitical nature of the colonel who ordered it done, I think it is obvious that others were involved, and that these officers must have been very high ranking. And yet, President Cristiani acts as though the case were closed."[13]

The Jesuits' murders marked the beginning of the end for the military dictatorship and started the beginning of the peace process. Studds returned to the region a month later in mid-February with the Speaker's Task Force. Five Republicans appointed by Minority Leader Bob Michel joined ten Democrats for a four-day trip. The congressmen visited the crime scene and met the surviving Jesuit leaders. They held separate meetings with military officials, President Cristiani, and the archbishop. Studds continued to suspect that the military officials were shielding the true organizers of the crime. As the delegation prepared to depart, Moakley called a news conference at the capacious, modern Camino Real Hotel, where they had lodged. With the grim-faced task force members arrayed behind him, Moakley insisted that there were still a lot of unanswered questions.

Over the next two months, McGovern and Woodward worked with the task force's chief informant, a Salvadoran exile named Leonel Gomez, a man with wide-ranging contacts, to craft an interim report. Released in April 1990, the one-hundred-page document suggested that the Salvadoran matter had reached a dead end. "As I see it," Studds wrote, "the stalled investigation into the Jesuit case is just the latest in a long line of broken promises about human rights and respect for democracy, and I will not be a party to any agreement that fails to acknowledge that fact."[14]

Studds's "no military aid for El Salvador" position probably helped Moakley and John Murtha, a Pennsylvania Democrat, to pass a new proposal in May. This measure cut military aid in half, from $85 to $42.5 million, and offered carrots and sticks to both sides to move the peace process forward. The bill passed the House by 250–163, was approved in the Senate, and was attached to a spending measure that Bush approved and signed.[15]

Studds's second contribution toward bringing peace to El Salvador was to free up Bill Woodward for the task force's staff. Woodward and Jim McGovern achieved a major breakthrough that August. Gomez, the Salvadoran exile, the Virgil to their Dante, drove the two men to the beach one day and instructed them to swim out to a certain spot. Shortly afterward, another man joined Gomez, and the two Salvadorans swam out to the two Americans. Nobody would be able to tape this conversation. There the informant, a colonel, confirmed what Moakley and Studds already suspected. The murders had been ordered by General Juan Rafael Bustillo and Colonel René Emilio Ponce, the very officers who had briefed the congressmen. They had ordered Colonel Benavides to organize the hit squad. This was widely known in military circles, and by Cristiani himself, but everyone was sticking to the story that Benavides initiated the murders. Obviously this informant wasn't going to come forward publicly either. After Woodward and McGovern reported their interview to the ambassador to El Salvador, William Walker, and later to the State Department, the Bush administration gradually folded its hand.[16]

The trial was held the following year and resulted in a pathetic outcome. Benavides and a few others were convicted and received light sentences. Bustillo, Ponce, and their co-conspirators were never brought to trial. Moakley issued a final report after the trial expressing his doubts that justice had been done, but naming no names. After the war concluded, a U.N. commission drew the same conclusions that Moakley had drawn. Many years later, a Spanish court (five of the victims were Spaniards) indicted the surviving generals, who at this writing were still facing extradition proceedings from the United States and El Salvador. Moakley later played a significant role in convincing the guerrillas that they could negotiate a peace; Jim McGovern would later be elected to the House himself and fight for economic aid to El Salvador after the war. Behind the scenes, Studds had set the whole process in motion. His aide Bill Woodward contributed significantly to the detective work and the writing of the task force reports. Gomez returned to his native country after the war, having been the crucial player in the entire drama.

The Soviet Collapse

Even as a member of the Foreign Affairs Committee, Studds could only watch the breathtaking events in the Soviet Union and eastern Europe that dominated the news in the incredible year 1989. The historic chain of events began with the withdrawal of Soviet troops from Afghanistan and concluded with the execution of the Romanian dictator Nicolae Ceaușescu on Christmas Day. In between, Gorbachev rejected the Brezhnev doctrine, which justified Soviet intervention in eastern Europe, and the Hungarian and Czech dictatorships fell. The climax came with the destruction of the Berlin Wall on November 10. In South Africa, the apartheid regime, sensing the beginning of the end, opened negotiations with the imprisoned Nelson Mandela. These breathtaking developments overshadowed the struggle in El Salvador and rendered the behavior of the generals and the Bush administration in the Jesuit case an absurd anachronism.

Studds paid these developments a great deal of attention. He had begun his political life as a Young Republican at Yale, helping to integrate Hungarian refugees into American life. In February 1990, Václav Havel, the formerly imprisoned dramatist, now president of Czechoslovakia, addressed a joint meeting of Congress. The speech left Studds "spellbound," he told his constituents. The historic changes taking place in eastern Europe were occurring so rapidly, he wrote, that "we have literally no time even to be astonished." A photographer captured Studds shaking hands with Havel; he looks more emotional than he does in any other picture as he clasps Havel's hand in both his own. Studds also greeted Poland's Lech Wałęsa with the same fervor. Bill Dugan was there with Studds, and spoke a few recently learned Polish words of greeting to Wałęsa.[17] In 1989 the world had changed so much more for the better than anyone had ever expected. Despite the horrors unfolding in El Salvador, the collapse of communism portended a foreseeable end to the war there as well.

17

Gay and Lesbian Warriors

KATE DYER was a sixteen-year-old Seattle high school student when she and a group of other teenagers left home to study for three months in Costa Rica. She had a spunky demeanor, an athletic physique, clean-cut good looks, a hundred-watt smile, and the sense of adventure that attracts young people to study abroad. The Seattle students were traveling in neighboring Nicaragua when Ronald Reagan was elected president in November 1980, and they could see that the Sandinistas were stunned by his victory. Dyer was shocked by the extensive damage still visible from the 1977 earthquake in that poverty-stricken country. She went on to college at Yale, where she majored in American studies and theater. Her early experience in Central America had given her the social justice bug, though, and after graduating, she applied for a job on Capitol Hill. Congressman Don Bonker of her home state of Washington offered her a paying job, and Gerry Studds offered her an internship. Dyer consulted with a friend. "Studds is brilliant," the friend said. "He doesn't speak often, but when he does, everyone listens." Dyer went to work for Studds in January 1987 as a volunteer, and was offered a full-time position a few months later.[1]

Shortly afterward, Dyer told Studds's aide Steve Schwadron that she was a lesbian. Schwadron looked surprised and said, "You should probably tell Gerry."

Dyer, feeling bashful, arranged to go into Studds's office, and told him.

"Why didn't you tell me before?" Studds asked.

"Well," Dyer said, "I didn't want to get the job over another applicant because I was a lesbian."

Studds smiled, shook his head gently, and said, "The times must be changing if you are worried that being a lesbian gives you an advantage." Dyer remembered, "He told other people that my being an American studies major from Yale didn't hurt."

The Pentagon Buries Its Own Report

There have always been gay men and, from the time the United States began admitting women into the armed services, especially from World War II onward, lesbians serving in the American military. Their numbers, according to author Randy Shilts, probably included Baron Friedrich Wilhelm von Steuben, drill master of the Continental Army; War of 1812 naval hero Stephen Decatur; and Tom Dooley, the famed navy medical doctor who treated Vietnamese refugees during the 1950s and was secretly dishonorably discharged for being a homosexual.[2]

During the Vietnam War, gay bars sprouted up all over Southeast Asia and a visible subculture emerged. After the war, when the military no longer needed them, the various branches began expelling gay service members. The signature case of the 1970s was that of air force technical sergeant Leonard Matlovich, a decorated Vietnam veteran. In March 1975, after twelve years of meritorious service, he formally notified his commanding officer that he was gay and was subsequently discharged. Matlovich took his case for reinstatement through the courts, raising the legal and ethical questions underpinning the exclusion of homosexuals from the military. By 1981 his discouraged lawyers advised him to accept a cash settlement that left these questions unresolved, but at least aired.[3]

Matlovich could sue for reinstatement because of gray areas in military regulations regarding what behavior constituted misconduct. To make the gray areas more black and white, the Defense Department issued a new policy in 1980 which stated that "homosexuality is incompatible with military service. The presence in the military environment of persons who engage in homosexual conduct or who, by their statements, demonstrate a propensity to engage in homosexual conduct, seriously impairs the accomplishment of the military mission. The presence of such members adversely affects the ability of the armed forces to maintain good order and morale." Homosexuality thus became a thought crime. Despite the new regulations, the military gay subculture expanded, and gay bars opened near military bases. The number of women volunteers dramatically increased. When some of these women refused the sexual advances of male colleagues, they sometimes found themselves accused of being lesbians. By the late 1980s, the armed forces were expelling two thousand accused gay men and lesbians a year. In this context, and in the aftermath of two spying cases, the Department of Defense in 1988 secretly commissioned a study whose real purpose was to reaffirm the old policy. Unfortunately for the Pentagon, the report, written by two meticulous researchers at the Defense Personnel Security Research and Education Center (PERSEREC) in Monterrey, California, came to conclusions opposite to those that its commissioners anticipated. The Pentagon buried the report.[4]

Kate Dyer had meanwhile been assigned to this issue in Studds's office. She got wind of the mysterious report through the office of Lambda Legal Defense Fund, a gay rights legal organization, and started making inquiries.

The Frank Affair

In late August 1989, problems in Barney Frank's private life wound up damaging his public career. He had taken under his wing a prostitute, Stephen Gobie, whom he later hired as an aide. Attempting to help the man, Frank used his influence to resolve Gobie's minor legal problems. Some time afterward, Frank learned that Gobie was running a prostitution ring out of the apartment they shared. Frank then realized that he had been hustled by a con man, and asked for an Ethics Committee investigation into his own behavior. A *Boston Globe* editorial, and several of the newspaper's columnists, urged Frank to resign. Frank apologized for his poor judgment and received a reprimand the following year. Newt Gingrich demanded that Frank be censured rather than reprimanded, but this time he failed, and Frank was reelected in 1990.[5]

Studds felt sympathetic to Frank's predicament, born, like his own earlier problems, out of the human need to be loved. Studds reminded reporters that congressmen are imperfect human beings and make personal mistakes. The editor of Boston's gay community newspaper *Bay Windows* pointed out that Frank's involvement with Gobie dated to the period when he was in the closet, and that the need to conceal one's gay identity often distorted the behavior of public people. Studds knew this only too well. He called Frank and told him, "Hold on, catch your breath, let time do some of its healing work." He told a reporter that "Barney is in great personal pain." He himself had walked a mile in those shoes.[6]

Frank's problems opened old wounds for Studds. Some writers pointed out that Frank's bad judgment was less injurious than Studds's had been in 1973. The *Globe* editorial urging Frank to resign stated outright that Studds's behavior had been worse, and that under current standards, he would have been expelled. *Globe* columnist David Nyhan, usually an astute observer of the political scene, wrote that Studds's influence had declined since 1983: "[The censure] eviscerated his effectiveness in the larger sense. He remains a 'local' congressman, dutifully servicing the fishing and boating interest of his district. . . . His ability to appeal to moral suasion . . . is ended." These words, coming from Nyhan, had to trouble Studds. He knew privately that Page X felt only goodwill toward him, yet he would never say this publicly in his own defense.[7]

Nyhan was wrong about Studds's supposedly declining influence. Studds reminded the reporter that by coming out, even involuntarily, he had transformed his life for the better. "These have been the five or six best years of my life," he said.[8] And in fact, Studds had been a national force for gay rights, for peace in Central America, and for the environment, and his authority was increasing.

PERSEREC Unearthed

After Kate Dyer called Lambda Legal Defense, word started to spread among military personnel exposed as being gay that there was someone in Gerry Studds's office who would help them. During 1988 and 1989, several dramatic cases involving gay and lesbian service members surfaced—a witch hunt against lesbians at Parris Island Marine Corps Recruit Training Depot, and a false accusation against a gay sailor killed in an explosion on the USS *Iowa,* among others. "Studds' emerging role gave gays in the military a champion of incalculable importance," Randy Shilts concluded.[9]

One afternoon in 1989, Dyer arranged a meeting between Studds, Democratic representative Jolene Unsoeld, and three servicewomen accused of being lesbians. The women, each from a different military branch, sat straight in their chairs as each related her story. One woman, a marine captain from Unsoeld's Washington State district, had come under suspicion for joining a softball team that included known civilian lesbians. "You're facing a dishonorable discharge because you played softball?" Unsoeld gasped. Another, a spit-and-polish navy petty officer, said glumly, "We just wanted to serve our country." The meeting was scheduled for half an hour and lasted for an hour and a half as the evening shadows darkened outside. After the visitors left, Studds turned to Dyer. "What an unspeakable waste that we are driving people like that out of the military," he said. "Let's do whatever we can to end this." That was the moment, Dyer knew, when Studds decided to throw his efforts into this issue wholeheartedly.[10]

In the spring of 1989, at a hearing before the Coast Guard and Navigation Subcommittee, Studds pursued the homosexuality policy as it applied to the Coast Guard. Although the Coast Guard was part of the Department of Transportation, its members could be integrated into the military, and it therefore followed the regulations barring homosexuals. "Studds noted that it was odd that he was a good enough man to be in charge of the Coast Guard for the House of Representatives but not good enough to swab decks on a Coast Guard vessel," observed Shilts.[11]

Meanwhile, Dyer persisted in her efforts to unearth the rumored report. News of its existence had reached Joe Steffan, a midshipman expelled from Annapolis whose case Studds backed. Staffers for Congresswoman Patricia Schroeder, who sat on the Armed Services Committee, journalists, and the National Gay and Lesbian Task Force were pursuing leads as well. Pentagon information offices gave Dyer the run-around. Studds and Dyer suspected that the report said something that the Pentagon did not want people to hear. In mid-October 1989, Studds and Schroeder finally scheduled a meeting with one of its authors, Dr. Ted Sarbin, and Maynard C. Anderson, the deputy secretary of defense for counterintelligence and security, whose office had commissioned the report.[12]

A day or two before the meeting, someone secretly brought Dyer a photocopy of the report. Fearful of being discovered, the informant insisted that Dyer re-copy it successively on five different machines and destroy the intermediate copies. Sarbin, a psychologist, and coauthor Kenneth E. Karols, a flight surgeon, had indeed come to conclusions that undermined Pentagon policy. The report, "Nonconforming Sexual Orientations and Military Suitability," found that sexual orientation "is unrelated to job performance in the same way as is being left- or right-handed." Studds put that line on page one of his introduction to the secret report, which he later had published.[13]

Schroeder joined Studds and Dyer at the meeting. Anderson claimed that the report said nothing new. Studds, tapping a manila folder purposefully on the table, replied, "I think you should know that I have the complete report right here, and I've read it." Anderson turned white, dropped his gaze, and murmured, "Oh." Dyer's press release summarized the report's conclusions and pointed out that the ban on gay service members echoed the military's segregation of blacks, which had ended forty years earlier. She quoted Studds, who called the document "a blockbuster." The story appeared on the front pages of the *New York Times,* the *Boston Globe,* and other newspapers.

A few days later Dyer unlocked the office door in the morning and found an unmarked envelope. There had been a second study, also commissioned through the Monterrey PERSEREC office, addressing several related, more narrow questions, reflected by its ponderous title, "Pre-Service Adjustment of Homosexual and Heterosexual Military Accessions: Implications for Security Suitability." Author Michael A. McDaniel concluded that "homosexuals show pre-service suitability-related adjustment that is as good as or better than the average heterosexual. Thus these results appear to be in conflict with conceptions of homosexuals as unstable, maladjusted persons." In addition to the second report, Dyer also obtained the interoffice memos arranging the suppression of both reports. "We want to give this as wide a public exposure as possible," Studds told the *Boston Globe.* "It has particular significance for impending court cases." A Pentagon spokesman told a reporter that they were commissioning another study, and then presumably retired to wipe the egg off his face.[14]

Meanwhile, a number of Reserve Officer Training Corps cadets, originally unaware of one another's actions, approached their commanding officers to report that they were gay. Among the most significant cases were those of Jim Holobaugh at Washington University in St. Louis, Rob Bettiker at MIT, and David Carney at Harvard. Bettiker and Carney were enrolled in nuclear science programs, making them unusually valuable potential naval officers. Holobaugh had an outstanding record in an army unit. These students had not lied. None believed himself to be gay at the time he applied for the scholarship. Each was told that he would have to return tens of thousands of dollars. From the military's perspective, it had invested in these young men and had been deceived.[15]

The cadets challenged the rulings and contacted Dyer, who helped connect them with attorneys and advised them to publicize their cases. Studds sent protest letters to the appropriate authorities, including Secretary of Defense Dick Cheney. In news releases he blasted the recoupment proceedings as an instance of "mean-spirited homophobia." Cheney ordered the service commanders to back down in these cases, and they did, but the broader policy remained. The cases of Holobaugh, Bettiker, Carney, and others sparked a new movement by gay students urging universities to enforce their antidiscrimination regulations and ban ROTC until the anti-gay policy was lifted. Many colleges did this.[16]

End of the Affair

Meanwhile, Gerry's relationship with Bill Dugan was unraveling. Despite their commonalities—a shared love of policy making, Provincetown, and the sea—they were twenty-five years apart in age. Dugan also had child support payments to make, and he worked two jobs to cover them. Gerry wanted Bill to be around more, but Bill wouldn't quit one of his jobs. Instead, in an impulsive act that Dugan deeply regretted immediately, he cleared his belongings out of their apartment while Gerry was away and moved out.

Gerry felt hurt and abandoned. Bill called to apologize and they met at a restaurant on June 7, 1990, so he could apologize again in person, but there was no attempt at reconciliation. Gerry teared up, but the relationship was over. This was going to cause further heartache for Gerry because his mother and Bill had bonded. They were both Irish, smoked, drank bourbon together, and shared a similar sensibility. But Bonnie had suffered a stroke earlier in the year, and Gerry did not want to deliver sad news.[17]

In a coincidence of cosmic unfairness, as the dejected Studds walked home that night, two young thugs assaulted him near Dupont Circle, the center of Washington's gay community. The assailants blindsided Studds, jumping him from behind, knocking him down, and kicking him. Luckily for Studds, passersby intervened, grabbed the two teenagers, and notified the police, who arrested them.[18]

Studds told reporters that the attack was "inexplicable," and never acknowledged that it had anything to do with his being who he was: "This kind of thing happens many times a day, and it is terribly important to emphasize that. . . . It is humbling and makes you put things in perspective about people who must live in a climate of violence every day." A few weeks later the assailants told reporters that they were only defending themselves because Studds had propositioned them. This was "an absolute lie that apparently took two weeks to concoct," Studds shot back. "This is obscene. This upsets me more than the original attack. I never looked at, said a word to, or paid any attention whatsoever to the assailants. . . . To this day I don't have the foggiest idea what they looked like." By the end of June, the teenagers, charged with assaulting a member of Congress and facing ten years in prison, changed their tune and pled guilty. Now claiming that they had acted in a drunken stupor, they were slapped on the wrist and sentenced to a period of probation.[19]

So what explained the "inexplicable"? The two muggers did not know Studds, and did not try to take his wallet. The likelihood is that they had gone to Dupont Circle, having screwed up their courage with booze, to beat up a gay man—"fag-bashing," as punks like these would have put it. After their story fell apart, the teenagers apologized so as to establish remorse. Studds generously declined to read more into the event than the record disclosed.[20]

Lesbian Vampires at Sea

That summer the navy faced a challenging test of the gay exclusion policy in the case of Karen Stupsky. Stupsky was a Harvard graduate and former ROTC cadet commissioned as an ensign, assigned to the USS *Sylvania*. There she finally acknowledged to herself that she was attracted to women. After consulting with fellow officers she reported her sexual orientation, and the navy initiated discharge proceedings against her. Planning for a fight, she contacted Dyer, who helped her secure legal representation. Thus far Stupsky had never had sex with a woman. Did her thoughts make her a lesbian, and therefore guilty of conduct unbecoming an officer?

Meanwhile, a female officer who had received a memo to high-ranking officers from Vice Admiral Joseph S. Donnell, the commander of the Atlantic Fleet, sent it to Dyer. In his memo Donnell complained that ships' captains had been lax about enforcing the anti-gay policy. Many, Donnell noted, were doing a good job of expelling male homosexuals but were failing to protect female sailors from the predatory advances of lesbians: "We must recognize that women who are targets for female homosexuals experience a unique form of sexual harassment which can be even more devastating and difficult to cope with than the more traditional harassment from men." Donnell further noted that lesbians as a group performed admirably on the job, but emphasized that that fact should not impede enforcement of the rules. As writer Randy Shilts observed, this argument bought heavily in to the "lesbian vampire from hell" stereotype that was widely shared by straight males.[21]

The female officer who forwarded the memo to Dyer was outraged. She had seen what Dyer had heard from other informants: that Donnell's memo was causing female sailors to submit to sexual advances from men they previously would have rejected, since every predator could now threaten any female sailor with an accusation of being a lesbian. Studds released the memo to the newspapers. It showed "an alarming display of Navy sexism as well as homophobia," he wrote. "If it's the Navy's policy to root out top performers, what is going on here?" Once again, Studds brought to light the failures of a counterproductive policy that was rooted in societal prejudices.

The year 1990 brought other challenges for gay rights advocates as well. Studds petitioned the Immigration and Naturalization Service and President Bush to remove the ban on visas for HIV-positive visitors to the United States. The annual International Conference on AIDS was to be held in the United States, and when some HIV-positive attendees were turned away, Studds protested and the INS quietly reversed course. Meanwhile, Barney Frank led the passage of a bill that was signed into law, ending the ban on gay immigrants, a major step toward the normalization of same-sex orientation. In April, Studds sponsored the display of the AIDS "NAMES Project" quilt in the rotunda of the Cannon House Office Building. "It's important for members of Congress to see it," Studds told his readers.[22]

Studds vs. the Airman

Studds seemed poised to repeat his easy electoral victory of 1988 again in 1990. Since 1980 he had used a consulting firm to poll the district and offer advice on electoral strategy. In the last two cycles he had not had to pay them much attention, and 1990 looked no different. He again faced Jon L. Bryan, a management professor and airline pilot, who had garnered a mere third of the vote in 1988. "Studds is certainly well-positioned to win a solid re-election," the consultants advised.[23]

During the spring and summer, however, the political environment shifted. In the governor's race, a Republican social liberal, Bill Weld, was facing off against a Democratic social conservative, John Silber, former president of Boston University and a cantankerous grouch who lost many voters when he gratuitously insulted a popular television anchorwoman. Weld, meanwhile, had the backing of a coterie of gay Republicans, while Silber was a homophobe. A number of Democrats defected to Weld. In August, Iraq's Saddam Hussein invaded the neighboring oil kingdom of Kuwait, and by October, President Bush began mobilizing an international coalition against the evil dictator. Public opinion rallied around the president. Nationally, the wind was beginning to fill Republican sails.

A July 1 article in the *Boston Globe* indicated that these new headwinds were blowing in Studds's face. " 'Family Values' Attract Supporters to Bryan," the headline ran. Two prominent Boston politicians endorsed the unheralded Republican contender—former mayor John Collins, a responsible moderate, now of Falmouth on Cape Cod, and Boston City Councilman Albert "Dapper" O'Neil, a colorful, abrasive social conservative from South Boston, both at least nominally Democrats. Bryan's newspaper ads showed him posed with his wife and children, demonstrating that he was a family man.[24]

Bryan started attacking Studds from every angle, even concocting bizarre charges out of thin air: Studds was cutting the Coast Guard budget; he was endangering dolphins; he was enriching himself at public expense and taking money from secretive political action committees. Studds was flabbergasted. The opposite was true in every case, and the secretive PAC Bryan had mentioned was the Democratic Party. "I have never in twenty years faced a less honest opponent than this guy," he fumed. Studds charged that Bryan, the erstwhile proprietor of a failed local restaurant, former pilot, and current professor, was somehow a millionaire whose actual sources of income remained unclear. This campaign never quite got around to topics like the fishing industry or the pending war with Iraq.[25]

When President Bush came to Massachusetts to campaign for Weld, Bryan had to sit in the audience. He was probably considered too nutty for the patrician Bush and Weld. Studds held an election eve rally at New Bedford's United Fishermen's Club hall that featured Ted Kennedy and Mayor John Bullard. When the *New Bedford Standard-Times* endorsed Bryan that day, Studds, borrowing a line from a recently deceased city councilman, declared, "To hell with the *Standard-Times!*"[26]

Studds won, but with only 53.4 percent of the vote. Bryan carried nineteen towns, capturing the votes of older, socially conservative Bostonians newly migrated to the district. Studds's margin of victory was just 17,588 votes, half of which came from New Bedford.[27] For a congressman poised to become chairman of the most important committee to his district's business interests, Studds had won a weak victory. What if a more formidable challenger, reading those same tea leaves, were to emerge in 1992?

"The Fall of the Policy Is Inevitable"

Studds continued his campaign to end the ban on gays in the military throughout the Bush years. He led thirty-nine colleagues in submitting a letter to President Bush, Defense Secretary Dick Cheney, and Chairman of the Joint Chiefs Colin Powell, the first black man to hold that position. Referring to President Harry Truman's 1948 executive order ending segregation in the armed services, the correspondents wrote: "We submit that discrimination on the basis of sexual orientation is as wrong as discrimination on the basis of race. The only difference is that gay people cannot be detected simply by the color of their skin."[28]

The Pentagon shot back that the ban on gays was "fundamentally differ-ent" from the segregation of African Americans. Some significant segment of the black community, especially its conservative Baptist ministers, held the same view, as did the now influential and widely respected Colin Pow-ell. The official response restated the "good order, morale and discipline" language of the regulations. To this old argument it added that "societal attitudes about homosexuals, however, derive from conduct that defines the class, not from a neutral characteristic such as skin color." The key word, of course, was "conduct." Many Americans still believed that gay men and lesbians had arbitrarily made a lifestyle choice to engage in same-sex behav-ior—a choice that was clearly condemned in the Bible. Studds saw right to the heart of this response. "The Pentagon is essentially saying that it has the obligation to mirror the worst of society's prejudices. That is ignorant and it is wrong," he said, pointing out that the same argument had been made in 1948, and that 81 percent of the public opposed the ban.[29]

Studds continued to support individual gay and lesbian service members. When air force captain Greg Greeley joined the Washington, D.C., annual Gay Pride parade, he was summoned before an investigatory panel and honorably discharged. Former naval cadet Joe Steffan was still demanding reinstatement at Annapolis. Steffan's and Greeley's lawyers discovered that additional studies had been conducted on the suitability of gays in the mili-tary, and Studds requested their release.[30]

Perhaps the most revealing case was that of the Washington State National Guard chief of nurses, Colonel Margarethe Cammermeyer, a twenty-seven-year veteran and holder of a Bronze Star for service in Vietnam. The Guard had sought her out to lead its national nursing program. She accepted the offer, but in her security clearance interview, like Joe Steffan, she felt "honor bound" to tell the truth when they got to the "have you ever had homosex-ual inclinations" question. The interviewers told her they wanted her for the position and implored her to lie, but she wouldn't. Republicans and Dem-ocrats in the Washington delegation joined Studds in advocating for her.[31]

Studds finally received from the Pentagon the document that was most relevant to the Steffan and Greely cases. Studds released that report, which found no correlation between homosexuality and espionage, just as he had released the others. Studds was growing hopeful. "The fall of the policy is inevitable," he declared. "The only question that remains is when it will occur." Defense Secretary Cheney, when questioned by Barney Frank in a hearing, confessed that the notion that gays might be subject to blackmail and therefore should not receive security clearances was "something of an old chestnut." During the Gulf War, gay activists had "outed" Pete Williams, the Pentagon news director, and Cheney had responded by saying, "So what?"[32] Just as in the Salem and McCarthy-era witch hunts, when the accusations rose higher in the social scale, the men in authority closed ranks around their social equals and disparaged the witch hunters.

If more confirmation was needed, the following year the Government Accounting Office released a report that had been requested by Studds and others on the manpower and financial costs of the gay exclusion policy. The GAO determined that about 1,500 service members had been discharged under this policy annually during the 1980s, and a majority of them were female. It found no evidence that the gay service members had disrupted discipline and estimated the costs of training their replacements at $270 million. "We always knew the anti-gay policy was wrong," Studds wrote his constituents. "Now we also know what we had long suspected: that it is also a colossal waste of our money."[33]

In October 1992 a Canadian court ordered its country's military to end its ban on gays. A majority of NATO member nations had arrived at this decision earlier, but the commonality of Canada's culture with America's further suggested that the ban was an anachronism. Studds again wrote to his constituents that the United States should catch up with changing times.[34]

The coming presidential election promised that it just might.

18

Gerry Gerrymandered

As the new Congress assembled in January 1991, Studds rethought his priorities in light of changing international developments. The wars in Central America were winding down. The Nicaraguan Sandinistas lost the election in 1990 to moderates and peacefully surrendered power. The negotiations by the Salvadoran parties advanced, and in January 1992 a final accord was signed.

In the Middle East, Saddam Hussein invaded Kuwait in August 1990, and President Bush assembled a "coalition of the willing" in Saudi Arabia. Studds submitted a bill to block the initiation of hostilities unless Congress declared war. "[Bush] was elected president—not king," Studds declared. Many Democrats urged that a U.N. deadline for Iraq's withdrawal be moved back to August 1991 to allow economic sanctions to work. Congress held a dramatic vote on the issue and gave the president authority to go forward, with a majority of Democrats, Studds included, voting for delay.[1]

Operation Desert Storm, during February and March of 1991, proved a spectacular success. Under attack, Saddam Hussein's unwilling conscripts abandoned their weapons and ran away. His army was destroyed from the air as they fled. The Americans lost fewer than three hundred soldiers in a one-sided battle. President Bush's popularity soared, and many thought the Democrats looked too indecisive to lead America as the world's lone superpower. Like most Democrats, Studds felt relieved but not triumphant with regard to the victory. "No one thought the casualties would be as light as they were," he told a reporter. This was true, but it sounded lame in light of the great victory. "If Kuwait's chief export was codfish, we would not have been in that war," he continued. That too was true, but meaningless.

Saddam Hussein would not have invaded a codfish kingdom in the first place. Jon Bryan, Studds's 1990 Republican opponent, warming up for a rematch, called him an "appeaser."[2]

Studds's interest in international relations was receding, and gay rights issues were becoming more central to him. He dropped off the Foreign Affairs Committee and joined Energy and Commerce. His goals were to establish a Canadian-style single-payer health care system; to increase funding for AIDS education, research, and care; and to develop a sensible energy policy. Most members of Energy and Commerce wanted to serve on the Telecommunications Subcommittee—regulating an emerging industry whose corporations contributed heavily to those who regulated it. Studds sat with his friend Peter Kostmayer before the Committee on Committees, which doled out the assignments. "Ka-ching!" Studds exclaimed, mimicking a cash register, as each bid for Telecom was announced. Studds and Kostmayer took seats on Health and the Environment, chaired by Henry Waxman, Congress's leading advocate for AIDS research and care; Studds also joined the Energy and Power Subcommittee. The new assignments brought his legislative portfolio more in line with the concerns of his constituents: health care, issues of aging, and energy costs.[3]

Fighting AIDS with a Volunteer Army

Studds's new committee assignment allowed him to work more directly on the AIDS crisis. He did this within a wider framework of advocating for single-payer health care, which he believed would provide insurance coverage to everyone while driving down health care costs. In 1990 the country spent 11.5 percent of its GNP on health care—the highest percentage of all the industrialized nations—at a cost of $2,354 per capita, while Canadians spent $1,683 per capita. Yet the United States still ranked thirteenth in life expectancy and twenty-second in infant mortality. Studds estimated that the Universal Health Care Act, H.R. 1300, would save the country $70 billion in its first year alone. In January 1992 he addressed an audience of six hundred at New Bedford High School to argue his case. The high rate of uninsured Americans, especially in poor communities like New Bedford, was making the goal of national health insurance seem possible.[4]

Should such a plan pass, it would ease the financial burden on those stricken by long-term diseases such as AIDS. On the eighth anniversary of the day the word "AIDS" was first spoken on the House floor, by Ted Weiss, Studds reviewed what had happened during the intervening period.

The American death toll from the disease stood at 100,000, and perhaps a million were infected, constituting "a public health emergency the magnitude of which our nation has never experienced," Studds informed his colleagues. The disease was spreading among intravenous drug users. The current research budget had grown to $1.92 billion, but scientists thought this was inadequate relative to the scale of the problem. Studds concluded by quoting activist Larry Kessler, who lamented that "the war on AIDS has been waged by a strictly volunteer army."[5]

Nonetheless, in 1990 Congress and President Bush took several significant steps forward regarding gay rights and the AIDS epidemic. The Hate Crimes Statistics Act included sexual orientation as a category for the first time. The Americans with Disabilities Act protected people with AIDS from discrimination, and courts later ruled that the law applied even to the asymptomatic.[6]

More important was the Ryan White Comprehensive AIDS Resources Emergency (CARE) Act, signed into law in August 1990. Ryan White was an Indiana teenager with hemophilia who had died four months earlier after contracting HIV through a blood transfusion. This law set grant amounts for cities with heavy AIDS caseloads. Henry Waxman was the bill's chief proponent in the House, and Ted Kennedy was its champion in the Senate. Waxman and his committee counsel, Tim Westmoreland, would have preferred to increase Medicaid money to provide for AIDS treatment, since Medicaid, a mandatory spending program, grows to meet demand. Grants, by contrast, are fixed amounts; people had to get on a waiting list to obtain treatment under the Ryan White Act. Waxman's committee monitored support for both programs in the House. In the Senate, however, Lloyd Bentsen, who chaired the Finance Committee, had no interest in AIDS, and it was his committee that oversaw AIDS appropriations. Ted Kennedy's committee had jurisdiction over grants, and so Waxman, Studds, and Westmoreland determined that a grant program, rather than an expansion of Medicaid, was the best deal they could get. Though less than Waxman and other proponents had hoped for, the CARE Act still represented significant progress from the Reagan years.[7]

During 1991, Studds hired Mark Agrast, a civil rights attorney, as his AIDS and gay rights staffer. Agrast, who held a Yale Law degree, had studied political theory at Oxford, and played classical piano, worked with Studds to develop AIDS policy; he attended subcommittee meetings and met with activists, administration officials, scientists, and other congressional staffers.

He also joined Tim Westmoreland to initiate a committee of gay and lesbian staffers on the Hill, most of whom were still in the closet during the Bush years.[8]

"Gerry really respected his staffers," Westmoreland recalled. "Not every congressman does. He listened, took advice, and didn't condescend. As a rule, congressmen and staffers don't socialize, but we did. Our bridge game pushed the prevailing norm. I was so inured to the custom that I called him "Mr. Studds" until he told me to call him by his first name." Still, there was a distracted side to Studds's personality, and he didn't always recognize people he knew. Once he passed Tom McNaught on the House floor without noticing him, and Cape Cod staffer Bob Nickerson recalled a similar incident. That was the absent-minded professor in him, however, not an indication of attitude.[9]

By 1993 Studds had become dissatisfied with the reauthorization funding levels in the Ryan White Care Act. The Bush administration cited the growth in absolute dollar amounts, but Studds and his allies pointed out that the increases had been mandated by the original act, and that six additional cities had reached caseload levels requiring appropriations that the new budget did not meet. Officials at the National Institute of Allergy and Infectious Diseases wanted more money for research and treatment, and Studds insisted that shortchanging its work was penny-wise and pound-foolish: "If the cost of AIDS for fiscal 1993 is frightening to the President, he should consider what his budget will mean ten years from now," Studds argued.[10]

To dramatize the shortfalls, Studds, at a February 1992 subcommittee hearing, called on the federal agencies to break down specifically the budget authorization requests for which funds had not been appropriated. "Now that we have recruited the scientists and built the nationwide network for clinical trials poised for productive work, we would be crazy to abandon them," he warned. Dr. Anthony Fauci at the National Institutes of Health told the committee that only 22 percent of research proposals were coming online. Studds blamed the president (although the House and Senate Appropriations Committees also bore major responsibility) and labeled Bush's AIDS research agenda "an extremely disheartening inventory of lost opportunities."[11]

Studds was similarly disappointed by the administration's AIDS treatment and education policies. In truth, President Bush performed better than his predecessor. First lady Barbara Bush held a baby born with the disease in her arms to show compassion for AIDS victims. Yet the president's priorities continued to disparage the societal outcasts who had contracted the disease—gay men and intravenous drug users. In a letter to William Roper, director of the Centers for Disease Control, Studds complained that "George Bush's silence on AIDS . . . is far from benign," and insisted that the public education campaign "must mention sex and condoms." He urged the CDC to issue educational materials that matched those developed by locally based community groups.[12]

One policy that would have been easy to change was the exclusion from the country of people with aids (PWAs), a regulatory problem that could have been ended by a bureaucratic edict. But the administration, fearing the reaction of an ignorant public, left it in place. As a result, Harvard University lost its bid to host the International AIDS Conference. Among other considerations, the estimated seven thousand visitors had been projected to spend millions of dollars, boosting the local economy. Studds issued an angry news release, but to no avail. In 1989 he had won an exemption for a Dutch PWA, who attended the San Francisco conference, but the rule remained in place.[13]

Studds's interest in health care was not limited to AIDS. He took seriously the relationship between health and the environment. He brought to his new assignment his experience as a conservationist. He learned that the Pacific yew tree, whose bark is a source of the anti-cancer chemical taxol, was being destroyed by timber companies. Studds introduced a bill to protect the tree. Cancer was a much bigger killer than AIDS, and support for its cure was broader. By July 1992 his bill had passed both chambers and was later signed into law. Taxol is still a valuable medication in cancer treatment. Studds also worked to fund medical research for "orphan" diseases, so called because they affect few people, and their treatment therefore offers little profit to pharmaceutical companies.[14]

Love and Death

In January 1991, while contemplating his pending vote on Operation Desert Storm, Studds stopped off at JR's Bar in Dupont Circle. There he noticed a familiar figure—Dean Hara, the tall, handsome man he had briefly dated eleven years earlier. They had liked each other then, and soon found that they still did. Hara was now thirty-two and working in human resources at a nonprofit. The twenty-year difference in their ages mattered less now, and by this time Studds was out of the closet. He invited Hara to give him a call.

To Hara's own surprise, he blurted out the office number. "Is that still it?" he asked. It was.

They had dinner at a Thai restaurant a few nights later. "I guess I put you away for ten years to age," Gerry said. Something clicked, and they agreed to meet again, and then again. Neither was seeing anyone else. Both older and wiser, they gradually became a couple, almost seamlessly, without the intensity of attraction and fear of commitment that often bedevils younger lovers. Gerry may have sensed that Dean had some qualities that his former lovers generally lacked; he radiated optimism, and possessed an even-tempered midwestern stability.

In July, Gerry's mother, Bonnie, died at home at age eighty-three after suffering a stroke two years earlier. The day of her stroke Gerry had called, and when she didn't answer, he phoned his brother Colin and sister-in-law Mary Lou. They discovered Bonnie, incapacitated. Colin and Mary Lou moved into the Black Horse Lane home and became her caregivers. Bonnie had always been a private person; she was proud of her eldest son's success but never intervened with a policy recommendation. She had tended, literally, to her own Cohasset garden, volunteered at a local charity shop, and enjoyed the company of her four grandchildren. Dean had not yet met Colin or Gerry's sister Gaynor. The funeral would not be the appropriate time for that, so he stayed away. Gerry was beginning to realize how comforting it might be to have a companion at his side.[15]

That summer Gerry took Dean to the White House picnic, where he met President Bush and the first lady; Dean thought Vice President Dan Quayle looked visibly nervous about meeting a gay couple at the White House. In December they attended the formal dress White House Christmas party, at which the guests and their spouses are announced. "Congressman Gerry Studds," the military attaché intoned. "No, it's Gerry Studds and Dean Hara," Studds corrected. Like all the other guests, the couple flanked the relaxed president and first lady and smiled for the camera in front of the Christmas tree. Hara later showed the picture to his mother. She was proud, but cautioned, "Don't let them know that you're gay!" Thus did Americans of goodwill lurch into a new era of social history.

The two men kept their separate apartments in Washington. They never lived together there. Dean would stay with Gerry in Provincetown. His first visit was on an unusually chilly Memorial Day weekend; ROTC cadet Jim Holobaugh, whose case Studds had supported, and his boyfriend stayed in the guest room. Gradually Studds was developing a contented personal life as part of a stable couple. Attending Washington social events became easier when he went with Dean, whose natural friendliness balanced Gerry's reserve. Even that characteristic seemed to mellow as Dean became a daily part of Gerry's life.[16]

The Ghost of Elbridge Gerry

One of the challenges facing Massachusetts's new Republican governor, William Weld, was to work with the Democratic legislature to redraw the state's legislative districts after the 1990 census, which indicated that Massachusetts would lose one seat in Congress and the state of Washington gain one. Brian Donnelly of the Eleventh District was about to retire, so his district seemed the obvious one to go. It extended from Dorchester in Boston's southeast corner eastward to Quincy and Weymouth and south through several smaller towns. Insiders recognized that Studds and Chester Atkins in the Fifth District were also likely targets of the governor. Neither congressman had cultivated any friends in the state legislature. By contrast, Joe Moakley in the Ninth District had grown up a few doors down from Massachusetts Senate president William Bulger in a South Boston housing project.

The political jockeying began in March 1991. Weld was backing his undersecretary for economic affairs, Dan Daly, in the Tenth District primary. He figured that if the Republicans could cut New Bedford out of the district and add some Republican towns, Daly might win the general election.[17] The problem was that New Bedford had been in the same district as Cape Cod for two hundred years because of their shared fishing and environmental concerns. Studds was poised to become chairman of the committee that oversaw the relevant federal agencies. Probably even some Republican businessmen could see that the state had a legitimate stake in keeping Studds in Washington.

Democratic legislators decided to make Atkins the sacrificial lamb, merging his district with Worcester's and forcing him into a primary that he would probably lose. But the first legislative plan to emerge also removed five Republican towns from the Tenth District and added five Democratic towns. The *Boston Globe*, advocating for a professional, nonpartisan approach to redistricting, blasted this Democratic map as "an incumbent protection plan." Governor Weld's plan, by contrast, would make Boston a single district, thereby concentrating Democratic votes; create a Merrimack Valley seat north of Boston; and remove New Bedford from Studds's district. There would have to be a compromise.[18]

Then in February 1992 a federal court tossed the entire jigsaw puzzle into the air, scattering the pieces. Massachusetts attorney general Scott Harsh-barger had sued to preserve the eleventh seat. The state prevailed. "This is stunning," a Republican operative expostulated. "No one thought that suit was going anywhere." The court found that the federal government had improperly counted federal employees who lived overseas. Weld could sus-tain a veto in the state Senate, and he had a horse, Daly, who he thought could beat Studds. He and Bulger moved New Bedford and its environs out of the Tenth and replaced them with Quincy, Weymouth, the eastern half of Brockton, and a few neighboring towns. Bulger knew that those were Democratic areas so it was fine with him. The governor signed the bill, after much huffing and puffing against it, some of it by Studds, in March.[19]

In response to the federal court decision Washington and other states appealed to the Supreme Court, further delaying the final outcome. Every Massachusetts congressman held his breath. In June a unanimous Court spoke: Massachusetts lost the seat. The legislature and governor huddled again. Studds could not reverse his loss of New Bedford, but some pun-dits observed that if Jon Bryan ran as an independent in a three-way gen-eral election, splitting the anti-Studds vote, Weld might turn out to have miscalculated.[20]

Although some fishermen had complained about Studds in 1991, the pros-pect of losing him as a congressman rankled. "Studds to Be Missed along New Bedford Waterfront," read a *Boston Globe* headline. "We want Studds," one interviewee said. "Studds is the good guy. He's for the fisherman." None of the new towns in Studds's district had fishing fleets. The *Quincy Patriot Ledger* ran a map of three revised districts, held by Studds, Moakley, and Frank, snaking their way south from Boston, and scoffed at the odd design. "Gerrymandering Leaves Mixed Result in Wake," read the headline, calling attention to the ancestral origins of Studds's first name. Sharing a similar puckish sense of humor, Bulger called this plan a "Weldamander" and Weld called it a "Bulgermander."[21]

Studds learned of the Supreme Court decision on the radio in his office on a hot, muggy Washington night. Hara was with him. The new district left him feeling dispirited. "We went out and walked around the Capitol after we heard it," Hara remembered. Studds voiced his misgivings aloud and said that he might quit. "This could be the first time you serve under a Democratic President that you like," Hara reasoned. "If you run and lose, you did your best, but if you win and Clinton wins, that would be great. You'd be committee chairman [elderly chairman Walter Jones was in failing health] and in a position to affect the issues you care about."[22]

Dean served as a relentlessly upbeat and encouraging voice in Gerry's ear and persuaded him to run. Studds hired Maureen Garde, a former staffer and now a seasoned professional at the Democratic National Committee, to direct the campaign, and even gave up his nightly martini. He was going to run hard.

The City of Presidents

Quincy is a blue-collar town populated by the descendants of Irish, Italian, and Finnish immigrants who had come to work in its famed granite quarries, which furnished the stone for the Bunker Hill Monument. To get the granite to Charlestown, workers constructed the nation's first railroad, running from the quarry to the shore. By 1992 the city's most important attribute was the now shuttered Fore River Shipyard, whose history dated back a century; it had been operated by General Dynamics from 1964 until its closing in 1986. Thousands of plumbers, shipfitters, riggers, machinists, electricians, and unskilled laborers lost their jobs when the yard shut down. Studds was poised to become chairman of the Merchant Marine and Fisheries Committee. He promised to use his clout to revive the yard.[23]

Because Quincy, Weymouth, and Brockton typically voted Democratic, Studds's biggest hurdle might turn out to be the primary election. Two formidable contenders announced: longtime Quincy city councilor and state senator Paul Harold, and Norfolk County district attorney William Delahunt. Both men had deep roots in Quincy, and both had planned to run in the now vanished Eleventh District. By contrast, Studds had no connections there or in Brockton, a gritty former shoe manufacturing town whose chief claim to fame was as the hometown of two boxing champions, Rocky Marciano and Marvin Hagler. Studds, a gay Yale grad from Cohasset whose signature issues had been the coastal environment, Central America, and gay rights, seemed particularly ill-suited to pull off a primary victory on this terrain.[24]

But with two Quincy politicians in the race, the city's Democratic vote was likely to be divided between them, and Studds would be the benefactor. Harold was a favorite son of a city that called itself the City of Presidents—the only city in the country to have produced two—yet it had not sent a native to Congress since John Quincy Adams. As a state senator, Harold did "stellar" constituent service work, as P. J. O'Sullivan, then a Delahunt aide, recalled, and he was promising to focus on urban transit and public works projects. Harold was part of a small group of independent-minded senators challenging Bulger for the leadership of the state Senate. Delahunt was a famously relaxed guy who sometimes came to work wearing a tracksuit, and he was more concerned about policy outcomes than about his own career. Studds met with Delahunt to discuss the race at the latter's Marina Bay apartment. Studds arrived in a jacket and tie; Delahunt wore sweatpants. Delahunt agreed to withdraw and threw his support to Studds.[25]

The long legislative and judicial reset made the contest harder for challengers. If Studds was unknown in Quincy, Harold was unknown on Cape Cod, where Studds had recently shown what seniority on Capitol Hill could do. Over the past few years, Studds had used his position to help the town of Chatham restore its fishing dock. The Army Corps of Engineers had first approved but then rejected a proposal by the town to rebuild the pier when beach erosion threatened to destroy it. The town fishermen (a local T-shirt advertised "Chatham: A Drinking Town with a Fishing Problem") closely examined the report reversing the earlier acceptance and discovered that the figures had been jury-rigged in the cost-benefit analysis. That money was now going to be spent in a Republican district. Just as Chatham was about to lose its fleet to this chicanery, the Bush administration brought a bill to the Merchant Marine and Fisheries Committee to approve a fishing treaty with Estonia, a tiny Baltic state newly emerged from the collapse of the Soviet Union. Studds worked out a deal behind the scenes: Chatham got its pier restored, and Estonia got its fishing treaty. To celebrate the occasion on June 13, 1992, Chatham unveiled a metal statue, *The Provider,* which displayed the bounty of the sea in its glorious variety. The sculptor dedicated his work to "the Fishing Industry of Chatham—Ever Changing to Remain the Same." Only outsiders missed the joke surrounding the strange flag that flew below the American flag. It was Estonia's. Did Cape Cod really want to be represented by a freshman congressman after such a show of clout?[26]

Campaign director Maureen Garde had a lot of national connections, and cash started flowing in from gays, Hollywood actors concerned about Central America, and environmentalists. She put out a brightly colored district map highlighting what Studds had done for each town. Meanwhile, the redistricting quandary had produced the shortest primary season ever: Harold had only two weeks after Labor Day to make his case. The two politicians actually held largely similar positions. The only significant differences between them involved the national health care plan, abortion, and gay rights.[27]

Studds hyped his pending committee chairmanship. Harold contended that that might matter in New Bedford but not in Quincy. Studds told the media at a labor-backed news conference that he expected to work with a Democratic president in 1993 to start rebuilding a U.S.-flagged merchant marine, and that Quincy was one of the places to do it. "I have nothing unkind to say about Paul Harold," he told reporters. "But there is a lot at stake here, and the people who represent the workers know that."[28]

Studds held his election night party at a Rockland hotel. Some polls showed a close election, but Studds had outspent Harold three to one, and Harold had conceded Cape Cod. The results astonished Studds: he won with 61 percent of the vote, carrying Cape Cod with 85 percent. Provincetown voted 1,442–47 for him, Chilmark on Martha's Vineyard 251–2. Harold won Quincy by 12,951–5,256, but barely carried Weymouth. Studds met Harold for breakfast the next day at Barry's Deli in the Wollaston section of Quincy, and the two former rivals toasted each other with coffee cups raised.[29]

"A Campaign of Hate"

Governor Weld's candidate Dan Daly won the Republican primary. Jon Bryan ran as an independent. This was the year of Ross Perot, the quirky billionaire whose chief issue was the budget deficit. Bryan expected that in November, Perot's voters would also vote for him. He had little to lose by running. He was furious at the Massachusetts Republican establishment for picking Daly. He, Jon Bryan, had just missed beating the unbeatable Gerry Studds in 1990, and his reward was to be thrown overboard by the party insiders. This same antiestablishment impulse would give birth to the "Tea Party" phenomenon during the Obama administration and the Donald Trump campaign of 2016.[30]

Bryan still loathed Studds, who had ignored him throughout their previous campaigns. He claimed not to be anti-gay but referred to the now twenty-year-old Page X affair as "rape." In early October, Bryan and his supporters were joined at a "stand out," by Dapper O'Neil, the socially conservative oddball Boston city councilor. As they held signs and waved to the passing traffic in Neponset Circle, on the border between Boston and Quincy, O'Neil told a reporter that Studds was a "faggot," "rapist," and "child molester." To this he added: "I believe in going for the jugular. When I get through with Studds, he'll wish he never heard of me." Studds's campaign spokesman, Tom Lyons, retorted: "We are well aware of what Jon Bryan stands for and that he will try to make this a campaign of hate. Our response is to be a campaign of hope."[31]

Studds pinned much of his own hope on the possibility of reviving the

Quincy shipyard. During the primary, Walter B. Jones, chairman of the Merchant Marine and Fisheries Committee, died. Studds became acting chair. He announced a plan to berth two cargo ships used in the Persian Gulf War at Quincy. Students at the Massachusetts Maritime Academy in Bourne on Cape Cod would train there, and the shipyard would get the berthing fees. The money could then be used to upgrade the yard so that General Dynamics might bid on naval repair contracts. Studds referred to his "clout" throughout the campaign, and this very likely persuaded many Quincy residents to vote for him. The shipyard had employed thousands only a few years earlier, and now it stood idle, its giant Goliath crane visible as a landmark of industrial decay. Daly derided the failed shipyard as proof that Studds didn't have any "clout." If he had so much power, where were the government contracts?[32]

On the one hand, this was manifestly unfair: Brian Donnelly had been Quincy's congressman, not Studds. Yet, on the other hand, Daly was pointing to an important problem that no one dared articulate—because it had few answers in a free market economy. During the Reagan and Bush administrations, the United States had de-industrialized at an alarming rate. Steel mills, auto plants, electrical appliance manufacturers, and shipyards were closing down as businesses moved facilities offshore, where labor was cheaper and government regulation sparse. There was little that workers could do about it. Daly would prove to be correct in this specific case. General Dynamics stayed closed; no shipbuilder would buy it, and twenty years later its giant construction crane was dismantled. As new Asian industrial economies emerged, there was little that legislatures could do in the face of historic global transformations.

The candidates held four debates in the closing weeks of the campaign. The second one, at North Quincy High School, was the nastiest. "Candidates Dive into Political Brawl," read the headline over a dramatic picture that showed Daly, his six-foot-four frame towering menacingly over a smirking, seated Jon Bryan. Bryan had pointed an accusatory finger at Studds, and because the seating arrangement placed Daly between them, the digit wound up under Daly's nose. "If you point that finger one more time, pal, there's going to be trouble," Daly snarled. "Do I make myself clear?" Studds, seated off to the side, regarded the eruption with a look of distressed bemusement. The audience roared with laughter. The contestants displayed more decorum in the next two debates. Studds pushed for a national health care plan, promised to work to lower water and sewage rates, defended his stand on a woman's right to choose, and vowed to deliver jobs to his district.[33]

Daly felt frustrated. Bryan was costing him the race. Out-of-state Republican donors stopped giving to him and contributed instead to candidates
who might win. Meanwhile, the Quincy Democrats united behind Studds,
Donnelly, Harold, and Delahunt all did their part. Studds introduced singer
James Taylor at a benefit concert in Plymouth's Memorial Hall that raised
$50,000 the same night Daly and Bryan clashed in a debate that Studds
skipped.[34]

A few days later Studds attended an event at the town hall in Holbrook,
a few miles south of Quincy. Afterward, as he entered his car to leave, a lone
picketer accosted him, pressing his face angrily against the windshield. "You
faggot!" the man jeered. "You should be in jail!" Studds sat stunned for a
moment, and then said to his driver: "Look at the hate on that man's face.
What kind of life does someone like that live?"[35] Just having to confront
such fury was taking its toll on him.

Studds returned to Rockland's Holiday Inn for the election night party.
He expected to win and wanted a majority, not just a plurality. Despite the
cold, rainy weather, the turnout had been high. Once again, he was stunned
by the result—an incredible 61 percent of the vote. The final tally was Studds,
189,343; Daly, 75,887; and Bryan, 39, 265. Studds carried Quincy with 22,336
votes to 9,918 for Daly and 4,904 for Bryan. Redistricting had helped two
Massachusetts Republican congressional candidates to win—Peter Blute in
Worcester and Peter Torkildsen on the North Shore. Studds was overjoyed
to be celebrating his victory along with the new love in his life, and to be
returning to a Washington led by a new Democratic president, William
Jefferson Clinton.[36]

19

Don't Ask, Don't Tell and a Memorable Address

GERRY STUDDS strongly supported only three presidential candidates in his life—John Kennedy, Gene McCarthy, and Ted Kennedy, all of whom ran when he was in the closet. Neither Jimmy Carter nor Walter Mondale nor Mike Dukakis, the three Democratic Party nominees of the 1980s, had said anything inspiring about gay rights or the AIDS crisis. By 1992, however, the national culture had changed so that for the first time in American history, the question of gay and lesbian rights had come onto the agenda, with military service the central issue. Studds was the nation's most prominent advocate for an end to the ban on gays serving in the armed forces.

Five major candidates contested the Democratic nomination in 1992: Iowa senator Tom Harkin, California governor Jerry Brown, Nebraska senator Bob Kerrey, former Massachusetts senator Paul Tsongas, and Arkansas governor Bill Clinton. Brown, Tsongas, and Clinton all earnestly supported gay rights, but as two perceptive writers put it, for gay people, Clinton was a "cipher." Closer examination revealed his record to be disappointing. Like most southern states, Arkansas had an anti-gay sodomy law. Clinton, who was attorney general when it passed, told gay activists that he had worked against it behind the scenes in 1977. No one could remember his doing so, and he would never have been elected governor if it were known that he had. As governor, Clinton did little to promote AIDS funding. Yet presidential candidate Clinton had several advantages with regard to the gay community. His friend David Mixner, with whom he had worked on the McCarthy campaign in 1968, brought the wealthy California gay community to Clinton's side. Moreover, Clinton's views were evolving as he appealed to a national electorate. At a Kennedy School of Government forum in 1991, he said that he opposed the ban on gays in the military and promised to appoint gays and lesbians to his administration, name an AIDS czar, and issue an executive order ending anti-gay discrimination in the federal government.[1]

Clinton bested his rivals in the early primaries and drove the others, except Brown, from the field by April. That's when Studds endorsed him. Clinton promised the Democratic congressional caucus an energetic campaign for AIDS education and research. "It was refreshing after twelve years and two presidents who were barely even able to say 'AIDS' much less show a real commitment to battle it. Clinton spoke right from the heart," he told his constituents.[2]

That was the real ace up Clinton's sleeve. He was a man of broad sympathies, a policy wonk who felt genuine emotions. Clinton may have been "straight" in his sexual orientation, but he was "hip"—a pot-experimenting saxophone player whose lifestyle brought him closer to outlaw cultures than most politicians dared venture. Clinton impressed the crowd at a gay and lesbian Los Angeles-fund raiser, and in the pre-Internet age, a video of the event went viral through the U.S. mail.[3]

Studds went to Madison Square Garden for the Democratic convention. He was in a tight primary race himself and was looking for money and allies. Hara came up from Washington with him. They were getting to be a familiar couple. San Francisco supervisor Roberta Achtenberg, a lesbian, and Robert Hattoy, a gay man with AIDS, addressed the delegates, 104 gay men and lesbians among them. "The 1992 convention was the most euphoric and heady convention we as a community had ever experienced," longtime activist Jean O' Leary later wrote.[4]

Clinton won the election, and the Democrats gained majorities in the House and Senate. The stars had come into alignment for lifting the military ban. Clinton could end it with a stroke of his pen by means of an executive order, and gay activists believed that he would. On the night before the inauguration, Studds spoke with a contact in the White House and then called David Mixner, who was putting on his tuxedo for an event honoring him. Studds had good news and bad news, and Mixner elected to hear the bad news first. As he later described the conversation, Studds told him:

> "I just talked to the White House. The President is not going to sign the executive order in the next couple of days."
>
> The knots in my stomach grew tighter. "Jesus Gerry, you better have good news now."

"Don't worry. It's all taken care of—I have their word. All parties—the Congress, the military, and the President—have reached agreement. There will be a six month study which will be used as a cooling off period. At the end of the six months the President has promised that he will sign the order."

I was still uneasy. "Gerry, are you convinced that he will do it in six months?"

"Yeah, David, I am. In fact, if you want, why don't you announce it tonight at your event?"[5]

Inauguration day was especially exhilarating for gays and lesbians. Clinton and Vice President Al Gore applauded as volunteers from the NAMES Project marched past, bearing panels from the AIDS quilt. Studds and Hara arrived a little late, riding the Metro with other exuberant members of the public. Newly chosen as chairman of Merchant Marine and Fisheries, Studds sat on the dais with his fellow committee chairmen. Hara, wearing a spousal security badge, was led through the warren of underground House hallways, all of a sudden emerging into the cold, bright morning air to be met by a military guard in full dress uniform. "Hello, Dean," the officer said. He was gay; Hara knew him. "I sat with the white-haired congressional wives," Hara remembered. He was placed alongside a southerner wearing fur and sporting big hair. "Hey, Dean," she welcomed him warmly, giving him a hug. "We all are gonna be on television today, honey!"[6]

After the ceremony, Studds and Hara attended a luncheon in Statuary Hall. Clinton came into the room, and they went over to say hello. "I want you to know," the new president said, one hour into his term, "we're going to keep this commitment."[7] Studds and Hara danced at the Triangle Ball, held at the National Press Club, the first gay inauguration gala, with two thousand festive revelers. Singer Melissa Etheridge, who had just come out, performed, and Joe Steffan, accompanied by a uniformed color guard, sang the national anthem.[8] Studds and Hara joined their friends Tim McFeeley, executive director of the Human Rights Campaign, donor Fred Eychaner, and their partners at an official black tie gala.[9] This was no longer Ronald Reagan's America.

Five days later, on Sunday, Clinton and his national security people met with the Joint Chiefs of Staff in the Roosevelt Room at the White House at four o'clock in the afternoon. Chairman Colin Powell had requested the meeting, at which the question of gays in the military would be one among others under discussion. That morning, Secretary of Defense Les Aspin had said on *Meet the Press* that if the Joint Chiefs didn't want to drop the ban,

the administration would maintain it. Powell concisely reviewed important security issues, and the group then spent the next hour and forty-five
minutes on the gay ban. Each of the four Joint Chiefs, and Powell himself,
explained why he wanted no change in the policy. Clinton listened intently.
He had taken some heat during the campaign for not having served in the
military during the Vietnam War. In addition, with the Cold War over, he
was about to cut the budget for each service branch to reduce the deficit.
He needed the willing cooperation of these military commanders, whose
subordinates might soon have to go into battle in Somalia or Bosnia. Clinton cited the statistics from the Government Accounting Office report that
Studds had solicited, showing that thousands of warriors were being discharged despite their strong performance, and protested that he had made
a campaign promise to lift the ban. Toward the end of the meeting, Powell
said, "We could stop asking about sexual orientation when people enlist."[10]

Thus was born the "don't ask, don't tell" compromise that many conservatives regarded as a concession to sin and many gay activists considered a
betrayal. Actually, the January meeting registered the deadlocked state of
the debate on an issue that had not yet been ventilated among the public.
Clinton agreed that the Joint Chiefs would study the matter for six months,
during which time they would suspend the expulsions. Defense Secretary
Aspin would produce a memorandum by July 15. Clinton did not want to
waste political capital on a matter that seemed extraneous to most people's
concerns, but he found himself backed into a corner. While he could have
issued an executive order lifting the ban, Congress could assert its ultimate
authority by statute. Clinton did not need a fight with Congress on gay
rights. In fact, it was Senate minority leader Bob Dole, already preparing
his own presidential campaign for 1996, who had moved the issue to the
foreground, along with some Democrats such as Sam Nunn of Georgia,
the chairman of the Senate Armed Services Committee. Few congressmen
welcomed a debate on a controversy that might spark an electoral challenge
if they voted their conscience.

Nor were gay activists prepared for a fight. They had simply assumed
that Clinton would issue an executive order and the case would be closed.
By reassuring activists that after six months he would sign the order, President Clinton had left the movement demobilized. Many gay activists were
culturally anti-military to begin with and had never prioritized the issue.
For a decade, their chief concerns had been AIDS funding, a federal anti-
discrimination bill, and repeal of the sodomy laws. There was not even a
single authoritative organization dedicated to fighting the ban, so the

activists formed Campaign for Military Service. In contrast, conservatives felt that their military citadel was being invaded by an alien, permissive culture, and they flooded their representatives with mail. Finally, neither of the two openly gay congressmen served on the Armed Services Committee, and both had demanding schedules of their own. The battle was joined, and the civil rights army looked to be asleep in its tent.[11]

"Homosexuals Are Not Cowards"

Studds understood that the case would not be closed even if Clinton did issue an executive order. Congress could override it, and very well might. He and Barney Frank were concerned that many movement activists did not grasp this. In the aftermath of Clinton's meeting with the Joint Chiefs, and a previously leaked congressional memo, Studds compared the task of the gay civil rights movement with that facing the African American freedom struggle during the 1960s. "I don't think the gay community can pull this off alone," Studds warned. "I marched with King from Selma to Montgomery and I marched with him in Washington in 1963, with people of all sexes and colors. This is the last major chapter of the two-century-old history of the civil rights movement in this country. It's a time for people of good will to come together again."[12]

As a former history teacher, he saw historic events, and Clinton's compromise, in long-term perspective. "I absolutely support the president's judgment. I don't remember any civil rights fight ever resolved by a single stroke of anyone's pen. They have always taken years or longer, and a lot of blood and sweat. This one is no different."[13]

To counter the Pentagon propaganda, Studds called attention to the findings of the PERSEREC and GAO reports. From 1986 through 1990, the military had conducted at least 3,663 investigations, just over two a day for four years, at an undetermined cost. Training one enlisted replacement cost $28,000, and $120,000 for an officer. Not one person discharged for being gay had been found unsuited to serve for other reasons. Responding to the charge that gays and lesbians disrupted good order and discipline, the GAO investigated police and fire departments that employed them and reported no problems. Studds concluded that only irrational homophobia motivated the ban.[14]

Studds was very busy in this period with his new responsibilities as committee chairman, but he made time to contribute to lesbian and gay rights issues. The state of Colorado had voted for Clinton in 1992 but simultaneously passed a binding referendum that overturned existing municipal anti-discriminatory measures. Most alarmingly, the referendum banned any further such measures in the future. Colorado had become headquarters for several national Christian conservative organizations, and their fund-raising overwhelmed the efforts of the state's civil rights community. Studds went to Denver at the behest of the Human Rights Campaign Fund to speak as the civil rights forces regrouped. The organization was suing in state court to overturn the referendum result, a case that would end with a victory for gays in the Supreme Court's landmark 6–3 *Romer v. Evans* decision.[15] Studds played his part in this case as a national spokesman.

Studds and Frank both raised the alarm about the need for *political* action. "The president wouldn't have to pause for a moment if members of Congress felt that they could do what they damn well know is right without paying an awful political price," Studds urged. They both spoke on *Face the Nation* as stories appeared in the press suggesting that only thirty senators would support lifting the ban. They called on gay activists in the Bay State to contact the two freshmen Republican congressmen, Peter Blute and Peter Torkildsen, to sway their votes. Both worried about the impending hearings that would be conducted by Senate Armed Forces Committee chairman Sam Nunn and their effect on public and congressional opinion.[16]

Meanwhile, gay activists mobilized for a March on Washington scheduled for Sunday, April 25. The call for the march preceded Clinton's election and the emergence of the military question. The organizers put together a list of speakers that represented the various elements of the gay movement, without prioritizing the new reality. As the date neared, the Park Service dragged its feet on issuing a permit. Studds helped to secure it.[17]

Coincidental to the march, Studds had a moving experience at an advance opening for dignitaries at the newly inaugurated Holocaust Museum. The museum personalizes the visit for each guest by randomly generating a card describing the story of one victim. Studds was stunned to receive the story of Willem Aronders, a Dutch artist who used his skills to falsify papers for Jews. The Nazis caught him and sentenced him to death. Aronders was also homosexual. Before being executed, he instructed his lawyer to tell people that "homosexuals are not cowards." Studds was particularly impressed by the museum's remembrance of gay victims of the Holocaust. He read into the *Congressional Record* the story of Aronders's arrest fifty years earlier. Its significance for the debate about gays in the military was manifest.[18]

Studds entered a whirlwind of activity the weekend of the march. On

Friday he hosted five meetings with visiting activists and attended two others. That night he spoke at a black tie dinner sponsored by the Human Rights Campaign Fund at the Mayflower Hotel, introducing gay and lesbian service people and veterans to the crowd. Saturday was even more hectic. Studds and Hara began the day on the Mall, where they read names of AIDS victims aloud for the NAMES Project. Next Studds was introduced to a big crowd at a luncheon sponsored by the Gay and Lesbian Victory Fund honoring their elected and appointed officials—sixty in all. Clinton loyalist James Carville gave the main address without mentioning the words "gay" or "lesbian," signaling how hot the topic remained inside the administration.[19]

From the Capitol Hilton, Studds raced off to the Dupont Plaza, where he delivered a brief address to the National Lesbian and Gay Law Association. Studds shared a panel with colleagues Eleanor Holmes Norton and Lynn Woolsey on Congress and the military issue. After collapsing at home for an hour, Studds headed off for a National Gay and Lesbian Task Force event honoring Pat Schroeder and Ron Dellums of the House Armed Services Committee. From there Studds departed for a Democratic Congressional Campaign Committee fund-raiser at Barney Frank's house, and then to a reception hosted by the Massachusetts AIDS Action Council, where he welcomed the guests. Here he was greeted by two old friends, Larry Kessler and former staffer Tom McNaught. His presence had to be particularly reassuring to the several hundred guests because national attention had shifted from AIDS to the military issue, and Studds had been a champion of both causes. The penultimate stop was at the Ritz-Carlton for a reception hosted by the Campaign for Military Service and the Lambda Legal Defense Fund, attended by veterans and active duty personnel with important cases pending. Finally, Studds attended the March on Washington Gala, where he warmed up the crowd for keynote speaker Jesse Jackson. With Colin Powell denying the relationship between the African American freedom struggle and the gay civil rights movement, Jackson's presence added significant moral authority to the cause.[20]

The March on Washington

The march marked a turning point in gay and lesbian history. The military question squarely raised the issue of the place of gay people in American life. It challenged their image in the straight mind, from that of irresponsible hedonists to fighting men and women committed to self-discipline. "We are different from you and your uptight culture!" rang the early gay manifestos. By 1993 the message had changed to "We are more like you than you think. Only our sexual orientation is different."

The organizers claimed that a million people marched. They departed from a staging ground on Constitution Avenue and filed past the White House for hours in contingents that included military personnel, AIDS activists, parents of gay children, and many others. The demonstration continued past Capitol Hill and on to the Mall. Studds and Hara, who was wearing a PTN (for "Provincetown") T-shirt, marched with the VIP contingent.

The list of speakers reflected the diversity of the gay movement and its allies. The organizers broadened the coalition to include Ben Chavis of the NAACP and Patricia Ireland of the National Organization for Women. Representatives of gay organizations and individual activists delivered spirited addresses. Larry Kramer of ACT UP blasted President Clinton as "Bill the Welcher" and declared that nothing had changed from the Reagan-Bush years: people were still dying of AIDS and the government was still doing nothing. Tim McFeeley of the Human Rights Campaign Fund presented an overview of the challenges facing the movement: AIDS, teen suicide, the military ban, and employment discrimination. Lesbian activists Virginia Apuzzo, Michelle Crone, Robin Tyler, and Urvashi Vaid addressed the crowd in language ranging from analytical to salty. Musicians played, the drag queen RuPaul strutted, actors offered their support, and tennis champion Martina Navratilova drew cheers. By the time David Mixner appeared, four hours into the event, the day had dragged on and the crowd was growing restive.[21]

Then a bugle sounded "Reveille" and the announcer intoned, "Ladies and gentlemen, dikes and fags, brothers and sisters, please welcome the combined forces color guard!" and the loudspeaker blared the stirring "Marines' Hymn" as uniformed color bearers marched smartly onstage presenting the American and rainbow flags. The announcer introduced a score more of soldiers, sailors, airmen, and marines, who saluted the flag as they passed while other familiar military anthems sounded—"Anchors Aweigh," "Stars and Stripes Forever," and "Wild Blue Yonder." The crowd ceased its murmuring and rose to its feet; some of the departing demonstrators turned around. Their faces reflected the growing awareness that they beheld onstage men and women who had risked their lives in service to their country and their careers in service to the cause of gay equality. The applause swelled.

The music stopped. "Ladies and gentlemen, now please welcome the highest-ranking elected gay official in the United States—please welcome Congressman Gerry Studds!" The applause continued but did not swell. Probably few people in the audience had heard of him. Studds wore a dark suit and red tie with diagonal stripes, looking every inch the dignified congressman, his bearing marking a contrast to some of the flamboyant entertainers who had come before. The crowd fell silent, and Studds delivered the most memorable address of his life. He spoke in bold declarative sentences, pausing for emphasis to let the words sink in. During his few short minutes on the podium, he was interrupted by applause nine times:

> Thirty years ago, Martin Luther King led one-quarter of a million people to this very place—to ask this country to keep a promise—a promise implicit in the Constitution, but not yet explicit in our laws. He helped us write a magnificent chapter in the history of civil rights.
>
> Today, a million Americans have come to this place to ask our country to help us write the last remaining, unfinished chapter in that history. Look—look around you. This is a history that is worth *fighting* for. This is a history that is worth *defending*. And that is why we *have* armed forces. But some people seem to have forgotten what it is they're supposed to defend. It is not just a piece of geography—every army does that. They're supposed to preserve, protect, and defend the Constitution of the United States: the land of the free and the home of the brave. Well, look out here on the mall, Senator Nunn, General Powell. There are a million people here, Senator. And they are very, very brave—especially, General, the ones in uniform. *But they are not yet free!*
>
> The question is not whether gay men and lesbians will serve in the armed forces. They always have, they do now—at every rank and level—and they always will. The question is whether they will be allowed to do so openly—with dignity and with pride—or whether they will be compelled to live a lie.
>
> The Department of Defense's rationale for the ban falls of its own weight—after roughly two seconds of reflection. Don't tell us about *security*. You cannot blackmail someone who has nothing to hide. And don't give us that tired old mantra about discipline, good order, and morale. We've heard that before, in 1948, the same words—*verbatim,* the same words—when President Truman issued an executive order ending racial segregation in the armed forces.
>
> We acknowledge the need for discipline and good order. And we have read the Navy's report on Tailhook. And we have concluded, nonetheless, that it would be wrong—fundamentally wrong—to ban heterosexuals from serving in the armed forces. The standard for *all* should be *conduct*—not status.

My friends, if at 12:00 tomorrow every gay and lesbian person in America stood up for two minutes—in the Army, in the Navy, in the Air Force, in the Marine Corps, in the House and in the Senate, every doctor, every lawyer, every carpenter, every teacher, every clergyman—this debate would be over.

Look—look around you, General Powell. Look, Senator Nunn. Here on the mall there *are* soldiers and sailors and airmen and marines, officers, enlisted men,—there *are* doctors and lawyers and teachers, and carpenters, and clergy—*and* members of Congress. Gay men and lesbians, Senator, General. And do you know how to spell that? H-U-M-A-N.

Look—look at this enormous family. Do you hear that, Senator Helms? *Family.* Look very carefully: look at the quilt, look at the faces. There is on this mall something more contagious by far than any virus—something called *self-respect.* And it is with this most powerful and benign of all contagions—and with immense pride—that we now call upon our country, in all of its magnificent diversity—black and white, male and female, straight and gay—to join us in concluding this final chapter in the history of the civil rights of us *all.*

Studds was followed by Dorothy Hajdys, the mother of Alan Schindler, a sailor who had been beaten to death on his ship by two haters. Hajdys stood flanked by two sailors in uniform, one bearing a photo of her son. When she finished, the color guard and service people marched offstage to chants of "Justice! Justice!" These dramatic presentations marked the emotional climax of the afternoon.

Studds had combined humor, outrage, and an appeal to the nation's best traditions in a speech that should endure as part of the nation's civil rights history. As did several other orators, he placed the gay civil rights struggle in the context of the African American movement, opening with an explicit reference to Martin Luther King, interweaving the desegregation of the military, and concluding with an implicit reference to Aretha Franklin, whose hit song "Respect" had once captured the mood of a people. The crowd giggled at his laugh line, when he referred to the Tailhook scandal, in which drunken male naval officers had harassed their female colleagues, a disgrace to their uniforms for which no one blamed all heterosexuals. Tailhook represented a genuine assault on good order and discipline. When Studds implored Senator Nunn and General Powell to look, look around on the Mall, the silence seemed to deepen, and the television cameras scanned the faces in the crowd, appearing thoughtful and somber. The biggest applause line came when he beseeched the crowd to "look at this enormous family. Do you hear that Senator Helms? *Family.*" Jesse Helms, a former segregationist, now played the role performed by George Wallace for the 1963 March on Washington. In truth, if the 1993 march was the equivalent of the 1963 demonstration, this was the gay civil rights movement's "I Have a Dream" speech.

The centrality of the military issue probably dawned on many in the crowd right at this moment. The implications of ending the ban were enormous. The homophobes believed that gays and lesbians, because of their weak character, had made an immoral choice in their lifestyles, which, in the case of gay men, was exemplified by their stereotypical effeminate behavior. Homophobic conceptions mirrored those of whites toward blacks before the Civil War. Whites who accepted slavery believed it to be justified by the inferior, naturally servile character of black people. When Lincoln agreed to form black regiments in 1863, many whites were horrified. The idea seemed to violate nature. So did matters seem to the homophobes in 1993. Should gay men openly demonstrate their courage at arms, they would undermine traditional notions of masculinity. Studds's brief speech had skewered these ideas.

Yet the march also revealed political divisions among the reformers. Larry Kramer hit the Democrats hard and received some mild applause. And when Congresswoman Nancy Pelosi of San Francisco rose to read a bland address from President Clinton, she was interrupted by chants of "Where's Bill?" The president had chosen not to be in town that day. Studds, not wishing to criticize the president, compared Clinton's role to that of President Kennedy in 1963. Clinton had recently met with leaders of gay organizations, just as Kennedy had met with African American leaders in 1963, but neither attended the event.[22]

Barney Frank later described the entire occasion in his memoir with considerable distaste, contrasting the decorum of the 1963 marchers with the exuberance of 1993. He referred disparagingly to one lesbian comedian, whose profanity-laced speech he found to be in extremely poor taste. The introduction of the soldiers with the line "Ladies and gentlemen, dikes and fags" exemplified the problem for him, as did the stereotypically clownish behavior of some of the soldiers just before they were called onstage. Tim McFeeley, executive director of the Human Rights Campaign, and a former Democratic Party ward leader in Boston, shared these concerns, and felt that he had been hustled off the stage by the prompter when he had barely begun his address. McFeeley also urged the organizers, without success, to demonstrate the movement's continuity with the African American civil rights movement by including Jesse Jackson on the main stage. Both Frank and McFeeley worried that countercultural displays would only provide grist for the conservative mill, making the work of congressional reformers more difficult. Frank was also right to criticize the failure of the leadership to organize a lobbying campaign.

Nevertheless, Frank mistakenly dismissed the power of mass action, especially for gays and lesbians, who, unlike African Americans, could assume invisibility. It is likely that millions of closeted people took heart from the demonstration and that many of them were inspired to announce their sexual orientation to family members. By such individual acts of courage the national atmosphere slowly changed, and led to the ending of the military ban seventeen years later.[23]

After the march, the hard-liners dug in and carried on as if the event had not taken place. Nunn's Senate Armed Services Committee conducted a series of hearings, some in the field, at which soldiers and sailors voiced their concerns about living in close quarters with gays. The hearings produced no evidence that one heterosexual service member had ever been harmed by a homosexual.[24]

Under these circumstances, Frank sought a way to salvage a compromise from impending defeat. Toward the end of the month, he floated a new idea to make the "don't ask, don't tell" compromise more palatable. In his judgment, which proved to be accurate, the game was lost. Frank's plan was that gay service people would have to abide by the rule while on duty, but not off duty. Thus, a soldier or sailor might acknowledge her or his sexual orientation under certain conditions.[25] This alternative might have saved the careers of thousands of gay and lesbian military personnel who would be discharged under the "don't ask, don't tell" policy. Yet in the aftermath of the demonstration, to a constituency emboldened by the seeming display of its own power, this looked like a capitulation to the status quo. Frank suffered a wounding critique from some gay movement activists who argued that he had given Clinton cover to retreat from his earlier position.[26]

Studds issued his own news release, headlined "Now Is Not the Time to Run Up the White Flag." Not mentioning Frank by name, Studds restated the fundamental principles and concluded, "I cannot endorse such a compromise at this time," thus leaving the door open to doing so in the future. "The country is only beginning to hear from our side in this debate, and I do not believe the American people have concluded that the debate is over. . . . The issue raised in this debate is one of fundamental civil rights. On this, there can be no compromise. Rosa Parks did not fight for the right to sit in the middle of the bus, and we cannot accept a compromise that continues to require us to live a lie."[27]

Studds thus reaffirmed the goal in stirring language, including another reference to a chapter from the civil rights movement. "It was very bitter for Gerry that Colin Powell could not see the analogy," Studds's aide Mark Agrast later recalled. "Powell could have turned the tide." Studds was also personally close to some of the military personnel and ROTC cadets who had challenged the ban. "We all believed that when we put up this parade of heroes in uniform," Agrast said, "it would sweep away the cynics because it was so obviously right . . . [but] we were naïve."[28]

There is much truth to Agrast's retrospective comment. That was the way Studds looked to Barney Frank—naïve. Years later Frank recalled, with considerable insight, that "Gerry was an odd political figure. He did not like the personal aspect of legislating. He did not get involved in the nitty-gritty." Frank acknowledged Studds's ability to state fundamental principles clearly as an orator but considered him, with some justice, to be a poor tactician.[29]

The divergence in views strained relations between Frank and Studds. "Things were tense between them for a while," McFeeley, who was a friend of both congressmen, recalled. Tom Iglehart visited Studds in his office and remembered Studds complaining that Frank had not consulted him before advancing his compromise.[30] Nevertheless, this was in essence a tactical disagreement whose significance is eclipsed by the fact that the military brass would not accept openly gay service members, and the president was in too weak a position to impose his will. The discussion was just beginning. The 1954 *Brown v. Board of Education* decision led to eleven years of turmoil until the passage of the Voting Rights Act, and another three years of violence culminating in the murder of Martin Luther King Jr. For the lesbian and gay civil rights movement and its relation to the broader public, by analogy, 1993 stood closer to 1954 than to 1965.

Studds fought a rear-guard action as the July 15 deadline approached for the Pentagon to submit its plan. With Patricia Schroeder and sixty-seven others, he issued a letter calling on Clinton to end the ban and urging the Pentagon to release a Rand Corporation study which reportedly concluded that the anti-gay policy was counterproductive. Two days later a GAO study came out, reviewing the policies of such allies as Canada, Sweden, Germany, and Israel, all of which had transitioned to an inclusive military.[31]

Studds and Frank met at the White House with Defense Secretary Aspin and Clinton's senior aide George Stephanopoulos to comment on the final draft. Studds issued an eloquent personal appeal to Clinton, thanking him for his efforts but mournfully concluding that "the draft finesses the question of whether homosexuality per se is incompatible with military service.

At the same time, however, it explicitly insists that lesbians and gay men will continue to be subject to investigation and separation from the service merely for speaking privately about their sexual orientation or engaging in private consensual conduct. . . . I respectfully renew my appeal to you to put before the Congress a plan that will allow lesbians and gay men to serve with dignity and pride."[32]

Three days later the president went to the National Defense University at Fort McNair and, flanked by the Joint Chiefs, announced to a large audience of officers the "don't ask, don't tell" compromise. In his memoir, Clinton called attention to its positive steps forward: "If you don't say you're gay, the following things will not lead to your removal: marching in a gay-rights parade in civilian clothes; hanging out in gay bars or with known homosexuals; being on homosexual mailing lists. . . . On paper, the military had moved a long way." Clinton, whose book appeared in 2004, nevertheless acknowledged that practice had not matched what was "on paper."[33]

In practice, commanding officers and judge advocates general showed arbitrary prosecutorial discretion, established clashing precedents, and produced confused outcomes. "I helped craft the rules at Defense," Mark Agrast recalled. "Once they were enacted, the parsing of the rules became a Talmudic exercise."[34] In some cases, of course, "don't ask, don't tell" saved some service members from being "outed." Nevertheless, many conservative officers still wanted an unalloyed ban, with everyone continuing to be "asked" upon enlistment. Thousands of good men and women were discharged from every service branch over the next seventeen years.

On Labor Day weekend, Studds and Hara flew together to New Orleans, where Studds was to speak at the annual convention of Parents, Families and Friends of Lesbians and Gays. "Sometimes anti-gay constituents demand to know if I am a 'practicing homosexual,'" he began. "I tell them, 'No, actually I'm pretty good at it by now." He offered an insider anecdote to explain his long-term optimism: lots of colleagues privately admitted that they voted against gay issues only because they feared public opinion. "If we had the president's proposal to revoke the ban on the floor, and we could vote on it in secret ballot, it would pass two to one." That, he postulated, would change over time as people came out of the closet and their parents spoke up their behalf. As for Sam Nunn stoking phony fears, Studds had another gag line: "I told him that if he raised one more red herring, I would assert jurisdiction over the debate in my capacity as chairman of the Fisheries Committee." And he concluded by reprising his own life story— that of a closeted, fearful man who would only cautiously jog near the 1979 demonstration, but who now stood before the public accompanied by his lover.[35] Studds mixed a cocktail of humor, historic perspective, and encouragement for the parents in his audience, reassuring them that openly showing pride in their gay son or lesbian daughter mattered. Ultimately, it did.

In late September 1993, Congress wrote a more restrictive version of the Pentagon regulations into law, codifying the ban on gays in the military, thus making the situation arguably worse than it had been before Clinton took office. The vote was 301–134, with mostly northern Democrats voting against the ban. A resolution to end it, put forward by Marty Meehan of Lowell, Massachusetts, failed. Studds was disappointed but felt undeterred. "We may lose some battles, but we shall prevail," his news release asserted. He remained optimistic about the future. "Despite our disappointment at this temporary defeat, we must not lose heart," he concluded. "*Every* civil rights movement has been an incremental progression, with setbacks and compromises along the way. We will lose some battles, as we have this week. But our cause is just, and we shall prevail. Our country shall yet rise up and live out the true meaning of its creed."[36] Few noticed what Studds said, but he was right.

Seventeen years later, a new generation of veterans, steeled by combat in Iraq and Afghanistan, fighting against an enemy that punished homosexuality by execution, had cast off the prejudices of the past. Led by one such veteran, Representative Patrick Murphy of Pennsylvania, Congress lifted the ban with a few votes to spare. President Barack Obama signed the bill into law, and no ill effects have followed.[37]

20

Saving the Whales ... but Not Much Else

Dᴜʀɪɴɢ ᴛʜᴇ ᴅᴇʙᴀᴛᴇ about "don't ask, don't tell," Studds was working hard as chairman of the Merchant Marine and Fisheries Committee. He now led one of only twenty-two House committees, with forty-eight members and seventy staffers, and five subcommittees that oversaw federal agencies wielding significant authority. Here he hoped to exercise his power to some effect. Unfortunately for the nation's shipbuilders, merchant sailors, and fishermen, globalization and overfishing had greatly diminished their industries, and no politician could have saved them. Nevertheless, Studds did achieve some successes in protecting the environment and the local landscape in ways that are still felt today.

Kilroy Was Here ... but Now He's Gone

James Kilroy worked as an inspector at Quincy's Bethlehem Steel shipyard during World War II. In those years the yard operated around the clock, employing 32,000 people. During the war, Bethlehem Steel turned out ninety ships. According to one version of the story, Kilroy scrawled the words "Kilroy was here" onto the hull when he approved the work, and the expression became famous to the World War II generation as an assertion of the ubiquity of the unknown working man. General Dynamics bought the yard in 1964 and operated it for the next twenty-two years, but in 1986 the company shut its doors, laying off thousands. Kilroy was gone.[1]

Over the next six years, the former employees made several unsuccessful efforts to bring the yard back. It seemed impossible to believe that this once mighty enterprise, and the accumulated skill of its workers, could go to waste. The Massachusetts Water Resources Authority acquired the property and used some of it as a staging area for its cleanup of Boston Harbor. The workers formed their own corporation and sought bids on jobs. None of it worked. In 1988 the MWRA sold off thousands of disused items at auction for pennies on the dollar. There matters stood when Studds became chairman of the Merchant Marine and Fisheries Committee.[2]

"The key to unlocking the yard's potential may rest with U.S. representative Gerry Studds," the local newspaper observed. Studds introduced legislation to make loan subsidies and tax incentives available to potential buyers in a risky, newly competitive market. He also worked to entice shipbuilders to buy the facility. "I myself have ushered through the yard several groups of potential investors, both corporate and individual, who have been looking at that yard at our request," Studds told a reporter. "It's a tough time for shipyards, and it's getting tougher as the defense budget continues to shrink." Studds, the peace advocate, was learning that peace could be hell for workers in an economy that had been permanently geared for war. By 1990 a mere fifty-seven shipbuilding companies employed only 71,000 workers nationwide.[3]

"The problem internationally was the rise of Korean and Japanese shipbuilding," former Studds staffer Gerard Dhooge pointed out years later. "Those industries were heavily subsidized by their governments, unlike American shipbuilding. And the problem in the Northeast was made worse by the Nixon administration, which deliberately shifted government contracts to southern and western shipyards." Born in Boston's working-class Dorchester neighborhood, Dhooge came to work for Studds through his position at the Seafarers International Union, which represented unlicensed sailors on merchant vessels. With his Irish name, labor background, and prior work for Boston mayor Kevin White, Dhooge brought to the team the street credibility Studds needed in Quincy and Weymouth. Moreover, Dhooge understood both the shipbuilding industry and the difficult working conditions facing sailors on all kinds of vessels.[4]

Studds's efforts to revive the shipyard took place in the context of the debate over the North American Free Trade Agreement. The idea for NAFTA, which its supporters promised would facilitate trade among Canada, the United States, and Mexico, had emerged during the Bush administration and was promoted by big business interests and establishment Republicans. New Democrats like Clinton believed that free trade would benefit the average working man as well, but labor unions were unanimously opposed, splitting the Democratic coalition. NAFTA posed a threat to American workers in low-wage jobs such as garment manufacturing and light assembly; workers in high tech, however, would see the export sector grow if NAFTA passed.[5]

Most Democrats were opposed. Studds stayed on the fence, telling reporters in September that he would study the matter. He looked carefully at economic forecasts regarding Mexican exports to the United States. The president lobbied him directly, and he held his own committee hearings. Representatives from the environmental groups Greenpeace and the Sierra Club offered testimony against NAFTA. He conducted an extensive discussion among his staff, with Dhooge arguing against NAFTA. Studds and Dhooge went to a Massachusetts AFL-CIO board meeting, at which Studds asked probing questions and listened carefully.[6]

To the disappointment of labor and environmentalists, Studds decided to back NAFTA. A week later, a small group of labor protesters demonstrated outside Studds's Quincy office. "I don't think Gerry would have voted for NAFTA if there wasn't a Democratic president," Dhooge reflected. "But ultimately he considered the question strictly on the merits, and on balance he believed NAFTA would be best for the district and the country. He was torn."[7]

The House passed NAFTA, 234–200, on November 18, with 102 Democrats voting in favor. Speaker Tom Foley voted aye, and party leaders Dick Gephardt and David Bonior voted nay. The Massachusetts delegation split right down the middle. Senator Kennedy voted against, but Senator John Kerry voted in favor. Democrats Moakley, Frank, Richard Neal, and John Olver, joined by Republican Peter Blute, voted no; Studds, Joe Kennedy (Ted's nephew), Marty Meehan, Ed Markey, and Republican Peter Torkildsen voted yes. The no votes came from districts with declining industry—namely, Boston, New Bedford, Springfield, Pittsfield, and Worcester.[8]

During the week that NAFTA passed, the House also approved, with the president's help, a $1.2 billion maritime subsidy program. The goal of the legislation was to preserve the U.S. shipbuilding industry and its merchant fleet. Some observers concluded that Studds voted for NAFTA to get the president's support for the maritime bill. Studds's aide Steve Schwadron denied that a deal had been struck.[9] Evidence of that possibility, however, came the following month when Studds announced at a news conference that the president's defense conversion plan would include a $230 million pledge of federal loan guarantees to a qualified purchaser of the yard. The president wrote to Studds reaffirming that domestic shipbuilding was vital to the national defense. Meanwhile, six potential purchasers had examined the property, some expressing strong interest, but Studds warned people not to get their hopes up.[10]

Did Studds have some under-the-table arrangement with the president's sausage makers as the clock ticked down to NAFTA's passage? Not likely. NAFTA's margin of victory was big enough without Studds. Two decades later, Gerard Dhooge scoffed at the idea: "A loan guarantee is a multi-leveled arrangement and is not actual money unless a qualified bidder has been vetted. The Congress only has to set aside 5 to 10 percent of the guarantee. It was an easy promise to make to a committee chairman." Studds's committee, and the House, did pass three bills providing subsidies for American shipbuilders, but all either died or were diluted in the Senate Commerce Committee.[11]

So it was back to the drawing board for shipbuilding advocates. Studds's committee reported a measure in 1994 that would raise $1.7 billion in subsidies over ten years through a "tonnage fee" on cruise and cargo ships entering U.S. ports, and Studds led the measure through the House, winning a vote on August 2, 1994. Yet this protectionist measure might invite foreign retaliation, so coal and grain exporters objected. The power of that lobby is stronger in the Senate, where, for example, a state like South Dakota gets two of one hundred votes, but only one of 435 in the House. Its senators killed the bill. This story reveals one of the hidden fault lines in American life—the competition between different industries as each, with scant concern for the national interest, lobbies to protect its own special prerogatives.[12]

In 1994 more potential buyers, including the Korean Daewoo conglomerate and the Japanese Mitsubishi enterprise, raised hopes that they might buy the yard. Then the Greek firm Regency, promising to build cruise ships in Quincy and employ up to three thousand workers, signed an agreement with the MWRA. Early in 1995, though, Regency pulled out of the agreement without an explanation. Another Greek company made a serious bid to purchase the facilities, but its financing proved shaky, and it could not qualify for the loan guarantees. A few years later, when the *Queen Elizabeth 2* encountered mechanical difficulties off Martha's Vineyard, an eighty-five-year-old shipyard veteran had to be called out of retirement to organize the repair job; there just wasn't anyone else around who knew what to do. The next generation of potential union shipfitters, riggers, and machine operators became independent contractors, small businessmen whose economic status conditioned them to be more individualistic and politically conservative than their fathers. In the face of these negative global trends, Gerry Studds served as the leading congressional advocate for the American shipbuilding industry during his chairmanship.[13]

Studds had no better luck preserving the American merchant marine. After World War II, American ship owners began dodging taxes by registering their ships under foreign flags, typically of nations such as Liberia and Panama. For a $250,000 fee they could save millions on taxes and hire less expensive foreign sailors. The potential problem with this sweetheart arrangement surfaced during the Persian Gulf War. The cheapest way to ferry supplies to the troops was by ship—but many foreign-flagged vessels refused to enter the war zone. The military vowed never to be caught in this situation again.

Nevertheless, maritime operators SeaLand and the American President Lines applied to the U.S. Department of Transportation to reflag their vessels under foreign flags in 1993. "If these ships are allowed to go foreign now, we will never get them back," Studds protested. By 1995, only 4 percent of global shipping sailed under U.S. flags; that figure had been 43 percent in 1950. Ranked fourth in merchant tonnage in 1960, the United States fell to sixteenth in 1992. Studds worked diligently throughout the year to write a new bill that would mesh commercial interests with national defense needs.[14]

With a show of bipartisanship, the House passed the Maritime Security and Competitiveness Act, largely crafted by Studds in collaboration with Republican Jack Fields of Texas, by a 347–65 vote. Studds added an amendment on the floor that prevented shipping companies from re-registering abroad for two years, and it passed. The measure offered financial encouragement to merchant vessels to register under the Stars and Stripes, but this bill died in the Senate Commerce Committee, probably because of lobbying efforts by the shipping lines.[15]

Government action could not roll back global trends in shipping registration. The new legislation allowed U.S.-flagged merchant supply ships to pre-position in potential conflict zones through the Military Sealift Command and National Defense Reserve Fleet. Twenty years later, the American flag flies over only about 450 merchant vessels, mostly engaged in domestic commerce.[16]

Studds also failed to preserve the South Weymouth Naval Air Station, New England's only training site for naval air reservists. With the Soviet Union dissolved, the Clinton administration established the Base Realignment and Closure Commission (BRAC) and charged it with rethinking the nation's military deployment posture. Studds had pledged to defend the base during the 1992 campaign and visited there to reassure its 250 civilian employees that he would fight for their jobs. After an initial victory, in which the New England congressional delegation persuaded the commissioners to keep the base open, in 1995 BRAC reversed itself. The training mission was relocated to an air base in Brunswick, Maine. Even dedicated peaceniks like Studds responded to the financial pressures of a war-based economy, an indication of how difficult the conversion to a peacetime economy has been.[17]

"The Bill Stinks"

The exclusion of foreign fishing vessels from American waters had resulted in a short-term windfall for fishermen, but scientists worried about the depletion of the catch in New England. Studds was disappointed by this outcome and later told his fisheries adviser Jeff Pike, "Thank God that bill got called the 'Magnuson Act' and not 'Studds-Magnuson.'" Environmentalists from the Conservation Law Foundation wanted to rein in the Americans. By 1990 fishermen were netting merely half of what they had caught when the Magnuson Act passed. Studds introduced the Groundfish Restoration Act in 1991, which required the New England Fisheries Management Council to draft a plan to double the stock over a ten-year period. The bill mandated a moratorium on new commercial fishing permits and created a buyout program to reduce the number of vessels, funded by a tax on diesel fuel. The bill, a *Boston Globe* editorial noted, was likely to draw the ire of fishermen.[18]

Indeed it did. "The bill stinks," one Marshfield fisherman told a reporter, saying of Studds: "He's been very good to us. He's been a fantastic congressman. Whatever brought him to this solution, I have no idea." The bill didn't pass.[19]

Studds was a conservationist, not merely a spokesman for the fishing industry. He succeeded in maintaining the Striped Bass Conservation Act, which he had authored in 1984. A Studds-sponsored study showed that recreational fishermen were depleting the stock too rapidly. Striped bass spawn in freshwater estuaries near the mouth of the Hudson and at Chesapeake Bay, and then migrate into the Atlantic. The 1984 law provided a monitoring system and banned net fishing for striped bass. It worked; the species bounced back. Fishermen were pleased, and the 1991 reauthorization passed easily.[20]

Studds also tried to stop drift net fishing. While it was illegal for Americans to use drift nets in international waters, fishing vessels from Japan, Taiwan, and Korea would suspend miles-long nets between two boats and scoop up everything in the sea. In 1987 Studds had passed a bill to study its effects. The study found that tens of thousands of dolphins, sea birds, and turtles had become collateral damage in this enterprise. Studds's bill would set trade sanctions and block port access for countries that countenanced drift net fishing. The bill passed the House in 1992 and later was signed into law.[21]

Studds was especially worried about overfishing in the Atlantic; even Chatham's 150 fishermen agreed that the stocks were in serious trouble when Studds met with them. He led the passage of a measure that allowed the secretary of commerce to impose fishing moratoriums on the Atlantic fisheries. In March 1994 he got the Commerce Department to set aside $30 million for boat owners who would have to refinance their loans. He wanted to allow the stocks to recover but also to protect individual boat owners. Studds was disappointed, however, by the Fisheries Council's refusal to act for the long-term good. "The result has been a paralyzed system of fisheries management that represents everyone's perceived immediate interests faithfully, the fundamental interests not at all," he lamented. Faced with a crisis at the end of 1994, the Commerce Department reduced the region's allowable catch by half. Studds saw no alternative. "This is obviously going to hurt the fishermen . . . [and] we need to do what we can to help them out," he said. The fishing industry, one reporter concluded, was becoming "a basket case."[22]

Amid this sad story of decline in America's shipbuilding, merchant marine, and fishing industries, Studds registered one important but little-noted success regarding human activity in the water. At 2:45 on the morning of September 22, 1993, a towboat operating near Mobile, Alabama, pushed a barge into a railroad bridge. Fifteen minutes later Amtrak's Sunset Limited derailed on the bridge and tumbled into the bayou below, killing forty-seven people. The disaster remains the worst in Amtrak's history.[23]

Studds had been concerned about such nautical accidents beginning with the 1976 *Argo Merchant* oil spill. "Huck Finn could not drift down the mighty Mississippi today without getting run over," Studds worried aloud. One year after the Amtrak disaster, he helped pass the Towing Safety Act, mandating better safety equipment and training for barge crews.[24]

That Dirty Water

One of the bodies of water most affected by the nation's declining interest in preserving clean water was Boston Harbor. While other cities faced similar problems, the cleanup of Boston Harbor was among the most challenging;

a 1965 rock tune whose refrain ran "Love that dirty water" had inspired in locals a perverse, gritty pride. Studds felt uniquely motivated to clean up that dirty water.

One day during the early 1980s, a Quincy official went running on the city's Wollaston Beach and stepped into a pile of human excrement washed up on the shore. Disgusted, Quincy's leaders joined environmental groups and other affected municipalities to sue the state for relief under the Clean Water Act. In 1985 a federal judge ordered state officials to clean up Boston Harbor. The ratepayers would now get stuck with the $7 billion bill, and water and sewer rates skyrocketed, reaching levels nearly equivalent to property taxes. Studds and other environmentalists worried that people would not be able to pay their water bills, and would then vote for politicians who would just repeal the Clean Water Act.

Meanwhile, the Massachusetts Water Resources Authority proceeded with the harbor cleanup as best it could. Studds and his Boston colleague Joe Moakley were able to secure $100 million annually in federal aid for four years for the job, so that ultimately the federal government covered 11 percent of costs. The centerpiece of this project was the construction of a new $3.8 billion sewage treatment facility on Deer Island in Boston Harbor. Its huge egg-shaped digesters would sanitize wastewater and recirculate the effluent nine and a half miles out into the Atlantic. Gradually swimmers and boaters returned to the harbor's coastline, and the result has been widely regarded as a magnificent environmental success story.[25]

Funding for the harbor cleanup was conditioned by the national debate over clean water. As chairman of the Environment and Natural Resources Subcommittee, Studds made it a priority to secure adequate funding for the Clean Water Act, first passed in 1972. The law allocated grant money to communities for sewage projects, and the nation's water quality improved dramatically; the Clean Water Act ranks as one of the Nixon administration's most important achievements. The Reagan administration weakened its funding mechanism by creating in its place a revolving loan fund made available to states. Its pending expiration sparked a congressional debate in 1993.[26]

Studds summoned a parade of urban officials, authorities from the Environmental Protection Agency, and environmentalists to testify. "Our country is about as far from achieving the objectives of the Federal Clean Water Act as we have ever been, and the reason . . . is that we do not have the money to do the job," he declared in his opening remarks. In truth, there had been significant improvement since 1972, but still one third of the nation's rivers and half its lakes did not meet federal standards. The EPA found that new infrastructure needs over the next twenty years would run to $111.5 billion.

Among his first witnesses was Quincy mayor James Sheets, who told the congressmen about the high costs of cleaning up Boston Harbor. He wanted the harbor cleaned up, but he was not happy that a judge had ordered the state to comply with federal standards, leaving the payment problem unresolved. Ratepayers therefore faced an unfunded mandate, and a national reaction against such procedures was setting in. Studds had a solution. He had commissioned a study by the Congressional Research Service, which agreed that his "Polluter Pays Principle" could yield $6 billion annually without inflicting new fees on ratepayers. The measure would also fund coastal zone management, estuaries, and wetlands protection programs.[27]

Senate Democrats took another tack. The senators ordered states to clean up entire watersheds, not just pollution sites. Studds's approach won the support of Clean Water Action, the group that had fought for the original law in 1972, and they lobbied for the Studds bill. Meanwhile, another House committee advanced yet a different measure, but the bills never made it onto their chambers' floor. Congress appropriated money to the states under the old Reagan formula, missing a chance to improve the nation's water quality. Americans began buying drinking water in plastic containers, further polluting the environment.[28]

To the Harbor Islands

Lying within Boston Harbor was a magnificent chain of thirty-one islands known collectively as the Harbor Islands. They were owned by various state agencies, regional authorities, and municipalities, which led to jurisdictional anarchy.

Both Studds and Boston congressman Joe Moakley sensed the recreational possibilities inherent in the underutilized islands, little gems largely inaccessible by public transport. At that point, ferry service ran only to George's Island, on which Fort Warren had been built in the mid-nineteenth century, a site unknown to most Bostonians. In Washington, Moakley and Studds operated from neighboring offices, both chaired House committees, and both their districts fronted the harbor. The harbor cleanup, the planned construction of a beautiful new federal courthouse on the waterfront, and the Central Artery/Third Harbor Tunnel Project raised the possibility that the Harbor Islands might be connected by ferry and merged into the National Park System.[29]

When Interior Secretary Bruce Babbitt came to visit on July 31, 1993, Studds led a delegation of two hundred movers and shakers on an island tour. Studds had secured a $250,000 appropriation for a one-year study to investigate how a new park might be created. Now he could only wait to learn the outcome, which would depend on the results of the study.[30]

Stellwagen Bank

In the 1850s the U.S. Coast Survey dispatched Lieutenant Commander Henry Stellwagen to map the fishing grounds off the northern tip of Cape Cod, using modern sounding devices. Stellwagen discovered that a shallow bank lay in Massachusetts Bay between Cape Cod and Cape Ann. Currents from the deep ocean brought nutrients to the surface where the water reached the bank, making it an ideal feeding ground for fish and the mammals that ate them. Stellwagen's commander named the bank for him.

By the late twentieth century, human activity threatened to despoil the place. Incredibly, ships were dumping radioactive medical waste near the fishing grounds. The area was also used for gravel mining. In 1982 Provincetown environmentalists led by marine scientist Charles "Stormy" Mayo of the Center for Coastal Studies promoted the idea of declaring Stellwagen a sanctuary. By 1991 the activists had presented National Oceanographic and Atmospheric Administration officials with over twenty thousand signatures requesting the sanctuary designation.[31]

Through Studds's efforts, Congress in October 1992 declared the area a national marine sanctuary, in which dumping, mining, and fishing were banned. The following year Studds joined Commerce Secretary Ron Brown and Senator John Kerry at Plymouth pier for the dedication ceremony. Studds told a reporter that whale watching could become a $100 million a year business, and in the following years, tourism boomed, with boats departing from Boston, Plymouth, and Provincetown carrying over a million passengers a year. The North Atlantic whales began to recover.[32]

A year earlier Studds had tried but failed to get reauthorization for the Endangered Species Act through Congress. Wildlife conservation was broadly popular with the public and had led to an increase in the grizzly bear and bald eagle populations. But when the recession began, western loggers sneered at limitations placed on the timber harvest because of its possible effect on spotted owls, and the issue came to symbolize for some the tensions between the "save the whales" crowd and working people. Studds's bill mandated that the Interior and Commerce departments draw up plans

to protect 601 endangered species, and allocated $517 million over five years
to the effort, but it made no headway in the 102nd Congress.[33]

Studds rejected what he saw as a false choice between preservation and
economic development. His stump speech on the subject stated that "less
than one-tenth of one percent [of economic development projects] were
halted as a result of endangered species." He insisted that species preservation made possible industries such as fishing. Endangered species functioned
as "canaries in a coal mine" regarding broader environmental collapse. All
living things are related in ecosystems to other living things, and humans
destroy those environments at their own peril. Nor would Studds countenance another dubious argument—that property owners should be compensated at full value even if only half their property were taken by eminent
domain proceedings. This looked to Studds like an ideological end run
around the Endangered Species Act on spurious constitutional grounds.
Studds also worked to adjust the Marine Mammal Protection Act. Originally passed in 1972, the law protects dolphins, whales, sea otters, and other
marine creatures.[34]

The Earthquake of 1994

Studds thus had achieved a record of mixed successes and failures during his
two years as committee chairman. Some of the problems under his purview,
such as the decline of shipbuilding and the merchant marine, were market
related and not amenable to legislative solutions; in other environmental
and recreational areas, Studds had made some progress. But neither he nor
anyone else foresaw the political earthquake coming in the midterm election
of 1994. No returning Democratic member of Congress would be more
affected by it than Gerry Studds.

That year Studds, the entire Massachusetts House delegation, and incumbent governor William Weld easily won reelection, but the state held its
breath as Senator Ted Kennedy narrowly defeated millionaire business con-
sultant Mitt Romney. Nationally, Republicans gained fifty-two House seats,
defeating Speaker Tom Foley and committee chairs Dan Rostenkowski and
Jack Brooks, giving them their first majority in forty years. Newt Gingrich
was elected speaker. Republicans won control of the Senate as well. Democrats felt stunned and Republicans were elated. Among the reforms House
Republicans enacted in January were the elimination of two minor committees and one major one: Merchant Marine and Fisheries. Its tasks were

parceled out among different committees, and any national focus regarding the marine environment was lost.[35]

With his committee dissolved, Studds became an internal exile. He felt dispirited, powerless in a place where he had once held power. "It really is a darn shame," Studds told a reporter. "It would be difficult for me to complain if they really had straightened out the place and created a committee structure that made sense. But they have kept intact a hodgepodge system that no rational person would ever come up with." His Republican friend and colleague Don Young agreed. "It was a bad thing to do," he remembered ruefully. "I fought against it."[36]

Yet the nation's shipbuilding, merchant sailing, and fishing glory days were over. Once, imaginary characters from Rosie the Riveter to Popeye the Sailor stood in for real figures in American life. Hundreds of thousands of Americans had only recently welded steel in shipyards, served on merchant vessels, and hauled in fishing nets at sea. When the Democrats took back control of Congress in 2007, they did not reconstitute that committee.

21

A True Defense of Marriage

THE DEFEAT of President Clinton's effort to repeal the ban on gays in the military felt like a powerful blow to many gay activists. Some concluded that Clinton had "betrayed" them, forgetting that the Republicans had moved the issue to the front burner before a protracted national discussion could take place, and that it had not been a priority for most activists either. Their first issue had been the AIDS epidemic, which continued to take its relentless toll during the Bush administration. Gay activists also fought to roll back discrimination against them, but that was not a life-or-death question. AIDS was.

The AIDS epidemic presented challenges in three broad areas: care and treatment; public health measures to reduce its spread; and the search for a cure or preventive vaccine. As a member of the Health and Environment Subcommittee of Energy and Commerce during Clinton's first term, Studds worked to influence each aspect of the epidemic. Although "don't ask, don't tell" dominated the news in 1993, the invention of the antiretroviral cocktail in 1996 made a diagnosis of HIV infection less than a death sentence. AIDS research funding during the Clinton administration contributed greatly to the achievement of this outcome.

The discussion about AIDS during Clinton's first term took place as the president tried to reform the health care system, which for most Americans was an unpredictable patchwork. Most people's access to medical care depended on their employer's health insurance plan. Many Americans, especially those employed by large corporations, enjoyed satisfactory coverage. Millions of others did not. People with preexisting conditions were excluded from many insurance plans or had to pay expensive premiums and deduct-ibles. This problem loomed most ominously for those in danger of dying from a protracted disease, such as AIDS. Should the Clinton health care ini-tiative pass, a government insurance plan that was open to all would greatly benefit those infected with HIV. Over the years, Studds had supported the Canadian-style single-payer system, which had never been a possibility given the views of Presidents Nixon, Ford, Carter, Reagan, and Bush.[1]

Studds, with his main assignment as chairman of Merchant Marine and Fisheries, did not play a major role in the health care issue, but he worked assiduously to secure appropriate AIDS funding. He joined Nancy Pelosi to introduce the HIV Prevention Act of 1993, which allocated $700 million for community-based education efforts to be administered by the Public Health Service. "In my own state of Massachusetts," Studds pointed out, "more than 5,500 cases of AIDS have been diagnosed," but on account of the apportionment scheme, the state had nonetheless lost a million dollars in federal funds since 1991. Studds had close ties with AIDS activists who provided testing and education services, and the new approach reflected their priorities.[2] In the early years of the Clinton administration, it seemed possible that the president's open attitude toward gays, and his reform of the health care system, might spark a new beginning in the fight against the epidemic.

In August, Studds hosted Clinton's recently appointed AIDS czar, Kris-tine Gebbie, when she visited AIDS clinics on Cape Cod and in Boston. Clinton was the first president to create this special White House position. One sign that AIDS had moved from the "unmentionable" category of the Reagan years to the status of an important national problem was that Rotary Clubs were raising money for AIDS treatment. Gebbie and Studds attended Rotary's Cape Cod fund-raising concert; later they held a news conference at Boston's Fenway Community Health Center. Although President Clinton had asked for an increase in treatment funding from $400 to $600 million, both Studds and Gebbie feared that Congress might not approve it. Studds also arranged for Gebbie to meet with Dr. Max Essex, the chairman of the Harvard AIDS Institute, to learn more about scientific research. By this point there had been 180,000 AIDS-related deaths, and no cure or preven-tive vaccine was in sight.[3]

Studds also fought to eliminate discrimination against people with AIDS. Despite the efforts of public health professionals, many Americans still believed that HIV could be spread through casual contact. Attorney General Janet Reno debunked this idea when she eliminated restrictions against people with AIDS coming to New York in 1994 for the Gay Games, an Olympic-style competition for gay and lesbian athletes. "We are the only advanced country in the world that imposes such restrictions in the first place," Studds said, "and they remain a national embarrassment."[4] The Clinton administration would later bring U.S. regulations in line with international norms.

Unlike gay men suffering from the disease, people who contracted AIDS through transfusions of tainted blood did enjoy public sympathy. Many of them were hemophiliacs, and it was their plight that inspired the 1990 Ryan White CARE Act, providing funding for the care of AIDS patients. That law, however, left open the question whether eight thousand hemophiliacs who contracted HIV in the early 1980s should be specially compensated because they had purchased a medical product that should have been regulated by government inspection. To address that question, Studds joined Republican colleague Porter Goss of Florida in introducing the Ricky Ray Hemophilia Relief Fund Act, named for a Florida teenager who died of AIDS in 1992 after receiving a transfusion of infected blood. Studds had been alerted to the problem by the family of William Modestino, a Scituate constituent who died of the same cause. "This disaster occurred because the government failed to take the steps that could have prevented it," Studds declared. "We must make restitution to the victims' families." The measure, which allocated $125,000 to the family of each victim, was later signed into law.[5]

When Republicans regained control of Congress in 1995, AIDS sufferers faced cuts in services as part of the new emphasis on "fiscal responsibility." One of the most potentially heartbreaking reductions came out of the House Appropriations Committee, which cut $186 million in housing opportunity grants for people with AIDS (HOPWA), folding a smaller sum into block grants. "HOPWA was created precisely because block grants had failed to meet the specific needs of this population," Studds insisted. He took to the House floor in March to protest. "We are talking about people who are fatally ill and have no home. . . . We are asking them to go away and die in the street. Today, when the programs are finally in place . . . some in the new congressional majority are doing everything they can to dismantle them." Studds's eloquence fell on deaf ears, and the House passed the cuts as part of a much larger "rescission" package. The Senate, however, allocated $156 million toward the project, and Massachusetts got almost $1 million through the funding formula.[6]

While any budget-cutting measure might be presented as fiscal prudence rather than an attack motivated by prejudice, Congressman Bob Dornan's move to discharge HIV-positive service members could not be classified as budget cutting. When soldiers or sailors contracted other fatal diseases, they were not expelled for falling ill. Dornan, a California Republican who was the new chairman of the House Armed Services Subcommittee on Military Personnel, proposed a measure to discharge all 1,214 armed forces members with AIDS, along with those who had tested positive for the HIV virus but were asymptomatic. "There is no shortage of problems that need our attention," Studds told a reporter. "There is no need to invent problems." The Pentagon was also opposed to the idea, which went nowhere. Dornan's proposal emerged shortly after Congressman Dick Armey of Texas referred to Barney Frank as "Barney Fag," and Newt Gingrich called for an end to "don't ask, don't tell" and returning to the old policy of asking recruits if they were gay. "A crass demagogic political judgment," Studds shot back at the speaker.[7]

Concerned congressmen fought hardest to reauthorize the Ryan White CARE Act, which was due to expire in 1995. At the time, AIDS was killing more Americans aged twenty-five to forty-four than any other disease. In 1995 Studds summoned Dr. Harold Cox, director of client services for the Bay State's AIDS Action Committee, to testify in Washington. Cox was able to explain why AIDS CARE money wasn't being wasted, why AIDS care was so expensive, and why, from a cold-blooded fiscal perspective, an ounce of prevention was truly worth a pound of cure. By 1995, 440,000 cases had been reported to the Centers for Disease Control and almost 250,000 Americans had died. Most congressional Republicans were not extremists on this issue, and many heard from the families of AIDS victims. The new Republican chairman of Health and the Environment, Michael Bilirakis, reported the reauthorization of the Ryan White CARE Act out of committee, receiving praise from Studds.[8]

The reauthorization still had to get past the hard-liners. Senate Republican leader Jesse Helms told a *New York Times* reporter that taxpayers should not have to pay to treat a disease caused by "deliberate, disgusting, revolting conduct." Studds retorted that the taxpayers were spending a lot more on diseases caused by smoking (Helms, from North Carolina, represented the tobacco lobby), and that Helms's comments "tell us more about ignorance and narrow-mindedness than about this disease."[9] The reauthorization went through in May 1996, and by 1998 CARE Act funding reached $1.15 billion. Critics on the left pointed out that this still represented less than 20 percent of government spending on AIDS care, because most patients were indigent and their bills were paid by Medicare. Some of these critics, like Studds's friend Tim Westmoreland, argued that activists might have done better by pressing for increases in Medicare spending.[10]

Studds and Hara lived through the epidemic, sharing the anxieties and tragedies along with millions of other gay men. "We went to funerals in those days the way other people went to weddings," Hara remembered. "People planned them. Hill staffers used committee meeting rooms for memorial services. Once, a friend of mine died while Gerry and I were on vacation, on a cruise ship. This was before e-mail and cell phones. Gerry was in communication with his office, and they told him. He decided not to tell me until we got off the ship. There was nothing we could have done, and I appreciated him sparing me the pain during a happy time together. People had to make difficult decisions like that all the time."[11]

To the Old Whaling Church

In October 1995, Studds announced that he would not run for reelection. He knew that 1994 would be his last race as early as the 1992 campaign. Years later, Dean Hara could not identify the exact moment when Studds decided not to run again but recalled that the decision was both personal and political. The political part was easy to identify. When the other party takes control of the House, committee chairmen typically become ranking members of the same committee. But the Republican takeover that year had wiped out Studds's committee. He felt disappointed that within the Democratic caucus he was relegated to a mid-level seniority ranking on his newly created committee, Natural Resources. "That hurt him more than anything else," Alaska's Don Young remembered.[12] Studds also felt that the Clinton administration had done a bad job of communicating with the Democratic congressional leadership.

Hara felt conflicted. Often in life, the spouse of a busier partner welcomes the opportunity to enjoy more relaxed time together, and Hara did feel this. He also knew that Studds was now unhappy in his work. Nevertheless, he recalled, "I also wanted him to stay because of his voice in Congress on gay and lesbian issues." But Gerry was through. He had been denied a normal youth and young manhood. When others were falling in love, he had had to bury himself in his work. He felt that it was time to enjoy a quiet domestic life. He didn't need a spotlight to be happy.[13]

Studds wanted to announce his retirement early, to give potential candidates a chance to consider their options. He invited his longtime chief aide Steve Schwadron and his wife out to dinner but found that he couldn't tell them the news in a public place. So he asked them to come over for an after-dinner drink. "Gerry, don't you have something to tell Steve?" Dean prompted. Studds's decision took Schwadron by surprise. He told the district office workers by conference call.

Fellow Massachusetts congressional Democrats could see it coming. "He was frustrated," Boston's Joe Moakley told a reporter. They had been elected together in 1972, and Moakley was now dean of the New England delegation. "He saw things unraveling and felt helpless to do anything about it." Marty Meehan, the representative from Lowell, told a reporter that "while [Studds] has great reverence for government he has no love for some of the buffoonery that has been displayed this year on the House floor."[14]

Studds picked Edgartown's Old Whaling Church as the place to make the announcement. Martha's Vineyard had been the site of his first open meeting, in early 1973, and with New Bedford no longer part of his district, Martha's Vineyard had given him his strongest support. Late in October, Studds and Hara flew up to Logan Airport. They spent the night in Cohasset with Colin and Mary Lou on Black Horse Lane. The next day they drove down to Hyannis and flew over to the Vineyard. Brendan Daly, Studds's media staffer in Washington, had notified reporters in advance, and a crowd of television trucks with their broadcast antennae surrounded the place.[15]

The Old Whaling Church is a classic whitewashed New England church, with a steeple marked by four signature spires and an entrance graced by slender columns in the Greek Revival style. Dean, Colin, Mary Lou, and Gaynor sat in the front pew. "You must have suspected there was some reason that, after twenty-three years of these gatherings, we finally offered coffee and donuts," Studds began with his trademark dry wit. "In case your grandparents failed to mention it," he reminded his audience that he had lost every town on the Cape and Islands in 1970 save one. But his core supporters—here he mentioned two who had died, Betty Bryant and Gratia Harrington—campaigned diligently for him over the years. "On the night of the 1992 primary, Betty called me to report that we had won in Gosnold [the Elizabeth Islands] by 33–0 and in Chilmark by 251–2—and that she had already identified the misguided Chilmark couple." He recalled his family's participation in the 1972 campaign, and how that congressional election had helped to end the war in Vietnam, his first big issue.[16]

He decried the rise of ugly partisanship in Congress, calling the Republicans "a wrecking crew," and regretted that "it is increasingly difficult today to imagine sharing a laugh, a constructive exchange, or anything else remotely genuine with a political opponent. Attack, distortion and demagoguery are now the tools of the trade." He was ready to retire, "to be a better partner, brother, uncle and friend," and looked forward to being "at least a minimal threat to the striped bass" off the Vineyard.

Putting his constituents at the center of the story, Studds reprised his work on the environment and issues of economic justice, and against the U.S. involvement in El Salvador. He placed his efforts on gay rights issues in the context of the broader civil rights movement by recalling his participation in the Selma to Montgomery march and lamenting the national failure to confront the AIDS epidemic. "Too many people in my own life have been touched by HIV," he confided. "For Dean and me, there are periods of time when our most common social gatherings are funerals of friends who have died far too young." He concluded with a tribute to the people of the district and a word of gratitude to his staffers: "They are devoted public servants, who spend inhuman hours to see that the potential of this region is realized in the federal arena."

Local residents, colleagues, and activists responded to his announcement. David Smith of the Human Rights Campaign declared, "Gerry demolished the myth that you can't be gay and serve this country in its highest elective offices." Others recalled Studds's efforts to pass the two-hundred-mile fishing limit, keep oil drilling out of Georges Bank, make Stellwagen Bank a marine preserve, and protect endangered species. Yet as the *Boston Globe* noted in a farewell appreciation, Congress was now moving in the opposite direction and had already voted to gut the Clean Water Act. "He is leaving on an ebb tide," the editorial concluded. As if to confirm Studds's point about lack of coordination with the White House, President Clinton called after the meeting and, unaware that he was too late, asked Studds to run again.[17]

"Emotional Speeches on the House Floor"

In 1990 Genora Dancel asked Ninia Baehr to marry her. Some lesbian and gay couples had been performing personal marriage ceremonies since the 1970s, but only two couples had taken their cases to court until then, one in Minnesota and one in Washington State, after their license applications were denied. By the early 1990s in Hawaii, where Dancel and Baehr lived, the state supreme court ruled on appeal that the state constitution, by forbidding discrimination on the basis of sex, made the law barring same-sex marriages unconstitutional. The opinion reasoned that the same-sex ban paralleled the anti-miscegenation laws that had been overturned by the United States Supreme Court and remanded the case for retrial.

Seizing upon the Hawaii ruling, cultural conservatives launched a wave of bills in state legislatures that defined marriage as a contract only between a man and a woman, or maintained that their state was not bound to respect the marriage of a gay couple legally consummated in another state. The strategy worked well. It rallied conservatives and divided gay groups on substantive and tactical questions. Some gay liberationists and straight feminists had argued that marriage was an oppressive institution—"patriarchy"—a dominant paradigm that should be subverted, not reinforced. Others felt neutral about the matter but concluded that the gay marriage battle could not be won, and therefore gay couples should not bother trying to establish legal precedents in states whose courts would surely rule against them. A few brave souls argued that the fight for gay marriage went straight to the heart of gay oppression: The homophobes declare that they are the ones fighting for "family values"? Well, we stand for family values too, and insist upon our right to marry and adopt children.[18]

After the 1994 election debacle, Clinton moved to the center politically and gained ground, "triangulating" his policies to co-opt some Republican ideas. The president's popularity surged after the 1995 bombing of the Oklahoma City federal building by right-wing terrorists which killed 168 people, and again when the House Republican leadership shut down the government, purportedly for fiscal reasons. The conservatives' overreaction to their 1994 victory weakened the hand of the party's presumptive 1996 presidential candidate, Bob Dole.

To strengthen Dole's chances, Republicans in both chambers put forward a Defense of Marriage Act (DOMA), hoping to portray themselves as champions of family values in contrast to their pro-homosexual Democratic opponents. In the House, the measure was assigned to the Judiciary Committee, on which Barney Frank sat. DOMA had two components. One was to declare that Article IV, section 1, of the Constitution ("Full faith and credit shall be given in each state to the public acts, records, and judicial proceedings of every other state") did not apply to marriage. Therefore, proponents insisted, the bill was necessary. Frank and Studds regarded the first provision as moot because regulating marriage was traditionally left to the states anyway. To Frank's dismay, some gay activists agreed with the Republican interpretation that under the Constitution, out-of-state gay couples might travel to Hawaii, marry, and return home legally wed. The second, clearly substantive section of DOMA stipulated that federal benefits would not accrue to partners in a legal same-sex marriage. In effect, DOMA reprised one question from the fight over slavery before the Civil War: Was

it a national institution that was banned in some states or a proscribed institution permitted in some states?[19]

Tactically, some pro-marriage activists worried that asking liberals for a no
vote on DOMA might compromise the chances for passage of the Employment Non-Discrimination Act (ENDA). This was a measure initiated by the
Human Rights Campaign Fund and crafted by legal scholar Chai Feldblum,
using the Americans with Disabilities Act as a model, to outlaw job discrimination. One restaurant chain, Cracker Barrel, had explicitly fired an
employee for being gay and issued a memo mandating the firing of all others. Studds, Frank, and Maryland Republican Connie Morella gathered 107
co-sponsors in 1994. Coretta Scott King spoke at the 1994 news conference
announcing the bill. Studds sponsored it again in 1995, and in September
1996 the bill failed in the Senate but by only one vote, representing a big step
forward.[20]

For some conservatives, gay marriage spelled the end of world civilization
as they knew it. The full enormity of the transformation that gay marriage
presents should not be underestimated. In 1996 the idea was shocking to
most Americans, and opposition to gay marriage did not necessarily imply
hostility to gay people or support for sodomy laws. Conservatives correctly
argued that the Judeo-Christian tradition held homosexuality in abomina-
tion, and that no society had ever sanctioned same-sex marriage. The debate
in the U.S. Congress therefore signaled a major turning point in the history
of gender relations. The acceptance of gays in the military had had a chance
to pass in 1993 because there was a template for solving that problem in
American life—the integration of black people into the military during
the Truman administration. The possible precedent for legalizing gay marriage, however—the Supreme Court's ruling in *Loving v. Virginia,* which
overturned Virginia's anti-miscegenation law—was disputed as a reasonable
analogy by conservative African American ministers, who had been less outspoken on the military issue.

During the deliberations on DOMA, Studds delivered an emotional, personal speech. Hara sat in the gallery, and for congressmen who knew Studds,
his presence helped to dramatize the stakes. Studds had asked Hara to be
his spouse in 1991, and Dean had accepted—a private arrangement with no
legal standing. "I have served in this House for twenty-four years," Studds
told his colleagues. "I have been elected twelve times, the last six times as
an openly gay man. For the last six years, as many members of this House
know, I have been in a relationship as loving, as caring, as committed, as
nurturing and celebrated, and sustained by our extended families as that

of any other member of this House. . . . The same is true of my other two openly gay colleagues."[21]

The third openly gay congressman was Steve Gunderson, who represented a rural Wisconsin dairy farming district. First elected in 1980, Gunderson had only come out during his most recent campaign, although many of his constituents knew that he had a male partner. Gunderson was a Lutheran, a pleasant, unassuming, likable midwestern guy. Unlike Studds or Frank, he wasn't naturally sarcastic, didn't come from Massachusetts, had not been censured or reprimanded—and he was a Republican. Gunderson's coming out suggested that being gay was "American" in a way that Studds's and Frank's did not. He attempted to work a compromise on DOMA, but his Republican colleagues, some of whom held him in contempt, rebuffed him.[22]

Referring to the key part of the bill, regarding federal benefits, Studds continued: "I have paid every single penny as much as every other member of this House has for that pension, but my partner, should he survive me[,] is not entitled to one penny. I do not think that is fair, Mr. Speaker. . . . Yet that is what the second section of this bill is about—to make sure that we continue that unfairness." And, referring to Dean again, he reminded his colleagues:

> He can be fired solely because of his sexual orientation. He can be evicted from his rental home solely because of his sexual orientation. I do not think most Americans think that is fair. Not so long ago in this very country, women were denied the right to own property, and people of color were property. Not so very long ago people of two races were not allowed to marry in many of the states of this country.
>
> Things change, Mr. Speaker, and they are changing now. We can embrace that change or we can resist that change, but God Almighty, as Dr. King would have said, we do not have the power to stop it.

Barney Frank, who had fiercely debated his colleagues on the Judiciary Committee, demanded to know how his potential marriage could hurt the marriage of any heterosexual. His argument went directly to the legal question of who had standing to bring a case into court. The bill's sponsors couldn't answer the question, a problem that would later vex opponents of gay marriage when Massachusetts and other states decided to permit it. Steve Largent of Oklahoma responded that gay marriage hurt the institution of marriage, but he couldn't say how he personally had suffered, or would suffer. Bob Barr of Georgia, the bill's chief sponsor, got to the real argument: "The flames of hedonism, the flames of narcissism, and the flames of self-centered morality are licking at the very foundations of our society, the family unit!" Barr himself was so pro–heterosexual marriage that he had been wed three times. His imagery nevertheless played well to the faithful. Gay marriage was the devil's work.[23]

In the House, the Defense of Marriage Act passed, 342–67. The Massachusetts delegation split, with Studds, Frank, Joe Kennedy, John Olver, and Ed Markey voting against. Gunderson was the only Republican "nay." The bill sailed through the Senate, and because Clinton signed it, the law never became an issue in the 1996 election.[24] After Clinton signed the bill, Dornan told Studds that Hara should return his spousal identification pin, which Dean did not do.[25] Yet Studds proved prophetic in defeat. The 1996 debate marked the beginning of the discussion, not the end.

Millions of Americans remember the debate about the Defense of Marriage Act. The issue did not go away, and DOMA was ruled unconstitutional in the June 2015 Supreme Court *Obergefell* decision. Few remember a page one *New York Times* headline from the day before the debate. Scientists meeting in Vancouver had announced a major breakthrough in treating HIV/AIDS. Two studies at New York City research institutions showed that a combination of drugs had suppressed the virus for a significant period of time. The Food and Drug Administration, moving at record speed, approved the first protease inhibitor, Saquinavir, classified as a "highly active antiretroviral therapy" (HAART)—the first drug "cocktail." In 1997, AIDS deaths decreased dramatically, by 40 percent over the previous year. Being HIV positive was no longer a death sentence but a chronic, manageable condition.[26]

President Clinton's commitment to AIDS care, and the work of congressional advocates like Henry Waxman, Ted Weiss, Gerry Studds, Nancy Pelosi, and Barney Frank in the House, and Ted Kennedy in the Senate, played a major role in the history of the epidemic, along with the ACT UP activists, the caregivers, and the scientists. For some, though, the new treatment came a little too late. Randy Shilts, the great chronicler of America's plague years, died of AIDS in 1994, just a few years before his life might have been saved by the scientific breakthrough.

Farewells

Studds enjoyed some sweet moments as his congressional career came to an end. His colleagues on the Natural Resources Committee conspired to amend an appropriations measure on the House floor at a moment when they knew he would be there, adding his name to the marine reserve he had worked so hard to create, making its formal title the Gerry E. Studds Stellwagen Bank National Marine Sanctuary. Don Young, his old friend and now committee chairman, organized the surprise, declaring, "Now that Gerry is leaving after twenty-four years of service, I believe this is a fitting tribute." A reporter observed that Studds "looked a little embarrassed but deeply touched." One after another, his colleagues rose to offer their accolades. "One would be hard pressed to find something that would have meant more to me than Stellwagen Bank," Studds said in thanks.[27]

There was a second triumph for the man who had made coastal preservation his life's work. In January 1995, the National Park Service study of the Boston Harbor Islands which he had commissioned was released. Studds and Peter Torkildsen, the North Shore Republican who had also worked on the issue, proudly announced that the study recommended that the islands be constituted as a national park. Studds toured the islands again in September with a boatload of officials and private-sector boosters. In December, Studds and Torkildsen, along with senators Kennedy and Kerry, held an upbeat news conference at the New England Aquarium. Their bill would leave ownership of the thirty-one islands in place but mandate their collective management as public resources by the Park Service. The private sector would jointly manage the park. In October 1996, Congress passed and the president signed the bill into law. "After four years of work, this is quite literally a career dream come true," Studds gushed.[28]

For the man who had as a boy raked Irish moss on the Cohasset coast, alone on a boat, his work had come full circle.

Epilogue

GERRY STUDDS wanted to live a quiet life in retirement, and that is what he did. Gerry and Dean left Washington for a garden duplex in Boston's gentrifying South End, splitting their time between Boston and Provincetown. With the aid of friend and architect Tom Green, they added a third floor to the Provincetown building. The Studds-Hara house is listed as a historic site in Provincetown's walking tour—the home of America's first openly gay congressman.

Dean, using his George Washington University MBA, transformed himself into a financial adviser, working for a financial services company. Gerry did a little consulting, mostly for ventures that didn't work out, such as a proposed aquarium to revitalize the New Bedford waterfront, and further attempts to revive the Quincy shipyard. They both got the travel bug. Gerry loved the water and discovered that he could see the world on ships. First they visited Asia and then voyaged around the tip of South America. Later they sailed more familiar seas: the Mediterranean, Aegean, and Baltic. Gerry was in his element—the water, the world, and its civilizations.

Travel had its price, and the price was Provincetown. The place had changed too much for Gerry. It was no longer the quiet Portuguese fishing village he first represented in 1973; by 2001 it felt too busy for him, and Dean was working in Boston. They sold the Provincetown house and relocated from Upton Street a few blocks away to a new building on Tremont Street in 2004. From their light and airy sixth-floor condo they could see the Back Bay skyline. Gerry, now in his mid-sixties, took up the piano, struggling through a weekly lesson. Dean teased Gerry that he wasn't getting his evening martini if he didn't practice an hour a day. The daily routine

Studds and Hara on their wedding day, May 24, 2004. *Photograph by Tom Iglehart, courtesy Dean Hara.*

included walking the dog, Bonnie, an English springer spaniel upon whom Gerry doted. Most of Gerry's neighbors didn't know that he had been a congressman; he was just a retiree, walking his dog. This quiet domesticity and its measured routines mirrored the family life of Elbridge Gerry Eastman Studds and Bonnie Murphy Studds, minus the children.

With Colin and Mary Lou Studds as witnesses, Dean and Gerry acquired a Massachusetts "domestic partnership" registration at Provincetown Town Hall in 1998, a "civil union" that bestowed some legal recognition on their marriage. Later, in 2004, less than a week after the Massachusetts Supreme Judicial Court legalized same-sex marriage, they held a simple wedding ceremony at the Beacon Hill home of their best friends, David Simpson and Tom Green, with whom they typically spent the holidays. They wanted to marry quickly in case the window of opportunity should close again, as it had in San Francisco earlier that year. After Tom performed the ceremony, another minister married David and Tom, who had been together since 1983.

A year later, on the first anniversary of same-sex marriage in Massachusetts, a local television news host, Emily Rooney, learned of the marriage when the *Quincy Patriot Ledger* reported it. Dean convinced Gerry that they should accept her invitation to discuss their marriage on her show.

On a sparkling New England autumn morning, Tuesday, October 3, 2006, Gerry took the dog out for her walk, as always. As always, Dean got breakfast ready. But Gerry didn't come home by 7:30, as he usually did. The phone rang fifteen minutes later. It was the South End Veterinary Clinic, asking what they should do with the dog. Gerry had fallen and been taken to the Boston Medical Center. Someone had called an ambulance and then brought the dog to the clinic.

Dean called his former neighbors Mark Smith and Mike Zamojski, and the three of them raced to the hospital. If it had not been for their 2004 marriage, Dean would have had no standing to act on Gerry's behalf. "I'm Gerry's partner, spouse, and husband," he announced to hospital staff, not sure what word was best.

Gerry had suffered a blood clot in his lung and had collapsed at the corner of Union Park and Tremont on the way home. When he fell, his head hit the pavement hard, and he'd suffered brain trauma. Each separate problem required a different treatment. Gerry was in emergency intensive care and couldn't talk.

Over the next ten days Gerry's condition improved, and the doctors moved him to a private room. Dean could eventually communicate with him, but the injury had disoriented him. "I like the sound of the waves," he told Dean, hearing the air conditioning hum on and off.

On the day he was to be moved to a rehabilitation center, Gerry's condition suddenly deteriorated. Around 4:30 in the afternoon, with the room full of doctors and nurses, the team leader pulled Dean aside. "Something's happened," he said grimly. Gerry's aorta, the main artery in the body, was collapsing. "We can keep him alive, but I don't know if he'll ever be the same."

"What are we talking about—days, weeks, months?" Dean asked.

"No, hours or minutes," the doctor replied.

The doctors could buy him a few more hours if they operated. Dean knew Gerry would not have wanted that. He started making calls, and Colin and Mary Lou rushed to the hospital. Tom and David, former neighbors Mark and Mike, and longtime friends Tom McNaught and John Meunier arrived at the bedside.

Dean could see that Gerry knew he was dying. His father had died at sixty-seven, and Gerry's paternal grandfather had died when Eastman was a boy. Gerry had not expected to live much longer than they did. He was comfortable and surrounded by family and friends. Still lucid, he said his good-byes to each one individually. He spoke with Gaynor in Buffalo by phone. Around nine p.m., with the morphine taking effect, Dean and Gerry were alone, holding hands. Dean woke up at a little after one in the morning to find Gerry was gone. It was October 14. Dean had never expected to be married—and now he was a widower before his fiftieth birthday.

Mindful of the political season, Dean scheduled the memorial meeting for December 2, well after the November election and Thanksgiving. Tom McNaught secured the John F. Kennedy Library's auditorium overlooking Dorchester Bay as the venue. McNaught wrote Gerry's obituary at Dean's request. On a stormy morning, five hundred people showed up, and outside a few rabid bigots of the Westboro Baptist Church appeared with their "God Hates Fags" placards. Dean assured people, "Gerry would have been happy that he pissed them off in death as well as in life." Gerry's family, most of the Massachusetts congressional delegation, Boston mayor Tom Menino, staffers, and friends came to honor and remember their friend and colleague.

Dean, Colin, Gaynor, Mary Lou, and their children sat in the front row. Page X sat behind Dean with Tom and David. He and Dean had met cordially for the first time over lunch in Boston a few weeks after Gerry died.

Bill Delahunt, Gerry's successor in the Tenth District, presided over a serene, tender, and funny farewell to their friend. Pointing to the sea behind them, he reminded the crowd how appropriate the setting was. The audience applauded when he said that Gerry would be happy to know that he, Delahunt, finally would be part of the House majority after the November election. Recalling Gerry's first campaigns in 1970 and 1972, Margaret Xifaras got a laugh by mentioning the "He's Younger, He's Tougher, and He's Going to Win" slogan. Speaking for the staffers, Kate Dyer recapitulated the campaign to end the military ban. Ted Kennedy spoke of Gerry's outstanding quality of perseverance—that would be the theme of his own memoir, *True Compass,* to be published posthumously, all too soon—and he concluded with John Masefield's poem "Sea-Fever." This touching farewell was balanced by Barney Frank's unscripted string of one-liners about his colleagues that provided some comic relief. Eugene Robinson, the Episcopal bishop of New Hampshire who had come out as gay, and who had received the Gerry Studds Visibility Award from Fenway Health, suggested how inspirational a figure Studds had been for the next generation of gay leaders.

The family was represented by Tyler Studds, Gerry's nephew, the thirty-one-year-old son of Colin and Mary Lou. Tyler looked a lot like his father and uncle. "You're not going to just get up there and read, are you?" Gerry had counseled him once, when as an undergraduate Tyler had introduced him at Kenyon College. Tyler's poignant youthful memory of watching the whales from Race Point on Provincetown's tip with his grandmother, parents, aunt, and uncle likely brought tears to a few eyes. And David Simpson gracefully concluded with an elegy to his friend, citing his Ciceronian eloquence, and one emblematic moment when he'd called out "Light alert!" to his assembled dinner guests to get them to look out at the interplay of the setting sun, the receding tide, and the Truro hills across Provincetown Harbor.

Dean had not been listed on the program. Traditionally, spouses do not speak at memorial events because they are expected to be too overcome by emotion. Dean simply appeared on the podium, unannounced, introduced himself in a calm voice, and, speaking without notes, thanked the congressional staffers and campaign volunteers. "He treasured each of you." Many of them had come, and this would have mattered to them all. "He didn't really like kissing babies," Dean continued. "He was a shy, reserved man who felt he had a calling to make the world a better place. And although he was a liberal in politics, in the classic sense he was a conservative fighting to preserve the environment and equal rights."

There had been a lovely musical presentation at the opening—"Alleluia" performed by a Boston LGBT chorus, and a male duet from Bizet's opera *Les pêcheurs de perles* as an interlude, the former symbolizing Gerry's spiritual, if unreligious, side and the latter another reference to the sea. At the darkest moment of Gerry's career, he had been sustained by a message of support from the San Francisco gay community and the words to "You'll Never Walk Alone" from *Carousel.* He had hummed that song to himself as he walked to the podium on Bastille Day, and the ceremony ended as a vocalist and a pianist performed it: "When you walk through a storm / Hold your head up high / And don't be afraid of the dark / . . . You'll never walk alone."

After Gerry's death, Dean applied to receive his pension, like the spouse of any other federal employee. Dean knew that the Defense of Marriage Act officially blocked his request, but he wanted to honor Gerry's memory and fight for what he thought was right, as Gerry had. He knew it would be a long uphill legal battle. For the next seven years Dean worked with Gay and Lesbian Legal Defenders (GLAD) in Boston. The Office of Personnel Management argued that Gerry had not completed the proper paperwork listing Dean as his spouse. Of course he hadn't: DOMA prohibited same-sex marriage.

For the legal proceeding, Dean solicited affidavits from family and friends attesting that the conduct of their relationship constituted a marriage. Gerry's former congressional colleagues Elizabeth Furse and Anthony Beilenson, along with Gaynor, David Simpson, Tom Green, Boston neighbor Mark Smith, and Tom McNaught, all offered written testimony. At a 2008 Merit Systems Protection Board hearing on Dean's case, Furse and Beilenson testified on Dean's behalf. Dean added the video of the Emily Rooney interview. In January 2009, the Merit Board ruled that solely because of DOMA, Gerry and Dean did not have a "marriage" and Dean was not a "spouse." Dean appealed to the U.S. Court of Appeals for the First Circuit.

Meanwhile, GLAD was preparing the long campaign to challenge the constitutionality of DOMA and the denial of federal benefits to legally married same-sex couples. In March 2009, GLAD filed *Gill v. Office of Personnel Management* on behalf of eight same-sex couples and three widowers. Mary Bonauto acted as lead attorney.

Dean was the most prominent of the plaintiffs. He made many television appearances, even venturing onto Fox News. "We need to look at this as not a red or blue issue but as about defending American family values," he told a skeptical interviewer. "No one's more pro-family than we are," he had told Emily Rooney earlier. The pitch was perfect and hard for opponents of gay marriage to deny.

After winning in the U.S. District Court in July 2010, and the U.S. Court of Appeals for the First Circuit in May 2012, *Gill v. OPM* went to the Supreme Court. On June 26, 2014, the Court ruled in *U.S. v. Windsor* that DOMA was unconstitutional. Almost another year passed as Dean's case wound its way back through the court system and the federal government before he started to receive the spousal benefits Gerry had spoken of on the House floor in 1996. Gerry's wish for Dean had come true.

The world has changed quickly in the short time since Gerry Studds died. Congress passed and President Obama signed the end to "don't ask, don't tell" in 2010. In 2015, marriage equality became law nationwide when the Supreme Court ruled in the *Obergefell* case. In the great history of American

civil rights reform, no other change has transpired as rapidly as the dimi-
nution of anti-gay prejudice. At the time of the 1969 Stonewall Inn battle,
same-sex behavior was legally proscribed, regarded as sinful by churches,
treasonous by the federal government, and a mental disorder by psychi-
atrists. In forty-six years, much of this social matrix had collapsed. Gerry
Studds played a significant if largely overlooked role in bringing about this
historic transformation.

Interviews

All conducted in person unless otherwise noted.

MARK AGRAST, February 21, 2014
RICHARD AIKEN, May 13, 2014
MICHAEL BARNES, June 10, 2015
MARYLOU BUTLER, February 3, 2014
GEORGE CARLISLE, June 17, 2015
BRENDAN DALY, February 20, 2014
GERARD DHOOGE, April 15, 2015
BILL DUGAN, June 26 (telephone), July 14, 2015
KATE DYER, September 23, 2014
PETER FLEISCHER, October 10, 2014 (telephone)
MARK FOREST, April 11, 2014
BOB FRANCIS, July 15, 2014 (telephone)
BARNEY FRANK, November 19, 2014
LEWIS GANNETT, May 29, 2015
MAUREEN GARDE, June 9, 2015
INES GONCALVES-DROLET, August 20, 2014
DEAN HARA, September 4, 2014; February 19, May 15, July 9, 2015
JIM HINKLE, May 13, 2014
DAVID HOEH, June 9, 2014 (telephone)
TIM HOGEN, May 5, 2014 (telephone)
TOM IGLEHART, June 2, 2015
LARRY KESSLER, December 9, 2014 (telephone)
PETER KOSTMAYER, June 24, 2015

Jim Litton, June 23, 2014

Patrick McCarthy, February 20, 2014

Tim McFeeley, June 11, 2015

Bob and Margaret ("Peg") McKenzie, June 24, 2014

Tom McNaught, October 28, 2014

Paul Nace, August 7, 2014 (telephone)

Bob Nickerson, June 9, 2015

P. J. O'Sullivan, February 13, 2015 (telephone)

Jeff Pike, February 21, 2014

Charles Read, June 18, 2015 (telephone)

Dave Schroeder, May 19, 2014

Steve Schwadron, February 19, 2014

Mark Segar, July 10, 2014 (telephone)

David Simpson, February 27, 2015

Mary Lou Studds, June 22, 2015

Maria Tomasia, August 20, 2014

John Weinfurter, February 20, 2014

Tim Westmoreland, June 11, 2015

Bill Woodward, February 22, 2014

Margaret Xifaras, June 20, 2014

Don Young, June 10, 2015

Notes

Abbreviations

CCT   *Cape Cod Times*
Globe   *Boston Globe*
Herald *Boston Herald*
NBST   *New Bedford Standard-Times*
NYT   *New York Times*
PL   *Quincy (Mass.) Patriot Ledger*

1. Wedding Day

1. The account in this chapter is from Dean Hara, author interview. Hereafter interviews by the author are cited only by the name of the person interviewed. See the list of interviews preceding these endnotes for additional information.

2. A New England Boyhood

1. E. Victor Bigelow, *A Narrative History of the Town of Cohasset: Early Times to 1898,* 4th ed. (Cohasset, Mass.: Committee on Town History, 2002).
2. Burtram J. Pratt, *A Narrative History of the Town of Cohasset, Massachusetts,* vol. 2 (Cohasset, Mass.: Committee on Town History, 1956), 62–87.
3. Unidentified article, November 29, 1898, in possession of Dean Hara. Hara's collection was being donated and catalogued at the Massachusetts Historical Society (MHS) during the writing of this book. "Hara Collection" refers to material in Hara's possession. "GES Papers" refers to the Gerry Eastman Studds Papers at the MHS.
4. Derived from census records, 1900–1940, retrieved on ancestry.com.
5. Gerry E. Studds, "Memoire" (hereafter GES, "Memoire"), 14–15, in Hara Collection; Mary Lou Studds.
6. "List of Persons Residing in the Town of Cohasset," 1946 annually through 1952, Cohasset Historical Society; GES, "Memoire," 14–17.
7. Jacqueline M. Dormitzer, *A Narrative History of the Town of Cohasset, Massachusetts, 1950–2000,* vol. 3 (Cohasset, Mass.: Committee on Town History, 2002), 1–28.
8. Gerry to Grandma, Uncle Bill, and Uncle Bud, August 24, 1949, Gerry Studds, Scrapbook 1, Hara Collection (hereafter GES Scrapbook); GES, "Memoire," 19.

9. This account is from GES, "Memoire," 14–20, quotation on 14; Mary Lou Studds.
10. GES, "Memoire," 21.
11. GES, "Memoire," 22–23, quotations on 23.
12. Playbill, *The Crucible,* February 1955, GES Scrapbook 1.
13. GES, "Memoire," 24; *The Grotonian* (1954), 37–41, in GES Scrapbook 1; David Schroeder.
14. This account is from GES, "Memoire," 21–31, quotations on 21, 24, 30.
15. GES, "Memoire," 33; *Globe,* March 18, 1958.
16. Gerry to family, May 8, 1957, GES Scrapbook 1.
17. "Security Investigation Data for Sensitive Position," January 11, 1965, in Freedom of Information Act folder, Hara Collection; GES, "Memoire," 63.
18. "Studds Receives Robert Millikan Award," *Yale Daily News,* March 18, 1958; unidentified clippings, GES Scrapbook 1.
19. GES, "Memoire," 36–37.
20. Tim Hogen; David Schroeder.
21. Linda Hirshman, *Victory: The Triumphant Gay Revolution* (New York: Harper Perennial, 2012), xi–xvii; Neil Miller, *Out of the Past: Gay and Lesbian History from 1869 to the Present* (New York: Alyson, 2006), 223–33; Jim Hinkle.
22. Miller, *Out of the Past,* 234–53.
23. GES, "Memoire," 36–38; David Schroeder.
24. Leslie Fiedler, *Love and Death in the American Novel* (New York: Criterion, 1960).
25. Hirshman, *Victory,* 29–59.
26. Ibid., 26–27.

3. "Bored with Trivia and Impatient with Stupidity"

1. This account is from GES, "Memoire," 40–45, quotations on 42, 44.
2. GES, "Memoire," 46–47; Yale University Graduate School registration form, Freedom of Information Act (hereafter FOIA) folder, Hara Collection.
3. This account is from GES, "Memoire," 47–50, quotations on 49, 50.
4. This account is from Ted Achilles to author, e-mail, April 27, 2014; Max Frankel, "Center for Crises—and Flaps," *NYT,* October 1, 1961, in GES Scrapbook 1. Subsequent newspaper clippings are from this scrapbook.
5. GES, "Memoire," 51–54; Mary Lou Studds.
6. GES, "Memoire," 54–55, quotation on 55; "Miss Giese Is Engaged to Mr. Studds," *Globe,* December 24, 1961.
7. George Chauncey, *Gay New York: Gender, Urban Culture, and the Making of the Gay Male World* (New York: Basic Books, 1994), 183.
8. Randy Shilts, *The Mayor of Castro Street* (New York: St. Martin's Press, 1982).
9. James E. McGreevey, *The Confession* (New York: Regan, 2006).
10. Robert McNamara, *In Retrospect: The Tragedy and Lessons of Vietnam* (New York: Times Books, 1995).
11. "40 Nations Asked to Skills Parley," *NYT,* September 3, 1962; "Job Secretariat to Aid 43 Nations," *NYT,* October 13, 1962; GES to 16 Black Horse Lane, telegram, October 12, 1962.
12. GES, "Memoire," 56–58.
13. Ed Wintermantel, "Domestic Peace Corps Plan Explained to Leaders Here," unidentified clipping; Carol Stevens, "Peace Corps Turnabout!" *Daily Illini,* January 8, 1963.
14. Dan Warner, "Direct Service Home Front Aim of Peace Corps," *Akron Beacon Journal,* April 17, 1963; "Official Explains National Service Corps to Tampans," *Tampa Tribune,* April 27, 1963; GES, "Memoire," 57–59.
15. GES, "Memoire," 59; Taylor Branch, *Parting the Waters: America in the King Years, 1954–1963* (New York: Simon and Schuster, 1988), 846–83.
16. GES, "Memoire," 57–58; David Schroeder.

17. Kenneth Auchincloss, obituary, March 6, 2003, nytimes.com; Department of State, Office of Security report, March 12, 1965, FOIA folder, GES Papers; GES, "Memoire," 61.

18. GES, "Memoire," 61–63. Although Studds does not identify Blackwell by name in the memoir, Blackwell is identified in Studds's Department of State Office of Security report.

19. Harrison A. Williams, obituary, November 20, 1001, nytimes.com.

20. GES, "Memoire," 63–67, quotation on 67; "Consultation with Dr. O. R. Langworthy, March 19, 1965," Hara Collection.

21. "Studds, McCarthy Oral History," box I, 1968 McCarthy file, GES Papers; GES, "Memoire," unpaginated (this version of the unpublished memoir courtesy of William Dugan); David Garrow, *Bearing the Cross: Martin Luther King, Jr., and the Southern Christian Leadership Conference* (New York: Vintage, 1988), 409–13.

22. GES, "Memoire," 60; David Schroeder.

23. Ted Morgan, *FDR: A Biography* (New York: Simon and Schuster, 1985), 677–84.

24. Franklin E. Kameny, "Government vs. Gays: Two Sad Stories with Two Happy Endings, Civil Service Employment and Security Clearances," in *Creating Change: Sexuality, Public Policy, and Civil Rights*, ed. John D'Emilio et al. (New York: St. Martin's Press, 2002), 188–207, quotation on 190.

25. Department of State, Office of Security report, March 12, 1965.

26. "Consultation with Dr. O. R. Langworthy."

4. With Gene McCarthy in New Hampshire

1. GES, "Memoire," 68.
2. Richard Aiken.
3. Bill Woodward.
4. Tom Iglehart.
5. Richard Aiken.
6. "Pic," St. Paul's School Pictorial, fall 1965, in GES Scrapbook.
7. GES, "Memoire," 69.
8. GES, "Memoire," 72–73.
9. GES, "Is Controversy Welcome?" *The Pelican,* November 21, 1967, in GES Scrapbook.
10. GES, "Memoire," 74–77.
11. Kirkpatrick Sale, *SDS* (New York: Random House, 1973); Todd Gitlin, *The Sixties: Years of Hope, Days of Rage* (New York: Bantam Books, 1987).
12. Melvin Small, *Antiwarriors: The Vietnam War and the Battle for America's Hearts and Minds* (Wilmington, Del.: Scholarly Research Books, 2002); George C. Herring, *America's Longest War: The United States and Vietnam, 1950–1975* (New York: Knopf, 1979).
13. William H. Chafe, *Never Stop Running: Allard Lowenstein and the Struggle to Save American Liberalism* (New York: Basic Books, 1993), 262–75.
14. Eugene J. McCarthy, *The Year of the People* (Garden City, N.Y.: Doubleday and Co., 1969), 16–50.
15. David C. Hoeh, *1968–McCarthy–New Hampshire: "I Hear America Singing"* (Rochester, Minn.: Lone Oak Press, 1994), 1–53.
16. Ibid., 67.
17. Ibid., 72–74, 92–93.
18. GES, "Memoire," 73; election statistics in box I, 1968 folder, GES Papers.
19. Hoeh, *1968–McCarthy–New Hampshire,* 86–90.
20. Chafe, *Never Stop Running,* 276–81; McCarthy, *Year of the People,* 58–60; David Hoeh.
21. GES, "Memoire," 79; Hoeh, *1968–McCarthy–New Hampshire,* 93–103, quotation on 100.
22. Hoeh, *1968–McCarthy–New Hampshire,* 105–12.
23. GES, "Memoire," 80.
24. Hoeh, *1968–McCarthy–New Hampshire,* 113–18.
25. GES, "Memoire," 80–81.

26. Ibid., 81.
27. McCarthy, *The Year of the People*, 66.
28. GES, "Memoire," 82; Hoeh, *1968–McCarthy–New Hampshire*, 132–38.
29. Hoeh, *1968–McCarthy–New Hampshire*, 135.
30. GES, "Memoire," 82; Hoeh, *1968–McCarthy–New Hampshire*, 153–54.
31. Hoeh, *1968–McCarthy–New Hampshire*, 179–91, GES quoted 183.
32. William J. Cardoso, "McCarthy Meets the Governor," *Globe*, January 28, 1968; Arlen J. Large, "New Hampshire: Icy Climate for a Dove," *Wall Street Journal*, January 31, 1968.
33. Herring, *America's Longest War*, 183–200.
34. Tom Henshaw, "How McCarthy Did It in N.H.," unidentified clipping, GES Scrapbook; "The Making of Gene McCarthy," *Newsweek*, March 25, 1968.
35. Thurston Clarke, *The Last Campaign: Robert F. Kennedy and 82 Days That Inspired America* (New York: Henry Holt and Co., 2008), 19–50.
36. GES, "Memoire," 85.
37. Mark Kurlansky, *1968: The Year That Rocked the World* (New York: Random House, 2004); GES, "Memoire," 86; edited transcript of unidentified 1991 interview with Studds, Hara Collection.
38. McCarthy, *The Year of the People*, 152–75; Clarke, *The Last Campaign*, 249–82; Bill Woodward; Studds interview, box I, McCarthy Oral History file, GES Papers.
39. McCarthy, *The Year of the People*, 197–236; Kurlansky, *1968*, 276–86; David Hoeh.
40. Studds interview, McCarthy Oral History file.
41. "Fake Convention Pass—Not-So Fake Arrest," *PL*, August 30, 1968; GES, "Memoire," 86; David Hoeh; Bill Markham, "Studds Speaks on Convention," *The Pelican*, September 18, 1961, GES Scrapbook.
42. Studds interview, McCarthy Oral History file.
43. GES, "Memoire," 77.
44. GES, "Statement Made before the Faculty—May 1968," Hara Collection; GES, "Memoire," 74–77; Bill Woodward.
45. Tom Iglehart.
46. Bill Woodward; Tom Iglehart.
47. Richard Aiken; David Hoeh; GES, "Memoire," 87. Aiken does not recall this incident.
48. GES, "Memoire," 87.
49. Ibid., 71, 86–87.
50. Tom Iglehart.
51. GES, "Memoire," 87–90.
52. Linda Hirshman, *Victory: The Triumphant Gay Revolution* (New York: Harper Perennial, 2012), 95–105.

5. Studds for Congress

1. "Gerry Studds, Candidate—and Quite a Guy," *South Shore Mirror* (Scituate, Mass.), July 9, 1970, GES Scrapbook; Charles Read.
2. "Gerry Studds, Candidate."
3. Bill Woodward.
4. Melvin Small, *Antiwarriors: The Vietnam War and the Battle for American Hearts and Minds* (Wilmington, Del.: Scholarly Resources, 2002), 95–112.
5. David R. Ellis, "Quiet Twelfth District Erupts in Political Battle," *Globe*, August 15, 1970.
6. John A. Farrell, *Tip O'Neill and the Democratic Century* (Boston: Little, Brown, 2001), 204–40; Raymond A. Schroth, S.J, *Bob Drinan: The Controversial Life of the First Catholic Priest Elected to Congress* (New York: Fordham University Press, 2011), 107–10.
7. David Ellis, "Keith Faces Challenge by Weeks," *Globe*, August 2, 1970.
8. Bob and Peg McKenzie.
9. Mark Forest.

10. Margaret Xifaras.

11. Jim Litton; Paul Nace.

12. Paul Nace.

13. Rachelle Patterson, "Drive to Unseat Rep. Keith Launched in 12th District," *Globe*, March 9, 1970.

14. Alex Ghiselin, "Two Years after Upset—McCarthy Returns to N.H., *Globe*, March 13, 1970.

15. "Cohasset Man to Challenge Rep. Keith," *Globe*, March 31, 1970.

16. Typescript, "Speech Given by Gerry E. Studds before the 12th Congressional Coalition Citizens Caucus, Plymouth, April 12, 1970," GES Scrapbook; Rachelle Patterson, "Studds Wins Caucus Vote," *Globe*, April 13, 1970; Margaret Xifaras.

17. Margaret Xifaras.

18. "He's younger, he's tougher" campaign brochures, GES Scrapbook,.

19. Ellis, "Quiet Twelfth"; Paul Nace.

20. Small, *Antiwarriors*.

21. Jim Litton.

22. Bill Hamilton to R. W. Apple, June 23, 1970, box I, 1970 file, GES Papers.

23. Mark Segar, "Dredging the Legitimate Channels," *Globe*, May 2, 1971; Margaret Xifaras.

24. Robert Healy, "Studds Reveals Campaign Skill," *Globe*, August 26, 1970; Bill Woodward.

25. Public Document 43, Election Statistics, Commonwealth of Massachusetts, 1970; David C. Cutler, "Studds Scores Impressive Victory in 12th District," *PL*, September 16, 1970; Jim Litton.

26. Robert Sales, "Studds Says Race 'No Gesture,'" *Globe*, September 20, 1970.

27. Margaret Xifaras.

28. "12th District," *Globe*, October 20, 1970.

29. Margaret Xifaras; Paul Nace.

30. Kenneth G. Campbell, "ADA State Convention Opposes Choice of Tauro to Head Court," *Globe*, September 28, 1970.

31. "Studds Cites Youth, Energy, Experience," *Globe*, October 25, 1970.

32. Robert Healy, "Keith Strays from Issues," *Globe*, October 28, 1970.

33. "Speech at Washington, D.C., Party for GES," typescript, Hara Collection; Drew Steiss, "Kennedy Giving Full Support to Gerry Studds," *Boston Herald Traveler*, undated clipping, GES Scrapbook; Jim Litton.

34. Public Document 43, 1970; Small, *Antiwarriors*, 31–132; Paul Nace.

35. "Rachel Patterson, "What the Vietnam War Referendum Showed," *Globe*, December 7, 1970.

36. David Nyhan, "Gerry Studds—in There Fighting," *Globe*, May 25, 1971.

37. Small, *Antiwarriors*, 133–36.

38. Michael Kenny, "Whatever Became of 1970 Congressional Candidates?" *Globe*, October 3, 1971.

39. David Nyhan, "Redistricting Bill Signed," *Globe*, November 13, 1971.

40. "Keith Says He May Not Run Again for House," *Globe*, January 13, 1972; "Weeks Seeks a 12th District Congressional Seat," *Globe*, June 2, 1972.

41. "Studds," *Globe*, April 1, 1972; Mary Lou Studds.

42. Stephen Wermiel, "Studds Again in 12th District Race," *Globe*, May 17, 1972; Wermiel, "Mass PAX Drinks Deep of Victory's Wine," *Globe*, May 22, 1972.

43. Joseph Rosenbloom, "Weeks Seeks a Twelfth District Congressional Seat," *Globe*, June 2, 1972; Rosenbloom, "Weeks Outspending Studds," *Globe*, October 26; Rosenbloom, "Party Symbols Fall as Studds, Weeks Comb New Bedford for Victory Votes," *Globe*, November 1, 1972.

44. Jim Litton.

45. Michael Kenny, "The Inevitable: Studds vs. Weeks in 12th," *Globe*, June 25, 1972; Margaret Xifaras; Jim Litton.

46. Michael Kenny, "Studds, Weeks, in TV Debate," *Globe,* September 4, 1972; Kenny, "Studds, Weeks Clash for 12th District in Campaign Season's First TV Debate," *Globe,* September 6, 1972.
47. Michael Kenny, "Studds Shoo-In Not at All Sure," *Globe,* September 19, 1972; Bob and Peg McKenzie.
48. Kenny, "Studds Shoo-In Not at All Sure"; David B. Wilson, "The Ivy League Fight," *Globe,* October 14, 1972.
49. "Studds News," October 1972, box I, 1972 file, GES Papers; Jim Litton.
50. "Studds Courts Portuguese, Weeks Woos Lebanese," *Globe,* November 2, 1972; "In 12th, Studds, Weeks Concentrate on New Bedford," *Globe,* November 5, 1972.
51. James M. Perry, "What's He Doing?" *National Observer,* October 28, 1972; Bruce Biossat, "On the Stump Kennedy Is the Best," *PL,* November 6, 1972.
52. Jeff Grossman, "Studds Wins 12th by 1,207 Margin, Recount Expected," *PL,* November 9, 1972; "The Election" (tally sheet), GES Scrapbook; Margaret Xifaras.
53. Ken Auchincloss to GES, telegram, November 8, 1972; GES to Auchincloss, December 12, 1972; Governor Francis Sargent to GES, November 8, 1972; John Kenneth Galbraith to GES, November 9, 1972; Bill Weeks to GES, telegram, December 14, 1972, all in GES Scrapbook; Jim Litton.

6. The Sacred Cod

1. "Weekly Report to the People," May 1973, box H, Report to the People file, GES Papers; Mary Lou Studds. The weekly reports are filed by year, so in subsequent references they are identified only as "Report" with the date; the file is not specified.
2. George C. Herring, *America's Longest War: The United States and Vietnam, 1950–1975* (New York: Scholarly Resources, 1979), 247–54.
3. Robert V. Remini, *The House: The History of the House of Representatives* (New York: HarperCollins, 2006), 429–32.
4. Charles E. Claffey, "Representative Studds Goes to Congress and Is 'Appalled,'" *Globe,* March 18, 1973.
5. Ibid.; "Studds Asks Federal Court to Rule in Cambodia Bombings," news release, May 7, 1973, box A, 1973 file, GES Papers; Remini, *The House,* 432–35. News releases are filed by year in GES Papers and are hereafter identified only by title and date.
6. Bob Francis.
7. Claffey, "Representative Studds"; "Report," May 1973; Mark Forest; Maureen Garde.
8. "Studds Decries Congressional Inequities," *Globe,* April 18, 1973; "Studds on the Presidency," *Globe,* October 26, 1973; "Studds Questionnaire Shows Dramatic Shift," *Globe,* December 7, 1973; "Studds to Vote for Impeachment," *Globe,* August 7, 1974; Robert Healy, "Political Circuit," *Globe,* January 16, 1974; "Report," August 9, 1974; Remini, *House,* 437–42.
9. Jeff Pike.
10. Mark Kurlansky, *Cod: A Biography of the Fish That Changed the World* (New York: Penguin, 1997), 18–29, 48–60, quotation on 59.
11. Ibid., 78–90.
12. Bob Francis.
13. Jeff Pike.
14. Kurlansky, *Cod,* 158–73.
15. Don Young.
16. "Studds Introduces 'Interim' 200 Mile Fish Protection Bill," news release, June 13, 1973; "Studds Key Speaker on Fishing during Busy Weekend Schedule," news release, September 11, 1973;. Ken Botwright, "Canada Wants to Extend Territorial Sea Limits," *Globe,* August 12, 1973.
17. Tony Chamberlain, "U.S. Fishermen Angling for 200 Mile Limit," *Globe,* January 20,

1974; "Testimony of Congressman Studds," news release, May 14, 1974; "Studds Explains Desperate Need for Studds-Magnuson Fish Bill," news release, June 6, 1974.

18. Stephen Wermiel, "Fishing Lobby Sails into Washington to Seek Support for 200-Mile Limit," *Globe*, June 11, 1974; "Studds Encouraged by Sail on Washington Results," news release, June 12, 1974.

19. "Studds 200-Mile Bill Gains Momentum," news release, August 22, 1974; "Studds-Magnuson 200 Mile Fight to Continue," news release, October 1, 1974; "Studds Meets with Ford on 200-Mile Fish Bill," news release, October 11, 1974.

20. "Studds to Attend Final 200-Mile Hearing in California," news release, October 16, 1974; "Studds-Magnuson Wins Senate Committee Approval," news release, November 26, 1974; "Studds-Magnuson Wins Overwhelming Senate Approval," news release, December 11, 1974; Stephen Wermiel, "Senate OK's 200-Mile Fish Bill, but Approval in House Is Doubtful," *Globe*, December 12, 1974.

21. "Report," March 14 and August 1, 1975; Ken Botwright, "Law of Sea Parley Buoys N.E. Hopes," *Globe*, April 6, 1974.

22. "Testimony at Oversight Hearing on International Fisheries Agreement, House Committee on International Relations," in "Report," September 24, 1975; "Remarks of Gerry Eastman Studds during General Debate on HR 200," in "Report," October 1, 1975; "Report," October 10, 1975; Stephen Wermiel, "House Approves 200-Mile Limit Fishing Bill 208–101," *Globe*, October 10, 1975.

23. "Senate Votes to Extend Fishing Limit 200 Miles," *Globe*, January 29, 1976; "Fishermen's Victory," *Globe*, January 31, 1976; "Ford OK's 200-Mile Fishing Limit, It Takes Effect March 1, 1977," *Globe*, January 31, 1976.

24. Don Young; Bill Woodward.

25. David Nyhan, "U.S. Says New England Seen Least Risky for Drilling," *Globe*, April 7, 1974; R. S. Kindleburger, "Offshore Oil Drilling Study Criticized by Studds," *Globe*, April 17, 1974.

26. "Studds Reports on Louisiana Hearings," news release, June 9, 1974.

27. "Report," July 11 and September 11, 1975; Jack Thomas, "Drilling Expected to Give Bay State 5400 New Jobs," *Globe*, July 17, 1975.

28. "Report," April 13, 1976.

29. "Report," July 22 and October 1976; Ian Menzies, "Big Oil Defeats Drilling Bill," *Globe*, October 11, 1976.

30. Editorial, "Spilling Oil in the Sea," *Globe*, December 18, 1976; Fletcher Roberts, "Who'll Pay for Spill Cleanup Is Unclear," *Globe*, December 19, 1976.

31. "Report," December 22, 1976.

7. The Congressman in the Closet

1. Bob Francis, Mark Segar, Jim Litton, Bob and Peg McKenzie, and Margaret Xifaras all offered some version of the same story.

2. GES, "Memoire," 123–24.

3. U.S. Congress, House, *Report of the Committee on Standards of Official Conduct on the Inquiry under House Resolution 12*, 98th Cong., 1st sess., July 14, 1983, 38–41.

4. "Report," September 7, 1973.

5. Vera Vida, "Congressman Studds Has No Time for Cupid," *PL,* undated article in GES Scrapbook.

6. Peter Fleischer; Mary Lou Studds.

7. For this account, see GES, "Memoire," 91–96.

8. Jeff Pike.

9. Randy Shilts, *The Mayor of Castro Street* (New York: St. Martin's Press, 1982); Shilts, *And the Band Played On* (New York: St. Martin's, 1987).

10. Chai R. Feldblum, "The Federal Gay Rights Bill: From Bella to ENDA," in *Creating Change: Sexuality, Public Policy, and Civil Rights,* ed. John D'Emilio et al. (New York: St. Martin's, 2000), 149–53.

11. GES, "Memoire," 97; Public Document 43, Election Statistics, Commonwealth of Massachusetts, 1974.

12. GES, "Memoire," 97–102; Sam Allis, "12th District Fight Getting Rough Early," *Globe,* July 31, 1976.

13. Neil Miller, *Out of the Past: Gay and Lesbian History from 1869 to the Present* (New York: Alyson, 2006), 366–81.

14. This account is from GES, "Memoire," 97–102, quotations on 99, 100, 102.

8. The Mashpee Wampanoag and the New Bedford Portuguese

1. Jack Campisi, *The Mashpee Indians: Tribe on Trial* (Syracuse: Syracuse University Press, 1991); Mark Forest.

2. Sam Allis, "Mashpee Residents, Studds Lock Horns," *Globe,* December 12, 1976; Allis, "Mashpee Organizes to Combat Indian Claims," *Globe,* January 3, 1977.

3. Allis, "Mashpee Residents."

4. "Report," February 9, June 1, September 16, and October 7, 1977; Stephen Wermiel, "Carter Assigns Representative to Indian Land Dispute in Maine," *Globe,* March 12, 1977; Wermiel, "Indian Land Cases Studied by Arbitrator," *Globe,* June 5, 1977; Wermiel, "Hope for Mashpee Solution Fades," *Globe,* September 17, 1977.

5. Alan H. Sheehan, "Jury Finding: No Indian Tribe in Mashpee, *Globe,* January 7, 1978; Mark Forest.

6. Mark Forest.

7. "Hammer Lesson Home," *CCT,* April 27, 1977; "Release Expected for Russian Ship," *NBST,* April 29, 1977; photo spread, *Brockton (Mass.) Enterprise,* May 9, 1977; "Studds Criticizes State Department for Interfering," *Falmouth (Mass.) Enterprise,* September 30, 1977; GES, "The 200 Mile Limit: One Year Later," March 9, 1978, box K, 1977 folder, GES Papers.

8. GES, "The 200 Mile Limit"; GES, "Beyond the 200 Mile Limit," *The New Englander,* undated clipping, box K, 1977 folder, GES Papers.

9. "Report," October 14, 1977; Frank Sargent, "Studds Rightly Sounds Oil Drilling Alarm," *Globe,* September 10, 1977.

10. Ian Menzies, "Big Oil Wins with Incredible Power Politics," *Globe,* October 31, 1977; GES, "Big Oil Could be Loser in Offshore Drilling," *Globe,* November 5, 1977; "Report," October 25 and November 2, 1977.

11. Stephen Wermiel, "States, Oil Firms Given More in US House Bill," *Globe,* February 3, 1978; "Report," February 3 and August 18, 1978.

12. Jeff Pike.

13. John A. Farrell, *Tip O'Neill and the Democratic Century* (Boston: Little, Brown, 2001), 461–71.

14. "Report," April 13 and June 22, 1979; Ines Goncalves-Drolet; Jeff Pike.

15. "Report," January 7, 1977.

16. "House Passes Tanker Safety Bill," *Globe,* September 13, 1978; "Report," September 22, 1978; Jeff Pike.

17. "Report," February 6 and May 4, 1979, January 29, February 8, April 25, and May 16, 1980.

18. Jeff Pike.

19. Leo Pap, *The Portuguese Americans* (Boston: Twayne, 1981); Maria Tomasia.

20. "Report," February 10, June 9, and July 23, 1976; Maria Tomasia.

21. "Report" January 28 and May 20, 1977.

22. "Report" May 27 and June 24, 1977; Jimmy Carter, *Keeping Faith: Memoirs of a President* (New York: Bantam Books, 1982), 51–55.

23. "Report," February 24, 1978; Carter, *Keeping Faith*, 152–86; David McCullough, *The Path between the Seas: The Creation of the Panama Canal, 1870–1914* (New York: Touchstone, 1977).

24. "Report," March 16, May 11, and June 1, 1979.

25. "Report," February 16, June 29, August 3, and September 7, 1979.

9. Knocks on the Closet Door

1. Jean O'Leary, "From Agitator to Insider: Fighting for Inclusion in the Democratic Party," in *Creating Change: Sexuality, Public Policy, and Civil Rights*, ed. John D'Emilio et al. (New York: St. Martin's Press, 2000), 81–95.

2. Randy Shilts, *The Mayor of Castro Street: The Life and Times of Harvey Milk* (New York: St. Martin's Press, 1982).

3. Neil Miller, *Out of the Past: Gay and Lesbian History from 1869 to the Present* (New York: Alyson, 2006), 366–81.

4. Nadine Smith, "Three Marches, Three Lessons," in D'Emilio et al., *Creating Change*, 438–42.

5. Brian McNaught, e-mail to author, February 1, 2014.

6. Lewis Gannett.

7. "Bill" to Chris Sands, December 16, 1977, in Hara Collection.

8. Lewis Gannett.

9. This account is from Dean Hara.

10. Lewis Gannett.

11. "The Democratic Battle Lines for the Massachusetts Primary," *Globe*, February 29, 1980; Adam Clymer, *Edward M. Kennedy: A Biography* (New York: Harper Perennial, 2009), 283–89.

12. Lewis Gannett.

13. "Report," June 27, July 25, August 25, and September 5, 1980.

14. Clymer, *Edward M. Kennedy*, 301, 308.

15. Sean Strub, *Body Counts: A Memoir of Politics, Sex, AIDS, and Survival* (New York: Simon and Schuster, 2014), 55.

16. Jeff Pike.

17. Al Larkin, "Gloves Off in the 12th District, Incumbent Studds Reacts to Challenger Doane," *Globe*, November 2, 1980.

18. Public Document 43, Election Statistics, Commonwealth of Massachusetts, 1980.

10. "The President Has Certified That . . . Black Is White"

1. Colman McCarthy, "Fact-Finding Missions," *Globe*, April 6, 1981.

2. Bill Woodward.

3. This account is from "Central America, 1981: Report to the Committee on Foreign Affairs, U.S. House of Representatives," March 1981, 97th Cong., 1st sess., U.S. Government Printing Office. quotations on 14, 33, 31.

4. This account is from William M. Leogrande, *Our Own Backyard: The United States in Central America, 1977–1979* (Chapel Hill: University of North Carolina Press, 1998), 10–71.

5. Ibid., 130–32, for the Inter-American Affairs Subcommittee (its name was later changed to Western Hemisphere Affairs); David Rogers, "O'Neill to Send Three Fact-Finders to El Salvador," *Globe*, February 11, 1982; Michael Barnes.

6. GES et. al., "Dear Colleague: Legislation to Terminate Military Aid to El Salvador," January 27, 1981, box J, El Salvador file, GES Papers. Subsequent letters and documents are from this file unless otherwise noted.

7. Rick Perlstein, *The Invisible Bridge: The Fall of Nixon and the Rise of Reagan* (New York: Simon and Schuster, 2014).

8. Ronald Reagan, *An American Life* (New York: Simon and Schuster, 1990), 471–87.

9. "Statement of Representatives Gerry E. Studds, Barbara Mikulski, and Robert Edgar before the Foreign Operations Subcommittee on Appropriations, February 25, 1981."

10. GES, "Dear Colleague," March 16, 1981; Edward J. Derwinski, March 19, 1981.

11. Leogrande, *Our Own Backyard*, 130–34; Bill Woodward; "Report," May 1, 1981.

12. "Report," June 12, 1981; Leogrande, *Our Own Backyard*, 86–89.

13. Bill Woodward; Leogrande, *Our Own Backyard*, 49, 234.

14. "Report," June 19 and August 7, 1981; news release, June 24, 1981; Thomas R. Melville, *Through a Glass Darkly: The U.S. Holocaust in Central America* (Bloomington, Ind.: Xlibris, 2005).

15. "Report," September 25, 1981.

16. "Report," November 6, 1981; Leogrande, *Our Own Backyard*, 77–79, 126–34.

17. This account is from "Review of U.S. Foreign Policy, November 12, 1981," box J, El Salvador Miscellaneous letters file, GES Papers; "Report," November 13, 1981.

18. "Report," December 11 and December 18, 1981.

19. This account is from Mark Danner, *The Massacre at El Mozote* (New York: Vintage, 1993), 214–17.

20. "Statement of Congressman Gerry E. Studds on Introduction of Resolution to Suspend Military Aid to El Salvador," February 2, 1981; Danner, *The Massacre at El Mozote*, 104–9.

21. Quotations are from "Transcript of Gerry Studds on MacNeill-Lehrer," February 2, 1982, box J, El Salvador Miscellaneous letters file, GES Papers.

22. "Report," March 5 and March 12, 1982.

23. Leogrande, *Our Own Backyard*, 158–65.

24. "Report," April 2, 1982.

25. "Report," March 19, 1982; Bill Woodward.

26. "Report," March 19 and May 14, 1982; Leogrande, *Our Own Backyard*, 291–94; "U.S. Arms for Argentina: House Panel Votes to Resume Sales with No Conditions," *Globe*, May 8, 1981.

27. "Report," May 28, June 25, and July 14, 1982.

28. "Report" July 14 and July 30, 1982; news release, July 27, 1982; Leogrande, *Our Own Backyard*, 171–73, GES quoted at hearing on 172.

11. The Fisherman's Friend Caught in a Net

1. This account is from GES, "Memoire," 3–13.

2. Lewis Gannett.

3. "Congressional Sex Charge Probed," *Globe,* July, 1, 1982.

4. David Rogers, "Capitol Hill Sex Probe Promised," *Globe,* July 2, 1982; Rogers, "Drug, Sex Probes Alarm Capitol Hill," *Globe,* July 3, 1982; Rogers, "Probe Reportedly Finds Six on Capitol Hill Use Cocaine," *Globe,* July 7, 1982; Rogers, "Columnist: Nine Named in Capitol Drug Probe," *Globe,* July 8, 1982.

5. H.R. 518, 97th Cong., 2nd sess., sec. 1, Hara Collection.

6. Joseph A. Califano, *Inside: A Public and Private Life* (New York: Public Affairs, 2004), 404–8.

7. Robert V. Remini, *The House: The History of the House of Representatives* (Washington, D.C.: HarperCollins, 2006), 442–54.

8. MaryLou Butler.

9. John F. Fitzgerald, "Gerry Studds Isn't Running for Cover," *Providence Journal,* May 20, 1984.

10. Maureen Garde.

11. Robert Turner, "Studds Faces Well-Known Foe," *Globe,* June 10, 1982; Andrew Blake, "Campaigns Heating Up as Primary Nears; Conway Is Giving Studds Tough 10th District Fight," *Globe,* August 22, 1982; Blake, "Miles Apart in the 10th Congressional District;

Gerry Studds Focuses on Ties to Home Base," *Globe*, October 17, 1982; David Farrell, "Campaign '82 Hopes to Unseat Incumbents Studds, Mavroules," *Globe*, October 17, 1982; John Powers, "Conway's Ears Told Him He Couldn't Win," *Globe*, November 3, 1982; Powers, "Studds on Way to a Big Win over Conway," *Globe*, November 3, 1982; MaryLou Butler.

12. *Report on Investigation by Committee on Standards of Official Conduct Pursuant to House Resolution 518*, 97th Cong., 2nd sess., December 14, 1982 (Interim Califano Report), 23–31.

13. See David J. Garrow, *Bearing the Cross: Martin Luther King, Jr., and the Southern Christian Leadership Conference* (New York: Vintage, 1988), 372–77.

14. *Report of the Committee on Standards of Official Conduct on the Inquiry under House Resolution 12*, 98th Cong., 1st sess., 39–40 (hereafter Califano Report).

15. Joseph A. Califano to Peter Fleischer, February 3, 1983, box 1983, file 2, Hara Collection. News reports and Interim Califano Report. Other documents are from this file unless otherwise noted.

16. Jeff Pike.

17. Bill Woodward.

18. George Clifford, "Columnist Names Kennedy, 8 More in Cocaine Case," *Washington Times*, April 28, 1983; Anne L. Millett, "Studds Laughs Off Columnist's Drug Charge, but Kennedy Is Incensed," unidentified clipping, GES Scrapbook; Patrick Buchanan, "Capitol Hill Coke Scandal Shows Double Standard," *Herald*, May 5, 1983.

19. Randy Shilts, *And the Band Played On: Politics, People, and the AIDS Epidemic* (New York: St. Martin's, 1987), 299–323.

20. Brian McNaught to author, e-mail, February 1, 2014; Mahoney to Studds, February 22, 1983; Steve Schwadron.

21. "Personal Statement of Representative Gerry Studds," typescript, June 22, 1983.

22. This account is from "Statement of Charles Francis Mahoney and Morris M. Goldings, Legal Counsel to Gerry E. Studds," undated typescript.

23. Joseph Califano to Charles F. Mahoney and Morris M. Goldings, June 27, 1983; Goldings and Mahoney to Califano, June 28, 1983; GES to the Honorable Louis Stokes, June 29, 1983; GES to Floyd Spence, July 11, 1983; Goldings and Mahoney to Califano, July 11, 1983; all in Hara Collection, box 1983, file 1.

24. GES, "Memoire," 103–4; Peter Fleischer.

25. I am grateful to Bill Dugan for this latter insight.

26. This account is from GES, "Memoire," 103–10.

27. Steve Schwadron; Bill Woodward.

28. Brian McNaught to author, e-mail, February 4, 2014.

29. David Rogers, "Georgia Republican Calls for Ouster of Studds, Crane," *Globe*, July 19, 1983.

30. "Two Members Censured," *Congressional Quarterly Almanac* (1983): 580–83.

31. GES, "Memoire," 110–13.

32. Califano, *Inside*, 410–12.

33. Ibid., 412–13.

34. David Rogers, "US House Censures Studds, Crane," *Globe*, July 21, 1983.

12. A Gay Man Runs for Congress

1. Mary Lou Studds.

2. GES, "Memoire," 115.

3. This account is from Susan Trausch, "Studds Discusses His Homosexuality," *Globe*, July 29, 1983.

4. MaryLou Butler.

5. Patrick McCarthy; John Weinfurter.

6. Robert E. Bauman, *The Gentleman from Maryland* (New York: Arbor House, 1986).

7. Phil Gailey, "Democrats Stress Gay Rights" (from *NYT*), *CCT,* July 30, 1983.
8. Robert L. Turner, "He Can Still Be Effective," *Globe,* n.d., in file 1, 1984 Campaign box; Fox Butterfield, "Cape Cod Residents Sharply Divided over Congressman's Political Future," *NYT,* July 27, "Studds Should Resign and Enter Special Election," *CCT,* August 28, 1983.
9. Brian McNaught, "Questions Raised in Studds Case," *Globe,* July 29, 1983.
10. Philip Dine, "New Bedford Has Cheers, Few Jeers, for Studds," *PL,* August 8, 1983; Diane Hinchcliff, " 'We're with You,' Crowds Tell Studds, *NBST,* August 8, 1983; Chris Black, "Studds Welcomed Home with Cheers," *Globe,* August 8, 1983; Mary Breslauer, "The Force of Gerry Studds," *Globe,* October 17, 2006.
11. Chris Black, "In Tisbury, Studds Finds Friendly Hall," *Globe,* August 12, 1983; Diane Hinchcliff, "A Warm Welcome," *NBST,* August 12, 1983; Jack White, "Studds Gets Cheers, Few Jeers," *CCT,* August 12, 1983.
12. William Mills, "A Day for Democrats," *CCT,* August 13, 1983.
13. Jon Marcus, "Studds Faces Angry Opposition," *CCT,* August 16, 1983; Kenneth J. Cooper, "Petitioners Ask Studds to Quit," *Globe,* n.d., file 1, 1984 Campaign box; "Studds Faces Calls for Resignation," *Cape Cod Oracle,* August 18, 1983; Janice Walford, "Rep. Studds Faces First Hostile Reaction at So. Dennis Meeting," *Cape Codder,* August 19, 1983.
14. Philip Dine, "Studds Reviews Damage," *PL,* August 18, 1983; Chris Black and Larry Collins, "Final Forum Gives Studds Mixed Review," *Globe,* August 18, 1983.
15. Steve Schwadron.
16. GES, "Memoire," 115.
17. Howie Carr, "Something about Being Gay," *Boston Magazine,* October 1984.
18. "Flynn May Be in for Studds' Seat," *Herald,* September 17, 1983; Elaine Allegrini, "Peter Flynn Tests the Water, May Oppose Gerry Studds," *Old Colony News* (Plymouth, Mass.), November 17, 1983; Joseph R. LaPlante, "Flynn Sets Date to Enter Race for Studds' Seat," *CCT,* January 28, 1984.
19. GES, "Memoire," 117.
20. "Flynn: I'll Talk about Studds Affair," *PL,* February 17, 1984.
21. "City Resident Plans to Run against Studds," *NBST,* December 1, 1983; Patrick Crowley, "Chris Trundy: The Liberal Alternative?" *Brockton Enterprise,* September 13, 1984; GES, "Memoire," 116–18.
22. "Flynn says Studds Campaign May Be 'Mortally Wounded,' " unidentified news article, file 1, 1984 Campaign box, May 7, 1984; Ernest J. Corrigan, "Foe Attacks Payment to Studds Aide," *NBST,* May 7, 1984.
23. "Flynn Labels Studds 'a Liar,' " *PL,* June 26, 1984.
24. Peter Fleischer; Steve Schwadron.
25. Peter Fleischer.
26. "A Survey of Voter Attitudes in the Tenth Congressional District of Massachusetts," David A. Cooper Associates, July 1, 1984, 19, box C; Dun Gifford and Lisa Port, "Poll: Studds Censure Not Key," *PL,* July 3, 1984.
27. Alan Levin, "Workers Still Loyal to Studds," *NBST,* August 26, 1984; Dean Hara.
28. GES, "Memoire," 118–19. Peter Fleischer heard this incident described afterward by Studds and X.
29. This account is from Patrick Crowley, "Studds Dodges Shot from Flynn," *Brockton Enterprise,* August 29, 1984; Joseph R. LaPlante, "Flynn Misses Mark in Debate," *CCT,* September 2, 1984.
30. GES, "Memoire," 119–20.
31. "Voters 'Censure' Flynn" and "Flynn Misses Mark in Debate," *CCT,* August 29, 1984; "Studds Dodges Shot from Flynn: Homosexual Censure Issue Fizzles in Forum," *Brockton Enterprise,* August 29, 1984; "Flynn Shifts Focus of Attack," *Brockton Enterprise,* September 8, 1984; "In 10th District Flynn for Dems," *Herald,* September 6, 1984.

32. "It's Studds against Crampton," *NBST,* September 19, 1984; Michael Lasalandra, "Studds Savors Win over Primary Rival," *Herald,* September 19, 1984; GES, "Memoire," 119–21.

33. "Kerry Squeaks Past Shannon, *Globe,* September 19, 1984; "It's Ray & Kerry," *Herald,* September 19, 1984.

34. Alan Levin, "Now Buttoned-Down, Crampton Flirted with Hippie Life in 60s," *NBST,* October 21, 1984.

35. Alan Levin, "Were Studds, Crampton Pals or Just Acquaintances?" *NBST,* October 21, 1984; MaryLou Butler.

36. Levin, "Studds, Crampton."

37. Stephen A. Shepherd, "Studds Assesses Opponent's Views," *PL,* October 17, 1984.

38. Robert A. Jordan, "In the 10th District, Script Not Followed," *Globe,* October 14, 1984; Stephen A. Shepherd, "Survey Shows Crampton 25 Points behind Studds," *PL,* October 4, 1984; Robert Jordan, "Aides Urge Crampton to Speak on Studds Censure," *Globe,* October 24, 1984; Bob Nickerson.

39. "Studds for Congress," news release, November 12, 1984.

40. Ian Menzies, "The Changing 10th District," *Globe,* November 13, 1984.

41. See "Report," e.g., March 16, May 11, and August 3, 1984; "League of Women Voters of Massachusetts Voters' Guide to Election 1984," *Globe,* October 23, 1984; Gayle Fee, "'Doc' Calls on Studds," *Herald,* October 22, 1984.

42. "Cape Cod & the Islands Election Result," *The Advocate* (Cape Cod), November 8, 1984.

13. Plague of Silence

1. John Ellement, States News Service dispatch, January 4, 1985, retrieved on Nexis by Tom McNaught, file in author's possession (hereafter McNaught file). News service dispatches and articles from newspapers outside Boston are from this file.

2. Lou Cannon, *President Reagan: The Role of a Lifetime* (New York: Simon and Schuster, 1991), 493–96; Robert V. Remini, *The House: The History of the House of Representatives* (New York: HarperCollins, 2006), 462–67.

3. Amfar.org.

4. Tom McNaught.

5. Tim Westmoreland.

6. Tom McNaught; Tim Westmoreland.

7. Cannon, *President Reagan,* 814; Tom McNaught.

8. Randy Shilts, *And the Band Played On: Politics, People, and the AIDS Epidemic* (New York: St. Martin's Press, 1987), 525–26, 534–36.

9. "Report," May 3, 1985; amfar.org.

10. Tom McNaught.

11. Lori Rozsa, "Gay Congressman Leads Fund-Raising Effort," *Miami Herald,* July 16, 1985; untitled UPI dispatch, July 1, 1985.

12. "Artists to the Aid of AIDS Victims," *Globe,* September 23, 1985; Bob Nickerson.

13. "Report," September 20, 1985.

14. David Farrell, *Globe,* September 23, 1985.

15. John Robinson, "Studds' Stature High Despite '83 Censure," *Globe,* November 24, 1985.

16. Daniel Beegan, "Massachusetts Democrat Is Comfortable as Congress' Only Open Homosexual," AP, November 11, 1985; Shilts, *And the Band Played On,* 573–82.

17. UPI dispatch, March 3, 1986.

18. Arlene Levinson, "4,000 March in Boston in Fund Drive for AIDS," *Globe,* June 1, 1986.

19. "Report," June 25, 1986; Wayne Woodlief, "The Return of Gerry Studds," *Herald,* January 4, 1987.

20. Cannon, *President Reagan,* 814–16.

21. Tom McNaught.

22. Amfar.org.

23. Quoted in William B. Turner, "Mirror Images: Lesbian/Gay Civil Rights in the Carter and Reagan Administrations," in *Creating Change: Sexuality, Public Policy, and Civil Rights,* ed. John D'Emilio et al. (New York: St. Martin's Press, 2000), 21–26, quotation on 23.

24. Barney Frank.

25. "Report," May 15, 1987; Dinah Wisenberg, "Studds Working to Combat AIDS," *Globe,* May 7, 1989; Kate Dyer.

26. John Robinson, "Dispute Delays Distribution of AIDS Report," *Globe,* June 10, 1987.

27. "Studds Demands Investigation of Reagan Inaction on AIDS Mailing," news release, October 1, 1987; "Report," October 2, 1987.

28. Tim Westmoreland.

29. "Report," July 3, 1987.

30. Barney Frank.

31. Barney Frank; Tim Westmoreland.

32. Barney Frank.

33. Robert E. Bauman, *The Gentleman from Maryland* (New York: HarperCollins, 1986), 30–31.

34. John Robinson, "Frank Discusses Being Gay," *Globe,* May 30, 1987; Barney Frank.

35. This account is from Kay Longcope, "Why a Gay Politician Came Out," *Globe,* May 31, 1987; Bill Woodward; Barney Frank; Barney Frank, *Frank: A Life in Politics from the Great Society to Same-Sex Marriage* (New York: Farrar, Straus and Giroux, 2015), 122–32.

36. Paula Charland, "Walking and Wilting for AIDS Research," *Bay Windows,* June 4, 1987; Larry Kessler. Massachusetts later passed an anti-discrimination bill.

37. Arthur S. Leonard, "From *Bowers v. Hardwick* to *Romers v. Evans:* Lesbian and Gay Rights in the U.S. Supreme Court," in D'Emilio et al., *Creating Change,* 57–64.

38. "Report," October 16, 1987.

39. Mark Perigard, "Gay Tidal Wave Floods Capital in March for Rights," *Bay Windows,* October 15, 1987; Barney Frank.

40. Judy Van Handle, "In the Public Eye," *Bay Windows,* October 22, 1987.

41. "US Unveils AIDS Mailing to Go to Every Household," *Globe,* May 5, 1988.

42. Dinah Wisenberg, "Studds Working to Combat AIDS," *Globe,* May 7, 1989; Sasha Alyson to author, e-mail, December 3, 2014.

43. "Report," May 6, 1988; Linda Hirshman, *Victory: The Triumphant Gay Revolution* (New York: Harper Perennial, 2013), 190–96; amfar.org.

44. "Report," August 5, 1988; Turner, "Mirror Images," 25–26. Years later, the movie *Dallas Buyers Club* dramatized this issue.

45. "Report," September 30, 1988. The 1993 movie *Philadelphia* tells a fictionalized version of one such story involving a lawyer dismissed by his firm for being gay.

46. Cannon, *President Reagan,* 819.

14. Studds versus the Contras

1. William M. Leogrande, *Our Own Backyard: The United States in Central America, 1977–1992* (Chapel Hill: University of North Carolina Press, 1998), 306–13.

2. "Report," April 15 and April 22, 1983.

3. "Report," April 28, 1983.

4. "Report," May 13 and June 10, 1983.

5. GES, *NYT,* June 13, 1983.

6. W. Dale Nelson, "House Debates Aid to Rebels," *Globe,* July 19, 1983; David Rogers, "House in Secret, Reportedly Hears Covert Action Criticism," *Globe,* July 20, 1983.

7. "Report," July 29, 1983.

8. "Report," August 5, 1983.

9. "Report," October 21,1983.

10. Michael Barnes.
11. "Report," October 28, 1983.
12. Leogrande, *Our Own Backyard,* 330–46.
13. Mike Shanahan, AP, January 30, 1985.
14. Matthew C. Quinn, UPI, February 19, 1985; "Shultz Assails Opponents of Aid to Contras," *Los Angeles Times,* February 20, 1985; Leogrande, *Our Own Backyard,* 410–13.
15. "Opening Statement of US Rep. GES for Subcommittee on Western Hemisphere Affairs," typescript, April 16, 1985, box J, GES and Nicaragua file, GES Papers. Documentary material is from this file unless otherwise noted.
16. Leogrande, *Our Own Backyard,* 422–26.
17. "Statement of US Representative GES on HJ Resolution 239, U.S. Assistance to Rebels in Nicaragua," typescript, April 23, 1985.
18. "Report," April 26, 1985.
19. Robert Parry, AP, April 25, 1985.
20. Leogrande, *Our Own Backyard,* 431–36.
21. Ibid., 431–36, 449; *Congressional Record,* June 12, 1985, box G, GES Speeches and statements binder, GES Papers; cspan.org.
22. GES speech, *Congressional Record,* March 19, 1986, box G, "Speeches and Statements" binder; Leogrande, *Our Own Backyard,* 454–57.
23. GES, "Declaration of War against Nicaragua," April 10, 1986; *Congressional Record,* April 16, 1986, box G, "Speeches and Statements" binder; cspan.org, April 10, 1986.
24. cspan.org, April 10, 1986; Lou Cannon, *President Reagan: The Role of a Lifetime* (New York: Simon and Schuster, 1991), 750.
25. Brian Barger, "Millions in Contra Aid Diverted," AP, June 12, 1986, McNaught file.
26. Leogrande, *Our Own Backyard,* 469–73.
27. *Congressional Record,* June 25, 1986.
28. Leogrande, *Our Own Backyard,* 476–80.
29. BW to GES, undated memo, GES Papers; "Nicaragua: More Tough Questions," *Time,* October 27, 1986, box J, "GES and Nicaragua" file, GES Papers.
30. William S. Cohen and George J. Mitchell, *Men of Zeal: A Candid Inside Story of the Iran-Contra Hearings* (New York: Viking, 1988); Theodore Draper, *A Very Thin Line: The Iran-Contra Affairs* (New York: Simon and Schuster, 1991); Cannon, *President Reagan.*
31. Sean Wilentz, *The Age of Reagan: A History, 1974–2008* (New York: Harper, 2008), 243–46, 249–63.
32. Cannon, *President Reagan,* 689, 652; "Report," January 30, 1987.
33. "Report," February 20, 1987.
34. "Report," March 13 and May 15, 1987; Leogrande, *Our Own Backyard,* 484–87.
35. Cohen and Mitchell, *Men of Zeal,* 275–81.
36. Leogrande, *Our Own Backyard,* 505–22.
37. "Report," August 7 and September 18, 1987.
38. cspan.org, October 13, 1987.
39. "Report," October 16, 1987.
40. "Report," March 4 and April 1, 1988 (quotation); Leogrande, *Our Own Backyard,* 526–42, quotation on 536.

15. Provincetown

1. David Simpson; Mary Lou Studds.
2. Bill Dugan; Dean Hara.
3. Peter Kostmayer.
4. Sasha Alyson to author, e-mail, December 5, 2014.
5. Dean Hara.
6. GES, "Memoire"; Peter Fleischer; Bill Dugan.

7. David Simpson.
8. Peter Kostmayer; Bill Dugan.
9. John Ellement, States News Service dispatch, February 4, 1985, McNaught file. Wire service clippings are from this file. See also *Globe*, August 22, 1985.
10. Tom Bowman, States News Service, June 27, 1985; Daniel Beegan, AP, November 20, 1985; "Report," May 6, 1986.
11. Tom Bowman, States News Service, August 12, 1986; Bob McHugh, "Experts Say Plastic at Sea Killing Millions of Animals," AP, August 12, 1986.
12. Mary Cranston, States News Service, August 12 and August 13, 1986; quotations from August 13.
13. John Ellement, States News Service dispatch, May 7, 1985; "Commerce Department Approves Tariff on Fish from Canada," *Globe*, January 4, 1986; "Report," May 2, 1986.
14. Tom McNaught; Jeff Pike; Mark Forest.
15. Masha Gessen, "Lesbians, Gays Speak at Democratic Meeting," *Bay Windows*, April 9, 1987.
16. "Dukakis Seeks to Mend Fences with Gay Community," *Globe*, January 20, 1988.
17. Mark Perigard, "ACT OUT Blasts Dukakis," *Bay Windows*, January 21, 1988; Bill Dugan.
18. Bill Dugan.
19. Herbert S. Parmet, *George Bush: The Life of a Lone Star Yankee* (New York: Transaction Publishers, 1997), 335–37, 350–52.
20. Sean Wilentz, *The Age of Reagan: A History, 1974–2008* (New York: Harper, 2008), 266–74; Parmet, *George Bush*, 349–56.
21. Editorial, November 7, 1988, *NBST;* "Democrats Solidify Gains in Congress," November 8, 1988, *NBST;* Peter Erbland, "Frank, Studds Returned to Office by Large Majorities," *Bay Windows*, November 10, 1988; Bill Dugan.
22. Bill Dugan.
23. Bill Dugan.

16. Spilling Oil, Spilling Blood

1. "Report," January 6 and February 17, 1989; news release, January 19, 1989.
2. William M. Leogrande, *Our Own Backyard: The United States in Central America, 1977–1992* (Chapel Hill: University of North Carolina Press, 1998), 553–54.
3. "Report," April 14, 1989; Leogrande, *Our Own Backyard*, 566–68.
4. "Report," April 14, 1989; Leogrande, *Our Own Backyard*, 554–58.
5. C-SPAN, "Alaskan Oil Spill, April 6, 1989," video recording.
6. Don Young.
7. C-SPAN, "Alaskan Oil Spill."
8. "Report," September 8 and November 10, 1989; Oil Pollution Prevention, Removal Liability and Compensation Act of 1990.
9. Don Young.
10. "Studds Urges Bush to Act on Global Warming," news release, February 9, 1989; "Report," February 23, 1989; John Robert Greene, *The Presidency of George Bush* (Lawrence: University of Kansas Press, 2000), 76–78.
11. Mark Robert Schneider, *Joe Moakley's Journey: From South Boston to El Salvador* (Boston: Northeastern University Press, 2013), 165–70; Bill Woodward, "Joe Moakley's Peace," unpublished typescript in author's possession; Bill Woodward.
12. "Report," January 8, 1990; "Special Report on Panama," January 10, 1990.
13. "Testimony Heard Jointly by Western Hemisphere Affairs and Human Rights and International Organizations Subcommittees," January 24, 1990, cspan.org.
14. Schneider, *Joe Moakley's Journey*, 177–78; "Report," May 4, 1990.
15. Schneider, *Joe Moakley's Journey*, 179.

16. Woodward, "Joe Moakley's Peace," 21.
17. "Report," February 23 and April 7, 1990; Bill Dugan.

17. Gay and Lesbian Warriors

1. This account is from Kate Dyer.
2. Randy Shilts, *Conduct Unbecoming: Gays and Lesbians in the U.S. Military* (New York: St. Martin's Press, 1993), 1–28.
3. Ibid. 194–95, 199–200, 207–11, 279–80, 365–66, 371.
4. Ibid., 378–79, 647–49.
5. Walter V. Robinson and Michael Kranish, "Republicans Call for Ethics Panel Probe; Democrats Predict He Will Survive," *Globe,* August 26, 1989; "Frank, in Shift, Seeks Inquiry into His Acts," *Globe,* August 29, 1989; Jonathan Kaufman, "The Problem with Being Too Frank," *Globe,* September 17, 1989; editorial, "Barney Frank's Future," *Globe,* September 17, 1989; Michael K. Frisby, "House Panel Details Frank Charges," *Globe,* July 21, 1990; Frisby, "Gingrich: Censure Frank," *Globe,* July 25, 1990.
6. Barney Frank; Carol Stocker, "Sympathy, Support for Frank Well Up from Gay Community," *Globe,* August 28, 1989; Michael K. Frisby, "Studds Reflects on His Censure—and Barney Frank's Future," *Globe,* October 3, 1989.
7. David Nyhan, "It's Stock-Taking Time for Frank," *Globe,* September 17, 1989; "Barney Frank's Future."
8. Frisby, "Studds Reflects."
9. Shilts, *Conduct Unbecoming,* 598–609, 649 (quotation), 653–80.
10. Kate Dyer.
11. Shilts, *Conduct Unbecoming,* 659–60.
12. Kate Dyer.
13. This account is from "Studds Releases Pentagon Report on Homosexuality and the Military," news release, October 23, 1989; Shilts, *Conduct Unbecoming,* 648–50, 680–82; Kate Dyer, ed., *Gays in Uniform: The Pentagon's Secret Reports* (Boston: Alyson, 1990), ix; Joseph Steffan, *Honor Bound: A Gay American Fights for the Right to Serve His Country* (New York: Villard, 1992), 206, 212–17, quotation on 215.
14. Michael K. Frisby, "Military Seeks Third Study of Policy on Gays," *Globe,* November 2, 1989; Kate Dyer.
15. Shilts, *Conduct Unbecoming,* 650–51, 686–87, 699–701, 709–10.
16. News releases, March 7, May 9, and May 18, 1990; Shilts, *Conduct Unbecoming,* 686–88, 699–701, 709.
17. Bill Dugan.
18. "Two Arrested in Attack on Studds," *Globe,* June 9, 1990; "Studds Calls Attack on Him 'Inexplicable,'" *Globe,* June 12, 1990.
19. "Representative Studds Denies Reported Charge That He Incited His Assailants," *Globe,* June 22, 1990; "Two Sentenced in Studds Attack," *Globe,* September 8, 1990.
20. Kate Dyer; Barney Frank.
21. This account is from Shilts, *Conduct Unbecoming,* 717–20; "Studds Releases Anti-Lesbian Navy Memo," news release, August 31, 1990.
22. Barney Frank, "American Immigration Law: A Case Study in the Effective Use of the Political Process," in *Creating Change: Sexuality, Public Policy, and Civil Rights,* ed. John D'Emilio et al. (New York: St. Martin's Press, 2000), 208–35; "Studds to Bush: Don't Jeopardize AIDS Conference," news release, April 4, 1990; "AIDS Quilt to Be Displayed on Capitol Hill," news release, April 17, 1990; "Studds Commends President for Signing AIDS Bill," news release, August 21, 1990.
23. "A Survey of Voter Attitudes in the 10th Congressional District," March 1990, Cooper and Secrest Associates, box C, book 3, GES Papers.

24. Brian McGrory, " 'Family Values' Attracts Supporters to Bryan," *Globe,* July 1, 1990.
25. Jack Stewardson, "Race for Congress Sizzles," *NBST,* November 1, 1990; Stewardson, "Studds Steps Up Campaign Pace," *NBST,* November 2, 1990; Stewardson, "Studds, Bryan Trade Barbs over Campaign Mailing," *NBST,* November 3, 1990; Brian McGrory, "Rhetoric Flows as Race Tightens in 10th District," *Globe,* November 3, 1990.
26. "GOP's Bryan Slighted for Not Chipping In," *NBST,* November 2, 1990; "Studds Has Traditional Rally in City," *NBST,* November 6, 1990.
27. Public Document 43, Election Statistics, Commonwealth of Massachusetts, 1990, for Tenth Congressional District.
28. "Studds to Bush: End Anti-Gay Military Policy," news release, March 15, 1991.
29. "Studds: Pentagon Response 'Insulting,'" news release, May 8, 1991.
30. "Studds to Cheney: Release Pentagon Documents," news release, June 28, 1991.
31. "Studds, Washington Delegation Fight for Local Lesbian Facing Army Discharge," news release, September 13, 1991; Kate Dyer.
32. Tim McFeeley, "Getting It Straight: A Review of the Gays in the Military Debate," in D'Emilio et al., *Creating Change,* 236–37; Barney Frank, *Frank: A Life in Politics from the Great Society to Same-Sex Marriage* (New York: Farrar, Straus and Giroux, 2015), 147–48.
33. "Studds Releases GAO Report on Wasteful Pentagon Anti-Gay Policy," news release, June 19, 1992.
34. "Studds Heralds Canadian Reversal of Gay Military Ban: Powerful Example for the U.S," news release, October 27, 1992.

18. Gerry Gerrymandered

1. "Studds Would Bar War without Congressional Consent," news release, January 3, 1991.
2. Patricia Nealon, "Bryan on Studds: Neville Chamberlain," *Globe,* March 24, 1991.
3. "Report," February 27, 1991; "Studds Co-Authors HIV/AIDS Medical Package," news release, March 12, 1991; Peter Kostmayer.
4. "Congressman Gerry Studds Reports on Health Care," "Report," winter 1991; "Report," January 15, 1992.
5. "Representative Studds on House Floor: Ten Years of AIDS," in "Report" June 7, 1991.
6. Joe Rollins, "Beating around Bush: Gay Rights and America's 41st President," in *Creating Change: Sexuality, Public Policy, and Civil Rights,* ed. John D'Emilio et al. (New York: St. Martin's Press, 2000), 34–35.
7. Tim Westmoreland.
8. Mark Agrast.
9. Tim Westmoreland; Tom McNaught; Bob Nickerson.
10. "Studds Criticizes 'Cynical' White House AIDS Budget," in "Report," February 12, 1992.
11. "Studds Warns of Inadequate AIDS Research Funding," in "Report," February 24, 1992.
12. "Studds Challenges Bush on Ineffective AIDS Education," in "Report," March 31, 1992.
13. "Studds Decries Loss of Harvard Conference, Urges AIDS Policy Change," in "Report," July 20, 1992.
14. "Studds Fights to Make Anti-Cancer Drug Available, Affordable," in "Report," March 4, 1992; "Studds Anti-Cancer Drug Bill Passed by the House," in "Report," July 7, 1992.
15. Mary Lou Studds; Dean Hara.
16. "Beatrice Studds, a Private Woman, Dies," *Cohasset Mariner,* July 18, 1991; Mark Forest; Steve Schwadron; Dean Hara.
17. Brian McGrory, "Taking Interest in Studds' Job," *Globe,* March 3, 1991; Nealon, "Bryan on Studds"; Scott Lehigh, "Weld Backs Daly in Bid for U.S. House," *Globe,* December 18, 1991; McGrory, "GOP District Plan Pits Eight Democrats in Matchups," *Globe,* December 22, 1991.
18. "Democrats to Issue Redistricting Plan," *Globe,* January 8, 1992; editorial, "The Gerrymander Preserved," *Globe,* January 14, 1992; "Weld Submits His Own Redistricting Plan,"

Globe, January 23, 1992; editorial, "Common Sense Redistricting," *Globe,* January 27, 1992; "GOP Remains Determined to Gain Delegates," *Globe,* February 22, 1992.

19. Frank Phillips, "A Ruling That Tips the Hand in Democrats' Favor," *Globe,* February 21, 1992 (quotation); Phillips, "Latest Redistrict Map Irks Studds," *Globe,* March 7, 1992; "New Map Sets '92 Election Showdown," *Globe,* March 15, 1992.

20. Frank Phillips, "Court Ruling Costs Massachusetts a US District," *Globe,* June 27, 1992; Phillips and Teresa M. Hanafin, "Reshaped Districts, Raised Stakes," *Globe,* July 12, 1992.

21. Tom Coakley, "Studds to Be Missed along New Bedford Waterfront," *Globe,* July 10, 1992; Jeremy Crockford, "Gerrymandering Leaves Mixed Result in Wake," *PL,* September 8, 1992.

22. Dean Hara.

23. H. Hobart Holly et al., *Quincy's Legacy: Topics in Four Centuries of Massachusetts History* (Quincy, Mass.: Quincy Historical Society, 1998), 138–40.

24. Frank Phillips, "Congressional Hopefuls Rethink Election Chances: Redistricting May Bring Withdrawals," *Globe,* July 11, 1992; Phillips, "Reshaped District, Raised Stakes."

25. P. J. O'Sullivan.

26. Mark Forest.

27. Maureen Garde.

28. Jeremy Crockford, "Union Leaders Endorse Studds," *PL,* September 1, 1992.

29. "Studds Buries Harold," *PL,* September 16, 1992; photo, *PL,* September 17, 1992.

30. Brendan Daly and Stephen Walsh, "State Independent Candidates Hope to Get a Boost from Perot," *PL,* October 2, 1992; Mark Forest.

31. Jeremy Crockford, "Bryan Camp: Bash Studds on Gay Issue," *PL,* October 5, 1992.

32. "The Passing of a Friend and Colleague," news release, September 15, 1992; Carolyn Ryan, "Students Will Train at Fore River Yard," *PL,* October 2, 1992; Brendan Daly, "Daly Challenges Studds' Claim of 'Clout,'" *PL,* October 26, 1992; Daly, "Daly Calls Studds Ad on Creating Jobs 'Outrageous,'" *PL,* October 29, 1992.

33. Brendan Daly, "Candidates Dive into Political Brawl," *PL,* October 15, 1992; Daly, "10th District Candidates Focus on Issues in Debate," *PL,* October 16, 1992; Daly, "Daly Challenges Studds' Claim of 'Clout,'" *PL,* October 26, 1992.

34. Robert Sears, "Sheets, Delahunt Lead Quincy Rally for Studds," *PL,* October 13, 1992; Jeremy Crockford, "Two Rivals Criticize absent Studds," *PL,* October 23, 1992; "James Taylor in Plymouth," *PL,* October 23, 1992.

35. Brendan Daly, "Studds Still Faces Hate Element on Trail," *PL,* October 27, 1992.

36. Brendan Daly, "Studds In, GOP Busts Monopoly," *PL,* November 4, 1992; Public Document 43, Election Statistics, Commonwealth of Massachusetts, 1992.

19. Don't Ask, Don't Tell and a Memorable Address

1. Chris Bull and John Gallagher, *Perfect Enemies: The Religious Right, the Gay Movement, and the Politics of the 1990s* (New York: Crown Publishers, 1996), 63–78, "cipher" on 73; Craig A. Rimmerman, "A Friend in the White House? Reflections on the Clinton Presidency," in *Creating Change: Sexuality, Public Policy, and Civil Rights,* ed. John D'Emilio et al. (New York: St. Martin's Press, 2000), 44–46.

2. News release, April 29, 1992.

3. Rimmerman, "A Friend in the White House?" 45.

4. Dean Hara; Jean O' Leary, "From Agitator to Insider: Fighting for Inclusion in the Democratic Party," in D'Emilio et al., *Creating Change,* 102–4, quotation on 102.

5. David Mixner, *Stranger among Friends* (New York: Bantam Books, 1996), 275–76.

6. Dean Hara; Cliff O'Neill, "Oh, What a Week It Was!" *Bay Windows,* January 28, 1993.

7. John Farrell, "Studds, Frank Say Small Gains a Beginning," *Globe,* January 30, 1993; Dean Hara.

8. O'Neill, "Oh What a Week It Was."

9. Tim McFeeley.
10. This account is from Colin Powell, *My American Journey* (New York: Ballantine, 1996), 570–75; Bill Clinton, *My Life* (New York: Knopf, 2004), 484–84; Barney Frank, *Frank: A Life in Politics from the Great Society to Same-Sex Marriage* (New York: Farrar, Straus and Giroux, 2015), 152–56.
11. David Rayside, *On the Fringe: Gays and Lesbians in Politics* (Ithaca: Cornell University Press, 1998), 215–47; Tim McFeeley, "Getting It Straight: A Review of the Gays in the Military Debate," in D'Emilio et al., *Creating Change*, 236–50; Bull and Gallagher, *Perfect Enemies*, 131–34.
12. Farrell, "Studds, Frank."
13. Paul Quinn Judge, "Clinton Acts to Modify Military's Ban on Gays," *Globe*, January 30, 1993.
14. "Statement of Congressman Gerry Studds Regarding the GAO Report on the Department of Defense Policy on Homosexuality," February 1, 1993, Hara Collection.
15. News release, January 28, 1993; Arthur S. Leonard, "From *Bowers v. Hardwick* to *Romer v. Evans:* Lesbian and Gay Rights in the U.S. Supreme Court," in D'Emilio et al., *Creating Change*, 66–77; Bull and Gallagher, *Perfect Enemies*, 97–24.
16. Marc S. Malkin, "Representatives Frank, Studds Say Pressure Is Key to Win," *Bay Windows*, February 4, 1993; Cliff O'Neill, "Gay Groups under Fire for Ban Response," *Bay Windows*, February 11, 1993.
17. Nadine Smith, "Three Marches, Many Lessons," in D'Emilio et al., *Creating Change*, 438–47; Mixner, *Stranger among Friends*, 299–300, 304–5; Mark Agrast.
18. News releases, April 21 and April 22, 1993.
19. "1993 March on Washington Weekend GES/DTH Schedule," Hara Collection; Mixner, *Stranger among Friends*, 315–16.
20. "1993 March Schedule."
21. This account is from cspan.org/video/?40062-1/gay-lesbian-march-washington. The Hara Papers include a draft or later transcription of the text of the speech: "Speech by Congressman Gerry E. Studds: March on Washington April 25, 1993."
22. "Hundreds of Thousands March for Gay Rights," *Globe*, April 26, 1993.
23. Frank, *Frank*, 157–60; Rayside, *On the Fringe*, 249–79; Tim McFeeley.
24. Rayside, *On the Fringe*, 215–46; Bull and Gallagher, *Perfect Enemies*, 146–48.
25. Ana Puga, "Frank Airs Compromise on Gays in the Military," *Globe*, May 19, 1993; "Barney Frank Breaks Ranks on Ban," *Bay Windows*, May 20, 1993.
26. Rayside, *Perfect Enemies*, 228–29, 274–79; Puga, "Frank Airs Compromise."
27. News release, May 18, 1993.
28. Mark Agrast.
29. Frank, *Frank*, 162. Frank recalled in his memoir that Studds already believed that the issue was unwinnable, which made his behavior seem self-serving to Frank. Studds, however, may have had no idea how individual colleagues would vote.
30. Tim McFeeley; Tom Iglehart.
31. News releases, June 23 and July 2, 1993.
32. Paul Quinn Judge, "Words Fly in Anticipation of Pentagon Plan on Gays," *Globe*, July 15, 1993; news release, July 16, 1993.
33. Clinton, *My Life*, 485.
34. Mark Agrast.
35. Network.lgbtv; "Gerry Studds at PFLAG, 1993," YouTube; Dean Hara.
36. Rayside, *On the Fringe*, 231; news release, September 29, 1993.
37. Alexander Nicholson, *Fighting to Serve: Behind the Scenes in the War to Repeal "Don't Ask, Don't Tell"* (Chicago: Chicago Review Press, 2012); Frank, *Frank*, 325–32.

20. Saving the Whales . . . but Not Much Else

1. Lawrence S. Rines and Anthony Sarcone, "A History of Shipbuilding at Fore River," pamphlet, n.d., Quincy Historical Society.

2. Della Klemovich, "State Remains Committed to Shipbuilding," *PL,* January 4, 1988; "Shipyard Gets Contract," *PL,* August 1, 1991; "Shipyard Changes Its Course," *PL,* November 6, 1992.

3. "Shipyard: An Uncertain Future," *PL,* May 24, 1993.

4. Gerard Dhooge.

5. Nigel Hamilton, *Bill Clinton: Mastering the Presidency* (New York: Public Affairs, 2007), 178–80, 228–30.

6. Ana Puga, "NAFTA Stance: Firmly Uncommitted State's Delegation Sits Squarely on the Fence," *Globe,* September 15, 1993; Gerard Dhooge.

7. Ana Puga, "The Great NAFTA Squeeze," *Globe,* November 11, 1993; "Unions: Fight Is Not Over," *Globe,* November 13, 1993; Gerard Dhooge.

8. Mark Schneider, *Joe Moakley's Journey: From South Boston to El Salvador* (Boston: Northeastern University Press, 2013), 206–8.

9. Meg Vaillancourt, "Foes See Link in Studds' 'Yes,' Shipyard Aid," *Globe,* November 14, 1993.

10. "Shipyard to Get $230 Million," *PL,* December 20, 1993; "US Gives Shipyard $230 Million Lift," *Globe,* December 21, 1993.

11. Gerard Dhooge; *Congress and the Nation: A Review of Government and Politics* (hereafter *C&N*), vol. 9, *1993–1996* (Washington, D.C.: Congressional Quarterly Press, 1998), 342.

12. Ibid.

13. "Greek Firm Scuttles Plan for Fore River Shipyard," *Globe,* March 23, 1995; Aaron Zitner, "Senate Vote Boosts Quincy Shipyard's Chance to Re-open," *Globe,* August 2, 1996.

14. Merchant Marine and Fisheries, news release, July 28 and July 29, 1993.

15. News release, August 2, 1994; *C&N,* 9:340–41.

16. Gerard Dhooge.

17. "Air Station Waiting Guardedly; Studds, Others Tour South Weymouth Base," *Globe,* March 9, 1993; "So. Weymouth Base on Pentagon Chopping Block," *Globe,* March 13, 1993; "Commission Spares South Weymouth Base," *Globe,* June 27, 1993; "Closings May Mean More Jobs for Region; S. Weymouth Sole Base to Be Shut," *Globe,* March 1, 1995.

18. "A Safety Net for Fisheries," *Globe,* July 17, 1991; Jeff Pike.

19. Brian McGrory, "Studds Bill Provokes Fishing Industry Wrath," *Globe,* August 4, 1991.

20. *C&N,* vol. 8, *1989–1992* (Washington, D.C.: Congressional Quarterly Press, 1993), 521; Jeff Pike.

21. "House Passes Studds Bill to End Large Scale Drift-Netting," news release, February 25, 1992; *C&N,* 8:528.

22. *C&N,* 9:427; news release, February 18, 1994; Colin Nickerson, "The Promise of Bounty Goes Bust for New England," *Globe,* April 18, 1994; Scott Allen, "New England Fishing Areas Shut Down," *Globe,* December 8, 1994.

23. theguardian.com/world/2013/nov/17-survive-deadliest-amtrak-train-crash.

24. Merchant Marine and Fisheries, news release, March 21 and June 22, 1994; *C&N,* 9:339.

25. Memos, Dan Ashe to GES, April 20, May 26, and June 13, 1994, GES Papers, box K, Boston Harbor Islands file.

26. *C&N,* 9:415.

27. "Financing Clean Water: A Long Term Funding Proposal—The Polluter Pays Clean Water Act" and "Clean Water: It's Not Cheap," GES, *Roll Call,* May 3, 1993; GES to Tom Foley, May 12, 1993; all in GES Papers, box K, Clean Water 1993 file.

28. *NYT,* February 2, 1994; memo, Dan Ashe and Barbara Jeanne Polo to GES, February 14, 1994; Merchant Marine and Fisheries, news release, March 18, 1994; all in GES Papers, box K, Clean Water 1993 file; *C&N,* 9:415.

29. Schneider, *Joe Moakley's Journey*, 57–58, 241–45.
30. Allen Scott, "U.S. to Consider Adding Harbor Islands to National Park System," *Globe*, July 31, 1993.
31. stellwagen.noaa.gov/about/history; "Sanctuary to Bear Studds' Name," *Cape Codder*, September 6, 1992; "National Marine Sanctuaries Annual Report," June 2002, both in GES Papers, box K, Stellwagen NMS file.
32. Editorial, "The Right Whale, the Right Protection," *Globe*, July 17, 1992; "Stellwagen Bank to Receive Sanctuary Status," *Globe*, October 9, 1992; "Congress Designates Stellwagen Sanctuary," news release, October 8, 1992; Indira Lakshmanan, "Officials Dedicate Marine Preserve," *Globe*, June 27, 1993; stellwagen.noaa.gov/about/history.
33. *C&N*, 8:521.
34. "The Endangered Species Act: Preserving Our Own Best Interests" and "Should the Endangered Species Act Be Amended to Provide Compensation for Takings of Private Property under the Act?" GES speeches, GES Papers, box K, Endangered Species file.
35. Robert V. Remini, *The House: The History of the House of Representatives* (Washington, D.C.: Library of Congress, 2006), 482–85.
36. "Dismay Is Voiced as GOP Affirms Bid to Kill Studds Panel," *Globe*, November 18, 1994; "In House, GOP Prepares to Scuttle Studds' Panel," *Globe*, December 3, 1994; Don Young.

21. A True Defense of Marriage

1. See, for example, Ana Puga, "Lawmakers Talk Health Care," *Globe*, December 19, 1993.
2. "Studds Co-sponsoring Landmark AIDS Prevention Bill," news release, March 30, 1993.
3. Gloria Negri, "Middle America Extends a Hand," *Globe*, August 26, 1993; Dolores Kong, "Clinton AIDS Leader Says Funding to Remain Tight," *Globe*, August 27, 1993; news releases, August 16 and August 24, 1993.
4. News release, March 22, 1994.
5. News release, February 23, 1995.
6. GES release, March 3, March 16, and June 26, 1995.
7. "Dornan Panel Clears Plan to Expel HIV Positive Soldiers," *Globe*, May 19, 1995; "Frank Cites Antigay Remark, Says It Exposes House Bigotry," *Globe*, February 17, 1995; Chris Black, "Gingrich Retreats from Ban on Gays," *Globe*, April 5, 1995.
8. News release, April 4, 1995.
9. "Studds Assails Comments by Helms on AIDS Spending," *Globe*, July 8, 1995.
10. John-Manuel Andriote, "The Ryan White CARE Act: An Impressive, Dubious Accomplishment," in *Creating Change: Sexuality, Public Policy, and Civil Rights*, ed. John D'Emilio et al. (New York: St. Martin's Press, 2002), 407–20.
11. Dean Hara.
12. Don Young.
13. This account is from Dean Hara.
14. "Rep. Studds to Announce He Will Not Seek Reelection," *Globe*, October 28, 1995; "A Journey: Power to Obscurity," *Globe*, October 29, 1995.
15. Dean Hara.
16. This account is from GES, "Memoire," 129–37.
17. "A Journey" and "Studds' Departure," *Globe*, November 4, 1995.
18. David L. Chambers, "Couples: Marriage, Civil Union, and Domestic Partnership," in D'Emilio et al., *Creating Change*, 281–96.
19. Barney Frank, *Frank: A Life in Politics from the Great Society to Same-Sex Marriage* (New York: Farrar, Straus and Giroux, 2015), 188–93.
20. Chai R. Feldblum, "The Federal Gay Rights Bill: From Bella to ENDA," in D'Emilio et al., *Creating Change*, 178–87; news releases, April 21, 1994, and June 15, 1995.
21. This account is from "Three Floor Speeches by Congressman Gerry Studds," in GES, "Memoire," 125.

22. Steve Gunderson and Rob Morris, *House and Home* (New York: Dutton, 1996); Peter Kostmayer.

23. Chris Black, "House OKs Bill Opposing Gay Marriage 342–67," *Globe,* July 13, 1995; Frank, *Frank,* 188–93.

24. Black, "House OKs Bill."

25. Dean Hara.

26. Kathy S. Stolley and John E. Glass, *HIV/AIDS* (Santa Barbara: Greenwood, 2009), 179–81; "Scientists Display Substantial Gain in AIDS Treatment," *NYT,* July 12, 1996.

27. Judy Mathewson, "A Fitting Honor Studds Can Bank On," *CCT,* September 5, 1996, GES Papers, box K, Stellwagen file; www.stellwagen.noaa.gov/about/history.

28. News releases, January 23, September 15, December 11, 1995, and October 3, 1996.

Index

Aaronson, Bernard, 188–89
Abrams, Elliott, 168, 170
Abzug, Bella, 80–81
Acquired Immunodeficiency Syndrome (AIDS), 148–55, 157–59, 205–8, 244–48, 254
Agrast, Mark, 206, 229–30
Aiken, Dick, 32–33, 45
Alyson, Sasha, 158, 174–75
Anderson, Jack, 119, 125
Argo Merchant, 74–75
Auchincloss, Ken, 13, 26, 52, 62–62
Arias, Oscar, 168–70

Baker, James, 183
Baring-Gould, Michael, 13
Barnes, Michael, 106, 111, 114, 162, 164, 168
Barr, Bob, 253–54
Bauman, Robert, 136, 156
Bennett, William, 153–54
Blackwell, Frederick, 27–28, 30
Boland, Ed, 160–61
Bonior, David, 170–72
Boston Globe, 65, 67, 136, 152, 194, 208, 250
Boston Harbor Islands, 240–41, 255
Bowers v. Hardwick, 157
Bryan, Jon L. 179, 200–201, 205, 214–16
Bryant, Anita, 96–97
Buchanan, Patrick, 125, 164
Bulger, William, 210–11
Bush, George H., 179, 183, 201, 204, 206, 208
Bustillo, Juan Rafael, 181, 190
Butler, MaryLou, 121, 135, 145

Califano, Joseph, 119, 125, 126, 132
Cammermeyer, Margarethe, 202
Cannon, Lou, 169
Cape Cod Times, 78, 136, 143
Carter, Jimmy, 75, 84, 86, 90, 99–100, 102
Casner, Mabel, 19–20, 31
Cheney, Dick, 197, 201–3
Clark, Blair, 38–39
clean water, 239–40
Clinton, Bill, 216–20, 230, 214–15, 251
Coast Guard, 87, 91–92, 175–176
cod, 67–69
Cohasset, 7–11
Constitutional amendments, 100–101
Conte, Silvio, 176
Conway, Jack, 121–22, 139
Crampton, Lew, 11, 29, 144–46
Crane, Daniel, 123, 130–33, 146
Cristiani, Alfredo, 181–83, 190

Daley, Richard, 43
Daly, Dan, 210, 214–16
Damon, Bill, 97–98
Dannemeyer, William, 129, 154
Danner, Mark, 112
D'Aubuisson, Roberto, 105, 113
Defense of Marriage Act (DOMA), 250–54
Delahunt, William, 212–13, 216, 259
Derwinski, Edward J. 107
Dhooge, Gerard, 233–35
Dinis, Edmund, 81–82
Doane, Paul, 102
Dodd, Chris, 106, 183

289